Media Ethics:

ISSUES AND CASES

EIGHTH EDITION

Media Ethics:

ISSUES AND CASES

EIGHTH EDITION

Philip Patterson
Oklahoma Christian University

Lee Wilkins
University of Missouri–Columbia

The McGraw·Hill Companies

MEDIA ETHICS: ISSUES AND CASES, EIGHTH EDITION

1 2 3 4 5 6 7 8 9 0 DOC/DOC 1 0 9 8 7 6 5 4 3

ISBN 978-0-07-3526249
MHID 0-07-352624X

Senior Vice President, Products & Markets: *Kurt L. Strand*
Vice President, General Manager, Products & Markets: *Michael Ryan*
Vice President, Content Production & Technology Services: *Kimberly Meriwether David*
Executive Director of Development: *Lisa Pinto*
Managing Director: *David Patterson*
Brand Manager: *Susan Gouijnstook*
Marketing Specialist: *Alexandra Schultz*
Managing Development Editor: *Penina Braffman*

Editorial Coordinator: *Adina Lonn*
Director, Content Production: *Terri Schiesl*
Project Manager: *Judi David*
Buyer: *Nicole Baumgartner*
Permissions Editor: *David W. Black*
Media Project Manager: *Sridevi Palani*
Cover Designer: *Studio Montage, St. Louis, MO*
Typeface: *10.5/12 Times Roman*
Compositor: *Laserwords Private Limited*
Printer: *R.R.Donnelley*

Library of Congres s Cataloging-in-Publication Data
Media ethics : issues and cases/[edited by] Philip Patterson, Oklahoma Christian University, Lee Wilkins, University of Missouri-Columbia.—Eighth edition.
    pages cm
  Includes bibliographical references and index.
  ISBN 978-0-07-352624-9 (acid-free paper)
  1. Mass media—Moral and ethical aspects. 2. Communication—Moral and ethical aspects.
I. Patterson, Philip. II. Wilkins, Lee.
P94.M36 2014
175—dc23

2012049102

To Amy, Andrew, Miranda and Joshua
Our equally bright and now-grown children,
unequally distributed between us

CONTENTS

FOREWORD

CLIFFORD G. CHRISTIANS
Research Professor of Communication
University of Illinois–Urbana

The playful wit and sharp mind of Socrates attracted disciples from all across ancient Greece. They came to learn and debate in what could be translated "his thinkery." By shifting the disputes among Athenians over earth, air, fire and water to human virtue, Socrates gave Western philosophy and ethics a new intellectual center (Cassier 1944).

But sometimes his relentless arguments would go nowhere. On one occasion, he sparred with the philosopher Hippias about the difference between truth and falsehood. Hippias was worn into submission, but retorted at the end, "I cannot agree with you, Socrates." And then the master concluded: "Nor I with myself, Hippias. . . . I go astray, up and down, and never hold the same opinion." Socrates admitted to being so clever that he had befuddled himself. No wonder he was a favorite target of the comic poets. I. F. Stone likens this wizardry to "whales of the intellect flailing about in deep seas" (Stone 1988).

With his young friend Meno, Socrates argued whether virtue is teachable. Meno was eager to learn more, after "holding forth often on the subject in front of large audiences." But he complained, "You are exercising magic and witchcraft upon me and positively laying me under your spell until I am just a mass of helplessness. . . . You are exactly like the flat stingray that one meets in the sea. Whenever anyone comes into contact with it, it numbs him, and that is the sort of thing you seem to be doing to me now. My mind and my lips are literally numb."

Philosophy is not a semantic game, though sometimes its idiosyncrasies feed that response into the popular mind. *Media Ethics: Issues and Cases* does not debunk philosophy as the excess of sovereign reason. The authors of this book will not encourage those who ridicule philosophy as cunning rhetoric. The issue at stake here is actually a somewhat different problem—the Cartesian model of philosophizing.

The founder of modern philosophy, René Descartes, preferred to work in solitude. Paris was whirling in the early 17th century, but for two years even Descartes' friends could not find him as he squirreled himself away studying mathematics. One can even guess the motto above his desk: "Happy is he who lives in seclusion." Imagine the conditions under which he wrote "Meditations II." The Thirty Years' War in Europe brought social chaos everywhere. The Spanish were ravaging the French provinces and even threatening Paris, but Descartes was shut away in an apartment in Holland. Tranquility for philosophical speculation mattered so much to him that upon hearing Galileo had been condemned by the Church, he retracted parallel arguments of his own on natural science. Pure philosophy as an abstract enterprise needed a cool atmosphere isolated from everyday events.

Descartes' magnificent formulations have always had their detractors, of course. David Hume did not think of philosophy in those terms, believing as he did that sentiment is the foundation of morality. For Søren Kierkegaard, an abstract system of ethics is only paper currency with nothing to back it up. Karl Marx insisted that we change the world and not merely explain it. But no one drew the modern philosophical map more decisively than Descartes, and his mode of rigid inquiry has generally defined the field's parameters.

This book adopts the historical perspective suggested by Stephen Toulmin:

> The philosophy whose legitimacy the critics challenge is always the seventeenth century tradition founded primarily upon René Descartes. . . . [The] arguments are directed to one particular style of philosophizing—a theory-centered style which poses philosophical problems, and frames solutions to them, in timeless and universal terms. From 1650, this particular style was taken as defining the very agenda of philosophy (1988, 338).

The 17th-century philosophers set aside the particular, the timely, the local and the oral. And that development left untouched nearly half of the philosophical agenda. Indeed, it is those neglected topics—what I here call "practical philosophy"—that are showing fresh signs of life today, at the very time when the more familiar "theory-centered" half of the subject is languishing (Toulmin 1988, 338).

This book collaborates in demolishing the barrier of three centuries between pure and applied philosophy; it joins in reentering practical concerns as the legitimate domain of philosophy itself. For Toulmin, the primary focus of ethics has moved from the study to the bedside, to criminal courts, engineering labs, the newsroom, factories and ethnic street corners. Moral philosophers are not being asked to hand over their duties to technical experts in today's institutions, but rather to fashion their agendas within the conditions of contemporary struggle.

All humans have a theoretical capacity. Critical thinking, the reflective dimension, is our common property. And this book nurtures that reflection in communication classrooms and by extension into centers of media practice. If the mind is like a muscle, this volume provides a regimen of exercises for strengthening its powers of systematic reflection and moral discernment. It does not permit those aimless arguments that result in quandary ethics. Instead it operates in the finest traditions of practical philosophy, anchoring the debates in real-life conundrums but pushing the discussion toward substantive issues and integrating appropriate theory into the decision-making process. It seeks to empower students to do ethics themselves, under the old adage that teaching someone to fish lasts a lifetime, and providing fish only saves the day.

Media Ethics: Issues and Cases arrives on the scene at a strategic time in higher education. Since the late 19th century, ethical questions have been taken from the curriculum as a whole and from the philosophy department. Recovering practical philosophy has involved a revolution during the last decade in which courses in professional ethics have reappeared throughout the curriculum. This book advocates the pervasive method and carries the discussions even further, beyond freestanding courses into communication classrooms across the board.

In this sense, the book represents a constructive response to the current debates over the mission of higher education. Professional ethics has long been saddled with the dilemma that the university was given responsibility for professional training precisely at the point in its history that it turned away from values to scientific naturalism. Today one sees it as a vast horizontal plane given to technical excellence but barren in enabling students to articulate a philosophy of life. As the late James Carey concluded,

> Higher education has not been performing well of late and, like most American institutions, is suffering from a confusion of purpose, an excess of ambition that borders on hubris, and an appetite for money that is truly alarming (1989, 48).

The broadside critiques leveled in Thorstein Veblen's *The Higher Learning in America* (1918) and Upton Sinclair's *The Goose Step* (1922) are now too blatantly obvious to ignore. But *Media Ethics: Issues and Cases* does not merely demand a better general education or a recommitment to values; it strengthens the communications curriculum by equipping thoughtful students with a more enlightened moral awareness. Since Confucius we have understood that lighting a candle is better than cursing the darkness, or, in Mother Teresa's version, we feed the world one mouth at a time.

PREFACE

As you glance through this book, you will notice its features—text, illustrations, cases, photos—represent choices the authors have made. I think it's as important to point out what's missing as what's there, and why. I'll begin with what's been left out and conclude with what you'll find in the text.

First, you'll find no media bashing in this book. There's enough of that already, and besides, it's too easy to do. This book is not designed to indict the media; it's designed to train its future employees. If we dwell on ethical lapses from the past, it is only to learn from them what we can do to prevent similar occurrences in the future.

Second, you'll find no conclusions in this book—neither at the end of the book nor after each case. No one has yet written the conclusive chapter to the ethical dilemmas of the media, and I don't suspect that we will be the first.

What, then, is in the book?

First, you'll find a diverse, up-to-date and classroom-tested compilation of cases in media ethics. Authors from many institutions and media outlets contributed real-life and hypothetical cases to this text to help students prepare for the ethical situations they will confront in whatever areas of the media they enter. We believe case studies are the premiere teaching vehicle for the study of ethics, and this book reflects what we think are the best available.

Second, the text binds these cases together and provides a philosophical basis from which to approach them. While it intentionally has been kept succinct, the text introduces students to the relevant ethical theory that will help eliminate "quandary ethics," which often results when cases are used as a teaching strategy.

Third, you'll find built-in discussion starters in the questions that follow each case. The questions at the end of the cases were written by the authors of each case, with the instructions that they were to be like concentric circles. The tightest circle—the micro issues—focuses only on the case at hand and the dilemmas it presents. The next circle—midrange issues—focuses on the problem in its context and sometimes manipulates the facts slightly to see if the decisions remain the same. The most abstract level—the macro issues—focuses on issues such as truth, equity, responsibility and loyalty. Properly used, the questions can guide discussion from the particular to the universal in any case in a single class period.

The book may be used either as the main text for a media ethics course or as a supplementary text for ethics modules in courses on newswriting, media and society, advertising and public relations and photojournalism. The book works well for teachers who like to use the Socratic method in their classes or as resource material for lecture classes.

Our approach in this text is best illustrated by an anecdote from a class. One student had the last hand up after a particularly heated case study. When I called on her, she asked, "Well, what's the answer?" I was surprised that she asked the question, and I was surprised that I didn't have a ready answer. I joked my way out of the question by asking if she wanted "The Answer" with a capital "a" or a lower-case one. If she asked today, I'd respond differently. I'd tell her that the answer exists within her, but that it won't emerge in any justifiable form without systematic study and frequent wrestling with the issues.

That's what this book is about. The chapters direct you in some systematic way through the philosophy that has explored these questions for centuries. The cases will make you wrestle with that knowledge in scenarios not unlike ones you might encounter while working. Together, they might not enable you to find "The Answer," but they might help you find *your* answer.

For the authors and contributors,

Philip Patterson

New to This Edition

The Eighth Edition of *Media Ethics: Issues and Cases* includes 29 new cases others have been updated. These are listed below and were written by academics and professionals who have personal knowledge of, or interest in the cases.

Chapter 1 Includes four new chapter-opening scenarios each with a different example of ethical decision making.

Chapter 2

Can I Quote Me on That? by Chad Painter, Eastern New Mexico University

News and the Transparency Standard, by Lee Wilkins, University of Missouri

NPR, the New York Times *and Working Conditions in China,* by Lee Wilkins, University of Missouri

Caught in the "WAR ZONE," by Mike Grundmann and Roger Soenksen, James Madison University

Murdoch's Mess, by Lee Wilkins, University of Missouri

Chapter 3

A Charity Drops the Ball, by Philip Patterson, Oklahoma Christian University

YELP!!! Consumer Empowerment or Small Business Extortion? by Lee Wilkins, University of Missouri

The Facts Behind the Ads: Oregon Changes a Campaign, by Lee Wilkins, University of Missouri

Chapter 10

ACKNOWLEDGMENTS

The ethical dilemmas that challenge us require a "moral compass" to help us find our way down the winding paths of life. My compass was given to me by my parents at an early age, and it has worked for more than four decades. No one can ask for a better gift than that, and I thank them for their part in placing me where I am today.

No book of this type is a solo effort, and this book is certainly the result of hard work and encouragement by many people. To begin, each of the authors in the text has been a pleasure to work with. Lou Hodges, Cliff Christians, Ralph Barney, Jay Black, Deni Elliott and others listened patiently to the idea in its many stages and offered advice along the way. Over the years I have been privileged to attend workshops on ethics sponsored by the Poynter Institute, the Freedom Forum and the University of Nebraska. To Bob Steele, Ed Lambeth, Steve Kalish and Robert Audi I owe a debt of gratitude for helping me continue to learn about ethics as I seek to teach my students.

A special thanks goes to the Ethics and Excellence in Journalism Foundation and to McGraw-Hill Higher Education for grants to cover costs incurred in this edition of the text. Finally, I thank my wife, Linda, and my children, Amy, Andrew and Joshua: I love you all.

p.d.p.

When ethics entrepreneur Michael Josephson opens his public speeches, he asks audience members to think of the most ethical people they know. Those people set ethical standards for others, by who they are and by what they inspire. It's fair for readers of this book to know who's on my list.

First, my mother, whose sense of human connection and compassion has been only incompletely copied by her daughter. Second, my father, who is the most principled human being I have ever met. Third, my stepmother, Carrie, who's managed to love the family she's married into—a feat worthy of far more than a Kantian sense of duty. My dissertation adviser and friend, Jim Davies, affirmed for me the ethical connection between people and politics. My former colleagues at the University of Colorado, Russ Shain, Steve Jones, Sue O'Brien and Risa Palm, have proved that connection to be a very human one, as have my colleagues at the University of Missouri. They have also been willing to listen—*another ethical activity that too often goes unmentioned.* Barrie Hartman and the staff of the Boulder *Daily Camera* were wonderful reality checks.

I've received intellectual help as well. I've attended a number of conferences designed to teach me about ethics. The Hastings House, Gannett, the Poynter Institute and the University of Nebraska have done their best to educate me in this field. The people connected with those efforts deserve special mention. Among them, Ed Lambeth, Ted Glasser, Deni Elliott, Cliff Christians, Lou Hodges, Martin Linsky, Roy Peter Clark, Don Fry, Sharon Murphy, Jay Black, Ralph Barney, Steve Kalish, Robert Audi and Stephen J. A. Ward have helped most profoundly. Many of them you will find mentioned in various contexts on the pages that follow. All of them have a special place in my intellectual psyche.

Three sets of acknowledgments remain.

For the past 32 years, my students at the state universities of Missouri and Colorado have taught me much more about ethics than I have taught them. They have suffered through portions of this manuscript with me. Their questions and their insights are evident on every page of this book.

Second, to Maureen Spada, without whom this book would not exist, let alone read as well as it does. Sometimes editors are friends, and you have been that and more to both of us.

Then there are Miranda and David—my daughter and my spouse. For the smiles, the hugs, the reading of first drafts, the talking, the listening, the suggestions, the lecture about using "skin" names, the films and all of the rest that being a family means. To David, particularly, for acting as the most tenacious permissions editor any author could ever have hoped for. Love and thanks. I could not have done this without you.

l.c.w.

1

An Introduction to Ethical Decision Making

By the end of this chapter, you should be able to:

- **recognize the need for professional ethics in journalism.**
- **work through a model of ethical decision making.**
- **identify and use five philosophical principles applicable to mass communication situations.**

MAKING ETHICAL DECISIONS

Scenario #1: You work as an intern for a start-up news organization that has a business model based on collecting broadcast coverage of specific stories from multiple news outlets, editing the coverage, adding studio-produced introductory comments, and selling the resulting packages to media outlets that have neither the staff time nor the facilities to produce high-quality, in-depth on-air or Web work. Your organization accurately credits those who produced the original coverage you aggregate. Most often packages are compiled from international news sources, although sometimes they include video and comments from bloggers, domestic on-air media critics, and others. The start-up is now in its third year; it has reached its capitalization goals, and while its subscriber base is modest, it includes Web outlets such as the Huffington Post. Part of your job is to help produce the packages the organization sells. But, you are also charged with scouring the Web for references to the story topics your organization is aggregating coverage about. When you find such a Web site, you are told to craft a laudatory response to the site content which must include a reference to similar content from the news organization you work for. In these messages, you are instructed not to disclose that you are an employee of the news organization you are required to mention. What should you do?

Scenario #2: According to documentarian Josh Fox, it all started with a letter he received from a natural gas company in 2009 offering to pay him $4,750 per acre

(Fox inherited 19 acres near Milanville, Pennsylvania, including the house he was born in, from his parents) for the right to drill for natural gas on his property which sits atop the Marcellus shale, a rich natural gas deposit. The drilling process the company will use is called hydraulic fracturing, "fraking" in the oil and gas business. Fox, who claimed to know little about the process or its potential monetary and environmental impact, took the letter as impetus to report, shoot and produce the documentary *Gasland* which, in 2010, was nominated for an Oscar for best documentary film. *Gasland,* which is based on first-person, point-of-view reporting, shot with a handheld camera and often crudely edited, has been politically influential, serving as part of the impetus to regulate fraking in several states. Early in *Gasland,* Fox's first documentary, Fox speculates about why so many average people were willing to talk to him about their experiences with fraking. "I guess if you have a camera in your hand, you know what you are doing," he says. With the advent of Op Docs in the *New York Times* and the emergence of first-person, point-of-view reporting in many media channels, what are the rules for "knowing what you are doing" in the making of documentary films or journalistic pieces that rely on these seemingly new information collection techniques?

Scenario #3: You work for a PR firm that represents pharmaceutical giant PharMedCo. The drug company has an herbal medicine used successfully in Europe to lower blood pressure. PharMedCo wants to sell it in the United States. It is planning a major national promotion, generating large fees for your firm. It wants to use "third-party strategy," hiring key opinion leaders in the medical world to help get the word out and create a buzz by talking up the advantages of herbal products, but they would not push PharMedCo's new herbal medicine directly. In doing some research, you discover a little-known piece of information: if the herb is used in combination with another over-the-counter drug, it can be abused to get high. You tell PharMedCo, but it wants you to go ahead without informing the third-party experts, who might possibly back out or even warn the public. What should you do?

Scenario #4: You are on a vacation car trip in another state when you narrowly miss becoming personally involved in a multiple-fatality car accident. You and your friends are not hurt, but you are on the scene before police and other first-responders arrive. The accident involves a striped-down van carrying 15 people, none of them wearing a seat belt because both seat belts and the seats themselves had been removed from the van. Several passengers have been thrown from the van and others are trapped beneath it. You have some minor first-aid training. Those responding initially are overwhelmed by the number of those injured and the seriousness of their injuries, so they ask you to help with the least seriously injured. You do so, and in the process overhear conversations among the police and medical personnel that those in the van are immigrants, that they are being driven to a manufacturing plant more than 50 miles from their homes on a daily basis by those who have brought them into the country, and that this sort of accident—while more lethal than most—is not the first to have happened in the area and to this immigrant population. You are badly shaken by what you have seen, but two days later when you get back home, you realize that the accident you witnessed is a potential "tip" to a significant news story. What might that story be? How do you, or do you, convince your newspaper editor to give you the time and resources to investigate what you, yourself, admit is a tragedy that happened in another state?

The Dilemma of Dilemmas

The scenarios above are dilemmas—they present an ethical problem with no single (or simple) "right" answer. Resolving dilemmas is the business of ethics. It's not an easy process, but ethical dilemmas can be anticipated and prepared for, and there is a wealth of ethical theory—some of it centuries old—to back up your final decision. In this chapter and throughout this book, you will be equipped with both the theories and the tools to help solve the dilemmas that arise in working for the mass media.

In the end, you will have tools, not answers. Answers must come from within you, but your answers should be informed by what others have written and experienced. Otherwise, you will always be forced to solve each ethical problem without the benefit of anyone else's insight. Gaining these tools also will help you prevent each dilemma from spiraling into "quandary ethics"—the feeling that no best choice is available and that everyone's choice is equally valid (see Deni Elliott's essay in this chapter).

Will codes of ethics help? Virtually all the media associations have one, but they have limitations. For instance, the ethics code for the Society of Professional Journalists could be read to allow for revealing or withholding the information in the scenarios above, two actions that are polar opposites. That doesn't make the code useless; it simply points out a shortfall in depending on codes.

While we don't dismiss codes, we believe you will find more universally applicable help in the writings of philosophers, ancient and modern, introduced in this chapter.

This book, or any ethics text, should teach more than a set of rules. It should give you the skills, analytical models, vocabulary and insights of others who have faced these choices, to make and justify your ethical decisions.

Some writers claim that ethics can't be taught. It's situational, some claim. Since every message is unique, there is no real way to learn ethics other than by daily life. Ethics, it is argued, is something you have, not something you do. But while it's true that reading about ethics is no guarantee you will perform your job ethically, thinking about ethics is a skill anyone can acquire.

While each area of mass communication has its unique ethical issues, thinking about ethics is the same, whether you make your living writing advertising copy or obituaries. Thinking about ethics won't necessarily make tough choices easier, but, with practice, your ethical decision making can become more consistent. A consistently ethical approach to your work as a reporter, strategic communication professional or copywriter in whatever field of mass communication you enter can improve that work as well.

Ethics and Morals

Contemporary professional ethics revolves around these questions:

- What duties do I have, and to whom do I owe them?
- What values are reflected by the duties I've assumed?

Ethics takes us out of the world of "This is the way I do it" or "This is the way it's always been done" into the realm of "This is what I should do" or "This

A Word about Ethics

The concept of ethics comes from the Greeks, who divided the philosophical world into separate disciplines. *Aesthetics* was the study of the beautiful and how a person could analyze beauty without relying only on subjective evaluations. *Epistemology* was the study of knowing, debates about what constitutes learning and what is knowable. *Ethics* was the study of what is good, both for the individual and for society. Interestingly, the root of the word means "custom" or "habit," giving ethics an underlying root of behavior that is long established and beneficial to the ongoing of society. The Greeks were also concerned with the individual virtues of fortitude, justice, temperance and wisdom, as well as with societal virtues, such as freedom.

Two thousand years later, ethics has come to mean learning to make rational decisions among an array of choices, all of which may be morally justifiable, but some more so than others. *Rationality* is the key word here, for the Greeks believed, and modern philosophers affirm, that people should be able to explain their ethical decisions to others and that acting ethically could be shown to be a rational decision to make. That ability to explain ethical choices is an important one for media professionals whose choices are so public. When confronted with an angry public, "It seemed like the right thing to do at the time" is a personally embarrassing *and* ethically unsatisfactory explanation.

is the action that can be rationally justified." Ethics in this sense is "ought talk." The questions arising from duty and values can be answered a number of ways as long as they are consistent with each other. For example, a journalist and a public relations professional may see the truth of a story differently because they see their duties differently and because there are different values at work in their professions, but each can be acting ethically if they are operating under the imperatives of "oughtness" for their profession.

It is important here to distinguish between *ethics,* a rational process founded on certain agreed-on principles, and *morals,* which are in the realm of religion. For example, the Ten Commandments are a moral system in the Judeo-Christian tradition, and Jewish scholars have expanded this study of the laws throughout the Bible's Old Testament into the Talmud, a religious volume running more than 1,000 pages. The Buddhist Eightfold Path provides a similar moral framework.

But moral systems are not synonymous with ethics. *Ethics begins when elements within a moral system conflict.* Ethics is less about the conflict between right and wrong than it is about the conflict between equally compelling (or equally unattractive) alternatives and the choices that must be made between them. Ethics is just as often about the choices between good and better or poor and worse than about right and wrong, which tends to be the domain of morals.

When elements within a moral system conflict, ethical principles can help you make tough choices. We'll review several ethical principles briefly after describing how one philosopher, Sissela Bok, says working professionals can learn to make good ethical decisions.

BOK'S MODEL

Bok's ethical decision-making framework was introduced in her book, *Lying: Moral Choice in Public and Private Life.* Bok's model is based on two premises: that we must have empathy for the people involved in ethical decisions and that maintaining social trust is a fundamental goal. With this in mind, Bok says any ethical question should be analyzed in three steps.

First, consult your own conscience about the "rightness" of an action. *How do you feel about the action?*

Second, seek expert advice for alternatives to the act creating the ethical problem. Experts, by the way, can be those either living or dead—a producer or editor you trust or a philosopher you admire. *Is there another professionally acceptable way to achieve the same goal that will not raise ethical issues?*

Third, if possible, conduct a public discussion with the parties involved in the dispute. These include those who are directly involved such as a reporter or their source, and those indirectly involved such as a reader or a media outlet owner. If they cannot be gathered—and that will most often be the case—you can conduct the conversation hypothetically in your head, playing out the roles. The goal of this conversation is to discover, *How will others respond to the proposed act?*

Let's see how Bok's model works in the following scenario. In the section after the case, follow the three steps Bok recommends and decide if you would run the story.

How Much News Is Fit to Print?

In your community, the major charity is the United Way. The annual fund-raising drive will begin in less than two weeks. However, at a late-night meeting of the board with no media present, the executive director resigns. Though the agency is not covered by the Open Meetings Act, you are able to learn most of what went on from a source on the board.

According to her, the executive director had taken pay from the agency by submitting a falsified time sheet while he was actually away at the funeral of a college roommate. The United Way board investigated the absence and asked for his resignation, citing the lying about the absence as the reason, though most agreed that they would have given him paid leave had he asked.

The United Way wants to issue a short statement, praising the work of the executive director while regretfully accepting his resignation. The executive director also will issue a short statement citing other opportunities as his reason for leaving. You are assigned the story by an editor who does not know about the additional information you have obtained but wants you to "see if there's any more to it [the resignation] than they're telling."

You call your source on the board and she asks you, as a friend, to withhold the damaging information because it will hinder the United Way's annual fund-raising effort and jeopardize services to needy people in the community because faith in the United Way will be destroyed. You confront the executive director. He says he already has a job interview with another nonprofit and if you run the story you will ruin his chances of a future career.

What do you do?

THE ANALYSIS

Bok's first step requires you to *consult your conscience*. When you do, you realize you have a problem. Your responsibility is to tell the truth, and that means providing readers with all the facts you discover. You also have a larger responsibility not to harm your community, and printing the complete story might well cause short-term harm. Clearly, your conscience is of two minds about the issue.

You move to the second step: *alternatives*. Do you simply run the resignation release, figuring that the person can do no further harm and therefore should be left alone? Do you run the whole story but buttress it with board members' quotes that such an action couldn't happen again, figuring that you have restored public trust in the agency? Do you do nothing until after the fund-raising drive and risk the loss of trust from readers if the story circulates around town as a rumor? Again, there are alternatives, but each has some cost.

In the third step of Bok's model, you will attempt to *hold a public ethical dialogue* with all of the parties involved. Most likely you won't get all the parties into the newsroom on deadline. Instead you can conduct an imaginary discussion among the parties involved. Such a discussion might go like this:

EXECUTIVE DIRECTOR: "I think my resignation is sufficient penalty for any mistake I might have made, and your article will jeopardize my ability to find another job. It's really hurting my wife and kids, and they've done nothing wrong."

REPORTER: "But shouldn't you have thought about that *before* you decided to falsify the time sheet? This is a good story, and I think the public should know what the people who are handling their donations are like."

READER 1: "Wait a minute. I am the public, and I'm tired of all of this bad news your paper focuses on. This man has done nothing but good in the community, and I can't see where any money that belonged to the poor went into his pocket. Why can't we see some good news for a change?"

READER 2: "I disagree. I buy the paper precisely because it does this kind of reporting. Stories like this that keep the government, the charities and everyone else on their toes."

PUBLISHER: "You mean like a watchdog function."

READER 2: "Exactly. And if it bothers you, don't read it."

PUBLISHER: "I don't really like to hurt people with the power we have, but if we don't print stories like this, and the community later finds out that we withheld news, our credibility is ruined, and we're out of business." [To source] "Did you request that the information be off the record?"

SOURCE: "No. But I never thought you'd use it in your story."

REPORTER: "I'm a reporter. I report what I hear for a living. What did you think I would do with it? Stories like these allow me to support my family."

EXECUTIVE DIRECTOR: "So it's your career or mine, is that what you're saying? Look, no charges have been filed here, but if your story runs, I look like a criminal. Is that fair?"

PUBLISHER: "And if it doesn't run, we don't keep our promise to the community. Is that fair?"

NEEDY MOTHER: "Fair? You want to talk fair? Do you suffer if the donations go down? No, I do. This is just another story to you. It's the difference in me and my family getting by."

The conversation could continue, and other points of view could be voiced. Your imaginary conversations could be more or less elaborate than the one above, but out of this discussion it should be possible to rationally support an ethical choice.

There are two cautions in using Bok's model for ethical decision making. First, it is important to go through all three steps before making a final choice. Most of us make ethical choices prematurely, after we've consulted only our consciences, an error Bok says results in a lot of flabby moral thinking. Second, while you will not be endowed with any clairvoyant powers to anticipate your ethical problems, the ethical dialogue outlined in the third step is best when conducted in advance of the event, not in the heat of writing a story.

For instance, an advertising copywriter might conduct such a discussion about whether advertising copy can ethically withhold disclaimers about potential harm from a product. A reporter might conduct such a discussion well in advance of the time he is actually asked to withhold an embarrassing name or fact from a story. Since it is likely that such dilemmas will arise in your chosen profession (the illustration above is based on what happened to one of the authors the first day on the job), your answer will be more readily available and more logical if you hold such discussions either with trusted colleagues in a casual atmosphere or by yourself, well in advance of the problem. The cases in this book are selected partially for their ability to predict your on-the-job dilemmas and start the ethical discussion now.

GUIDELINES FOR MAKING ETHICAL DECISIONS

Since the days of ancient Greece, philosophers have tried to draft a series of rules or guidelines governing how to make ethical choices. In ethical dilemmas such as the one above, you will need principles to help you determine what to do amid conflicting voices. While a number of principles work well, we will review five.

Aristotle's Golden Mean

Aristotle believed that happiness—which some scholars translate as "flourishing"—was the ultimate human good. By flourishing, Aristotle sought to elevate any activity through the setting of high standards, what he called exercising "practical reasoning."

Aristotle believed that practical reason was exercised by individuals who understood what the Greeks called the "virtues" and demonstrated them in their lives and calling. Such a person was the *phrenemos,* or person of practical wisdom, who demonstrated ethical excellence in their daily activity. For Aristotle, the highest virtue was citizenship, and its highest practitioner the statesman, a politician who exercised so much practical wisdom in his daily activity that he elevated the craft of politics to art. In contemporary terms, we might think of a *phrenemos* as a person who excels at any of a variety of activities—cellist Yo-Yo Ma, poet Maya Angelou,

CALVIN AND HOBBES © 1989 Watterson. Dist. By UNIVERSAL UCLICK.
Reprinted with permission. All rights reserved.

filmmakers George Lucas and Steven Spielberg. They are people who flourish in their professional performance, extending our own vision of what is possible.

This notion of flourishing led Aristotle to assert that people acting virtuously are the moral basis of his ethical system, not those who simply follow rules. His ethical system is now called *virtue ethics.* Virtue ethics flows from both the nature of the act itself and the moral character of the person who acts. In the Aristotelian sense, the way to behave ethically is that (1) you must know (through the exercise of practical reasoning) what you are doing; (2) you must select the act for its own sake—in order to flourish; and (3) the act itself must spring from a firm and unchanging character.

It is not stretching Aristotle's framework to assert that one way to learn ethics is to select heroes and to try to model your individual acts and ultimately your professional character on what you believe they would do. An Aristotelian might well consult this hero as an expert when making an ethical choice. Asking what my hero would do in a particular situation is a valid form of ethical analysis. The trick, however, is to select your heroes carefully and continue to think for yourself rather than merely copy behavior you have seen previously.

What then is a virtue? *Virtue lies at the mean between two extremes of excess and deficiency,* a reduction of Aristotle's philosophy often called the "golden mean" as shown in Figure 1.1. Courage, for example, is a mean between foolhardiness on one hand and cowardice on the other. But to determine that mean for yourself, you have to exercise practical wisdom, act according to high standards and act in accordance with firm and continuing character traits.

Unacceptable behaviors (deficiency)	Acceptable behaviors	Unacceptable behaviors (excess)
Cowardice . . . . .Courage . . . . Foolhardiness
Shamelessness . . . . Modesty . . . . Bashfulness
Stinginess . . . . Generosity . . . . .Wastefulness

FIGURE 1.1. Aristotle's golden mean

In reality, therefore, the middle ground of a virtue is not a single point on a line that is the same for every individual. It is instead a range of behaviors that varies individually, while avoiding the undesirable extremes. Candor is a good example of a virtue that is most certainly contextual—what is too blunt in one instance is kind in another. Consider two witnesses to a potential drowning: one onlooker is a poor swimmer but a fast runner, the other is a good swimmer but a slow runner. What is cowardice for one is foolhardiness for the other. Each can exhibit courage, but in different ways.

Seeking the golden mean implies that individual acts are not disconnected from one another, but collectively form a whole that a person of good character should aspire to. A virtue theory of ethics is not outcome-oriented. Instead, it is agent-oriented, and right actions in a virtue theory of ethics are a result of an agent seeking virtue and accomplishing it. As Aristotle wrote in *Nicomachean Ethics:* "We learn an art or craft by doing the things that we shall have to do when we have learnt it: for instance, men become builders by building houses, harpers by playing on the harp. Similarly we become just by doing just acts, temperate by doing temperate acts, brave by doing brave acts."

Far from being old-fashioned, Aristotle's concept of virtue ethics has been rediscovered by a variety of professions. As Kenneth Woodward (1994) states in a *Newsweek* essay entitled "What Is Virtue?" a call for virtue is still relevant today:

> But before politicians embrace virtue as their latest election-year slogan, they would do well to tune into contemporary philosophy. Despite the call for virtue, we live in an age of moral relativism. According to the dominant school of moral philosophy, the skepticism engendered by the Enlightenment has reduced all ideas of right and wrong to matters of personal taste, emotional preference or cultural choice. . . . Against this moral relativism, advocates of the "ethics of virtue" argue that some personal choices are morally superior to others.

Kant's Categorical Imperative

Immanuel Kant is best known for his *categorical imperative* which is most often stated in two ways. The first asserts that an individual should act as if the choices one makes for oneself could become universal law. The second states that you should act so that you treat each individual as an end and never as merely a means. Kant called these two rules "categorical" imperatives, meaning that their demands were universal and not subject to situational factors. Many readers will recognize the similarity between Kant's first manifestation of the categorical imperative and the Bible's golden rule: Do unto others as you would have others do unto you. The two are quite similar in their focus on duty.

Kant's ethical theory is based on the notion that it is in the act itself, rather than the person who acts, where moral force resides. This theory of ethics is unlike Aristotle's in that it moves the notion of what is ethical from the actor to the act itself. This does not mean that Kant did not believe in moral character, but rather that people could act morally from a sense of duty even if their character might incline them to act otherwise.

For Kant, an action was morally justified only if it sprang from duty—psychological motivation was irrelevant—and in Kant's moral universe there were two sorts of duties. The strict duties were generally negative: not to murder, not to break promises, not to lie. The meritorious duties were more positive: to aid others, to develop one's talents, to show gratitude. Kant spent very little time defining these notions, but philosophers have generally asserted that the strict duties are somewhat more morally mandatory than the meritorious duties.

Some have argued that in Kant's ethical reasoning consequences are not important. We prefer a somewhat less austere reading of Kant. While Kant's view is that the moral worth of an action does not depend on its consequences, those consequences are not irrelevant. For example, a surgeon may show moral virtue in attempting to save a patient through an experimental procedure, but the decision about whether to undertake that procedure requires taking into account the probability of a cure. This framing of Kantian principles allows us to learn from our mistakes.

The test of a moral act, according to Kant, is its universality—whether it can be applied to everyone. For instance, under Kant's categorical imperative, journalists can claim few special privileges, such as the right to lie or the right to invade privacy in order to get a story. Kant's view, if taken seriously, reminds you of what you give up—truth, privacy and the like—when you make certain ethical decisions.

Utilitarianism

The original articulation of *utilitarianism* by Englishmen Jeremy Bentham and later John Stuart Mill in the 19th century introduced what was then a novel notion into ethics discussions: *The consequences of actions are important in deciding whether they are ethical.* In the utilitarian view, it may be considered ethical to harm one person for the benefit of the larger group. This approach, for example, is the ethical justification for investigative reporting, the results of which may harm individuals even as they are printed or broadcast in the hope of providing a greater societal good.

The appeal of utilitarianism is that it has proven to mesh well with Western thought, particularly on human rights. Harvard ethicist Arthur Dyck (1977, 55) writes of Mill:

> He took the view that the rightness or wrongness of any action is decided by its consequences. . . . His particular understanding of what is best on the whole was that which brings about the most happiness or the least suffering, i.e., the best balance of pleasure over pain for the greatest number.

The benefit of utilitarianism is that it provides a principle by which rightness and wrongness can be identified and judged, conflicts can be resolved and exceptions can be decided. The utilitarian calculus also has made possible the "quantification of welfare" Dyck says, allowing governments to make decisions that create the most favorable balance of benefits over harms.

With its focus on the consequences of an action, utilitarianism completes a cycle begun with Aristotle (see Table 1.1). Aristotle, in developing the golden mean, focused on the *actor.* Kant, in his categorical imperative, focused on the *action,* while Mill, in his utilitarian philosophy, focused on the *outcome.*

Utilitarianism has been condensed to the ethical philosophy of the "greatest good for the greatest number." While this pithy phrase is a very rough and ready characterization of utilitarian theory, it also has led to an overly mechanistic application of the principle: just tally up the amount of good and subtract the amount of harm. If the remaining number is positive, the act is ethical. However, when properly applied, utilitarianism is not mechanical.

To do justice to utilitarian theory, it must be understood within a historical context. Mill wrote after the changes of the Enlightenment. The principle of democracy was fresh and untried, and the thought that the average person should be able to speak his mind to those in power was novel. Utilitarianism as Mill conceived of it was a profoundly social ethic; Mill was among the first to acknowledge that the good of an entire society had a place in ethical reasoning.

Mill was what philosophers call a *valuational hedonist.* He argued that pleasure—and the absence of pain—was the only intrinsic moral end. Mill further asserted that an act was right in the proportion in which it contributed to the general happiness. Conversely, an act was wrong in the proportion in which it contributed to general unhappiness or pain. Utilitarianism can be subtle and complex in that the same act can make some happy but cause others pain. Mill insisted that both outcomes be valued simultaneously, a precarious activity but one that forces discussion of competing stakeholder claims.

TABLE 1.1. The Shifting Focus of Ethics from Aristotle to Mill

Philosopher	Known for	Popularly Known as	Emphasized
Aristotle	Golden mean	Virtue lies between extremes.	The actor
Kant	Categorical imperative	Act so your choices could be universal law; treat humanity as an end, never as a means only.	The action
Mill	Utility principle	An act's rightness is determined by its contribution to a desirable end.	The outcome

In utilitarian theory, no one's happiness is any more valuable than anyone else's, and definitely not more valuable than everyone's—quantity and quality being equal. In democratic societies, this is a particularly important concept because it meshes well with certain social and political goals. In application, utilitarianism has a way of puncturing entrenched self-interest, but when badly applied, it can actually promote social selfishness.

Utilitarianism also suggests that moral questions are objective, empirical and even in some sense scientific. Utilitarianism promotes a universal ethical standard that each rational person can determine. However, utilitarianism is among the most criticized of philosophical principles because it is so difficult to accurately anticipate all the consequences of a particular act. Different philosophers also have disputed how one calculates the good, rendering any utilitarian calculus fundamentally error prone.

While utilitarianism is a powerful theory, too many rely exclusively on it. Taken to extremes, the act of calculating the good can lead to ethical gridlock, with each group of stakeholders having seemingly equally strong claims with little way to choose among them. Sloppily done, utilitarianism may bias the user toward short-term benefit which is often contrary to the nature of ethical decisions.

Pluralistic Theory of Value

Philosopher William David Ross (1930) based his ethical theory on the belief that there is often more than one ethical value simultaneously "competing" for preeminence in our ethical decision making, a tension set up in the title of his book: *The Right and the Good.* Commenting on the tension, ethicist Christopher Meyers (2003, 84) says:

> As the book title suggests, Ross distinguished between the *right* and the *good*. The latter term refers to an objective, if indefinable, quality present in all acts. It is something seen, not done. Right, on the other hand, refers to actions. A right action is something undertaken by persons motivated by correct reasons and on careful reflection. Not all right actions, however, will be productive of the good.

In acknowledging the competition between the good and the right, Ross differs from Kant or Mill, who proposed only one ultimate value. To Ross these competing ethical claims, which he calls duties, are equal, providing the circumstances of the particular moral choice are equal. Further, these duties gain their moral weight not from their consequences but from the highly personal nature of duty.

Ross proposed these types of duties:

1. Those duties of *fidelity,* based on my implicit or explicit promise;
2. Those duties of *reparation,* arising from a previous wrongful act;
3. Those duties of *gratitude* that rest on previous acts of others;
4. Those duties of *justice* that arise from the necessity to ensure the equitable and meritorious distribution of pleasure or happiness;
5. Those duties of *beneficence* that rest on the fact that there are others in the world whose lot we can better;

6. Those duties of *self-improvement* that rest on the fact that we can improve our own condition; and
7. One negative duty: the duty of *not injuring others.*

We would recommend two additional duties that may be implied by Ross's list but are not specifically stated:

1. The duty to tell the truth, *veracity* (which may be implied by fidelity); and
2. The duty to *nurture,* to help others achieve some measure of self-worth and achievement.

Ross's typology of duties works well for professionals who often must balance competing roles. It also brings to ethical reasoning some affirmative notions of the primacy of community and relationships as a way to balance the largely rights-based traditions of much Western philosophical theory.

Like Kant, Ross divided his duties into two kinds. *Prima facie* duties are those duties that seem to be right because of the nature of the act itself. *Duty proper* (also called actual duties) are those duties that are paramount given specific circumstances. Arriving at your duty proper from among the prima facie duties requires that you consider what ethicists call the *morally relevant differences.* But Ross (1988, 24) warns that:

> . . . there is no reason to anticipate that every act that is our duty is so for one and the same reason. Why should two sets or circumstances, or one set of circumstances *not* possess different characteristics, any one of which makes a certain act our prima facie duty?

Let's take an example using one of Ross's prima facie duties: keeping promises. In your job as a reporter, you have made an appointment with the mayor to discuss a year-end feature on your community. On your way to City Hall, you drive by a serious auto accident and see a young child wandering, dazed, along the road. If you stop to help you will certainly be late for your appointment and may have to cancel altogether. You have broken a promise.

But is that act ethical?

Ross would probably say yes because the specific aspects of the situation had a bearing on the fulfillment of a prima facie duty. You exercised discernment. You knew that your commitment to the mayor was a relatively minor sort of promise. Your news organization will not be hurt by postponing the interview, and your act allowed you to fulfill the prima facie duties of beneficence, avoiding harm and nurturing. Had the interview been more important, or the wreck less severe, the morally relevant factors would have been different. Ross's pluralistic theory of values may be more difficult to apply than a system of absolute rules, but it reflects the way we make ethical choices.

Ross's concept of multiple duties "helps to explain why we feel uneasy about breaking a promise even when we are justified in doing so. Our uneasiness comes from the fact that we have broken a *prima facie* duty even as we fulfilled another" (Lebacqz 1985, 27).

Communitarianism

Classical ethical theory places its dominant intellectual emphasis on the individual and individual acts by emphasizing concepts such as character, choice, liberty and duty. But contemporary realities points out the intellectual weakness in this approach. Consider the environment. On many environmental questions, it is possible for people to make appropriate individual decisions—today I drive my car—which taken together promote environmental degradation. My individual decision to drive my car (or to purchase a hybrid car) doesn't matter very much; but when individual decisions accumulate, the impact is profound not only for a single generation but for subsequent ones as well.

Communitarianism, which has its roots in political theory, seeks to provide ethical guidance when confronting the sort of society-wide issues that mark current political and business activity. Communitarianism returns to Aristotle's concept of the "polis"—or community—and invests it with moral weight. People begin their lives, at least in a biological sense, as members of a two-person community. Communitarian philosophy extends this biological beginning to a philosophical worldview. "In communitarianism, persons have certain inescapable claims on one another that cannot be renounced except at the cost of their humanity" (Christians, Ferré and Fackler 1993, 14). Communitarians assert that when issues are political and social, community interests trump individual interests but does not trample them.

Communitarianism focuses on the outcome of individual ethical decisions analyzed in light of their potential to impact society. And when applied to journalism, you have a product "committed to justice, covenant and empowerment. Authentic communities are marked by justice; in strong democracies, courageous talk is mobilized into action. . . . In normative communities, citizens are empowered for social transformation, not merely freed from external constraints" (Christians et al. 1993, 14).

Communitarianism asserts that social justice is the predominant moral value. Communitarians recognize the value of process, but are just as concerned with outcomes. History is full of "good" processes that led to bad outcomes. For example, democratic elections led to the 1933 takeover of Germany by a minority party headed by Hitler. It was a democratically written and adopted Constitution which included the three-fifths clause where African-Americans were equal to three-fifths of a single Caucasian for purposes of population count. Under communitarianism, the ability of individual acts to create a more just society is an appropriate measure of their rightness and outcomes are part of the calculus.

Communitarian thinking allows ethical discussion to include values such as altruism and benevolence on an equal footing with more traditional questions such as truth telling and loyalty. Indeed, Nobel Prize—winning work in game theory has empirically demonstrated that cooperation, one of the foundation stones of community, provides desirable results once thought to be possible only through competition (Axelrod 1984). Cooperation is particularly powerful when the "shadow of the future," an understanding that we will encounter the outcome of our decisions and their impact on others in readily foreseeable time, is taken into account.

Communitarianism suffers from a lack of a succinct summary of its general propositions. But any notion of a communitarian community begins with the fact that its members would include, as part of their understanding of self, their membership in the community. "For them, community describes not just what they have as fellow citizens but also what they are, not as a relationship they choose (as in a voluntary association) but an attachment they discover, not merely an attribute but as a constituent of their identity" (Sandel 1982, 150). Communitarian community resembles family more than it resembles town.

Under communitarianism, journalism cannot separate itself from the political and economic system of which it is a part. Communitarian thinking makes it possible to ask whether current practice (for example, a traditional definition of news) provides a good mechanism for a community to discover itself, learn about itself and ultimately transform itself.

Communitarian reasoning allows journalists to understand their institutional role and to evaluate their performance against shared societal values. For instance, the newsroom adage "if it bleeds it leads" might sell newspapers or attract viewers, but it also might give a false impression of community and its perils to the most vulnerable members. Communitarianism would not ban the coverage of crime but would demand context that would help viewers or readers decide if they need to take action.

Thinking as a communitarian not only mutes the competition among journalistic outlets, it also provides a new agenda for news. Rape stories would include mobilizing information about the local rape crisis center. Political stories would focus on issues, not the horserace or personal scandals, and the coverage would be ample enough for an informed citizenry to cast a knowledgeable ballot. Writers have linked communitarian philosophy with the civic journalism movement. But like the philosophy of communitarianism, the practice of civic journalism has not yet been embraced by the mainstream of society.

THE "SCIENCE" OF ETHICS

Life in the 21st century has changed how most people think about issues, such as what constitutes a fact and what does or does not influence moral certainty. But ethical theory, with its apparent uncertainties and contradictions, appears to have taken a back seat to science. As people have become drawn to ethics they seek "the answer" to an ethical dilemma in the same way they seek "the answer" in science. Consequently, the vagaries of ethical choice as contrasted with the seeming certainty of scientific knowledge casts an unfair light on ethics.

We'd like to offer you a different conceptualization of "the facts" of both science and ethics. Science, and the seeming certainty of scientific knowledge, has undergone vast changes in the past 100 years. Before Einstein, most educated people believed that Sir Francis Bacon had accurately and eternally described the basic actions and laws of the physical universe. But Bacon was wrong. Scientific inquiry in the 20th century explored a variety of physical phenomena, uncovered new relationships, new areas of knowledge and new areas of ignorance. The "certainty" of scientific truth has changed fundamentally in the last 100 years, and there is every reason to expect similar changes in this century, especially in the areas of nano technology. Science and certainty are not synonymous, despite our tendency to blur the two.

Contrast these fundamental changes in the scientific worldview with the developments of moral theory. Aristotle's writing, more than 2,000 years old, still has much to recommend it to the modern era. The same can be said of utilitarianism and of the Kantian approach—both after 100 years of critical review. Certainly, new moral thinking has emerged—for example, feminist theory, but such work tends to build on rather than radically alter the moral theory that has gone before. Ethical philosophers still have fundamental debates but these debates have generally tended to deepen previous insights rather than to "prove" them incorrect. Further, thinking about global ethics uncovers some striking areas of agreement. We are aware of no ethical system, for example, that argues that murder is an ethical behavior, or that lying, cheating and stealing are the sorts of activities that human beings ought to engage in on a regular basis.

From this viewpoint, there is more continuity in thinking about ethics than in scientific thought. When the average person contrasts ethics with science, it is ethics that tends to be viewed as changeable, unsystematic and idiosyncratic. Science has rigor, proof and some relationship to an external reality. We would like to suggest that such characterizations arise from a short-term view of the history of science and ethics. In our view, ethics as a field has at least as much continuity of thought as developments in science. And while it cannot often be quantified, it has the rigor, the systematic quality and the relationship to reality that moderns too often characterize as the exclusive domain of scientific thinking.

Suggested Readings

ARISTOTLE. *The Nicomachean ethics.*
BOK, SISSELA. 1978. *Lying: Moral choice in public and private life.* New York: Random House.
BORDEN, SANDRA L. 2009. *Journalism as practice.* Burlington, VT: Ashgate.
CHRISTIANS, CLIFFORD, JOHN FERRÉ, and MARK FACKLER. 2011. *Ethics for public communication.* New York: Oxford University Press
GERT, BERNARD. 1988. *Morality: A new justification of the moral rules.* New York: Oxford University Press.
MILL, JOHN STUART. *On liberty.*
POJMAN, L. 1998. *Ethical theory: Classical and contemporary readings.* Belmont, CA: Wadsworth Publishing Co.
ROSS, W.D. 1930. *The right and the good.* Oxford, England: Clarendon Press.

CHAPTER 1 ESSAY

Cases and Moral Systems

DENI ELLIOTT
University of South Florida—St. Petersburg

Case studies are wonderful vehicles for ethics discussions with strengths that include helping discussants

1. appreciate the complexity of ethical decision making;
2. understand the context within which difficult decisions are made;

3. track the consequences of choosing one action over another; and
4. learn both how and when to reconcile and to tolerate divergent points of view.

However, when case studies are misused, these strengths become weaknesses. Case studies are vehicles for an ethics discussion, not its ultimate destination. The purpose of an ethics discussion is to teach discussants how to "do ethics"—that is, to teach processes so that discussants can practice and improve their own critical decision-making abilities to reach a reasoned response to the issue at hand.

When the discussion stops short of this point, it is often because the destination has been fogged in by one or more myths of media case discussions:

Myth 1: Every opinion is equally valid.

Not true. The best opinion (conclusion) is the one that is best supported by judicious analysis of fact and theory and one that best addresses the morally relevant factors of the case (Gert 1988). An action has morally relevant factors if it is likely to cause some individual to suffer an evil that any rational person would wish to avoid (such as death, disability, pain, loss of freedom or pleasure), or if it is the kind of action that generally causes evil (such as deception, breaking promises, cheating, disobedience of law or neglect of duty).

Myth 2: Since we can't agree on an answer, there is no right answer.

In an ethics case, it may be that there are a number of acceptable answers. But there also will be many wrong answers—many approaches that the group can agree would be unacceptable. When discussants begin to despair of ever reaching any agreement on a right answer or answers, it is time to reflect on all of the agreement that exists within the group concerning the actions that would be out of bounds.

Myth 3: It hardly matters if you come up with the "ethical thing to do," since people ultimately act out of their own self-interest anyway.

Any institution supported by society—manufacturing firms or media corporations, medical centers, etc.—provides some service that merits that support. No matter what the service, practitioners or companies acting only in the short-term interest (i.e., to make money) will not last long. Both free-market pragmatism and ethics dictate that it makes little sense to ignore the expectations of consumers and of the society at large.

The guidelines below can serve as a map for an ethics discussion. They are helpful to have when working through unfamiliar terrain toward individual end points. They also can help you avoid the myths above. While discussing the case, check to see if these questions are being addressed:

1. What are the morally relevant factors of the case?
   (a) Will the proposed action cause an evil—such as death, disability, pain, loss of freedom or opportunity, or a loss of pleasure—that any rational person would wish to avoid?
   (b) Is the proposed action the sort of action—such as deception, breaking promises, cheating, disobedience of law or disobedience of professional or role-defined duty—that generally causes evil?

2. If the proposed action is one described above, is a greater evil being prevented or punished by allowing it to go forward?
3. If so, is the actor in a unique position to prevent or punish such an evil, or is that a more appropriate role for some other person or profession?
4. If the actor followed through on the action, would he be allowing himself to be an exception to a rule that he thinks everyone else should follow? (If so, then the action is prudent, not moral.)
5. Finally, would a rational, uninvolved person appreciate the reason for causing harm? Are the journalists ready and able to state, explain and defend the proposed action in a public forum or would a more detached journalist be ready to write an expose?

CHAPTER 1 CASE

CASE 1-A

How to Read a Case Study

PHILIP PATTERSON
Oklahoma Christian University

When you look at the photo on page 19, it stirs your emotions. It's the last moment of one girl's life (the younger survived). It's a technically good photo—perhaps a once-in-a-lifetime shot. But when you learn the "back story" of this photo, a world of issues emerge and the real discussions begin. And that's the beauty of cases as a way of learning media ethics.

For this case, here is what you need to know. One July afternoon, *Boston Herald* photographer Stanley Forman answered a call about a fire in one of the city's older sections. When he arrived, he followed a hunch and ran down the alley to the back of the row of houses. There he saw a 2-year-old girl and her 19-year-old godmother, on the fifth-floor fire escape. A fire truck had raised its aerial ladder to help. Another firefighter was on the roof, tantalizingly close to pulling the girls to safety. Then came a loud noise, the fire escape gave way and the girls tumbled to the ground. Forman saw it all through his 135 mm lens and took four photos as the two were falling.

The case study has several possible angles. You can discuss the gritty reality of the content. You can factor in that within 24 hours, the city of Boston acted to improve the inspection of all fire escapes in the city and that groups across the nation used the photos to promote similar efforts. You can talk about the ingenuity and industry of Forman to go where the story was rather than remain in front where the rest of the media missed it. You can critique his refusal to photograph the girls after impact. You can debate why the Pulitzer Prize committee gave Forman its top prize for this photo and add in the fact that more than half of the various "Picture of the Year" awards over decades are of death or imminent death. You can argue whether the *Boston Herald* profited off of the death

www.stanleyformanphotos.com Pulitzer Prize 1976. Used with permission.

and injury of the girls and what Forman's role was once he witnessed the trag-edy. And you can ponder what happens when this photo hits the Web, stripped of context.

You can talk about any or all of these issues or imagine others. That's the beauty of a case study—you can go where it takes you. From this one case you can argue taste in content, media economics ("If it bleeds, it leads"), personal vs. professional duty, etc.

Perhaps you will want to role play. Perhaps you will ask yourself what Kant or Mill would do if he were the editor or whether a communitarian would approve the means (the photo) because of the end (better fire escape safety). Perhaps you want to talk about the "breakfast test" for objectionable content in the morning paper, whether it passes the test or whether the test ought to exist. Or what values led the paper to run the photo and the committee to give it an award.

During the semester, you can do more than just work through the cases in this book—you can find your own. All around you are cases of meritorious media behavior and cases of questionable media behavior. And, quite frankly, there are cases where good people will disagree over which category the behavior falls into. Good cases make for good discussion, not only now but also when you graduate into the marketplace as well.

So dive in, discuss and defend.

2

Information Ethics:
A Profession Seeks the Truth

By the end of this chapter, you should be familiar with:

- **both the Enlightenment and pragmatic constructions of truth.**
- **the development and several criticisms of objective news reporting as a professional ideal.**
- **why truth in "getting" the news may be as important as truth in reporting it.**
- **how to develop a personal list of ethical news values.**

INTRODUCTION

Each traditional profession has laid claims to a central tenet of philosophy. Law is equated with justice; medicine with the duty to render aid. Journalism, too, has a lofty ideal: the communication of truth.

But the ideal of truth is problematic. We often consider truth a stable commodity: it doesn't change much on a day-to-day basis, nor does it vary greatly among members of a community. However, the concept of truth has changed throughout history. Human beings since ancient times have acknowledged that how truth is defined may vary. Since Plato's analogy of life as "truthful" in the same way that shadows on the wall of a cave resemble the physical objects that cast those shadows, people have grappled with the nature of truth. Today, while we accept some cultural "lies"—the existence of Santa Claus—we condemn others—income tax evasion or fabricating an employment history. Most of the time, we know what the boundaries are, at least when we deal with one another face-to-face.

Compounding the problem is the changing media audience. When a profession accepts the responsibility of printing and broadcasting the truth, facts apparent in face-to-face interaction are subject to different interpretations among a diverse group of readers and viewers. Ideas once readily accepted are open to debate. Telling the truth becomes not merely a matter of possessing good moral character but something that requires learning how to recognize truth and conveying it in the least distorted manner possible.

A CHANGING VIEW OF TRUTH

One pre-Socratic Greek tradition viewed truth—*alethea*—as encompassing what humans remember, singled out through memory from everything that is destined for *Lethe,* the river of forgetfulness (Bok 1978). Linking truth with remembrance is essential in an oral culture, one that requires information be memorized and repeated so as not to be forgotten. Repeating the message, often in the form of songs or poetry, meant that ideas and knowledge were kept alive or true for subsequent generations. Homer's *Iliad* and *Odyssey* or much of the Bible's Old Testament served this function.

This oral notion of truth, as noted in Table 2.1, was gradually discarded once words and ideas were written down. However, it has come to the fore with the advent of television and its computer cousins like YouTube that allow viewers to hear the words of the president rather than wait for those words to be passed down to them. When we see something on television or our computer screen, we assume that it closely corresponds to reality. The maxim "Seeing is believing" reminds us that truth has become entangled with pictures, an oral concept of truth that has been a dormant form of knowledge for hundreds of years until technology made "seeing" events live worldwide possible.

While the ancient Greeks tied truth to memory, Plato was the first to link truth to human rationality and intellect. In *The Republic,* Plato equated truth with a world of pure form, a world to which human beings had only indirect access. In Plato's vision, there was an ideal notion of a chair—but that ideal chair did not exist in reality. What people thought of as a chair was as similar to the ideal chair as the shadows on the wall of the cave when a chair is illuminated. To Plato, truth was knowable only to the human intellect—it could not be touched or verified. We're living in the cave.

Plato's metaphor of the cave has had a profound influence on Western thought. Subsequent centuries and thinkers adhered to Plato's view. Medieval theologians believed truth was revealed only by God or by the Church. The intellectual legacy of the Reformation centered on whether it is possible for the average person to ascertain truth without benefit of a priest or a king. About 200 years later, Milton suggested that competing notions of the truth should be allowed to coexist, with the ultimate truth eventually emerging (see Table 2.1).

Milton's assertions foreshadowed the philosophy of the Enlightenment, from which modern journalism borrows its notion of truth. The Enlightenment cast truth in secular terms, divorced from the Church, and developed a "correspondence theory" of truth still held today. The correspondence theory asserts that truth should

TABLE 2.1. A Philosophy of Truth Emerges

Source	Truth Equals
Ancient Greeks	What is memorable and is handed down
Plato	What abides in the world of perfect forms
Medieval	What the king, Church or God says
Milton	What emerges from the "marketplace of ideas"
Enlightenment	What is verifiable, replicable, universal
Pragmatists	What is filtered through individual perception

correspond to external facts or observations. The Enlightenment concept of truth was linked to what human beings could perceive with their senses harnessed through the intellect. Truth acquired substance. It was something that could be known and something that could be replicated.

This Enlightenment notion of truth is essential to the scientific method. Truth has become increasingly tied to what is written down, what can be empirically verified, what can be perceived by the human senses. Enlightenment truth does not vary among people or cultures. It is a truth uniquely suited to the written word, for it links what is written with what is factual, accurate and important.

Truth and Objectivity

This Enlightenment view of truth is the basis for the journalistic ideal of objectivity. While objectivity has many definitions, minimally it is the requirement that journalists divorce fact from opinion. Objectivity is a way of knowing that connects human perception with facts and then knowledge. Objectivity is also a process of information collection (Ward 2004). Journalists view objectivity as refusing to allow individual bias to influence what they report or how they cover it. It is in journalism that all facts and people are regarded as equal and equally worthy of coverage. Culture, an individual sense of mission, and individual and organizational feelings and views do not belong in objective news accounts. An Enlightenment view of truth allowed objectivity to be considered an attainable ideal.

However, philosophy was not the only reason, or even the most important reason, that objectivity became a professional standard in the early 1900s. The early American press was not really a mass press, and it garnered much of its financial support from political advertising and most of its readership through its avowedly partisan political reporting. As America became more urban in the late 1800s, publishers realized that to convince potential advertisers their advertising would be seen, they had to make certain that their publications would be read. Partisan publications could not ensure that, for strong views offended potential readers. What publishers at the turn of the 20th century needed was a product that built on an Enlightenment principle that facts would be facts, no matter who was doing the reading. Opinion would be relegated to specific pages and both facts and opinion could be wrapped around advertising (Schudson 1978).

The normative ideal of objectivity came along at an advantageous time. The mass press of the early 1900s was deeply and corruptly involved in yellow journalism. Fabricated stories were common; newspaper wars were close to the real thing. Objectivity was a good way to clean up journalism's act with a set of standards where seemingly none had existed before. It fit the cultural expectations of the Enlightenment that truth was knowable and ascertainable. And it made sure that readers of news columns would remain unoffended long enough to glance at the ads.

The Enlightenment view of truth also was compatible with democracy and its emphasis on rational government. People who could reason together could arrive at some shared "truth" of how they could govern themselves. Information was essential to government, for it allowed citizens to scrutinize government. As long as truth was ascertainable, government could function. Under this view, *information provided the social glue as well as the grease of society.* Citizens and government needed information in order to continue their rational function. Information, and the notion that it corresponded in some essential way with the truth, carried enormous promise.

The 20th-century pragmatists—most notably Americans John Dewey, George Herbert Mead, Charles Sanders Pierce and William James—challenged the Enlightenment view of truth. To them truth depended on how it was investigated and on who was doing the investigating. Further, they rejected the notion that there was only one proper method of investigation—that is, the scientific method. Borrowing from Einstein, pragmatists argued that truth, like matter, was relative.

The pragmatists proposed that knowledge and reality were not *fixed by* but instead were *the result of* an evolving stream of consciousness and learning. Reality itself varied based on the psychological, social, historical or cultural context. Additionally, reality was defined as that which was probable, not as something intrinsic (the Platonic view) or something determined by only one method of observation (the Enlightenment view). Pragmatism found a comfortable home in the 20th-century United States. Under pragmatism truth lost much of its universality, but it was in remarkable agreement with the American value of democratic individualism. Soon pragmatism filtered through literature, science and some professions, such as law.

Pragmatism provided a challenge to objectivity. No sooner had the journalistic community embraced objectivity than the culture adopted more pragmatic notions of truth. That clash fueled criticism of objectivity. Several questions surfaced. If truth is subjective, can it be reported by an impassive, objective and detached reporter? Does such a reporter exist? Is truth a construct that relies on context?

Postmodern philosophy (see *The Matrix* that follows) has taken these questions to their logical extension, suggesting that the concept of truth is devoid of meaning. Postmodernism asserts that context is literally everything, and that meaning cannot exist apart from context, which is directly opposed to fact-based journalism which assumed that facts were facts regardless of context.

The last 40 years have added yet another level of complexity to the problem: the information explosion. Facts and truth come to us quickly from all over the globe. Today, the Internet has removed the financial imperative of objectivity and made it once again financially viable to operate a partisan press, especially a virtual one. While objective reporting is still *one* standard, it is not the *only* standard. The ratings success of MSNBC and Fox News compared with that of CNN might indicate that the partisan press can be made profitable. With the advent of blogs such as Huffington Post, which include not just words, but images, aggregated from many sources, yet a different notion of truth is resurfacing—what philosophers call the convergence or coherence theory of truth. Under this view, truth is discovered not through any single method of investigation but by determining which set of facts form a coherent mental picture of events and ideas investigated through a variety of methods.

Convergence journalism—which uses sounds, images and words to cover stories—is one professional response to the coherence theory of truth and the technological possibilities of the Internet and the personal computer. Of course, convergence journalism requires an active audience. All too often, it is possible to be overwhelmed by the information available to us rather than devoting the time and effort required to make sense of it. Telling your readers and viewers the truth has become a complicated business as Sissela Bok points out:

> Telling the "truth" therefore is not solely a matter of moral character; it is also a matter of correct appreciation of real situations and of serious reflection upon them. . . . Telling the truth, therefore, is something which must be learnt. This will sound very shocking to anyone who thinks that it must all depend on moral character and that if this is blameless the rest is child's play. But the simple fact is that the ethics cannot be detached from reality, and consequently continual progress in learning to appreciate reality is a necessary ingredient in ethical action. (Bok 1978, 302–303)

WHO'S DOING THE TALKING ANYWAY?

The pragmatic's critique of objectivity has called attention to the question of who writes the news. Journalists—primarily male, Caucasian, well educated, and middle to upper class—are often asked to cover issues and questions that life experiences has not prepared them to cover. Stephen Hess (1981) noted that journalists (particularly the Eastern "elite" media), in terms of their socioeconomic status, look a great deal more like the famous or powerful people they cover than the people they are supposedly writing for. Work on the national press corps has shown similar results (Weaver, Beam, Brownlee, Voakes and Wilhoit 2007). Journalists generally are better paid and better educated than the audience for their product.

In the past few decades, almost every professional journalistic organization has developed programs specifically to attract and retain women and minorities with only incremental and sporadic success. This lack of access to the engines of information has not been lost on a variety of minority groups—from religious

The Matrix: A Postmodern Examination of Truth

"Do you ever have that feeling where you're not sure whether you are awake or still dreaming?"

"Yeah, all the time. . . . It just sounds to me like you might need to unplug, man . . . get some R&R?"

Thus begins Neo's journey down the rabbit hole (like Lewis Carroll's *Alice in Wonderland*) where reality literally turns inside out on itself. A computer wizard, and unknown genetic mutation, Neo—who is awakened to the possibilities courtesy of Morpheus—literally unplugs himself from the reality of a computer simulation where human beings serve as batteries for machines that run the world. Reality for most people is nothing more than a computer code invented by the artificial intelligence and inserted electronically into their neural systems from infancy onward. Neo is the person who has the capacity to crack and overcome the code.

The Matrix set the early standard for smart films about the potential of the computers that power the information age. The film was stylish. In fact, the long, black trench coats Keanu Reeves and Carrie-Anne Moss wore were eerily predictive of the attire worn by the Columbine High School shooters. The special effects and set design, based as they were on a comic book reality, gave form to one vision of hyper-reality, as did the film's other-worldly, violent content.

Besides being provocative, the film provides an accessible discussion of the postmodern approach to truth.

Postmodernism is a logical outgrowth of pragmatism. Instead of suggesting that truth varies with receiver, or sender or context, postmodernism suggests that truth—if it exists at all—is unknowable. Those who believe they know the truth, like Neo at the beginning of the film,

discover that their "reality" is false consciousness, founded on invalid assumptions that shift constantly in a chaotic environment.

Postmodernism rejects the correspondence theory of truth, or the Platonic ideal that truth is knowable only as an intellectual construct. In postmodernism, revealed truth does not exist, and the marketplace of ideas yields babble. In the film, dreams are real, reality shifts and absolutely nothing is what it seems. Control, in the form of computer programs (malleable by both the programmers and the programmed), and death, in the form of biological waste, remain.

Most journalistic endeavors reject postmodern thinking on the grounds that the essence of humanity itself provides an irrefutable challenge to postmodernism's premise. Others have noted that postmodernism too easily falls into the trap of solipsism—the notion that it is impossible to know anything outside of one's individual thoughts and perceptions.

While traditional theory and theorists may reject postmodernism, contemporary culture sometimes embraces what Morpheus calls "the desert of the real." If postmodernism is an appropriate worldview, does that mean journalists and persuasion professionals should abandon their jobs or their ancient foundations?

We think not.

Neo and Morpheus still have to act. They learn to think in new ways, but their actions remain centered on their belief in human independence and the "rightness" of thinking about and connecting with others. Even in this postmodern vision, ethical thinking still has a place. Neo's goal, after all, is to dismantle one matrix so humanity can make its own choices.

fundamentalists, who have in some cases established their own broadcasting networks, to racial minorities, who fail to find themselves either as owners or managers of media outlets. To them, news is *about* middle-class Caucasians, *for* middle-class Caucasians. Even the 2008 election of the nation's first African-American president did little to change the way media covered "ordinary" minorities, and attempts to both employ and cover minorities have traditionally been slow and sporadic.

In the beginning of the 21st century, worldwide newspaper readership and broadcast viewership continued to decline. How individual journalists and the corporations they work for should remedy the situation is unclear. But as demographics changed us from a culture that is predominantly Caucasian to one that is not, the mass media, particularly newspapers, will play a decreasing role unless journalists find a way to report news that is of interest to the new majority of their readers. The winners in all this change: the Internet (including newspaper Web sites) and magazines that focus on celebrities rather than public affairs (Thorson, Duffy and Schumann 2007). Traditional journalists faced an audience in open rebellion with no clear strategy to regain the "eyeballs" advertisers desire or the public focus that civic engagement requires.

SEEING ISN'T BELIEVING

More than 80 years ago, journalist Walter Lippmann (1922) said, "For the most part, we do not first see, and then define, we define first and then see." He added that we tend to pick out what our culture has already defined for us, and then perceive it in the form stereotyped for us by our culture.

In one classic study (Rainville and McCormick 1977), a blind New York journalism professor claimed he could predict the race of football players being described in the play-by-play by what was said about them. Caucasian athletes were described as intellectually gifted while African-American athletes were described as physically gifted. In a culture that values brains over brawn, African-American football players were the subject of repeated stereotypical insults—all couched as praise. And even though the study is now more than 50 years old, the tendency to revert to these stereotypes continues on sports broadcasts today in which athletes are called "smart" and which are called "athletic." In the former, the quality was obtained by hard work; in the latter, it was a gift of genetics.

Women, elderly people and the gay community have conducted studies with similar results. Their conclusion has been that while journalists maintain that they are objective, they (like their readers and viewers) bring something to the message that literally changes what they see and what they report (Lester 1996). Culture also has an impact, an issue we will ask you to consider in the third case study in this chapter.

In a *Columbia Journalism Review* cover story entitled "Rethinking Objectivity," author Brent Cunningham (2003) says that "objectivity can trip us up on the way to truth. Objectivity excuses lazy reporting. If you're on deadline and all you have is 'both sides of the story,' then that's often good enough." Cunningham points to a study of 414 Iraq war stories broadcast on ABC, CBS and NBC leading up to the 2003 conflict. All but 34 originated from the White House, the Pentagon or the State Department. The result: the "official truth" becomes the received truth, and only the bravest journalists dared depart from it. Timothy Crouse in his classic campaign memoir *The Boys on the Bus* reported the same phenomenon—stories outside the mainstream were not rewarded, they were spiked.

E. J. Dionne (1996) claims that the press is in internal contradiction. It must be neutral, yet investigative. It must be disengaged, but have an impact. It must be fair-minded but have an edge. The conflicts make objectivity virtually impossible to define and even harder to practice.

DEFINING AND CONSTRUCTING THE NEWS

News reflects certain cultural values and professional norms. In a classic study, sociologist Herbert Gans (1979) studied how stories became news at *Newsweek* and CBS and found that almost all news stories reflected these six cultural values: (1) ethnocentrism; (2) altruistic democracy; (3) responsible capitalism; (4) individualism; (5) an emphasis on the need for and maintenance of social order; and (6) leadership. These dominant values helped shape which stories were printed and what they said, what communication scholars call "framing."

Gans called these values the "para-ideology" of the media. He added that "the news is not so much conservative or liberal as it is reformist." Researcher James Carey (quoted in Cunningham 2003) says that it is this para-ideology that results in charges of liberal bias against the media. "There is a bit of the reformer in anyone who enters journalism. And reformers are always going to make conservatives uncomfortable."

News stories about middle-class or upper-class people, those who tend to successfully adopt the culture's values, made the American news "budget," according to Gans. While Gans focused on journalism about the United States, other scholars have noted the same phenomenon, called *domesticating the*

NON SEQUITUR © Wiley Miller. 1993 Dist. By UNIVERSAL UCLICK. Reprinted with permission. All rights reserved.

foreign, in international coverage (Gurevitch, Levy and Roeh 1991). Journalists working for U.S. media outlets tell stories about international events in cultural terms Americans can readily understand but which also sacrifice accuracy. For example, routine coverage of elections in Britain or Israel is conveyed in horse-race metaphors even though both countries employ a parliamentary system where governing coalitions are common and who wins the horse race is not nearly so important.

PACKAGING THE STORY: NEWS AS MANUFACTURED PRODUCT

The goal of telling a "good story" also raises other ethical questions, specifically those that focus on packaging to highlight drama and human interest. These questions have intensified as all media channels—from newspapers to documentary film to entertainment programming—have focused on coherent storytelling and the need for a powerful story to capture audience interest. Current research suggests that narratives are memorable; but news narratives are not always neat and the facts from which they emerge can be both chaotic and contradictory.

This drive to package has led to a profession that values finding an "event" to report and to be there first. Few consumers realize it, but news is "manufactured" daily, just as surely as furniture, cars or the meal at your favorite fast-food restaurant—and often the process can be messy. Journalists start the day with a blank computer screen and with press time or broadcast time looming. They end the day with a print story, a video package or a Web page—or often all three. And adding to the built-in tension of deadlines is the challenge to be fair, complete, accurate and, above all, interesting. Whole industries—particularly public relations or "strategic communications"—have emerged to help journalists package their daily stories on deadline.

The need to find an event has meant journalists have missed some important stories because they were not events but rather historic developments with both a past and a future. For example, major social developments such as the women's movement (Mills 1989), the civil rights movement and the anti–Vietnam War movement were under-covered until their leaders created events such as sit-ins and demonstrations for the media to report. Director Michael Moore said he began his career with the 1989 film *Roger and Me* about the devastation of General Motors layoffs on his hometown of Flint, Michigan, because he "didn't see on the silver screen or the television screen what happened to people like us" (Smith 1992).

Reporting on the Occupy Wall Street movement—and its sister protests—represents a current example of the traditional media finding a story "late" and being baffled by a group without the sort of organizing structure that promoted ready media access, formal spokespersons and routinized events. The same is true of political candidates in the United States as the media often make decisions on whom to cover based, oddly enough, on who is getting covered.

The preoccupation with events affects coverage of science, too, which is most frequently reported as a series of discoveries and "firsts" rather than as a process (Nelkin 1987). We are treated to stories about the new cures often without the necessary context—political, economic, etc.—to interpret the latest research results. Nelkin says that the twin dramas of "new hope" and "no hope" drive most science reporting. Former Vice President and Nobel Laureate Al Gore's documentary *An Inconvenient Truth* was an example of making an "event" out of more than 50 years of science, all in an attempt to spur public debate.

Other stories are missed or misreported when they lack the easy "peg" editors look for. When thousands of lives were lost in Bhopal, India, by a malfunctioning plant, coverage focused entirely on the event and not the socioeconomic, scientific and political causes that led to the disaster. Instead, news coverage focused on the picture-friendly event (Wilkins 1987). A deeper look at news coverage of the 1986 Chernobyl nuclear disaster, something Charles Perrow calls a "normal accident" in his book of the same title, found coverage echoed the stereotype of American superiority and Russian inferiority rather an approach focusing on science and risk (Patterson 1989). More recently, the *Washington Post*'s Pulitzer Prize–winning stories on conditions at Walter Reed Army Medical Center emerged only after dismayed veterans and their families contacted the newspaper multiple times.

Because of their nature, slow-onset disasters such as topsoil erosion, climate change and waste management have historically been underreported. Phenomena not linked to specific events such as the growth of a permanent American underclass go unreported for years waiting for an appropriate news peg. For instance, the Great Recession that began in 2008 supplied a needed event to help complex stories of corporate and bank fraud make the larger news agenda. Under event-oriented journalism, elections become horse races with "frontrunners" and the "rest of the pack" counted and handicapped daily with each new poll. But reporting an election as a contest fails to focus on the policy issues, which is what democratic elections are supposed to be about.

The phenomenon of "pack journalism" has been chronicled in several films, dating back to the classic *The Front Page* and later *The Boys on the Bus* (Crouse 1974) and the book *Feeding Frenzy* (Sabato 1992). All emphasize journalistic excesses and an unwillingness to engage in independent thought that would disturb enlightened and pragmatic philosophers alike. They also expose a too easily manipulated system, particularly as newsroom staffs have shrunk. This unwillingness to leave the "pack" with a breakout story has caused some of the hottest political stories of the new century to be reported first on the Web where these institutional pressures do not exist.

Journalists have also been cowed by the threat of litigation. The film *The Insider* presents a fictionalized but nonetheless fact-based account about the impact of litigation on reporting stories critical of big tobacco. Seymour Hersh's original reporting of the My Lai massacre during the Vietnam War, which eventually appeared in the *New York Times,* was held up because no other reporter had a similar story. Some 30 years later, it wasn't until CBS broadcast images of prisoner abuse at the notorious Abu Ghraib prison in Iraq that Hersch's initial reporting of the scandal in the Atlantic received serious national attention.

Truth is more than just a collection of facts. Facts have a relationship to one another and to other facts, forming a larger whole. Yet analytic coverage of American institutions, of science and technology, of politics and of social movements is rare. What is more common—especially on cable news outlets—is to invite two or more parties with conflicting views, allot them too little time to discuss the issue at hand and then sit back and let the resulting heated exchange take the place of reporting. If the role of the mass media is not only to detail events and issues but to make the relationship among them clear, is merely rounding up conflicting talking heads sufficient? Or do we need to do it better?

Stephen Hess (1981) has argued that journalists need to engage in reporting that looks more like social science than storytelling. Gans (1979) argues for news that is labeled as originating from a particular point of view. If readers and viewers are alerted to the worldview of those who have selected the news (as they were during the era of the partisan press) they would be better able to place news in context. Other scholars argue for news that is analytical rather than anecdotal, proactive rather than reactive and contextual rather than detached. On a practical level, working reporters and editors insist that individual journalists need to do a better job of understanding their own biases and compensating for them.

The accumulated evidence, both anecdotal and scholarly, today strikes at the core of objectivity and shows that intellectually we are living in a pragmatic era, but professionally we seem to be unable to develop a working alternative to the Enlightenment's view of truth. Because of this, mainstream media are increasingly seen as irrelevant, particularly to a younger audience for whom truth is more likely to be a segment on *The Colbert Report,* who in 2012 won a Peabody Award for his coverage of the impact of Super PACs on elections, than a report on the network's dwindling nightly newscasts.

ON THE ETHICS OF DECEPTION

In a profession that values truth, is it ever ethical to lie to editors? To readers? To sources, who may be liars themselves? Are there levels of lying? Is flattering someone to get an interview as serious a transgression as doctoring a quote or photograph? Is withholding information the same thing as lying? If you can get only one side of the story, do you go with it? Does it matter today if opinion mingles with news?

Crises of credibility have faced media outlets of all sizes including spectacular instances at both *USA Today* and the *New York Times* that resulted in front-page editorial apologies and multipage retractions. The case of the *Times* started when a 27-year-old reporter, Jayson Blair, fabricated all or part of more than 40 stories. After his resignation from the paper, the *Times* ran four full pages of corrections documenting every error discovered in Blair's reporting. The *Times'* correction made it clear that the *Times* had failed to correct the problem earlier, in part because of his race. Blair was African-American, and he had been hired as part of the *Times'* diversity program. His mentors at the paper, Executive Editor Howell

---

Errors in Journalism: Inevitability and Arrogance

Confounding truth and deception in journalism is the problem of errors. Inadvertent mistakes in stories are common. One freelance fact checker (Hart 2003) wrote in the *Columbia Journalism Review* that she had not experienced an error-free story in three years of fact checking for *CJR,* one of journalism's leading watchdog publications. Her calls to fellow fact checkers at other publications led her to believe that articles with errors are the rule, not the exception.

However, mistakes are different from fabrication and do not indicate a lack of dedication to the truth. Some, if not most, mistakes are matters of interpretation, but others are outright errors of fact. In her article, "Delusions of Accuracy," Ariel

Hart says that hearing journalists proudly claim to have had no errors or fewer errors than the *Times* found in Blair's writing is "scary, not the least because it encourages delusions of accuracy."

One problem seems to be audience members so disconnected from the media that they don't bother to correct our mistakes or, worse, assume as readers of the *Times* evidently did, that fabrication is *de rigueur* for journalists. "Journalists surely make mistakes often, but I think we don't—or can't—admit it to ourselves because the idea of a mistake is so stigmatized. . . . So mistakes need to be destigmatized or restigmatized and dealt with accordingly. They should be treated like language errors," Hart argues.

Raines and Managing Editor Gerald Boyd, who also was African-American, were among Blair's strongest supporters. Both eventually resigned in the fallout. While the *Times* denied that race was the reason that Blair had been promoted, Blair himself did not.

Pulitzer Prize–winning reporter Rick Bragg also resigned from the *Times* after it became public that he, too, had published stories based largely on the reporting of stringers who did not receive a byline in the *Times.* Furthermore, some of his stories filed with non–New York datelines had been written on airplanes and in hotel rooms where Bragg was functioning more as a rewrite editor rather than doing actual on-the-scene reporting. Bragg said his practices were known at the *Times* and common in the industry. That comment aligns with one heard frequently in the Blair incident that sources did not complain to the *Times* about incorrect stories *since they felt that fictionalizing stories was just the way things are done.* This cynical appraisal of journalism threatens journalists' credibility, which is the chief currency of the profession.

So, how do journalists feel about deception? A survey of members of Investigative Reporters and Editors (IRE) provides some insight into the profession's thinking (Lee 2005). Journalists think about deception on a continuum. At one end, there is almost universal rejection of lying to readers, viewers and listeners. IRE members regard such lies as among the worst ethical professional breaches. At the other end, more than half of the IRE members surveyed said they approved of flattering a source to get an interview, even if that flattery was insincere.

PEARLS BEFORE SWINE © 2003 *Stephan Pastis. Reprinted with permission of UNIVER-SAL UCLICK. All rights reserved.*

In the same survey, lies of omission—such as withholding information from readers and viewers and also editors and bosses—were considered less of a problem than fabricating facts in a story or fabricating entire stories, which was almost universally condemned. IRE members were more willing to withhold information in instances when national security issues were involved. The journalists also said some lies were justified; they approved of lying if it would save a life or prevent injury to a source.

The journalists surveyed also noted that there were outside influences on these judgments. Broadcast journalists were more accepting of hidden cameras and altering video than were print journalists, although that difference might be changing as more print journalists get video experience via their newspaper's Web sites. And, those who worked in competitive markets were more willing to accept deception than were those who saw themselves in less competitive environments. The more experienced a journalist was, the less likely he or she was to accept any form of deception. Finally, the survey revealed what journalists worry about is the impact such reporting methods have on the believability of news accounts and on journalists' ability to cover subsequent stories if caught in an ethical lapse.

Is it ethical to lie to liars? Is withholding information the same thing as lying? If not, under what circumstances might it be appropriate? If it is, are there ethically based justifications for such an act? Sissela Bok (1978) has written eloquently on lying to liars. She argues that such an act raises two questions: Will the lie serve a larger social good, and does the act of lying mean that we as professionals are willing to be lied to in return?

Bok suggests that most of the time, when we lie we want "free rider" status—gaining the benefits of lying without incurring the risks of being lied to. In other words, some journalists may believe it's acceptable to lie to a crook to get a story, but they professionally resent being lied to by any source, regardless of motive.

Lying is a way to get and maintain power. Those in positions of power often believe they have the right to lie because they have a greater than ordinary understanding of what is at stake. Lying in a crisis (to prevent panic) and lying to enemies (to protect national security) are two examples. In both circumstances journalists can be—either actively or without their knowledge—involved in the deception. Do journalists have a right to counter this lying with lies of their own, told under the guise of the public's need to know? Does a journalist have the responsibility to print the truth when printing it will cause one of the evils—panic or a threat to national security—that the lie was concocted to prevent?

Then there is the "omission versus commission" issue. In the first, the lie is that some part of the truth was conveniently left out; in the latter, the lie is an untruth told purposefully. Bok asserts that a genuinely white lie may be excusable on some grounds, but that all forms of lying must stand up to questions of fairness and mutuality. According to Kant's categorical imperative, the teller of the white lie must also be willing to be lied to. Even lying to liars can have its downside as Bok points out in her book, *Lying.*

> In the end, the participants in deception they take to be mutually understood may end up with coarsened judgment and diminished credibility. But if, finally, the liar to whom one wishes to lie is also in a position to do one harm, then the balance may shift; not because he is a liar, but because of the threat he poses (Bok 1978, 140).

Reporting *via* the Internet has given new urgency to the issue of lying by omission. In most instances failing to identify yourself as a reporter when collecting information electronically from news groups, chat rooms or other modes of public discussion is considered problematic. Journalists, when pressed, note that the U.S. Supreme Court has ruled Internet transmissions are public. The ethical issue emerges when most of those involved in the discussion are not aware of the legal standards and expect, instead, the more ethically based relations of face-to-face interactions. Ethical thought leaves journalists with difficult choices.

Reporting *on* the contents of the Internet—and cable television—raises another series of challenges. How should journalists go about debunking Internet rumors? Conventional wisdom for the legacy media holds that re-printing or re-broadcasting rumors only furthers them. However, people seem to believe what they see on the Internet, no matter how implausible. News organizations in New Orleans covering Hurricane Katrina dealt with a series of difficult news decisions in face of the rumors sweeping the city. In some instances, they elected to print or broadcast that they could not substantiate rumors prevalent in the networked world. The same problems continue to plague journalists in stories as distinct as news of Michael Jackson's death, terrorist attacks in India, or a variety of sophisticated hoaxes perpetrated on officials and journalists alike. Another equally serious challenge is how to treat information from well-known sources when it is false. Journalists covering campaigns are frequently put in the position of airing information that is dubious in its content but nonetheless newsworthy because it was stated by the candidate. Calling someone a liar, at one level, seems the height of nonobjective journalism. But, when the facts suggest that a source is lying—even if that source is not held to the same standards of truthtelling as journalists are—what becomes an acceptable professional mechanism to hold nonjournalist sources to account? We will ask you to grapple with this issue in Case 6-A.

ETHICAL NEWS VALUES

Most mass media courses present a list of qualities that define news. Most such lists include proximity, timeliness, conflict, consequence, prominence, rarity, change, concreteness, action and personality. Additional elements may include notions of mystery, drama, adventure, celebration, self-improvement and even ethics. While these lists are helpful to beginning journalists, they probably will not help you decide how to recount the news ethically.

We suggest you expand your journalistic definitions of news to include a list of ethical news values. These values are intended to reflect the philosophic tensions inherent in a profession with a commitment to truth. If news values were constructed from ethical reasoning, we believe the following elements would be emphasized by both journalists and the organizations for which they work.

Accuracy—using the correct facts and the right words and putting things in context. Journalists need to be as independent as they can when framing stories. They need to be aware of their own biases, including those they "inherit" as social class, gender and ethnicity, as well as learned professional norms.

Confirmation—writing articles that are able to withstand scrutiny inside and outside the newsroom. Media ethicist Sandy Borden (2009) refers to this as the "discipline of confirmation," a concept that reflects how difficult it can be to capture even a portion of the truth in sometimes complex news situations.

Tenacity—knowing when a story is important enough to require additional effort, both personal and institutional. Tenacity drives journalists to provide all the depth they can regardless of the individual assignment. It has institutional implications, too, for the individual cannot function well in an environment where resources are too scarce or the corporate bottom line too dominant. In addition, news organizations need to trust journalists when they report independently rather than expect them to act as part of a pack.

Dignity—leaving the subject of a story as much self-respect as possible. Dignity values each person regardless of the particular story or the particular role the individual plays. Dignity allows the individual journalist to recognize that news gathering is a cooperative enterprise where each plays a role, including editors, videographers, designers and advertising sales staff.

Reciprocity—treating others as you wish to be treated. Too often, journalism is "writing for the lowest common denominator." Reciprocity demands respect for the reader. It also rejects the notion of journalism as benevolent paternalism—"We'll tell you what we think is good for you"—and recognizes that journalists and their viewers and readers are partners both in discovering what is important and in gleaning meaning from it.

Sufficiency—allocating adequate resources to important issues. On the individual level, sufficiency can mean thoroughness, for example, checking both people and documents for every scrap of fact before beginning to write. On an organizational level, it means allocating adequate resources to the newsgathering process. With virtually every media outlet suffering from declining readers or viewers, thanks mainly to the Web, this is probably the central issue of the current media landscape.

Equity—seeking justice for all involved in controversial issues and treating all sources and subjects equally. Equity assumes a complicated world with a variety of points of view. Equity demands that all points of view be considered, but does not demand that all sides be framed as equally compelling. Equity expands the journalistic norms of "telling both sides of the story" to "telling all sides of the story."

Community—valuing social cohesion. On the organization level, a sense of community means that media outlets and the corporations that own them need to consider themselves as citizens rather than mere "profit centers." On the individual level, it means evaluating stories with an eye first to social good.

Diversity—covering all segments of the audience fairly and adequately. There appears to be almost overwhelming evidence that news organizations do not "look like" the society they cover. While management can remedy part of this problem by changing hiring patterns, individual journalists can learn to "think diversity" regardless of their individual heritages.

In 2011, the Corporation for Public Broadcasting decided to make an ethical news value—transparency—the cornerstone of its new standards and practices policy. We'll ask you to take a look at the impact of that ethical news value—and its implication for the other values we have listed—in a case study in this chapter. Regardless, no list of ethical news values should be considered conclusive. Collectively, they provide a framework within which informed ethical choices can be made.

Suggested Readings

Bok, Sissela. 1978. *Lying: Moral choice in public and private life.* New York: Random House.

Gans, Herbert. 1975. *Deciding what's news: A study of CBS Evening News, NBC Nightly News, Newsweek, and Time.* New York: Pantheon.

Jamieson, Kathleen Hall. 1992. *Dirty politics.* New York: Oxford University Press.

Lippmann, Walter. 1922. *Public opinion.* New York: Free Press.

Plato. *The republic.*

Weaver, David H., Randal A. Beam, Bonnie J. Brownlee, Paul s. Voakes, and G. Cleveland Wilhoit. 2007. *The American journalist in the 21st century: U.S. news people at the dawn of a new millennium.* Mahwah, NJ: Lawrence Erlbaum & Associates.

Cases on the Web

www.mhhe.com/mediaethics8e

"Columbine: News and community—A balancing act" by Lee Wilkins

"The doctor has AIDS" by Deni Elliott

"Taste in photojournalism: A question of ethics or aesthetics" by Lou Hodges

"Reporters and confidential sources" by Steve Weinberg

"Rodent wars and cultural battles: Reporting hantavirus" by JoAnn M. Valenti

"Too many bodies, too much blood: A case study of the 'family-sensitive newscast'" by Bill Silcock

"Nine days in Union: The Susan Smith case" by Sonya Forte Duhé

"SARS: The bug that would not go away" by Seow Ting Lee
"The spouse is squeezed: A South Carolina TV reporters' attempt to conceal her source" by
    Sonya Forte Duhé

CHAPTER 2 CASES

CASE 2-A

Can I Quote Me on That?

CHAD PAINTER
Eastern New Mexico University

During an Aug. 19, 2012, interview with St. Louis television station KTVI-TV, Missouri Senate candidate Todd Akin said women cannot get pregnant from "legitimate rape" because their bodies have ways to block unwanted pregnancies. Republican presidential contender Mitt Romney quickly condemned the comments, calling them "insulting, inexcusable, and frankly, wrong" and saying that he found the comments "offensive" and "entirely without merit," according to an article in the *National Review Online.*

But did Romney actually say those words?

There is question because government and campaign officials regularly grant interviews to journalists only under the condition of quote approval, according to *New York Times* writer Jeremy Peters. Quote approval, *Time* media critic James Poniewozik wrote, is when a journalist agrees to send his or her source quotes to be "redacted, stripped of colorful metaphors, colloquial language and anything even mildly provocative."

Peters wrote that Romney and his campaign advisers almost always require quote approval from any conversation, and that journalists quoting any of Romney's five sons use only quotations approved by his press office. Quote approval also is the accepted norm for President Barack Obama, his top strategists, and almost all of his midlevel aids in Chicago and Washington.

Several major news organizations—including *The New York Times, The Washington Post, Reuters, Bloomberg, Vanity Fair,* and *National Journal*—have accepted the practice of quote approval in political stories, according to Peters. (There also is a long-standing, problematic tradition of quote approval for celebrity news and certain types of sports stories.) One reason for the acquiescence by reporters, Poniewozik wrote, is that a reporter who does not accept the condition could be scooped by another reporter who did. A second reason is that reporters often are desperate to pick the brains of a politician or his top strategists. Finally, each of the reporters Peters interviewed said that the meanings of quotes were not altered, and that changes were always small and seemingly unnecessary.

Many journalists perform accuracy checks with sources, ensuring that the quotes and information gained from a source are correct. Some publications require accuracy checks. However, quote approval is quite different from an accuracy check.

The quote approval requirement really is a struggle between reporters and politicians for power and control. News is a construction of reality (Gulati, Just and Crigler 2004) dependent on the relationship of a news organization with other institutions, interests, or groups in a society (Baldasty 1992; Shoemaker and Reese 1996). News about political campaigns is an ongoing negotiation—or power struggle—between journalists, editors, and owners on one side, and candidates, campaign staffers, and party activists on the other (Gulati et al. 2004). The media need a steady, reliable flow of the raw material of news (Herman and Chomsky 2002). Journalists become reliant on their sources because of this constant need for new information, and this reliance allows sources to dictate terms of coverage.

Politicians and their campaign staffs also could be asserting control, calling off the hounds of an attack-dog press. Sabato (2000) suggests that attack journalism during presidential campaigns causes candidates to become increasingly secretive because of their fear of reporters. The result is that politicians limit press access except under highly controlled situations (Sabato 2000). The ultimate highly controlled situation is for a politician to grant interviews only when he or she knows any quote can be deleted or changed.

Micro Issues

1. Citizens need information about candidates' and politicians' views on issues. However, what should journalists be willing to give up in order to obtain that information?
2. How reliable is information obtained after a politician or his or her advisers have massaged or altered quotes?
3. Are there certain sorts of stories, for example stories about science or finance, where this practice might be more acceptable? Why or why not?

Midrange Issues

1. Quote approval is for newspaper journalists. Should there be such a thing as video approval? What would be the morally relevant distinctions?
2. Should reporters disclose to their readers when they have submitted a story for quote approval? Kovach and Rosentiel (2007) argue that journalism's first obligation is to the truth, and journalists' first loyalty is to citizens. Journalists should report honestly to their readers (Associated Press 2012) and should disclose unavoidable conflicts (Society of Professional Journalists 2012).
3. How is quote approval related to truth?

Macro Issues

1. Media based on social responsibility is premised on the idea that freedom of expression is a positive freedom (Nerone 1995). The moral right of freedom of expression is not unconditional (The Commission on Freedom of the Press 1947) but a right granted to do moral good (Neron 1995). By agreeing to "quote approval" are reporters opening the debate as to whether they are serving the best interests of the public or serving the interests of politicians? How would you respond to this question?
2. How does the notion of citizen journalism influence the concept of quote approval? Of candidates' willingness to speak "off the cuff" with citizens?

CASE 2-B

News and the Transparency Standard

LEE WILKINS
University of Missouri

By many measures, 2010 and 2011 were very bad years for the Corporation for Public Broadcasting and its radio arm, National Public Radio. CPB found itself under attack by members of the Tea Party and some other Republicans for what they viewed as a "liberal" media agenda. Congress threatened to cut CBP's $320 million funding, a move that would have placed the financial future of about 50 percent of public radio and public television stations (most of those in smaller markets) in fiscal jeopardy. At the same time, the Great Recession that began in 2008 also took a financial toll; audience fund-raising activity—and corporate support—weakened.

Finances were not the only problem. These years included a series of significant controversies, beginning with the firing of NPR's Juan Williams for comments he made about Muslims that were broadcast on Fox News, where he also was a commentator. Ultimately NPR's top news manager, Ellen Weiss, was forced to resign over the incident. Just weeks later NPR's top executive, Vivian Schiller, who had come to public radio after working at the *New York Times,* was forced to resign after an audiotape of one of the organization's top fund-raisers, Ron Schiller (no relation), surfaced on the Internet. In that audiotape, Ron Schiller called some congressional Republicans and particularly members of the Tea Party racist, unchristian, and anti-intellectual. Schiller also said he believed that NPR and CPB would, over the long run, be better off without congressional funding support. Both Vivian Schiller and Ron Schiller were forced out.

All this came in the midst of professional successes, including a listening audience for NPR of more than 27 million people—much above those watching television network and cable news—and reporting that won every professional prize.

CPB had last changed its editorial and organizational standards in 2005, but beginning in 2009 launched a multiyear project to update those standards and to apply them to all aspects of CPB efforts—from program selection to fund-raising to news. The intent was a single set of standards that would inform best practices throughout the corporation. Executives hoped these consistent standards would strengthen ties with audience members and funders, including Congress. Those new standards were adopted in June 2011 and may be accessed at http://www.pbs.org/about/editorial-standards/. In many ways, these standards were similar to those that had informed the organization since its inception.

Those new standards included standards for the news organization that audiences know as National Public Radio. The standards were based on a normative framework for NPR's journalism and included an acknowledgment of the following principles: fairness, accuracy, balance, responsiveness to the public (accountability), courage and controversy, substance over technique, experiment and innovation, exploration of significant subjects and subsections on what would be considered unprofessional conduct, unacceptable production methods, and NPR's use of social media, particularly as a source for news stories. Third on the normative list was the standard of objectivity, which those who developed the updated standards linked to transparency in this way:

> Beyond that, for a work to be considered objective, it should reach a certain level of transparency. In a broad sense, this spirit of transparency means the audience should be able to understand the basics of how the producers put the material together. For example, the audience generally should be able to know not only who the sources of information are, but also why they were chosen and what their potential biases might be. As another example, if producers face particularly difficult editorial decisions that they know will be controversial, they should consider explaining why choices were made so the public can understand. Producers should similarly consider explaining to the audience why certain questions could not be answered, including why, if confidential sources are relied on, the producers agreed to allow the source to remain anonymous. And the spirit of transparency suggests that if the producers have arrived at certain conclusions or a point of view, the audience should be able to see the evidence so it can understand how that point of view was arrived at. One aspiration implicit in the idea of transparency is that an audience might appreciate and learn from content with which it also might disagree.
>
> Opinion and commentary are different from news and analysis. When a program, segment, digital material or other content is devoted to opinion or commentary, the principle of transparency requires that it be clearly labeled as such. Any content segment that presents only like-minded views without offering contrasting viewpoints should be considered opinion and should identify who is responsible for the views being presented.
>
> No content distributed by PBS should permit conscious manipulation of selected facts in order to propagandize.

Individual media outlets—both television and radio—may decide whether to adopt these voluntary standards.

Micro Issues

1. Are there certain sorts of agreements between journalists and their sources that would be jeopardized by the transparency standard?
2. Are there certain sorts of activities journalists do—for example, deciding which stories to cover—that might benefit from a transparency standard?
3. Does being transparent about process add unproductively to a journalist's workload?
4. Is transparency best considered a component of objectivity?

Midrange Issues

1. Take a news story from any media source and evaluate how well it meets the CPB normative guidelines.
2. What values on the CPB list do you find internally consistent? Contradictory? Could you adopt these standards as part of your best practices?
3. Do you think labeling something news or opinion matters to most audience members? What about entertainment programming such as *The Daily Show with Jon Stewart?*

Macro Issues

1. Should the U.S. taxpayer fund media organizations such as the Corporation for Public Broadcasting? (Answer this question now, and then see if you agree with your answer after reading Chapter 7.)
2. What definition of truth do you believe CPB is applying to news content—at least as reflected in its professional standards?

CASE 2-C

NPR, the *New York Times* and Working Conditions in China

LEE WILKINS
University of Missouri

On January 6, 2012, Ira Glass, host of Chicago Public Media *This American Life,* devoted a 39-minute segment to a report on working conditions at manufacturing plants in China.

The show was based extensively on a single source, Mike Daisey, who recounted what he had seen and what he had been told through an interpreter on a visit to a Foxconn factory in China, a plant that makes parts for the popular iPhone and iPad. Daisey recounted stories about working conditions and stated some workers in the plant had been poisoned during the manufacturing process.

Less than a month later, the *New York Times* ran a series of investigative stories on working conditions at Chinese plants making Apple products (http://www.nytimes.com/2012/01/26/business/ieconomy-apples-ipad-and-the-human-costs-for-workers-in-china.html?pagewanted=all).

"Mr. Daisey and the Apple Factory" quickly became the most popular *This American Life* podcast, with about 880,000 downloads. Daisey, a performance artist, became something of a celebrity and Apple critic, granting numerous interviews about his experiences. Faced with the publicity, Apple responded, announcing that it would for the first time allow third-party inspections of its Chinese manufacturing facilities.

National Public Radio's marketplace reporter Rob Schmitz also had spent a great deal of time in China and reported on working conditions there. He, too, heard the Mr. Daisey segment—and he told his bosses at NPR that there were facts included in it that did not ring true. He was given the go-ahead to do independent reporting.

Less than three months later, Glass aired the following retraction (http://www.thisamericanlife.org/blog/2012/03/retracting-mr-daisey-and-the-apple-factory/):

> I have difficult news. We've learned that Mike Daisey's story about Apple in China—which we broadcast in January—contained significant fabrications. We're retracting the story because we can't vouch for its truth. This is not a story we commissioned. It was an excerpt of Mike Daisey's acclaimed one-man show "The Agony and the Ecstasy of Steve Jobs," in which he talks about visiting a factory in China that makes iPhones and other Apple products.
>
> The China correspondent for the public radio show Marketplace tracked down the interpreter that Daisey hired when he visited Shenzhen China. The interpreter disputed much of what Daisey has been saying on stage and on our show. On this

week's episode of *This American Life,* we will devote the entire hour to detailing the errors in "Mr. Daisey Goes to the Apple Factory."

Daisey lied to me and to *This American Life* producer Brian Reed during the fact checking we did on the story, before it was broadcast. That doesn't excuse the fact that we never should've put this on the air. In the end, this was our mistake.

Subsequent inspections at Foxconn plants did reveal numerous violations of agreements to working conditions there. Daisey, in subsequent interviews, has said that while the specifics of his allegations were fabrications, the overall indictment of Apple is "true."

Micro Issues

1. Justify Schmitz's decision to go to his editors, who work for the same organization that broadcasts *This American Life,* asking to reinvestigate this story.
2. Download the original Mr. Daisey piece and the *New York Times* investigative report. Examine the sources for each. What principles regarding "knowing" and "telling" the truth emerge?
3. Was the retraction that Ira Glass provided ethically justifiable? Why or why not?

Midrange Issues

1. Many reporters work in countries where they do not speak the native language(s). What are the risks to accurate reporting when the individual journalist does not understand the words that are being spoken? Should "helpers" such as translators receive some byline or on-air credit for their assistance with such coverage?
2. What journalistic norms made Daisey's accounts so believable? How do you see those norms expressed in other investigative reports?
3. The *New York Times* has never had to retract any of its reporting on this issue. Evaluate the distinctions between the *Times* report and the Mr. Daisey piece based on the ethical news values outlined in this chapter.

Macro Issues

1. How should journalists treat sources that lie to them, particularly after the lie has been discovered? Is what Ira Glass did in his retraction ethical?
2. Is Mike Daisey right—even though his facts were wrong? Was the overall story "true"? What definition of truth do you use in responding to this question?

CASE 2-D

When Is Objective Reporting Irresponsible Reporting?

THEODORE L. GLASSER
Stanford University

Amanda Laurens, a reporter for a local daily newspaper, covers the city mayor's office, where yesterday she attended a 4:00 p.m. press conference. The mayor,

Ben Adams, read a statement accusing Evan Michaels, a city council member, of being a "paid liar" for the pesticide industry. "Councilman Michaels," the mayor said at the press conference, "has intentionally distorted the facts about the effects of certain pesticides on birds indigenous to the local area." "Mr. Michaels," the mayor continued, "is on the payroll of a local pesticide manufacturer," and his views on the effects of pesticides on bird life "are necessarily tainted."

The press conference ended at about 5:15 p.m., less than an hour before her 6:00 p.m. deadline. Laurens quickly contacted Councilman Michaels for a quote in response to the mayor's statement. Michaels, however, refused to comment, except to say that Mayor Adams's accusations were "utter nonsense" and "politically motivated." Laurens filed her story, which included both the mayor's accusation and the councilman's denial. Laurens's editor thought the story was fair and balanced and ran it the following morning on the front page.

The mayor was pleased with the coverage he received. He thought Laurens had acted professionally and responsibly by reporting his accusation along with Michaels's denial. Anything else, the mayor thought, would have violated the principles of objective journalism. The mayor had always believed that one of the most important responsibilities of the press was to provide an impartial forum for public controversies, and the exchange between him and the councilman was certainly a bona fide public controversy. Deciding who's right and who's wrong is not the responsibility of journalists, the mayor believed, but a responsibility best left to readers.

Councilman Michaels, in contrast, was outraged. He wrote a scathing letter to the editor, chiding the newspaper for mindless, irresponsible journalism. "The story may have been fair, balanced and accurate," he wrote, "but it was not truthful." He had never lied about the effects of pesticides on bird life, and he had "never been on the payroll of any pesticide manufacturer," he wrote. "A responsible reporter would do more than report the facts truthfully; she would also report the truth about the facts." In this case, Michaels said, the reporter should have held off on the story until she had time to independently investigate the mayor's accusation; and if the accusation had proved to be of no merit, as Michaels insisted, then there shouldn't have been a story. Or if there had to be a story, Michaels added, "it should be a story about the *mayor* lying."

By way of background: The effects of pesticides on bird life had been a local issue for nearly a year. Part of the community backs Mayor Adams's position on the harmful effects of certain pesticides and supports local legislation that would limit or ban their use. Others in the community support Councilman Michaels's position that the evidence on the effects of pesticides on bird life is at best ambiguous and that more scientific study is needed before anyone proposes legislation. They argue that pesticides are useful, particularly to local farmers who need to protect crops, and because the available evidence about their deleterious effects is inconclusive, they believe that the city council should not seek to further restrict or prohibit their use. The exchange between Mayor Adams and Councilman Michaels is the latest in a series of verbal bouts on the subject of pesticides and the city's role in their regulation.

Micro Issues

1. Did Laurens do the right thing by submitting her story without the benefit of an independent investigation into the mayor's accusations about Councilman Michaels?
2. Is the mayor correct in arguing that Laurens acted responsibly by providing fair and balanced coverage of both sides of a public controversy without trying to judge whose side is right and whose side is wrong?
3. Is the councilman correct in arguing that Laurens acted irresponsibly by concerning herself only with reporting the facts truthfully and ignoring the "truth about the facts"?

Midrange Issues

1. Is it sufficient when covering public controversies to simply report the facts accurately and fairly? Does it matter that fair and accurate reporting of facts might not do justice to the truth about the facts?
2. Does the practice of objective reporting distance reporters from the substance of their stories in ways contrary to the ideals of responsible journalism?
3. If reporters serve as the eyes and ears of their readers, how can they be expected to report more than what they've heard or seen?

Macro Issues

1. What distinguishes fact from truth? For which should journalists accept responsibility?
2. If journalists know that a fact is not true, do they have an obligation to share that knowledge with their readers? And if they do share that knowledge, how can they claim to be objective in their reporting?
3. Justify or reject the role of objectivity in an era when more media outlets are available than ever before.

CASE 2-E

Caught in the "War Zone"

MIKE GRUNDMANN AND ROGER SOENKSEN
James Madison University

"War Zone" blared the giant headline above photos of fire, vandalism and drunken students being arrested by police in riot gear. This was an out-of-control Springfest, the annual pre-finals block party at James Madison University in Virginia. The Virginia event is but one rite of spring held on college campuses across the nation. Iowa State calls it "Veishea" and that event has turned ugly more than once over the years. At the University of Colorado's similar event, more than 10,000 people show up to smoke pot.

By 2010, on the campus of the University of Virginia, Springfest had ballooned thanks to notices on Facebook that drew students and nonstudents from other states. The 2010 number, estimated to be about 8,000, was about four times larger than previous years according to the *Post,* and the "block party" began to get out of control. Two photographers for *The Breeze,* the twice-weekly student newspaper, had taken hundreds of photos of the event and continued as the crowd grew more unruly, spilling into a nearby neighborhood.

According to the *Post,* President Linwood H. Rose e-mailed the entire 18,500 student campus the following Sunday. "Your collective behavior was an embarrassment to your university and a discredit to our reputation," he wrote. "No one is opposed to some fun on a beautiful spring weekend, but public drunkenness, destruction of property, and threats to personal safety are unacceptable outcomes."

Five days after the melee, the chief local prosecutor, Marsha Garst, was pursuing claims that both attendees and police as well had been assaulted. In trying to find the perpetrators who might have escaped the police dragnet, Garst's office asked *The Breeze* editor, Katie Thisdell, and a faculty adviser to turn over any unpublished photos so offenders could be identified and arrested. Both refused, on grounds that the paper could not make itself an arm of the law and must remain independent.

The next day, Garst, joined by the campus police chief and other law officers, raided the newsroom with a search warrant. It demanded all Springfest photos under threat of confiscating all computers, cameras, cellphones and other devices that could contain the photos. The number of photos seized in this manner was more than 900, according to the *Washington Post.*

Acting on the advice of the Student Press Law Center (SPLC), Thisdell refused, citing the federal Privacy Protection Act (PPA), which shields newspapers from such seizures until they can be challenged in court. The PPA was passed in 1980 just after the state of California had successfully pursued a newsroom search and seizure over the objection of the editors. Interestingly, this case, too, also sprang from a college campus—Stanford University, where the students had photos of a riot on campus and had refused to turn them over.

However, this congressional action did not sway Garst, who stuck to her ultimatum. Thisdell, who considered a newsroom emptied of its tools an unacceptable option, relented and turned over all the photos.

Thisdell and her advisers alerted news media in the region, and the story went national, including a *Washington Post* editorial condemning Garst. *The Breeze* also provided continuous coverage of its own story, but not using any of the staffers directly involved. The state attorney general, Ken Cuccinelli, at a speaking engagement in town, was asked his opinion of Garst's actions. He supported them.

A lawyer provided free by the SPLC finally convinced Garst of the Privacy Protection Act's provisions and persuaded her to surrender the photos to a neutral third party so negotiations over the next step could begin.

The lawyer advised Thisdell: You can stand by your principle and refuse to turn over any of the photos, but with a plurality of conservative judges, there was a risk of a court order essentially matching the search warrant. Or you can negotiate with Garst to turn over the few photos that show suspects Garst is after.

Thisdell, her advisers and her photographers considered the consequences of both choices. Refusing could mean a newsroom shutdown, public accusations of shielding criminals, and weeks, months or years of court appearances. Compromising could embolden future prosecutors, harm *The Breeze*'s journalistic reputation and discourage important future sources.

Thisdell decided to compromise and ultimately turned over 20 photos. As part of the bargain, *The Breeze* won a public apology from Garst, who said she regretted frightening the student journalists and would follow the law next time.

Rober Boag, "The Breeze"

Rober Boag, "The Breeze"

Micro Issues

1. How should the editor have responded to the prosecutor's initial, nonthreatening request for the photos and why?
2. Thisdell made a pragmatic decision: a newsroom without its human and physical tools was "unacceptable." Is this pragmatic decision also an ethical one? What is the difference in the two forms of justification?

Midrange Issues

1. If the editor was right in the initial withholding of the photos, can she then also be right in turning over some of the same photos? What is the ethical justification for making the change?
2. What are the ethical issues in the paper alerting other news media to its plight? Does the alert by the student newspaper play into a stereotype of student-run media as being weaker than traditional media when interacting with public officials?
3. What are the ethical issues in the paper covering its own story? Can any medium be objective when the story—in whole or in part—is about it?
4. In covering events like "Springfest," are the media culpable for encouraging attendees to act outrageously to get on-camera? As television adds to the likelihood that "acting out" will happen, do they have a moral obligation to tone down the rowdy activities?

Macro Issues

1. In looking at the typology of duties outlined by Ross in Chapter 1, do the news media have a duty to help law enforcement when it asks for information that only a newsroom has?
2. What are the implications of a newsroom allowing itself to be used as an arm of the law?
3. If the public accuses your news organization of shielding criminals, is that a price worth paying for sticking to the journalistic principle of independence?
4. How could you counter any claims that the media cooperated in the end to get in good favor with the police?

CASE 2-F

Murdoch's Mess

LEE WILKINS
University of Missouri

It may have begun as an instance of "watching the watchdog." For two years, *Guardian* reporter Nick Davies had been doggedly investigating whether Britain's tabloid press—particularly the Rupert Murdoch–owned *News of the World*—had been engaging in unethical activities to report the news. Specifically Davies was investigating whether the voice-mail messages left on cell phones (most of the British public uses cell phones) had been accessed to gain information. In most instances such practices would be illegal. A 2005–2007 investigation concluded that only celebrities, the royal family and politicians had been the subjects of phone hacking and that the hacking had been conducted by a single reporter. The rest of the British press dropped the story, and the public didn't seem to care.

Murdoch continued to build his media empire, which included a sizable financial stake in BSkyB, the most lucrative broadcast holding in the United Kingdom. During this same period, Murdoch purchased the U.S. *Wall Street Journal,* adding it to his U.S. holdings that include several other newspapers and, most prominently, the Fox network including both its news and entertainment divisions.

Davies worked for *The Guardian,* an unusual publication on any continent. *The Guardian* is owned by a trust; it is not a traditional profit-making enterprise and its exemplar journalistic status is a relatively recent phenomenon. *Guardian* employees are required to take public transportation to cover most stories, and the paper itself conducts and publishes an ethical audit once a year that includes the paper's impact on the environment and its role as a citizen of its local community. In the British media market—almost all of which is focused in London—*The Guardian* competes fiercely with Murdoch publications, both tabloid and more traditional news organizations.

In July 2011, Davies reported that phone hacking extended beyond a single journalist and those usual and seemingly acceptable suspects. Voice-mail messages to families of British soldiers serving in Afghanistan, victims of the July 2007 London tube bombings and, most egregious, the voice-mails of murdered British schoolgirl Milly Dowler also had been hacked. In fact, according to Davies and subsequent investigations, Dowler's voice-mail had not merely been hacked, it had been altered, leaving her family with the impression that the child remained alive after she had been murdered. Davies's later reports also revealed that the journalists involved appeared to have bribed Scotland Yard as part of the newsgathering effort. The outrage was immediate: major advertisers withdrew from the *News of the World* and many others threatened to follow. On July 10, 2011, the 168-year-old paper published its last edition. About 200 journalists lost their jobs, and James Murdoch, Rupert Murdoch's son and heir apparent, conceded that the paper had been irrevocably "sullied by behavior that was wrong."

On July 13, 2011, Murdoch announced he was withdrawing his bid to take over BSkyB. The announcement was made just a few hours before the British Parliament was scheduled to debate a resolution, supported by all political parties, calling on Murdoch to withdraw from the process. Despite the announcement, the House of Commons unanimously passed the resolution. On July 16 and 17, Murdoch published full-page apologies to the British public for the scandal and its impact. The next month, Wireless Generation, a News Corp. subsidiary, lost a no-bid contract with the state of New York to build an information system to track student performance. New York State Comptroller Thomas DiNupoli said the revelations of corporate and individual malfeasance had made awarding this bid to Wireless Generation "untenable."

The elder Murdoch was politically influential on both sides of the Atlantic, but his power reached to the highest levels in Britain. At the time the phone hacking scandal broke, a former Murdoch employee was serving as Prime Minister David Cameron's chief communications officer.

Rupert and James Murdoch were called before Parliament. Both admitted that the hacking had occurred, but each denied, in different terms, the existence of a corrosive organizational culture that could have led to a widespread ethical and legal breach. Rupert Murdoch testified that he was a victim of a cover-up. Concurrently there were high-level resignations throughout the Murdoch empire, including that of Wes Hinton, who had been serving as the chief executive of Dow Jones, owner of the *Wall Street Journal* and a longtime Murdoch employee. Hinton had testified to Parliament that there was never any evidence of phone hacking beyond the actions of a single employee.

However, as the scandal continued to unfold, it became apparent that other Murdoch-owned news organizations had engaged in similar newsgathering tactics. The FBI opened an investigation into whether any phone hacking had occurred in the United States, with potential targets the victims of the 9/11 bombing among others.

About a year later, a British inquiry ruled that Murdoch was not a "fit and proper" person to be allowed to own or acquire media outlets in the UK. In the meantime, multiple lawsuits were filed over the scandal—and the Murdoch empire has paid more than 1 million pounds to settle them. As of this writing, there have been more than 30 arrests of Murdoch current or former employees. In November 2012, indictments for bribing a public official, the most serious charge to emerge from the scandal to date, were filed against Brooks and David Coulson, former communications chief for Britain's Prime Minister Glen Cameron. To find updates of the latest events, access http://www.guardian.co.uk/media/phone-hacking.

Rupert Murdoch has been called the last of the media barons and the criticisms of him and his business practices parallel those leveled against Joseph Pulitzer and William Randolph Hearst at the height of the yellow journalism era in the United States. All were accused of building media empires that lacked an ethical foundation. Journalism professor Karl Grossman, State University of New York at Old Westbury, accused Murdoch of building the most "dishonest, unprincipled and corrupt" media empire in history and turning the notion of public service journalism on its head. He also accused Murdoch of changing the newsroom culture at his most recent acquisitions, among them the *Wall Street Journal*. *Newsweek* in July 2011 quoted one of Murdoch's top executives as follows:

> This scandal and all its implications could not have happened anywhere else. Only in Murdoch's orbit. The hacking at *News of the World* was done on an industrial scale. More than anyone, Murdoch invented and established this culture in the newsroom, where you do whatever it takes to get the story, take no prisoners, destroy the competition, and the end will justify the means. . . . In the end, what you sow is what you reap. Now Murdoch is a victim of the culture that he created. It is a logical conclusion, and it is his people at the top who encouraged law-breaking and hacking phones and condoned it.

In July 2012, executives with News Corp. decided to break the company into two parts: one part devoted exclusively to newspapers, including the *Wall Street Journal,* and a second, far more profitable part, devoted to broadcasting and entertainment, including Fox News. Rupert Murdoch also reigned from multiple boards controlling both corporations in the same month.

While many were willing to blame Murdoch personally, other critics noted that the 24/7 nature of competitive news on the Internet had created the sort of atmosphere in which hacking was not merely tolerated but encouraged. These critics noted that hidden cameras, lurking on Web sites, publishing stories before checking facts—all in the drive to increase Web hits—were merely less illegal, but not less ethically questionable results, of the 24/7, celebrity-driven news cycle.

Micro Issues

1. Phone hacking is illegal, but is it unethical? Why or why not?
2. How would you, or could you, justify Davies's pursuit of this story about one of his major competitors?
3. In most of the phone hacking cases, none of the victims have said that the information collected about them was untrue. Is the way a journalist collects information a component of the truthfulness of the story?
4. Contrast phone hacking to the other deceptive techniques evaluated by investigative reporters and editors and reviewed in this chapter. How are they alike and different in an ethical sense?

Midrange Issues

1. What is the role of competition in the concept of "watching the watchdog"? Does the same sort of thinking apply to the media's watchdogging of other major institutions in society?
2. Does the 24/7 nature of the news cycle—and the sometimes Wild West nature of the Internet—encourage working at the very edge of acceptability? If you answer yes, then what sort of rules or guidelines or training might encourage contemporary journalists to stay on the "right" side of the ethical boundaries?
3. In light of this case, how do you respond to those who say that all journalists will do anything to get a story?

Macro Issues

1. What should be the role of democratic governments in policing the ethical behavior of corporate media owners?
2. Evaluate the notion of an ethical newsroom culture. Contrast the culture of *The Guardian* with that of the *News of the World*. What makes the ethical difference?
3. One role for the mass media as an institution is that of collaboration. Yet, journalists have historically been suspicious of the sort of collaboration and political influence Rupert Murdoch has had. Analyze what you believe is the most ethically defensible role relationship between the mass media as an institution and powerful political and economic institutions. See if your answer changes after reading Chapter 6.

3

Strategic Communication: Does Client Advocate Mean Consumer Adversary?

By the end of this chapter, you should be familiar with:

- how new technologies raise old ethical questions.
- the balance and cognitive dissonance persuasion theories and their role in persuasion.
- the amplified TARES test for evaluating the ethics of individual messages.
- why the relationship between the media and public relations is both symbiotic and strained.

REACH OUT AND TOUCH SOMEONE

Most of the readers of this book are in their early 20s, and are most often seeking *someone* in addition to the *something* of a college education. Many of you will conduct your search for friends and life partners online—and increasingly on sites such as eHarmony. Visitors to that site and others like it pay a subscription fee, complete various sorts of profiles and are linked with possible matches. The non–virtual world and that human thing called chemistry seem to take it from there.

Not much of an ethical issue involved—that is, until you learn how such Web sites really make their money. They do it not exclusively through the matching service they advertise, but more predominantly by attaching cookies to subscribers' computers, and then selling that information—willingly provided in the form of the profile—to marketers who seek a specific demographic; for example, people of a certain age, or a certain income, and with specific likes and dislikes. Those electronic lists the Web sites sell—a process you must agree to in order to use the matching service—then allow marketers to push specific sorts of messages at you electronically and at times of their choosing, employing what the industry now terms *behavioral marketing*.

In addition to the technology of the cookie—which you can find and delete from your computer—marketers also are increasingly placing Web beacons—which can be neither spotted nor deleted by the average user—on your machine as part of the tracking process. While the marketers never know your specific identify—in other words your name—they know enough about you for selling purposes, right down to the fact that you like terrier dogs but not cats and that your favorite musician is Kanye West.

It's all part of the brave new world of *strategic communication,* or the seamless connections between what professionals used to refer to as advertising and public relations.

And strategic communication, just like news, is facing a new economic reality: a business model that is no longer successful. What used to be the case—that entertainment or news content on either television or in a print medium was designed to deliver an audience to advertisers—is now increasingly problematic because people are finding ways to dodge persuasive messages as never before. Whether it's TiVo and skipping through commercials or getting news "for free" on the Web, strategic communication professionals are being forced to find novel ways to get their messages to "eyeballs"—or people acting in their roles as consumers. Strategic communication professionals are also faced with the reality of an active audience—an audience that not only buys products or services but also expects to be able to evaluate those services and products in public ways. These audience-based measures of products and services have added new dimensions to efforts to "control the message" that has been part of both advertising and public relations for decades. Companies that once used to purchase advertising expertise are also experimenting with user-generated advertising content—an effort that bypasses the industry entirely.

These novel approaches can raise serious individual ethical issues—issues that once seemed more the realm of the journalist. Students who once said, "I went into advertising because I don't feel comfortable forcing people to talk to me and I don't have to think about invading people's privacy," are now facing decisions about whether and how to use computer-based technologies to do precisely these things—only this time to promote sales of various products and lifestyles.

For example, in the summer of 2012, Orbitz, the travel Web site, announced that it was going to "show" Mac users pricier hotel options than those accessing the site using a PC. The reason: statistically, those who own Macs have higher incomes and tend to book more expensive hotels. By obtaining information about the user electronically—and inferring something about household income, a "fact" most Americans consider quite private—the marketing pitch changes. It's not that the computer itself is private—it's the information that comes along with it. While such an approach might be considered a savvy marketing choice, it also raises questions of privacy and equity that are troubling. Phrased in the student's vernacular, the computer is talking to Orbitz without the knowledge or permission of its owner, and what it is talking about is potentially quite private. All for the end of booking hotel rooms. The Orbitz effort provides just one illustration of the ethical problems that both journalists and strategic communication professionals share.

These facts of new media life also do not blunt some of the deepest continuing criticisms of persuasion, that the nature of the persuasive message itself—short, highly visual and intentionally vague—is overly reliant on stereotypes, spins the truth, glorifies consumerism at the expense of community and as an institution warps nonpersuasive content in significant ways. The ease of bypassing persuasive messages also challenges one of the most significant justifications for advertising: that without the funding it provides, broad-ranging political discourse would not be possible in developed democracies such as the United States. These new economic realities have heightened the need for clear ethical thinking for those entering the persuasive end of the business.

TECHNOLOGY: A ROOM OF REQUIREMENT OR A SYSTEM OF VALUES?

Many of the issues raised by activities such as behavioral marketing or data mining for selling purposes arise because technology makes certain activities possible. Such activities, which most often require the enormous data processing capacities of the computer, also present professionals with two different ways of thinking about technology itself.

The first approach equates technology with efficiency. Those who subscribe to this school of thought assert that technology itself raises no ethical issues, but rather the ethical issues arise in how the technology is put to use. Think of the room of requirement in *Harry Potter.* In book five of the series, *The Order of the Phoenix,* Harry and his friends stumble on the room of requirement when they need a place to practice magic—specifically defense against the dark arts. (Professor Dumbledore apparently "found" the room during his student days when he was in desperate need of a "chamber pot.") The room of requirement is always equipped to fulfill the seeker's needs. Both Dumbledore's and later Harry's use of the room are done for "good" purposes.

Yet, in book six, *Harry Potter and the Half-Blood Prince,* the room of requirement serves an evil purpose. Malfoy uses the room to repair the connecting closet that allows the death eaters to enter Hogwarts and kill Dumbledore. Same room—but in book six its use results in great evil. The room itself is not to blame; it is merely an efficient way of serving the needs of those who use it. It is in the intent of the user—not the existence of the room itself—that the capacity for ethical choice lies.

The second approach asserts that any technology is embedded with values. Think of the technology you are using right now: the written word and the printing press. What does writing value? It values a specific definition of truth, as reviewed in Chapter 2 of this book. It values a specific standard of evidence; for example, written documents and sources for them are important. It values specific ways of organizing human community and of placing economic value on some activities. The act of writing and the technology of the printing press have made much of contemporary human community possible—but those communities maximize some values while minimizing others.

In this view, articulated by French theologian Jacques Ellul, technology is at core a system of values that must be understood before any decision to adopt a technology can be made. Failure to understand the values embedded in a technology can have many unintended consequences, some of them quite horrible.

Being a competent and ethical professional does not require you to resolve this deeply philosophical debate. But it does require you to acknowledge that it exists, and to think clearly about whether, in the process of claiming efficiency, you have overlooked important questions of values.

THINKING ABOUT THE AUDIENCE: FROM PERSUASION THEORY TO PHILOSOPHICAL ANTHROPOLOGY

Psychologists first began to try to understand persuasion by working with a stimulus–response model. This early behaviorist approach led many to believe that the media could act as a "hypodermic needle" or a "magic bullet," sending a stimulus/message to an unresisting audience. These researchers, called "powerful effects theorists," found examples to support their theory in the public panic after Orson Welles's *War of the Worlds* broadcast on Oct. 30, 1938, and in the success of propaganda during both world wars.

But, the stimulus–response model proved a poor predictor of much human behavior. Later, communication theorists focused on cognitive psychology. Rather than analyzing persuasion as a simple behavioral reaction to a sufficient stimulus, these scholars theorized that how people think and what they brought to the persuasive situation helped explain persuasion. According to these theories, people strain toward cognitive balance. Simply put, we are most comfortable when all of our beliefs, actions, attitudes and relationships are in harmony, a state theorists called "symmetry."

Such theories have become known as "balance theories," since they stress the tendency of people to strive for cognitive balance in their lives. A person achieves balance only when his or her attitudes, information and actions are in harmony. Leon Festinger (1957) coined the term *cognitive dissonance* to describe the state where a message and an action give conflicting and uncomfortable signals. Think of it as knowing the

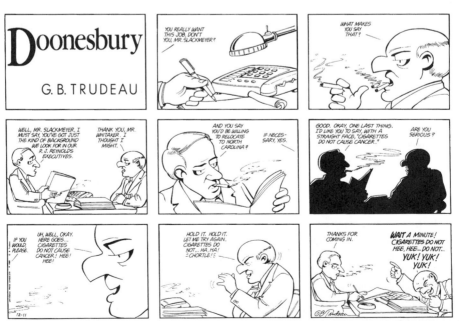

DOONESBURY © G. B. Trudeau. 1988 Reprinted with permission by UNIVERSAL UCLICK. All rights reserved.

hazards of smoking but choosing to smoke anyway, setting up a classic brain–action dissonance. The desire to eliminate that dissonance is a strong one, sometimes strong enough to influence purchasing behavior and voting habits—at least some of the time.

Advertisers use this theory. Knock a consumer off balance early in the commercial and then promise restoration of that balance through the purchase of a product. For instance, the opening scene of a commercial might suggest that your dandruff is making you a social outcast, and the subsequent copy promises you social approval if you use the correct shampoo.

Balance theories also explained why persuasive messages were sometimes quite effective while at other times inconsequential. No consequences to the problem, no lack of balance and subsequently no sale. This individually focused approach also provided the ultimate practical justification for advertising, the ancient Roman phrase *caveat emptor,* "Let the buyer beware." The creators of the ads were willing to assume little responsibility for the impact of their work, and academic studies gave them partial cover: if you can't prove that something's been effective, then it's unreasonable to suggest you take some responsibility for it. Even the Federal Trade Commission allows "puffery in advertising but not deception"—but it never tells you where it plans to draw the line.

Anthropologists assert that human rationality exists on equal footing with daily experience, language and symbols. Culture and our personal experience balance rationality (Wilkins and Christians 2001). If philosophical anthropology is correct, then ethical analysis of advertising founded in "Let the buyer beware" is morally unsustainable.

Instead, the ethical goal of advertising should be the empowerment of multiple stakeholders—from those who need to buy, those who need to sell, those who live in a community fueled by commerce and tax dollars and finally those who depend on advertising-supported news to be participatory citizens in a democracy.

If the concept of human being as creator of culture and then a dynamic user of symbols becomes an ethical foundation for thinking about the audience, advertising practitioners should be expected to operate within the following framework:

- Clients and the public need information that gives them "a good reason to adopt a course of action" (Koehn 1998, 106). The reason needs to be nonarbitrary and capable of helping people support one action instead of others.
- Rather than offering only expert opinion, advertising should foster ongoing discussion so that people can explore when options are sound and when practical knowledge (common sense) is superior.
- Advertising, just like news, can help foster reflective community, including the community of consumers. Just like the Super Bowl results are discussed at work the next day, often the creative ads that supported it are part of the social experience as well.
- Advertising needs to take seriously the role of culture in our lives. That means that advertising must authentically reflect the diverse voices that comprise our culture.
- Advertising will speak to the role of organizations in our lives. Questions of history and background can be conveyed in ads, but that must be done accurately and in context.

Given these general guidelines, let's explore a specific framework that puts ads to an ethical test.

THINKING ABOUT THE MESSAGE: A SYSTEMATIC TEST

The original TARES test is a checklist of questions the creators of every persuasive message should ask themselves to determine the ethical worthiness of the message (Baker and Martinson 2001). While the TARES test takes its inspiration from the "symbol formation" function of both advertising and news, public relations practitioners have added the significant element of advocacy to an ethical evaluation of public relations messages. Advocacy means "understanding and valuing the perception of publics inside and outside organizations" (Grunig, Toth and Hon 2000). Advocacy also means communicating those perceptions to other publics, an effort that has become more complex because it involves relationships with multiple stakeholders "in a world of increasingly diverse and more active publics who are empowered by and connected through the Internet" (Fitzpatrick and Bronstein 2006, *x*).

Those who support the advocacy model argue that any misleading information put out by strategic communication professionals will be somehow "self-corrected" by the gatekeepers of the media or by the self-righting "marketplace of ideas." Those who reject the advocacy model do so on two grounds. First, they assert that advocacy too easily morphs into distortion and lies. Second, they argue that the long-term health of many enterprises, from business to government programs, is ill-served by "spin" and better served by honest, timely communication—even at the expense of short-term losses.

> "Of course, public relations professionals do not enjoy the special status of the "Fourth Estate." Indeed, as representatives of *special* interests—as compared to the *public* interest—they and their clients and employers may have less protection from judicial forays into questions of ethics. Public relations professionals must consider both whether the special obligations associated with the freedom to communicate are being met and whether, in the absence of effective *self*-regulation, the government might step in to hold practitioners accountable for irresponsible behavior" (Fitzpatrick and Bronstein 2006, 16) [italics in the original].

To help you think through the ethical issues that persuasion raises—particularly in the world of strategic communication where most professionals will be asked to meld traditional advertising and public relations, we have connected the approaches in both fields through a single, ethically based test of specific messages.

The first element of the test—**T**—stands for **truthfulness.** Are the claims, both verbal and visual, truthful? If the message communicates only part of the truth (and many ads do this), are the omissions deceptive? Conversely, a message would pass the test if it meets a genuine human need to provide truthful information, even if some facts are omitted. Does the technology used to convey the message obscure or help reveal the truth about the claims? In addition, practitioners should be able to verify with clients the truthfulness of client claims, and they should provide information to their audiences that will allow them to verify the truthfulness of claims in messages aimed at the public.

The Amplified TARES Test of Ethical Persuasion

T   Are the ad claims **Truthful?**

A   Is the claim an **Authentic** one?

R   Does the ad treat the receiver with **Respect?**

E   Is there **Equity** between the sender and the receiver?

S   Is the ad **Socially** responsible?

The Cheerios television ads that emphasize eating Cheerios as part of a heart-healthy lifestyle could easily pass the first element of the TARES test. People do have to eat, and the ads provide needed information. The ads also omit some information—for example, the other components of a heart-healthy lifestyle or the fact that other breakfast cereals also meet these requirements. But the omitted information does not lead the mature consumer to make false assumptions and bad choices.

In addition, telling the truth in times of crisis, such as becoming an advocate rather than an adversary in the long-term health care of a particular client, tests the foremost professional principles for public relations practitioners. The history of the field would suggest that businesses and agencies whose actions demonstrate that public health and safety are more important than short-term profits—telling the truth even when it hurts—are quite likely to profit and survive in the long term.

Step two in the amplified TARES test—**A** for **authenticity**—is closely linked to step one. Authenticity suggests that it's important not only to do the right thing, but also "to do it with the right attitude" (Pojman 1998, 158). We link this notion to the concept of sincerity. First, is there a sincere need for this product within the range of products and services available? Second, are the reasons given to the consumer purchasing the product presented in such a way that they also would motivate the person who developed and wrote the message? Simply put: would you buy your own reasoning about the uses and quality of the product advertised?

Authenticity, used in this way, is closely linked to disclosure, an important standard for public relations messages. The ethical end of disclosure is the generation of trust among and between various publics. "Ethical public relations professionals are forthright and honest and counsel clients and employers to adopt responsible communication policies built on principles of openness and transparency" (Fitzpatrick and Bronstein 2006, 13). Disclosure also demands providing information about who is paying for the message and who stands to profit from its success. Direct advertising of pharmaceuticals to consumers—once banned by law—often fails this part of the test.

Let's take a set of strategic communication messages about products designed to help elderly or infirm people live more independently. Although some of these products—for example, devices that turn on lights in response to a hand clap—may seem little more than high-tech toys, anyone with a grandparent in a wheelchair, a sibling disabled by an illness like rheumatoid arthritis or even a young person suffering from the imposed immobility of a broken leg can readily understand the need for such devices.

Others, such as advertisements for extended care facilities or supplements to existing insurance plans, attempt to focus on the human desire of independent living. But in making this point, if the messages stereotype elderly people as frail, helpless, weak or easily panicked, or if they knock otherwise healthy individuals off balance to sell a product based on fear, they do not authentically reflect the reality of life beyond age 65. The ad lacks authenticity based on an unrealistic stereotype of the early retiree. The TARES test would require rethinking the specific appeal in the ad to one that scares and stereotypes less and informs more. For creative people, such a switch is readily accomplished if they think about it. Just as important, a fresher approach might well sell more.

The **R** in the test stands for **respect,** in this case, respect for the person who will receive the persuasive message. However, as a shorthand way of thinking through this element of the test, it might be appropriate for advertising practitioners to ask themselves, "Am I willing to take full, open and personal responsibility for the content of this ad?"

Take the recent anti-texting-while-driving public service campaign that began with an ad of an actual car crash filmed from inside the car and its devastating aftermath. Even though the ad itself, which originated with a European government and went viral through YouTube, was filmed as a documentary, the campaign was criticized for its "scare" tactics. However, while the campaign relied on fear as a primary emotional tactic, it also provided rational reasons to not text and drive. Even though it was created by a government agency, the ad and its emotional appeal provide evidence of respect for human life.

The **E** in the amplified TARES test stands for **equity.** We conceptualize equity as follows: is the recipient of the message on the same level playing field as the ad's creator? Or, to correctly interpret the ad, must that person be abnormally well informed, unusually bright or quick-witted and completely without prejudice? Equity is linked to **access** for public relations professionals, and it takes its ethical power from the role of free speech in a democratic society. Free people are the autonomous moral actors that philosophers have long insisted must be the foundation of ethical choice and access to information equalizes an individual's ability to participate in the marketplace of ideas.

Think about this corporate image ad for ExxonMobil—the one with the pristine scenery, glorious sunset and an oil tanker. The ad claims that the company has the best interest of the environment at heart by building tankers with double hulls. While ExxonMobil's claim—that it builds double-hulled tankers—is literally true, correctly interpreting the ad requires a recall of recent history. ExxonMobil, and all other oil companies, were required by Congress to build double-hulled tankers after the single-hulled tanker, the *Exxon Valdez,* ran aground and spilled an enormous amount of oil in Alaska, an environmental disaster of the first magnitude. For the image ad to work, it counts on the average person not knowing—or not being able to connect—legal requirements with corporate behavior. The ad assumes (and actually depends on) an imbalance between the knowledge of the person who created the ad and the consumer. It flunks the concept of equity. Similarly, an airline company that brags about a point of customer service that has actually been codified by the congressionally mandated Passenger Bill of Rights, is relying on customer ignorance or forgetfulness to score points for behavior required by law.

Finally, the **S** in the amplified TARES test: Is the ad **socially responsible?** This is perhaps the most difficult element of the test for the simple reason that advertising practitioners have duties to many groups, among them their clients, the agencies for which they work, consumers, people exposed to the ad whether they buy or not and society at large.

Because this text emphasizes social ethics, we suggest interpreting this portion of the TARES test in the following fashion:

- If everyone financially able to purchase this product or service did so and used it, would society as a whole be improved, keeping in mind that recreation and self-improvement are worthy societal goals?
- If there are some groups in society that would benefit from using this product as advertised, are there others that could be significantly harmed by it? Are there ways to protect them?
- Does this ad increase or decrease the trust the average person has for persuasive messages?
- Does this ad take the notion of corporate responsibility, both to make money and to improve human life and welfare, seriously and truthfully?

For public relations practitioners, social responsibility also may be defined as **process,** whether public relations advocacy impedes or contributes to the robust functioning of the marketplace of ideas. An evenhanded process encourages both the journalists who use PR-generated information for news stories and various audiences who must rely on those stories as part of their decision making to use the information provided.

Using this concept of social responsibility should enable you to think ethically about television's decisions to air condom advertising. MTV, the network targeted at teenagers, chose to air such ads in 2000. More traditional network television outlets still do not. Which decision do you believe is more ethically justified? Why? Does the notion of social responsibility, and the process of democratic functioning, have any place in your analysis?

Or try this dilemma. With all the talk about global warming, there is one organism that thrives in a warmer subtopic environment—the mosquito that perpetuates dengue fever, a painful disease totally preventable by mosquito control. Does the "first world" have a right to advertise the comforts of energy consumption when a single degree's change in the world's climate allows more latitudes for the disease-bearing mosquito?

The amplified TARES test is a demanding one. But asking these questions, particularly during the process of creating an ad, can also be a spur to better, more creative execution and can be rewarded in the capitalistic marketplace. The TARES test may help advertising practitioners warn their corporate clients about the kind of advertising that could do them, as well as society at large, great long-term harm.

ADVERTISING'S SPECIAL PROBLEMS: VULNERABLE AUDIENCES

Advertising in a mass medium reaches large, heterogeneous audiences. Often, advertising intended for one group is seen by another. Sometimes the results are humorous, and maybe even a little embarrassing, as when ads for contraception or personal hygiene products make their way into prime-time programming.

However, in the case of Camel cigarettes' "Joe Camel" ads, this "confusion" of intended audience with actual recipients appeared quite deliberate. A few years ago, the tobacco company agreed to withdraw the cartoon spokesperson "Joe Camel" from magazines and billboards after internal documents revealed the industry targeted underage smokers and sales figures bore out its success.

In other cases—for example, the beer industry—no such ban exists. Advertising intended for adults is often seen by those who cannot legally drink but do remember the catchy commercials and the presentation of drinking as something connected with fun and good times. Even young children remembered the once used Budweiser talking bullfrogs and other creative beer ads. These ads air in a society where most adult alcoholics report having had their first drink when they were underage.

Are there certain types of audiences that deserve special protection from advertising messages? U.S. law says yes, particularly in the case of children. Legal restrictions on advertising targeted at children cover everything from Saturday-morning television programming to types of products and the characters that advertisers may employ. Children, unlike adults, are not assumed to be autonomous moral actors. They reason about advertising imperfectly, and in an attempt to protect them, American society has accepted some regulation of commercial speech.

However, the issue gets murkier when the target audience is formed of subgroups of adults—for example, ethnic consumers. Exactly when advertisers began to actively court ethnic consumers is uncertain. Brooks (1992) quotes a 1940 *BusinessWeek* article that reported an organization was established in Los Angeles to help guide advertisers who wished to garner the patronage of African-American consumers. Amazingly, the businesses were cautioned against using such words as "boss," "boy" and "darkey" in their ads. Instead, the advertisers were urged to refer to African-American consumers as "Negroes" who want the same things as other shoppers.

America is on its way to being a nation with no ethnic majority, and the real attempt to court ethnic audiences began when those audiences acquired buying power. Hispanics are now the largest minority in the United States. The buying power of African-American consumers now tops more than $300 billion. The Asian-American market has also increased substantially.

Yet, a relative handful of advertisements reflect this emerging demographic reality, and commercials designed to appeal to this market segment sometimes employ troubling stereotypes or encounter other difficulties. For example, R.J. Reynolds Tobacco Company spent millions developing a cigarette aimed at African-Americans and put billboards in African-American neighborhoods to announce it, only to pull the product when consumer outrage caught up to Reynolds's plan.

Magazines pointed at teenage girls seldom reflect the reality of teenage bodies. Studies have shown that women who are exposed to such advertising images find their own bodies less acceptable. The same goes for facial features. Scholars have noted that the ideal image of beauty, even in magazines targeted at African-Americans, is a Caucasian one of small noses, thin lips and lighter skin tones. African-American women simply don't see themselves in these advertisements. Scholars in cultural studies argue that the impact of these repeated images is "cumulative." Ultimately, culture comes to accept without question what is nothing more than a gender or a racial stereotype and ultimately the stereotype becomes a "truism."

Few scholars have suggested that adults who are minorities need special protection from advertising. What they have noted is that ads that abuse the trust between consumer and advertiser have consequences. In the short term, products may not sell or may find themselves the target of regulation. In the long term, cynicism and societal distrust increases. People sense they are being used, even if they can't explain precisely how. The buyer may resort to avoiding advertising itself rather than to using advertising to help make better decisions.

JOURNALISM AND PUBLIC RELATIONS: THE QUINTESSENTIAL STRUGGLE

Public relations began as a profession in the late 19th century when newsmakers sought to find a way to get past journalism's gatekeepers to get their stories told from simple press releases to elaborate publicity stunts (such as the "torches of freedom" march for women smokers envisioned by Edward L. Bernays in the early years of the 20th century). For the client, PR practitioners offered free access to the audience; for the newspapers, they offered "free" news to publishers.

Despite the occasional animosity between journalists and public relations practitioners, the relationship is truly symbiotic—they simply could not live without each other. No news organization is large enough to gather all the day's news without several public relations sources. Business pages are full of press releases on earnings, new product lines and personnel changes, all supplied by writers not paid by the media. Travel, entertainment and food sections of newspapers would be virtually nonexistent if not for press releases. On the other hand, media outlets provide the all-important audience for an institution wanting the publicity.

With this common need, why are the two professions sometimes at odds? Much of the problem stems from how each of the two professions defines news. To the public relations professional, the lack of breaking news is newsworthy. Plants that operate safely and are not laying off any employees, nonprofit organizations that operate within budget and provide needed services, companies that pay a dividend for the 15th consecutive quarter are all signs that things are operating smoothly and make for a story that the public should hear. To the journalist, the opposite is true. Plants make news only when they endanger the public safety. Employees are at their most newsworthy when they bring a gun to work, not when they show up every day for 30 years.

The average news consumer rarely observes this constant struggle for control, yet he or she is affected by it. How should we evaluate a profession with the goal of persuading in a manner that does not look like traditional persuasion or the goal of preventing the dissemination of information that might harm the illusion that has been created? By undermining the concept of independent and authentic news messages accepted as credible by the public, are strategic communication practitioners undermining the central content vehicle for their messages? Doesn't persuasion need the contrast of news to succeed?

More recently, the focus of animosity has centered on the concept of "synergy," or the notion that consumers should receive multiple messages for distinct sources, thereby increasing sales or public perception of particular issues. At the ethical core of synergy is the concept of independence—for the journalists who report on the news and for the consumers of both news and persuasive messages who need to make independent decisions about them. The current economic pressures on both strategic communication and journalism have intensified this tug-of-war over independence. Contemporary research suggests that synergistic concerns, particularly for those corporations that own both news and entertainment properties, is having an impact on soft-news program content (Hendrickson and Wilkins 2009).

OF MARKETS AND MORALS

Let's say you're a famous Broadway producer—Joe Papp—and in the mid-1970s decide that while Broadway productions are terrific, it would be even better if the average New Yorker could see classics for free. Shakespeare in the Park was born. Each summer, New York City's Public Theater puts on free outdoor Shakespeare performances in Central Park, subsidized by taxpayer dollars. All New Yorkers have to do is stand in line—and sometimes it's a long one—to get the tickets.

Enter Craigslist and services that will wait in line for you: at a cost of $125 per hour. Suddenly, the free tickets weren't so free. New York is not the only place you can hire someone to stand in line. Washington D.C. has an industry fueled by Linestanding.com where surrogates will stand in line for seats to U.S. Supreme Court arguments or at congressional hearings. Homeless people are often hired to do the work. And, of course, if you want to move to the front of the line at Disney World, you just have to pay more for the tickets. Or, if you want to drive in the high-occupancy lane in some metropolitan areas—without benefit of a car pool—you can pay for the privilege, even if there is no one in your vehicle but you.

What's wrong with that? In a market economy, goods and services change hands and no one really gets hurt. Or do they? In the case of Shakespeare in the Park, New York's attorney general (later governor) Andrew Cuomo pressured Craigslist to stop the ads, arguing that selling tickets that were meant to be free deprived New Yorkers of one of the more unusual benefits of their political community.

The chance to stand in line for a chance to see Al Pacino play Shylock is something that should not be for sale, according to Harvard political philosopher Michael Sandel. In his best-selling 2012 book *What Money Can't Buy: The Moral Limits of Market*s, Sandel argues that in this century, economic language—where literally everything has to be marketed and incentivized—has not only crowded out moral thinking but has sometimes changed our conception of what it means to have a good life in the sense that Aristotle meant it—to have a life with authentic flourishing. Whether it's paying kids to get good grades, the naming opportunities for everything from sports stadiums to national parks to newborns, to the selling of everything from blood to kidneys, Sandel argues that there are places and areas of life where the market simply doesn't belong.

Sandel notes two sets of basic objections to thinking that everything should be the subject of commerce. The first is the notion of fairness, which is highlighted by the example of hiring someone to stand in line for a free ticket. Those with money move to the front. Shakespeare might have objected (after all, he wrote jokes for the groundlings who couldn't afford the expensive seats); Sandel most certainly does. Line jumping just is not fair. In addition, it's coercive—those involved in

OF MARKETS AND MORALS *(continued)*

the case the citizens of New York haven't given their permission for "free" tickets to be sold to the highest bidder. And, they have no recourse to change the system that emerges, unless they become unwilling participants.

The second set of objections to thinking about everything in terms of a market begins with the capacity to fuel corruption. This objection is not new. Paying money for priestly indulgences in the Roman Catholic Church, a corruption of the concept of forgiveness of sins, is one of the reasons for the Protestant Reformation more than 500 years ago. God, and forgiveness, simply could not and should not be bought—even though they were for sale. As Sandel notes, you can buy sports memorabilia or even a sports team. What you cannot do is buy the actual experience of hitting a home run in the World Series or scoring the winning touchdown in the Super Bowl. Moneyball will take you only so far, and the experiences are not equivalent.

In many areas of life, money does not incentivize better behavior. Students who were offered a monetary incentive to raise money for a charity raised less money then those who were offered nothing. Citizens of a community in Switzerland volunteered to become the locus of a nuclear waste repository. But, when the same problem was presented to them with an economic inducement, they turned down the same proposal. Traditional economists tend to think that qualities such as altruism, generosity, solidarity and civic duty are scarce. Sandel argues that they are like

a muscle: they grow with repeated use. They speak to notions of the good life, and when market language is substituted for the language of morals, our concept of the good life itself is degraded. Corruption and degradation are the second set of reasons that market thinking fails to capture what human beings truly want and need.

Sandel concludes his book with the following, "The disappearance of the class-mixing experience once found at the ballpark represents a loss not only for those looking up but also for those looking down. Something similar has been happening throughout society. At a time of rising inequality, the marketing of everything means that people of affluence and people of modest means lead increasingly separate lives. . . . Democracy does not require perfect equality, but it does require that citizens share in a common life. . . . For this is how we learn to negotiate and abide our common differences, and how we come to care for the common good" (Sandel 2012, 203).

Contemporary education in strategic communication emphasizes the how—of consumer behavior, of target marketing, of strategic planning and of synergy. These are important professional skills, but they are most often funded by market logic and utilitarian thinking. Equally important is purpose. What is it that's being marketed? Does the appeal corrode or degrade our conceptualization of a life well lived? The skill of seeing beyond market logic is just as essential for creative strategic communication as technique.

PERSUASION AND RESPONSIBILITY

Hodges (1986) says that the notion of professional responsibility can be summed up in a single question: To what am I prepared to respond ably? In other words, what have my education and my experience equipped me to do and to assume responsibility for? Ask a strategic communication practitioner, "To what are you ably equipped to respond?" and he or she might answer, "To respond to a crisis for a client" or "To generate favorable media attention for a client" or "To generate increased sales for my client." However, there are greater responsibilities.

Hodges further states that responsibilities come from three sources. First, there are those that are *assigned,* such as employee to employer. Second, there are those that are *contracted,* where each party agrees to assume responsibilities and fulfill them. Third, there are the *self-imposed* responsibilities, where the individual moral actor takes on responsibilities for reasons indigenous to each individual. It is our contention that public relations, practiced ethically, will not only fulfill the assigned or contracted responsibilities with the employer or the paying client but also take on the greater calling of self-imposed responsibilities. These self-imposed responsibilities could include such constructs as duty to the truth and fidelity to the public good. The more self-imposed responsibilities the strategic professional assumes, the more ethical the profession will become as practitioners see their personal good as being synonymous with the public good.

Suggested Readings

BAKER, S., and D. MARTINSON, 2001. "The TARES test: Five principles of ethical persuasion." *Journal of Mass Media Ethics,* 16, Nos. 2 and 3.

FITZPATRICK, K., and C. BRONSTEIN, eds. 2006. *Ethics in public relations: Responsible advocacy.* Thousand Oaks, CA: Sage.

HODGES, LOUIS. 1986. "Defining press responsibility: A functional approach." In D. Elliott (ed.), *Responsible journalism.* (pp. 13–31). Newbury Park, CA: Sage.

LEISS, WILLIAM, STEPHEN KLINE, and SUT JHALLY. 1986. *Social communication in advertising: Person, products and images of well-being.* New York: Methuen.

O'TOOLE, JOHN. 1985. *The trouble with advertising.* New York: Times Books.

SANDEL, MICHAEL. 2012. What money cant buy: The moral limits of markets. New York: Farrar, Straus and Giroux.

SCHUDSON, MICHAEL. 1984. *Advertising: The uneasy persuasion.* New York: Basic Books.

Cases on the Web

www.mhhe.com/mediaethics8e

"A case of need" by Deni Elliott

"Exxon's whipping cream on a pile of manure" by JoAnn M. Valenti

"A sobering dilemma" by Beverly Horvit

"Superman's Super Bowl miracle" by Renita Coleman

"The plagiarism factory" by John P. Ferré

"Handling the media in times of crisis: Lessons from the Oklahoma City bombing" by Jon Hansen

"Public relations role in the Alar scare" by Philip Patterson

"Endowment or escarpment: The case of the faculty chair" by Ginny Whitehouse

"The gym shoe phenomenon: Social values vs. marketability" by Gail Baker

"Taking it for a spin: Product samples in the newsroom" by Philip Patterson

"Breaking through the clutter: Ads that make you think twice" by Fritz Cropp

CHAPTER 3 CASES

CASE 3-A

A Charity Drops the Ball

PHILIP PATTERSON
Oklahoma Christian University

Susan G. Koman for the Cure is a global organization dedicated to finding a cure for breast cancer, educating the public about the disease and aiding patients who have been diagnosed with cancer. The organization has raised nearly $2 billion in more than three decades of operation. Its signature event, the Susan G. Komen Race for the Cure, draws on a network of activists, survivors and volunteers to create an event that is one of the largest in all U.S. charities. Since 1982, the Komen organization has been a trusted brand in its chosen field of breast cancer research.

In February of 2012, the leadership of Komen announced that it would end its long-standing relationship with Planned Parenthood, a women's health resource. Planned Parenthood delivers reproductive health care, sex education and information to its clients worldwide. Its 800 centers in the United States serve nearly 5 million clients each year. According to its publicity information, one in five women in the United States has visited a Planned Parenthood health center at least once in her life. Nearly three-quarters of a million breast exams are provided by the organization each year. Three percent of the health care provided by Planned Parenthood are abortions or abortion referrals. This keeps the organization at odds with many religious groups and conservative causes as well.

Prior to the decision by Komen, it had been announced that Planned Parenthood was under congressional investigation to determine if the organization had used federal funding to finance abortions. (This charge is a long-standing one and has been repeatedly rebutted by Planned Parenthood as well as multiple congressional inquiries.) In the midst of the inquiry, Susan G. Komen for the Cure announced that it would suspend its funding of Planned Parenthood—at the time a total of $680,000 annually.

Backlash to the decision was swift and came from many sources. Children's author Judy Blume was one who condemned the Komen organization publicly saying, "Susan Komen (the namesake of the charity) would not give in to bullying or fear. Too bad the organization bearing her name did." Other criticism came from various sources around the country.

Days later, the Komen organization leaders apologized for their actions and reinstated the funding to Planned Parenthood. Karen Handel, Komen policy chief, resigned after the public apology. Handel had been an outspoken critic of abortion and Planned Parenthood dating back to an unsuccessful run for the governorship in Georgia, and most members of the media believed that her resignation was not voluntary. However, in her resignation letter and in interviews afterward, Handel said that while she had a role in the decision, both the Komen board and top executives were onboard with her decision.

In the months that followed, Katrina McGhee, executive vice president and chief marketing officer; Nancy Macgregor, vice president of global networks; and Joanna Newcomb, director of affiliate strategy and planning, all resigned. Organizers of the signature Komen event of 5K races and walks that constitute the bulk of Komen fund-raising claimed that participation declined by as much as 30 percent (Wallace 2012).

Then, in August of 2012, Liz Thompson, president, and Nancy Brinker, founder and CEO, both resigned their positions at the charity, bringing to seven the number of resignations for the year, according to the Associated Press (Wallace 2012). Brinker, who founded the charity in 1982 after her sister, Susan G. Komen, died of breast cancer, said that she would remain in a fund-raising role after stepping down as CEO of what had become the nation's largest breast cancer foundation.

The announcement of the resignations by the top two officials made no reference to the earlier problems with Planned Parenthood.

Micro Issues

1. Does a charity such as Susan G. Komen for the Cure have a duty to reflect the views of its donors in its policies and its affiliations?
2. Does the average donor even know his or her money might go to any number of agencies that the donor might or might not agree with? Should donors have a right to shape the way their funds are used after they have given them?
3. If the original decision to drop the funding had the support of the Komen board, why did Handel have to resign?
4. What should Komen spokespersons have said to journalists who were writing news stories about these decisions and the resignations that followed? To donors?

Midrange Issues

1. The decision to break the affiliation with Planned Parenthood by Komen came in the midst of a congressional inquiry with largely Republican support. Was the subsequent decision of Komen to reinstate Planned Parenthood politically motivated?
2. If you are a spokesperson for a group, is it incumbent that you agree with all of its actions? Would you have resigned as Handel did? Why or why not? Does your opinion about abortion have anything to do with your decision?

Macro Issues

1. This controversy involved two of America's largest charities for women's health care. Much of the funding of these charities comes from large corporate donations. In light of that, what is your opinion of Komen's initial action against Planned Parenthood? What about its subsequent reversal?
2. Donations to organizations like Komen are tax deductible. To what extent does that give the government a right to regulate them?

CASE 3-B

YELP!!! Consumer Empowerment or Small Business Extortion?

LEE WILKINS
University of Missouri

In the middle of the last decade, San Franciscan Jeremy Stoppelmen had an idea to empower consumers online by harnessing something that was happening on social media. If you like a local business, or if you feel abused by one, let you friends know. YELP promised to bring that information to the world.

For about five years, from 2005 to 2010, YELP dominated a class of Web sites—Google is now in the business—that allowed consumers to post their unfiltered opinions about local businesses, including restaurants, shops, and other sorts of local services. The site and its content were both successful and powerful. Local businesses particularly thrived with positive mentions; they were punished by negative reviews. YELP's imitators now include Angie's List, a subscription service. In some ways, YELP is an online version of something travelers are familiar with: Zagat ratings, which come in book/magazine form in many cities throughout the world. YELP's initial business model did not allow anyone other than individual consumers to post their opinions on the site.

But, when YELP turned the power of rating local firms over to individual consumers, it ran into a buzzsaw of criticism and ultimately legal action. Small businesses filed lawsuits against YELP, complaining that consumer reviews posted on the site were manipulated depending on which companies advertise on the site. In one 2010 suit, a Long Beach, California, veterinary clinic sued when it alleged that the site had published a false and defamatory review and then refused to help, instead demanding about $300 per month in the form of advertising to hide or remove the review in question.

YELP's vice president of communication provided this statement in response to the lawsuits: "YELP provides a valuable service to millions of consumers and businesses based on our trusted content. The allegations are demonstrably false, since many businesses that advertise on Yelp have both negative and positive reviews. These businesses realize that both kinds of feedback provide authenticity and value."

But, as YELP matured, it also decided that it had to find a way to allow local businesses to respond to the comments on the site. Beginning in April 2009, it allowed small-business owners to respond publicly to reviews, in large part because local businesses had been demanding more of a voice on the site. YELP's chief operating office Geoff Donaker noted of the responses, "as long as it's done in a respectable way, it's good for the consumer and good for the business owner."

In general, local business owners welcomed the opportunity. Peter Picataggia, the owner of Tart, a Los Angeles restaurant and a YELP advertiser, was quoted in the *New York Times* as saying that while his staff responded privately to almost every YELP review, he welcomed the opportunity to respond publicly.

These business model tweaks apparently worked in another way. In March 2012, YELP offered sales of stock in the business—which in financial terms is called an initial public offering (IPO)—to investors. The stock offering was successful and the price of YELP stock, three months later, was about $6 per share above its initial price of $15.

Micro Issues

1. What is the ethical responsibility of members of the public who have a bad experience with a local business to tell the truth or accurately report what happened?
2. What is the ethical responsibility of someone who reads such a post?
3. In an ethical sense, should businesses be allowed to respond either privately or publicly to such criticism?
4. In an ethical sense, is it the responsibility of the business owner to monitor what is said about that business in the "online" environment? Does the same responsibility apply to the consumer?
5. Does the same thinking apply to sites such as Ratemyprof.com? How about a site such as Ratemychurch.com?

Midrange Issues

1. What is the ethical responsibility of those who develop such sites to make certain that criticism and praise are both truthful and civil?
2. Should such sites offer advertising to local businesses? Distinguish in an ethical sense between the policy of YELP and similar sites and those of Angie's List.
3. Businesses reviewed in Zagat seldom asked for correction or a chance to respond. Why would YELP and other such sites be different?
4. How should such sites ensure that negative reviews were not "planted" by competitors?

Macro Issues

1. Evaluate the statement that such a site needs both positive and negative reviews to promote authenticity.
2. Develop a public relations/strategic communication plan for a local business that specifically addresses how the local business should respond to both critical and positive Web reviews.
3. Are individual consumers bound by the same sort of ethically based expectations when they write such reviews as journalists or strategic communication professionals? If they are not, what are the ethical expectations for consumer comment and why are they distinct from those of professionals "in the business"?

CASE 3-C

The Facts Behind the Ads: Oregon Changes a Campaign

LEE WILKINS
University of Missouri

Beginning in 2010, the Oregon lottery employed an ad campaign with the slogan that "97 cent of every dollar comes back to Oregon." Print ads for the next two years sometimes went even further. One that ran in the *Oregonian* in 2012 claimed that "ninety-seven cents represents over $500 million that is returned to Oregonians every year to help support job creation, schools, state parks and watersheds."

Oregon, like many states, established a lottery in the 1980s through an amendment to the state's Constitution that was approved by the voters. The Oregon lottery was approved in the midst of the 1984 recession, and supporters hoped that lottery proceeds would help turn around the state's economic situation. Voters also have specified how they want the money to be spent through various ballot measures. Since its inception, lottery officials say that the lottery has paid out more than $19 billion in prize money and more than $7 billion to support activities specified by the voters. The statute enacting the program specified that at least 50 percent of the lottery proceeds be awarded as prize money and that no more than 16 percent of the gate fund administrative activities.

Lotteries have always been controversial. President Thomas Jefferson favored them as a form of painless taxation. Contemporary public officials have noted that because gambling is so common, legalizing it and regulating it to ensure the integrity of the system is important. States have also used lottery proceeds to plug budgetary holes. Critics have objected to lotteries for a variety of reasons ranging from a moral objection to "games of chance" to a public policy–based concern that relying on revenues from gambling—which are not always consistent—shifts the burden from traditional taxpayers to the vagaries of gamblers who may not contribute the same amount of money to a state's general fund from year to year. Phrased more simply, this criticism asserts that it is too big a gamble to fund important public programs such as education or environmental preservation on lottery winnings.

Oregon's lottery became a particularly important revenue stream. The state is one of a very few that charges no sales tax; property taxes in Oregon are high in comparison to neighboring states and its income tax is higher than some surrounding states as well. But, without a sales tax—and Oregonians have defeated statewide sales tax proposals multiple times—that state itself has fewer consistent revenue streams than most. Like all state lotteries, Oregon's lottery is heavily marketed, and claims that the state benefits from the lottery have always been part of the marketing pitch.

In June 2012, the lottery decided to phase out its two-year-old campaign. The reason: the campaign had been given a "pants on fire" truthfulness rating by PolitiFact Oregon. The "pants on fire" rating was not only a way of questioning the truth of the claims, it suggested that the claims themselves were ridiculous in the extreme.

As reported by the *Oregonian,* the lottery campaign's claims were based on math that included something called "churn"—a process whereby a gambler's initial bet of, say $20—is added to a player's "winnings" of, say $10—resulting in $30 of revenue even though the $10 winning never existed as money in the system. The claim also assumes that all winners were from Oregon (unlikely) and that the winners spent all of their winning within the state (equally unlikely). State representative Carolyn Tomei, a Democrat from the Portland suburb of Milwaukie, asserted that all the winnings were not going back to the state. "I looked at that ad and thought, 'What is the public supposed to take away from that?' It's so people will feel good about the lottery, and what is the point of that?"

It took the lottery less than a week to mothball the "97 cent campaign" after the Oregon PolitiFact rating. Lottery spokesperson Chuck Baumann told the *Oregonian* that the lottery was moving on to a new campaign but that it still stood by the 97 cent figure.

Micro Issues

1. What sorts of advertising claims should be examined by organizations such as Oregon PolitiFact? Why?
2. Would it be more truthful to note that playing the Oregon lottery is part of what Jefferson called a painless tax? What might be the likely outcome of such an inclusion?
3. Do you think those who play state lotteries are aware that they are paying additional taxes? Should it matter? Is let the buyer beware an appropriate ethical standard in the case of a state-regulated and voter-approved lottery?
4. Do you find this ad and its claims deceptive? Is making residents feel good about the lottery itself ethical?

Midrange Issues

1. Advertisers often use something called creative vagueness in crafting slogans and claims. Should the claims in ads be as fact-based as the information in news stories?
2. Should advertisements for products and services be subject to the same sort of scrutiny as ads that support governmental activities?
3. Did the Oregon lottery respond appropriately to the "pants on fire" judgment?

Macro Issues

1. Is a lottery an adequate mechanism to support something as crucial as public education?
2. Develop what you believe is a ethical campaign for a local lottery.

CASE 3-D

Sponsorships, Sins and PR: What Are the Boundaries?

LAUREN BACON BRENGARTH
University of Colorado at Colorado Springs

Sponsorships are a complicated, yet essential tool for nonprofit organizations. Sponsorships from the for-profit world provide funds that are critical for nonprofit growth and operations, yet they come at a cost. Consider, for example, the for-profit University of Phoenix and a nonprofit organization that administers local Head Start services and provides free preschool to children living in poverty.

While interviewing the Communication Manager of the nonprofit, I asked him if he felt that social media enabled the organization to serve a news-producing function in the community. He affirmed that he not only believes that the organization is a news producer, but that the group's success in driving social media has led to new dollars coming to the organization. Some of those new dollars had raised troubling questions.

For example, contributions from the for-profit University of Phoenix included an exchange of promotional mentions and opportunities by the nonprofit preschool. For example, the preschool promoted the University of Phoenix as the lead sponsor of its annual fundraising breakfast through Facebook and Twitter posts.

Additionally, at the breakfast, the nonprofit hosted a University of Phoenix "cyber café" where event attendees were encouraged to log on and tell others that they were at the event.

In previous years the University of Phoenix local staff members volunteered at the preschool through events such as reading to the children, providing "literacy totes" filled with school supplies and books for the kids, and several other activities. The relationship between the two organizations prompted the preschool to nominate the University of Phoenix for a Head Start Corporate award for model corporate/community partnerships, which it won.

Meanwhile, the University of Phoenix has come under fire for its high tuition rates and tendency to cater to low-income students who often leave campus with a pile of debt, minimal job prospects, and no degree. Because of the substantial federal financial aid that students receive, graduation rates have received heightened government scrutiny (Gramm 2012).

Additional University of Phoenix criticisms highlight its reliance on part-time instructors and a pattern of pushing students through course curriculum in half the time of traditional postsecondary schools (Dillion 2007). In 2009, the institution paid a $78.5 million settlement when two whistleblowers filed a False Claim Act lawsuit against the university regarding its student recruitment practices. Officials counteract widespread critiques by saying that the university structure caters to working students that many traditional schools ignore.

The University of Phoenix has experienced a sharp dip in enrollment because of widespread national criticism adding to a negative public image. In the third quarter of 2012, reports from the University of Phoenix reflect a 15% drop in average degreed enrollment and an 8% decline in new student starts. Net revenue for the Apollo Group (the operator of the University of Phoenix) shows a 9.2% decline in the third quarter of fiscal year 2012; however, the company still brought in $3.3 billion in revenue.

Micro Issues

1. If working, lower-income students make up a large portion of the University of Phoenix student body, how does this partnership cause potential ethical conflicts?
2. Should nonprofits partner with for-profit organizations?
3. What are the appropriate conditions and parameters for a nonprofit to promote its sponsor(s)?
4. What do for-profit organizations hope to gain by partnering with nonprofits?
5. What are nonprofits willing to sacrifice in order to gain for-profit capital?

Midrange Issues

1. What differentiates sponsorships from advertising?
2. Many for-profit corporations encourage employees to volunteer their time and dollars to a variety of local and national organizations. What, if anything, should for-profit organizations expect for this effort?

Macro Issues

1. How do politics influence the appropriateness of sponsorship relationships and promotion (for example, the U.S. Olympic Team received apparel from Ralph Lauren that was manufactured in China)?
2. How does social responsibility influence the appropriateness of sponsorship relationships (for example, Budweiser sponsoring football tailgates for a major university)?
3. What should nonprofits do to adequately research the history and practices of the for-profits that want to sponsor them?
4. Chapter 6 discusses the role of the corporate citizen as one element that can have a positive impact on the bottom line. Do you believe sponsorships such as the one described in this case contribute to the concept of the "good" corporate citizen? Do motives matter?

CASE 3-E

Corporate Responsibility: Doing Well by Doing Good?

CHRISTINE LESICKO
University of Missouri

Being environmentally conscious is the wave of the present. In an effort to go green, top water purification system manufacturer, Brita, has launched a campaign Web site designed to influence people to stop using water bottled in plastic.

The Web site, filterforgood.com, includes statistics on plastic bottle waste, a pledge one can take, plus statistics of how many bottles have been saved by those who took the pledge. The Web site also includes links to the NBC show "The Biggest Loser," a weight-loss reality show, and where to buy Brita products. The site also promotes Nalgene reusable bottles, a bike race for the environmental cause and a college grant program.

Facts included on filterforgood.com are, "America used 50 billion water bottles in 2006 and sent 38 billion bottles to landfills, the equivalent of 912 million gallons of oil." The Web site reports, "The energy we waste using bottled water would be enough to power 190,000 homes."

If Web site visitors opt to pledge to reduce plastic bottle waste, they receive a coupon and more information about Brita filtration systems. Visitors can also purchase a "handy kit" to help become more eco-friendly which includes a Filter-For-Good Nalgene bottle, 10 On the Go sticks from Crystal Light, Kool-Aid and Country Time, along with other offers and coupons.

Brita's campaign is obviously not hiding its affiliation with sponsors. However, as a news article in the *New York Times* noted, Clorox—Brita's parent company—does not take back used water filters, which means there is no effective way to recycle them. Beth Terry, who developed the Web site TakeBacktheFilter.org, notes "in order to give up bottled water, you have to switch to another plastic product that's not recyclable."

The Web site includes a petition to Clorox to initiate a recycling program plus collecting used filters for recycling. The site also notes, "while the original European Brita GmbH Company has created a take-back recycling program for its filter cartridges, Clorox has no such program in place for reusing or recycling Brita cartridges." The site commends Clorox for what it is doing, but also notes the underlying irony of the campaign itself.

Micro Issues

1. Should those who developed the Brita campaign have investigated whether the filters could be recycled before they went public with the effort?
2. Should news journalists investigate campaigns of this sort and write about what they find?
3. How does this effort at corporate social responsibility seem like or unlike others—for example, turning in the tops of yogurt containers in exchange for corporate donations to breast cancer research?

Midrange Issues

1. Evaluate Brita's campaign using the expanded TARES test.
2. Evaluate the need for bottled water—which used to be uncommon in the United States—according to the expanded TARES test.
3. Should consumers base their purchasing decisions, in part, on efforts such as these?

Macro Issues

1. Take the notion of a campaign for a supposedly environmentally friendly disposable diaper, assuming there is one. What would a campaign like this look like from a communitarian philosophy? A utilitarian one? How would the campaigns be similar? How would they differ?
2. Does the concept of transparency apply to corporate social responsibility? If so, how? If not, why not?
3. In this and similar cases, to whom should the strategic communication professional be loyal? Why?

CASE 3-F

Was That an Apple Computer I Just Saw? A Comparison of Product Placement in U.S. Network Television and Abroad

PHILIP PATTERSON
Oklahoma Christian University

Michael Scott, the buffoon-like office manager in the Emmy Award–winning NBC comedy *The Office,* shows up at casual Friday encouraging his shocked employees to check out his backside in his new Levi's jeans. In the wildly popular ABC drama/comedy *Desperate Housewives,* Gabrielle (played by Eva Longoria) gets desperate enough for cash to model beside a Buick LaCrosse at a car show and for a mattress firm. In the now-canceled *American Dreams,* which portrayed American life in the 1960s, such American icons as Campbell's Soup and the Ford Mustang were woven into the show.

Hollywood calls it "brand integration." Its critics—some of them the very writers for shows using product placement—call it much worse. But by any name, the phenomenon is growing. During the 2004–2005 television season, more than 100,000 actual products appeared in American network television (up 28 percent in one year) according to Nielsen Media Research, generating $1.88 billion (up 46 percent in a year) according to PQ Media (Manly 2005). Advertising agencies have set up product placement divisions. Research organizations have cropped up to take on the task of measuring the effectiveness of product placement. And television shows in the United States seem to have an insatiable appetite for what they offer.

"The fact is, these brands are part of our lives, and brands exist in these television environments, so why not showcase them," said Ben Silverman, chief executive of the firm that produces *The Office* (Manly 2005, A14).

However, not everyone is pleased. In a 2005 meeting in New York during "Advertising Week," television writers protested outside a panel discussing the state of brand integration in television programming. Among their gripes: they want more of a say in how products will be placed and, inevitably, a share of the profits generated from writing a product into the script.

Most see the move as one of survival. Taking a cue from radio and its "soap operas," the original television shows were named for the sponsors (*The Colgate Comedy Hour* and *Texaco Star Theater*), and the audience had little option but to watch the ads. But while commercials undergirded the television industry for the first 50 years, the advent of the remote, and more recently TiVo have allowed consumers to avoid the very commercials that make the programming free.

"The advertising model of 10 years ago is not applicable today," according to Bruce Rosenblum, president of Warner Bros. Television Group. "At the end of the day, if we are unable to satisfy advertisers' appetites to deliver messages in new ways to the viewer, then we're destined to have a broken model" (Manly 2005, A14).

However, for government-sponsored television in Europe, the practice of product placement remains a sticky issue.

In a 2005 edition of *Spooks,* a BBC drama, a logo for an Apple computer appeared in early airings of the show and then was removed in subsequent showings after British print media alleged that the Apple logo and others had slipped into BBC programming in exchange for cash and favors, which violates BBC rules. In Germany, firings occurred after public broadcaster ARD was found to have had shows full of illegal product placements for years (Pfanner 2005).

Not every European country has such a ban. In Austria, public broadcaster ORF airs more than 1,000 product placements a year on its shows and provides the ORF with about $24 million in funds to supplement its budget of approximately $1 billion. The ORF says that allowing the placements actually regulates what happens anyway. "If you don't regulate it, it exists anyway, in a gray zone," said Alexander Wrabetz, chief financial officer for ORF (Pfanner 2005, A15).

And even within the BBC, which has not announced any intent to change its ban on product placement, there are differing opinions. One BBC executive, speaking to the *International Herald Tribune* off the record said, "Back in the '50s, everything was called Acme, or we stuck stickers over all the brand names. There isn't a TV company in the world that does that now. Viewers don't find it convincing" (Pfanner 2005, A15).

Ultimately, success in product placement still comes down to whether the placement fits the plot. "The needle we have to thread," according to Jonathan Prince, creator of *American Dreams* and now working on Madison Avenue, "is to have brand integration that is effective enough to have resonance, but . . . subtle enough so that it doesn't offend" (Manly 2005, A16).

Micro Issues

1. Would you personally prefer to go back to the days where made-up names like "Acme" were placed on products to conceal the true brand names of the products?
2. Does the authenticity that real products such as name brand computers bring to a television show outweigh the intrusiveness of inserting a product into the plot of a show?
3. Are products placed into television shows the "price" you pay for free television, just as watching 30-second commercials were the "price" your parents and grandparents paid?

Midrange Issues

1. News magazines such as *Newsweek* will often run multipage special sections on issues such as "Women's Health," and all of the ads within the section will be for products promoting women's health. What do you see as the difference between this practice and product placement on television shows?
2. Do you see a difference in whether product placement should occur in scripted dramas and comedies as opposed to reality television?
3. How does product placement in television shows differ from naming sports stadiums or college bowl games after corporate sponsors, where presumably they will be mentioned on air for free during newscasts? Should newscasters avoid the corporate names of these places and events?
4. When a news show ends with rolling credits that attribute the wardrobe of the anchor to a certain store, is that product placement? Is that an intrusion on the objectivity of the news? Justify your answers.

Macro Issues

1. If consumers are "zapping" and "TiVo-ing" through commercials in free television, what will happen to the medium if product placement fails to deliver the needed revenue to keep the programming free? What will happen to the United States if free television is eliminated?
2. In trying to "thread the needle" between effectiveness and offensiveness, what are some of the guidelines you would write for product placement?
3. Is the argument made by Wrabetz in this case an ethical one? Compare the argument to the five standards of the TARES test found in this chapter and see how it measures up.

CASE 3-G

In the Eye of the Beholder: Dove's Campaign for Real Beauty

BRANDI HERMAN-ROSE
University of Missouri–Columbia

In the summer of 2005, Dove, a division of Unilever Corporation, launched its campaign for real beauty in the U.K. This marketing campaign—initially to promote skincare products such as a firming lotion—has expanded to include public service ads and promotions that simply question what constitutes real beauty.

Dove's campaign has drawn extensive media attention because it features six very unconventional models. They range in dress size from 6 to 14 and have different body types. Some have tattoos. Others have larger thighs. Dove touts these models as "real women" with "real beauty."

To view a number of the ads that have run as part of this continuing campaign, go to the following Web sites: www.Dove.com or www.Campaignforrealbeauty.com.

These ads feature six women in no-frills white bras and panties. All six are in their 20s. They are of different races, sizes and shapes. One has a large tattoo on her thigh. They vary in height. One is lily white, others have curly hair.

Women are pictured large on billboards and print ads that ask about each woman's characteristics. One 95-year-old woman is pictured with the two words "Wrinkled or wonderful?" Another larger-than-average woman is pictured smiling broadly at the camera with the words "Overweight or outstanding?" Each ad features women who are outside the conventional modeling stereotype. Each image also asks whether the model should be described with a positive or negative word or phrase.

In an advertisement featured on TV for Dove's hair care products, women are seen walking the streets with identical blonde coifs. At a given point, these women pull off their wigs to reveal curly-, straight-, blonde-, brown- and black-haired women. This ad ran in multiple countries and emphasized the beauty found in each woman's unique hair type.

Other companies have tried to showcase real women in their ads without boosting sales or receiving the same recognition as Dove's real beauty campaign. So, how did Dove come up with this campaign idea? Did Dove push for this creative direction or was the idea the work of Ogilvy and Mather, Dove's advertising agency?

Dove's campaign for "real beauty" was the result of an extensive research initiative that studied 3,200 women in Argentina, Brazil, Canada, France, Italy, Japan, the Netherlands, Portugal, Britain and the United States. Of the women sampled, only 2 percent considered themselves "beautiful." Another 5 percent described themselves as "pretty" and only 9 percent described themselves as "attractive."

For the survey, Dove commissioned the services of StrategyOne and MORI International to ensure that the study met criteria and codes of conduct established by global research associations. In addition, Dove utilized leading independent thinkers and academic institutions for research design and data analysis. Finally, Dove ensured that the study itself contained no reference to the brand or its parent, Unilever, and participants remained unaware of their sponsorship of the study (Lagnado 2004).

Dove, a company whose entire success is tied up in the actions and beliefs of women, is highly invested in research about women's belief systems. In a report entitled "The Real Truth about Beauty," the researchers (Etcoff, Orbach, Scott and D'Agostino 2004) claim:

> Women's interest in and preoccupation with beauty, is not some easily dismissed concern. This study shows conclusively that women now judge beauty as important and even crucial as they navigate today's world. In attempting to democratize and make accessible to all the idea of beauty, women are eager to see a redefinition and expansion of the ideals, along the lines they see it and away from the limiting, narrowed and restricted body shapes and sizes we see in moving images and in print.

The campaign for real beauty launched in the summer of 2005 in the U.K. to wide acclaim in the British press, and that same media attention spread throughout the United States and worldwide. This global campaign has received a mixture of praise and ridicule.

Alicia Clegg, a writer for www.brandchannel.com, wrote about the real beauty campaign after its launch in the U.K. "By showing a wider range of skin types and body shapes, Dove's advertising offers a democratized view of beauty to which all can aspire. The campaign also has an implied moral purpose, one that takes on the ethical issues of consumerism" (Clegg 2005).

Despite the positive comments that Dove received, still others felt that the methods of marketing used for this campaign were nothing more than a veiled attempt to convince women of their imperfections. "Some people think that the ads were just a ploy for Dove to make money by trying to boost a woman's confidence, while at the same time catering to her insecurities by selling her a firming cream" (Marchese 2005). Still others (Gogoi 2005) have suggested that the only reason that this campaign showcasing "real women" works well at this time is because of the prevalence of reality television within the past few years.

When held up against other campaigns for beauty products, Dove is doing something considerably different. Campaigns for brands like Olay and Jergens, two of Dove's main competitors, feature long-legged, very thin women in sexy poses, choices that Ogilvy, with Dove's direction, avoided.

Dove's campaign has received more positive reception in the U.K. Citizens of the United States responded well to the ads for hair products, but getting U.S. women to see overweight women as beautiful has been a more difficult task.

Micro Issues

1. What about this ad represents an attempt to "cut through the clutter"?
2. Using the TARES test outlined in the chapter, how would you evaluate this ad?
3. What is the role of authenticity in getting consumers to buy products that make them look "better" than they really do?

Midrange Issues

1. The Dove campaign has been praised as an example of ethical advertising. Evaluate this statement.

2. What role does stereotyping—specifically about beautiful women—play in the creation of this ad? Is that use of stereotyping ethically distinct from ads that feature more traditional models?
3. To whom or what have the ads' creators been loyal?

Macro Issues

1. Examine the literature on eating disorders. What role do you believe ads play in the development of those disorders? How important is advertising compared to some other influences?
2. Since the population of the planet is aging, is what Dove is doing really just smart marketing? What role do you believe ethical thinking played in the campaign?

CASE 3-H

Channel One: Commercialism in Schools

ROZALYN OSBORN
University of Missouri

PHILIP PATTERSON
Oklahoma Christian University

Channel One is a 12-minute newscast designed for teenagers—middle school through high school—broadcast via satellite into classrooms across the United States. At its peak, the channel's programming was viewed in more than 350,000 classrooms, in 12,000 schools, and by about 8 million students every day—about 40 percent of the nation's total students in this age group.

Channel One was first developed by Chris Whittle of Whittle Communications in 1989 in Knoxville, Tennessee. The program was later owned by Primedia Inc., the owner of the *Weekly Reader, New Yorker* magazine, and *Soap Opera Digest* and most recently by Alloy Media and Marketing creators of "Gossip Girl" and other teen fare deemed "raunchy" by its critics.

The original appeal of *Channel One* was that it offered to provide each subscribing school with a satellite dish, networked cable wiring, a VCR, and a television for every classroom. The equipment was provided, installed, and maintained at no cost to the school. In return, schools agree to air *Channel One* to a large majority of their students every day.

What lies at the center of the debate over *Channel One* and programs like it is advertising. As part of the twelve-minute program, students view 2 minutes of advertising. In one school year, students who view *Channel One* see the equivalent of about one day of class time in commercials.

Channel One supporters maintain the technology and information the outlet provides are invaluable, particularly in poorer schools. They contend that brief exposure to advertising is worth the gain in technology and materials. But critics focused on the outlet's commercial aspect, maintaining that schools should be a protected environment. By accepting the commercialization that comes with *Channel One,* opponents argue that schools are targeting a captive audience.

Commercial Alert, a Washington, D.C., watchdog group, claimed that "*Channel One* doesn't belong in schools because it conveys materialism and harmful messages to children, corrupts the integrity of the schools, and degrades the moral authority of schools and teachers" (Kennedy 2000, 21). Eventually the critics of *Channel One* went silent and the owners of the program continued to make money off of a guaranteed audience with thirty second commercials commanding a fee of up to $200,000. And advertisers had good reason to pay the money. Not only did they have a captive audience, they had an alert one. A 2006 study by the American Academy of Pediatrics proved that children remembered the two minutes of commercials more than the ten minutes of news. At various times, *Channel One* had forged arrangements for copy from both NBC and CBS.

In the summer of 2012, a Boston non-profit called Campaign for a Commercial-Free Childhood (CCFC) re-ignited the controversy when they urged states to drop the 12-minute newscast, which had won a Peabody Award in 2005 for its coverage of the conflict in Sudan, saying that it was nothing more than a business ploy to subject children to commercials. In addition, the CCFC claims that some of the *Channel One* content was questionable.

The Boston group wrote letters to 42 state superintendents urging them to take a look at the content of the program which reached thousands of students daily. In addition to questioning the number and content of the ads, CCFC claimed that *Channel One* spent time promoting its website, which the group says advertised a $7.49/minute psychic and promoted other websites with questionable material. The group also claimed that one full day of instruction time is lost just to the two minutes of commercials that *Channel One* was contractually allowed to air.

Josh Golin, the associate director of CCFC, claims that the network is being coy with ads which show a different version in the classroom from that shown online version where parents could, presumably, monitor the content. Golin claims that *Channel One* also has consistently refused to produce a list of the advertisers on the site accessed on August 11, 2012.

A review of the *Channel One* website in the summer of 2012 revealed ads for Puma, Vistaprint and Lowes and also a link to the URL.com website which CCFC claims has had such stories as "Reader Hookup Confession: My BF's Mom Caught Me Giving Him Oral Sex!"

Alabama school Superintendent Tommy Bice told FoxNews.com that *Channel One* programming was now under review by his state, but added that decisions about using *Channel One* were local decisions. And on the local level, many districts did vote to opt out of the programming. In 2011, the reach of *Channel One* had shrunk to less than 230,000 classrooms down from 440,000 in 1999.

Obligation, Inc., a watchdog group for childhood education and a long-time critic of *Channel One,* claimed that *Channel One* had "a long history of fudging their audience claims in their sales literature." Eventually *Channel One* lowered its claims of "nearly six million" viewers to "nearly 5.5 million" viewers. In discussing the problems at *Channel One,* Obligation, Inc.'s Jim Metrock said:

> Schools no longer have time for *Channel One*'s nonsense. Academic time can't be wasted anymore. The silliness and the often age-inappropriateness of *Channel One*'s content is angering school administrators, teachers, parents, and students. *Channel One*'s recent partnership with white board manufacturer Promethean in an effort to muscle into elementary schools will be a financial disaster for both firms. The downward spiral is accelerating for *Channel One.* The recent loss of half of their news anchors shows the employees are heading for the exits.

Micro Issues

1. How is *Channel One* different from the student newspaper or yearbook that sells advertising? From the PTA fund-raiser?
2. Are there certain sorts of ads that should be censored from *Channel One?*
3. A news service called ZapMe! installs and maintains computer labs for schools, providing the schools agree to log 4 hours per day per computer and allow ZapMe! to place ads of marketers on their Internet connections. It also tracks student demographic information. The company asks your local school district for permission to sign a contract. Do you write an exposè of the practice or an editorial praising it?

Midrange Issues

1. Are there certain areas of U.S. life that should be protected from commercialization? Why or why not?
2. How would you respond to the argument that *Channel One* helps students learn, particularly about difficult issues?
3. Campaign for a Commercial-Free Childhood (CCFC) has called *Channel One* "nothing more than a business ploy to subject children to commercials." How do you respond to that?
4. Would a preferable funding mechanism for schools be local taxes or state taxpayer support, or should schools just simply learn to do with less?

Macro Issues

1. Democracy works best with a well-informed citizenry. After going to it Web site and viewing some of the headlines, does *Channel One* fulfill that?
2. What other sorts of commercialism appears in public schools? How is *Channel One* like or unlike those forms of commercialism?
3. What responsibility does *Channel One* have for heightening desires in children for the products advertised when their socioeconomic status leaves little chance that the child will be able to have the service or product?
4. Critique the statements of Metrock in the case. Do you agree or disagree with him? Justify your answer after viewing a few of the 12-minute newscasts (some entire episodes can be found at http://www.obligation.org).

4

Loyalty: Choosing Between Competing Allegiances

By the end of this chapter, you should:

- **understand why the articulation of loyalties is important in professional ethics.**
- **know Royce's definition of loyalty and at least one of the major problems with that conceptualization.**
- **understand how journalists' role in society provides them with an additional set of loyalties to consider.**
- **be familiar with and able to use the Potter Box as a justification model for ethical decision making.**

LOYALTY AS PART OF THE SOCIAL CONTRACT

Decisions involving loyalty occur routinely for media professionals. When journalists make a decision to air or not to air a story, they have decided to whom they will be loyal. When recording executives cancel the contract of a controversial artist to avoid a boycott, they have chosen a loyalty. In fact, most ethical decisions come down to the question "To whom (or what) will I be loyal?"

The original discussion of loyalty in Western culture was written by Plato in *The Trial and Death of Socrates* (see Russell 1967). In Plato's *Phaedo,* Socrates bases his defense against the charges brought against him on his loyalty to divinely inspired truth. When asked by his accusers if he will stop teaching philosophy, Socrates responds:

> Men of Athens, I honor and love you: but I shall obey God rather than you, and while I have life and strength I shall never cease from the practice and teaching of philosophy, exhorting any one whom I meet. . . . For know that this is the command of God; and I believe that no greater good has ever happened in the State than my service to God.

While the word *loyalty* is not present in English translations of the *Phaedo,* the overall tone of the work is a tribute to loyalty, in this case a willingness to die for a cause.

Social contract theorist Thomas Hobbes was the first major Western philosopher to assert that God did not have to be the focus of loyalty. In his historic work, *The Leviathan,* Hobbes asserted loyalty is a social act and asserted that the agreement allows people to form a "social contract" that is the basis of political society. Unlike Socrates, Hobbes acknowledged that people could have more than one loyalty at a time and might, at certain times, be forced to choose among them—a notion most philosophers hold today.

Hobbes, unlike Socrates, also asserted that loyalty has limits. Loyalty to the ruler stops when continued loyalty would result in a subject's death—the loyalty to self-preservation being higher than loyalty to the ruler. The turmoil surrounding how the United States responds to terrorist acts and activities is a vivid example of how being loyal can inform decisions.

THE CONTRIBUTIONS OF JOSIAH ROYCE

American theologian Josiah Royce, who taught at Harvard in the early 1900s, believed that loyalty could become the single guiding ethical principle. In *The Philosophy of Loyalty* (1908), Royce wrote, "My theory is that the whole moral law is implicitly bound up in one precept: 'Be loyal.'" Royce defined loyalty as a social act: "The willing and practical and thoroughgoing devotion of a person to a cause." Royce would be critical, therefore, of the journalist who gets a story at all costs and whose only loyalty is to himself or the public relations professional who lets loyalty to an employer cause her to bend the truth in press releases or annual reports. To Royce, loyalty is an act of choice. A loyal person, Royce asserted, does not have "Hamlet's option"—or the leisure not to decide. For in the act of not deciding, that person has essentially cast his loyalty.

Loyalty also promotes self-realization. Royce spent much of his academic career fascinated with the new Freudian psychology and he viewed loyalty in its light. As a person continued to exercise loyalty, Royce believed, he or she would develop habits of character that would result in systematic ethical action. Like other aspects of moral development (see the last chapter of this book), loyalty can be learned and honed, Royce believed.

Loyalty as a single ethical guide has problems. *First,* loyalty, incompletely conceived, can be bias or prejudice thinly cloaked. *Second,* few people maintain merely a single loyalty and if loyalty is to become a guiding ethical principle, we need to develop a way to help distinguish among competing loyalties. *Third,* in a mass society, the concept of face-to-face loyalty has lost much of its power. *Finally,* the most troubling question: whether it is ethical to be loyal to an unethical cause; for example, racism or gender discrimination.

However, Royce suggested a way to determine whether a specific cause was worthy of loyalty. A worthy cause should harmonize with the loyalties of others within the community. For instance, the loyalty of the journalist should be in harmony with the loyalty of the reader. The loyalty of the advertising agency should not conflict with the loyalty of either its client or the consumer. Our loyalty to free and unfettered political discussion as the basis of modern democracy and journalism meets Royce's test of loyalty but is also the core of the debate over campaign finance laws.

To Royce, the true problem of loyalty as an ethical principle was not the poor choice of loyalties but failure to adhere to proper loyalties: "The ills of mankind are largely the consequence of disloyalty rather than wrong-headed loyalty" (Royce 1908). Causes capable of sustaining loyalty, Royce noted, have a "super-individual" quality, apparent when people become part of a community. A spirit of democratic cooperation is needed for Royce's view of loyalty to result in ethical action. For instance, advertising agencies demonstrate an ethical loyalty when they view their role as providing needed information for intelligent consumer choice, but more often they opt for loyalty to the bottom line because they suspect that competing agencies do.

Royce's thought has been criticized on a number of grounds. First, some philosophers assert that Royce's concept of loyalty is simplistic and that the adoption of loyalty as a moral principle may lead to allegiance to troubling causes. For instance, the advertising copywriter who scripts distorted television spots about a political opponent in the belief that she must get her candidate elected is demonstrating a troubling allegiance to a politician over the democratic process. Similarly, a reporter who must get the story first, regardless of its completeness or accuracy, would be demonstrating a misplaced loyalty to beating the competition.

Second, others have noted that Royce provides no way to balance among conflicting loyalties. Media professionals such as journalists are faced daily with a barrage of potential loyalties—the truth, the audience, the sources, the bottom line, the profession—and choosing among them is among the most basic of ethical decisions. Other professions have similar dilemmas such as the documentarian who must be loyal to the truth in her art while at the same time being loyal to the producers who want large numbers of the ticket-buying public to see the final product.

Third, it is unclear how Royce's ethical thinking would balance majority notions against minority views. Strictly interpreted, Royce's notion of loyalty could inspire adherence to the status quo or strict majority rule. For instance, advertisements that stereotype groups of people despite evidence to the contrary help perpetuate incorrect images. The ads work because they appeal to the majority, but by stereotyping, they have crowded out more accurate impressions.

Yet despite these criticisms, Royce's thought has much to recommend it. First, Royce speaks to the development of ethical habits. Second, Royce reminds us that the basis of loyalty is social and loyalty requires we put others on an equal footing with ourselves. Most important is the overriding message of Royce's work: *when making ethical choices, it is important to consider what your loyalties are and how you arrived at those loyalties.*

JOURNALISM AS A PROFESSION

Loyalty is not a fixed point but a range within a continuum. In *Loyalty: An Essay on the Morality of Relationships,* Fletcher (1993) identifies two types of loyalty. The first is minimal: "Do not betray me." The second is maximal: "Be one with me."

Between these two poles is a range of possibilities for allegiance and for corresponding media behavior. The location on the continuum for YouTube will differ from that of *The Nation* magazine.

One of the problems modern news media face is that a large percentage of the U.S. public subscribes to the notion that if the media are not maximally loyal—that is, one with government, the military and so forth—then they are traitorous. The media are routinely called disloyal by politicians, often for no greater sin than fulfilling the watchdog role, and it plays very well on the campaign trail.

Loyalty can be linked to role. A role is a capacity in which we act toward others. It provides others with information about how we will act in a structured situation. Some roles are occupationally defined—account executive, screenwriter, editor. Others are not: mother, spouse and daughter. We all play multiple roles and they help us define ourselves and know what is expected of us and others.

When the role you assume is a professional one, you add the ethical responsibilities of that role. Philosophers claim that "to belong to a profession is traditionally to be held to certain standards of conduct that go beyond the norm for others" (Lebacqz 1985, 32) and journalism qualifies as one of those professions with a higher expected norm of conduct.

However, not all journalists agree in practice. Hodges (1986) makes the distinction in this manner: when asked what she does for a living, one journalist says, "I am a journalist" while another says "I work for the *Gazette*." Hodges claims the first speaker recognizes her responsibility as a professional while the latter merely acknowledges her loyalty to a paycheck. The first would be expected to be loyal to societal expectations of a journalist; the second may or may not.

Journalists and their employers have debated whether journalism should be considered a profession. Advocates of professionalism assert that professionalism among journalists will provide them with greater autonomy, prestige and financial rewards. Critics see the process of professionalization as one that distances readers and viewers from the institutions that journalists often represent.

Despite these debates, we sense that journalists have two central responsibilities that are distinct in modern society. First, they have a greater responsibility to tell the truth than members of most professions. Second, journalists also seem to carry a greater obligation to foster political involvement than the average person.

Philosophers note that while ethical dilemmas are transitory, roles endure. Role expectations carry over from one situation to another. Loyalty to the profession means loyalty to the *ideals* of the profession. To Aristotle, loyalty to a profession also would mean maintaining high professional standards. The Aristotelian notion of virtue means being the best television producer or advertising executive you can be in the belief that you are being loyal to the profession and its ideals.

CONFLICTING LOYALTIES

As you can see, we are no longer talking about merely a single loyalty. We live in an age of layers of loyalties, creating added problems and complications.

Sorting through competing loyalties can be difficult, particularly when loyalties in one role appear to conflict with the loyalties of another. Much has been written about this issue and we have adapted one such framework from William F. May (2001), who outlined these layers of loyalties for college professors, but they are adaptable to those who work in the media. He offers four types of loyalty.

1. Loyalties arising from shared humanity:

   - demonstrate respect for each person as an individual.
   - communicate honestly and truthfully with all persons.
   - build a fair and compassionate environment that promotes the common good.

2. Loyalties arising from professional practice:

   - fulfill the informational and entertainment mission of the media.
   - understand your audience's needs.
   - strive to enhance professional development of self and others.
   - avoid the abuse of power and position.
   - conduct professional activities in ways that uphold or surpass the ideals of virtue and competence.

3. Loyalties arising from employment:

   - keep agreements and promises, operate within the framework of the law and extend due process to all persons.
   - do not squander your organization's resources or your public trust.
   - promote compassionate and humane professional relationships.
   - foster policies that build a community of ethnic, gender and socioeconomic diversity.
   - promote the right of all to be heard.

4. Loyalties arising from the media's role in public life:

   - serve as examples of open institutions where truth is required.
   - foster open discussion and debate.
   - interpret your professional actions to readers and viewers.
   - serve as a voice for the voiceless.
   - serve as a mirror of society.

The problem of conflicting loyalties is evident in the reality that most media professionals work for a corporation. They owe at least some loyalty to their corporate employers. However, such loyalty seldom involves a face-to-face relationship. Corporations demand employee loyalty but are much less willing to be loyal in return. The fear is that one's allegiance to the organization will advance the interest of the organization without any reciprocal loyalty to the employee. This is particularly true in the first years of this century when many news organizations, particularly newspapers, are going out of business or facing severe economic cutbacks.

Most ethical decisions, however, are not about loyalties to corporations or loyalty to an abstract concept such as freedom of the press or the public's right to know. Most everyday loyalty decisions are about how you treat the subject of your interview or how you consider the consumer of your advertising. Such ethical decisions bring to the forefront the notion of *reciprocity*. Simply articulated, reciprocity requires that loyalty should not work against the interest of either party.

Ed Stein © 1989 Reprinted with permission of UNIVERSAL UCLICK. All rights reserved.

Even in a time of shifting loyalties, there are some loyalties that should only be reluctantly abandoned such as loyalty to humanity and loyalty to truth. *Virtually no situation in media ethics calls for inhumane treatment or withholding the truth.* You can probably articulate other loyalties you would rarely, if ever, abandon. Even if you can't foresee every possible conflict of loyalty in your media profession, knowing where your ultimate loyalties lie is a good start to avoiding conflicts.

THE POTTER BOX

Ethical decision-making models, such as the one in Chapter 1 by Sissela Bok, help you make an ethical choice. In this chapter, you will learn a second decision-making model, one that incorporates loyalties into the reasoning process. The model was developed by Harvard theologian Ralph Potter and is called the Potter Box. Its initial use requires that you go through four steps to arrive at an ethical judgment. The case below will be used to help familiarize you with the model.

> You are the assistant city editor for a newspaper of about 30,000 circulation in a western city of about 80,000. Your police reporter regularly reports on sexual assaults in the community.
>
> While the newspaper has a policy of not revealing the names of rape victims, it routinely reports where assaults occur, the circumstances and a description of the assailant, if available.
>
> Tonight the police reporter is preparing to write a story about a rape that occurred in the early-morning hours yesterday on the roof of the downtown bus

station. Police report that the young woman who was raped went willingly to the roof of the bus station with her attacker. Although she is 25, she lives in a group home for the educable mentally disabled in the city, one of seven women living there.

She could not describe her assailant, and police have no suspects.

Your reporter asks you for advice about how much detail, and what detail, he should include in the story.

The Potter Box has four steps (see Figure 4.1) that should be taken in order. They are (1) understanding the morally relevant facts, (2) outlining the values inherent in the decision, (3) applying relevant philosophical principles and (4) articulating a loyalty. You proceed through the four steps in a counterclockwise fashion, beginning with the factual situation and ending at loyalties. We will examine each step individually.

Step One: Understanding the facts of the case. In the scenario, the facts are straightforward. As the newspaper editor, you have the information. Your ethical choice rests with how much of it you are going to print.

Step Two: Outlining values. Values is a much abused word in modern English. People can value everything from their loved ones to making fashion statements. In ethics, however, values takes on a more precise meaning. When you value something—an idea or a principle—it means you are willing to give up other things for it. If, as a journalist, you value truth above all things, then you must sometimes be willing to give up privacy in favor of it. In the foregoing case, such a value system would mean that you would print every detail, because you value truth and would risk invading the privacy of a person who is in some important ways unable to defend herself. If, as a journalist, you value both truth and privacy, then you may be willing to give up some truth, the printing of every detail, to attempt to preserve the victim's privacy.

Values often compete and an important element of using the Potter Box is to be honest about what you really do value. Both truth and privacy are lofty ideals. A less lofty ideal that most of us value is keeping our jobs. Journalists often value getting the story first or exclusively. A forthright articulation of all the values (and there will be more than one) in any particular ethical situation will help you see more clearly the choices that you face and the potential compromises you may have to make.

Step Three: Application of philosophical principles. Once you have decided what you value, you need to apply the philosophical principles outlined in the first chapter. For example, in the previous scenario, a utilitarian might argue that the

Facts	**Loyalties**
Values	**Principles**

FIGURE 4.1 The four steps of the Potter Box

greatest good is served by printing a story that alerts the community to the fact that some creep who rapes women who cannot defend themselves is still out there. Ross would argue that a journalist has duties both to the readers and to the victim and they must be weighed before making a decision.

Aristotle's golden mean might counsel a middle ground that balances printing every detail against printing no story at all. Kant would suggest that the maxim of protecting someone who cannot protect herself is a maxim that could be universalized, making a decision to omit some information justifiable. He would also argue to not use the woman as a means to your end—an exclusive story in this instance.

In this case, application of several ethical principles leads to the general conclusion that the newspaper should print some story, but not one that inadvertently reveals the victim's identity or that makes her out to be hopelessly naive in her trust of strangers.

However, you should be alert that while different ethical principles in this scenario lead to the same conclusion, many, if not most, ethical dilemmas may not produce such a happy result. The principles point to different and even mutually exclusive actions on your part, leaving you to decide your ultimate loyalty. But this is why the Potter Box demands that you apply more than one ethical principle, so that if (or when) they vary, you are able to explain why.

Step Four: Articulation of loyalties. Potter viewed loyalty as a social commitment and the results of using the Potter Box reflect that ethic. In the fourth step, you articulate your possible loyalties and decide whether they are in conflict. In the case above, you have a loyalty to the truth, to the community, to the woman and to your job—just for starters.

But, your loyalties are not in severe conflict with one another unless you adopt an absolutist view of the truth the community needs to know. It is possible to counsel your reporter to write a story that tells the truth but omits some facts (for example, the woman's residence in a group home and her mental disability), alerts the community to a danger (there's a creep out there who police haven't caught), protects the victim's privacy (you won't print her name or where she lives) and allows you to take pride in the job you've done (you've told the truth and not harmed anyone).

However, use of the Potter Box often highlights a conflict between loyalties. In these instances, we refer you to Royce's concept: what you choose to be loyal to should be capable of inspiring a similar loyalty in others who are both like and unlike you. Journalists are often accused of being "out of touch" with their viewers or readers, a fact for which we are highly criticized.

Our experience with the Potter Box has been that the vast majority of ethical decisions will allow you to sustain a variety of loyalties—they are sometimes not mutually exclusive as we saw above. However, those decisions that are most troubling are ones where a loyalty becomes so dominant that you are forced to abandon other loyalties that once seemed quite essential.

While you may initially find the stepwise process of the Potter Box somewhat cumbersome, as you learn to use it you will become fluent in it. The following case study, "The Pimp, the Prostitute and the Preacher," illustrates how you might use the Potter Box when making an ethical decision.

The Pimp, the Prostitute and the Preacher

You are the court reporter for a daily newspaper in a city of about 150,000 in the Pacific Northwest. About a year ago, the local police force began to crack down on prostitutes working the downtown mall. However, the department sought to limit prostitution by arresting pimps rather than by arresting either the prostitutes or their customers. The first of those arrests has now come to trial, and your paper has assigned you to cover it.

In his opening statement, the local assistant district attorney tells the jury that in order to convict a person of pimping under state law, the state must prove first that money was exchanged for sexual favors, and second that the money was then given to a third party, the pimp, in return for protection, continued work, etc. During the first two days of the trial, he calls as witnesses four young women, ages 14 to 16, who admit they have worked as prostitutes in the city but are a great deal less clear on the disposal of their earnings. Your story after the first day of the trial summarizes the details without disclosing their names.

Near the end of the second day, the prosecutor calls as witnesses men caught paying one or more of the women to have sex with them. Among those who testify is a middle-aged man who in an almost inaudible response to a question lists his occupation as a minister at one of the more conservative Protestant churches in the city. He admits to having paid one of the young women for sex, and that day's portion of the trial ends soon after his testimony is complete.

About 45 minutes later you are back in the office to write the story when the newsroom secretary asks you if you have a few minutes to speak with "Reverend Jones." You look up and realize you are facing the minister who testified earlier. In the open newsroom he begs you, in tears and on his knees, not to print his name. He even holds out a copy of the story you wrote on page one of this morning's paper outlining why the names of the prostitutes had not been used. He asserts that, should a story with his name appear, his marriage will crumble, his children will no longer respect him and he will lose his job.

After a few minutes the paper's managing editor realizes what is happening and calls you, the minister and the news editor into his office for a conference.

Using the Potter Box, determine how you would report this story. Your decision will reflect a set of loyalties as well as the values and principles you have chosen. Others may choose differently. A justification model such as Potter's or Bok's does not eliminate differences. What it will do, ideally, is ensure that your choices are grounded in sound ethical reasoning and justifiable on demand.

When you are finished, the final casting of loyalties will inevitably create another fact for the first quadrant of the box. For instance, in this case, if the decision is to run the name, anything that might subsequently happen to the minister as a result—firing, divorce, even possible suicide—is now a hypothetical "fact" for the first quadrant of the Potter Box. With this new "fact" you return to the first quadrant of the Potter Box and go through it again. If you decide not to run the minister's name and his parishioners discover his actions, the newspaper loses credibility. This is also a "fact" to be entered into the first quadrant of the Potter Box. Considering these additional although hypothetical "facts," you may want to go through the process again to see if your decision will remain the same. (You might search the Web or see the Web site for this book for the story of Admiral Boorda, who committed suicide after it was revealed that he wore medals on his uniform he had not earned.) Regardless of your initial decision about the story, would the possibility of that subsequent "fact," obviously not known to the journalist at the time, make a difference in a later use of the Potter Box?

Now that you've made a decision about revealing the name of the minister based on the facts, we'd like to introduce additional facts. Read them and go through the Potter Box again focusing less on the minister and more on larger issues that affect how the story is written and how it is run in the newspaper. This time, think about the notions of stereotyping, how minorities are portrayed in news reports and what exactly we mean by "objectivity" and "truth."

> As the trial continues, it becomes clear that there are other factors at work. In your largely Caucasian community, the only people arrested for pimping have been African-American. All the young women who work as prostitutes are Caucasian, as are the customers who testify. As far as prostitution goes, your Pacific Northwest version is relatively mild. There are no reports of drug use among the prostitutes and their customers, and none of the prostitutes has complained of physical violence. Further, the prosecuting attorney cannot make any of the young women admit under oath that they ever gave the pimps any money. The jury verdict in this case is not guilty.

Do the new facts change your loyalties? Do they change the way you look at the trial? If so, in what way?

We recommend that you try using both the Bok and Potter justification models at various times in your ethical decision making. Becoming a competent practitioner of both methods will provide you with greater flexibility and explanatory power. We also recommend, regardless of the approach you use, that an unvarnished and critical discussion of loyalty become part of your ethical dialogue. We believe it will enable you to anticipate situations as well as react to them.

Suggested Readings

FLETCHER, GEORGE P. 1993. *Loyalty: An essay on the morality of relationships.* New York: Oxford University Press.

FUSS, PETER. 1965. *The moral philosophy of Josiah Royce.* Cambridge, MA: Harvard University Press.

HANSON, KAREN. 1986. "The demands of loyalty." *Idealistic Studies,* 16, pp. 195–204.

HOBBES, THOMAS. 1958. *Leviathan.* New York: Bobbs-Merrill.

OLDENQUIST, ANDREW. 1982. "Loyalties." *Journal of Philosophy,* 79, pp. 73–93.

POWELL, THOMAS F. 1967. *Josiah Royce.* New York: Washington Square Press, Inc.

Cases on the Web

www.mhhe.com/mediaethics8e

"She chose before losing the choice" by Tom Lyons
"Standing behind a reporter: The CBS/*News Journal* Controversy" by John Sweeney
"The anchor as activist" by Fred Bales
"The wonderful world of junkets" by Ralph Barney

CHAPTER 4 CASES

CASE 4-A

Who's Facebook Page Is It Anyway?

AMY SIMONS
University of Missouri

Barrett Tryon joined the Colorado Springs *Gazette* staff in April 2012. He was hired to help draw users to the newspaper website, providing updates on breaking news and enterprise stories.

Tryon was no stranger to the Colorado Springs market. He'd spent more than a decade working for KRDO-TV, an ABC affiliate. In 2011, he won an Emmy for "Best Newscast" in a medium-sized market. That same year, the station's website—of which Tryon was the managing editor—was given the award for best website by the Associated Press. On his station bio, he was described as "the face behind KRDO.com and KRDO's Facebook and Twitter pages." As the face of those pages, Tryon drew in more than 200 new followers to the station's sites each week.

If there was one thing Barrett Tryon was confident he knew, it was how to use social media responsibly.

That's why what happened to him at the *Gazette* surprised so many.

It started with a *Los Angeles Times* story published on June 12, 2012, announcing Freedom Communications Holdings Inc.'s sale of the *Orange County Register* and six other newspapers to a Boston investment group. One of those papers: the *Gazette.*

Tryon posted a link to that story to his Facebook page, along with a pull quote highlighting his employer's direct involvement.

Three hours later, Tryon's boss, Carmen Boles, told him via email that the Facebook post was a violation of Freedom Communication's social media policy, stating the *LA Times* article "does not meet our standards of factual information." Soon after, in a second email, she included this passage:

> Freedom Communications, Inc.'sAssociate Handbook/Confidentially and Propri-
> etary Rights policy prohibits you from posting disparaging or defamatory . . . state-
> ments about the company or its business interests, but you should also avoid social
> media communications that might be misconstrued in a way that could damage the
> company's goodwill and business reputation, even indirectly.

Tryon maintained he was acting within his rights under the First Amendment. He told his boss in an email, "it's on my personal account, and from an *LA Times* article, I'm not removing it."

The email exchange continued for several hours, and Boles told Tryon that corporate human resources would be handling the matter. Tryon, standing his ground, told Bowles "it's only natural for someone to be interested in something that directly affects you . . . I think there's a huge difference between saying 'eff off' versus pulling a quote. But, since I violated the policy, I'll deal with the consequences."

The human resources department scheduled a meeting with Tryon for June 14, 2012, two days after the initial post. But, that meeting never happened because, Tryon told the *Colorado Springs Independent,* he insisted on bringing an attorney. Instead, Freedom Communications put Tryon on administrative leave. Meanwhile, the paper's decision ignited debate over the ethics and legality of social media policies.

Almost all news organizations and professional associations have some kind of social media policy or guideline. Many, like NPR, the *New York Times* and the *Roanoke Times,* even make them public. Most read like a list of common sense reminders: identify yourself as a journalist and a representative of your newsroom, maintain standards of confirmation and attribution, maintain copyright by linking to content instead of reposting, assume anything you post is public, etc. Some, such as the Associated Press and the American Society of Newspaper Editors urge journalists not to break news on social networks, but to do it through conventional publishing channels (meaning on a news organization's website and not on a personal blog or Facebook page), and to keep "company confidential information confidential."

According to the National Labor Relations Act, which gives workers the right to organize, unionize and bargain collectively, some of these widely shared guidelines might be illegal. In response to Tryon's case, Poynter.org published a memo issued by the National Labor Relations Board that ruled the following social media policy provisions unlawful:

- "Avoid harming the image and integrity of the company."
- "Do not express public opinions about the workplace, work satisfaction or dissatisfaction, wages, hours or work conditions."
- "Don't comment on any legal matters, including pending litigation or disputes."
- Instruction not to "reveal non-public company information on any public site."

"I really want to emphasize this—I think this is so important—is that this is not an effort for me to slam the *Gazette,* to slam Freedom Communications, to slam the new owners, 2100 Trust. That's not what I'm doing," Tryon told the *Colorado Springs Independent,* in its report of Tryon's unwanted administrative leave and the reasons behind it.

"I'm standing on principle that what I posted absolutely was not breaking any type of social media policy; I didn't interject any opinion. And the fact of the matter is, it was on my personal account. I have a vested interest in what's happening with the new owner; and like anyone else in the country, if they were getting bought out by a new company would damn well do your research—as a reporter, or not—to look into that new company."

On June 19 2012, about a week after Barrett Tryon posted the *LA Times* story to his Facebook page, his bosses at Freedom Communications called him with an offer to reinstate him. Tryon resigned instead. He announced his decision to followers on Twitter, referencing a hit song by the musical group, Goyte.

"I think after I realized there was support from so many people locally and nationally that I'm not really interested in working for an organization [where] we would even have this conversation; that there was never a dialogue to begin with—and that's unfortunate," he told the *Colorado Springs Independent.* "I hope that the takeaway is that people realize that, if you do have a social-media policy in place, it's important that you know what it is, and how it can be interpreted or misinterpreted."

Micro Issues

1. Did Barrett Tryon violate Freedom Communications' social media policy?
2. Was Freedom Communications within its right to demand Tryon remove the post from his Facebook page?
3. What risks does an employee take when posting about his or her employer on social media? A competitor? A news story that has already been published or broadcast?
4. What loyalties did Tryon's boss demonstrate in how she handled her initial objections to the first Facebook posting?

Midrange Issues

1. Should news organizations expect employees to follow social media policies and guidelines on their personal accounts?
2. Evaluate the social media policy that suggests that news should not be broken on social media but through more traditional channels.
3. What, if any, types of social media posts should be fireable offenses for a journalist?

Macro Issues

1. Should news agencies publish their social media policies for public view?
2. Is there such a thing as "private" social media presence for a journalist? Should anything published under a journalist's name uphold all journalistic standards?
3. Tyron said he had a First Amendment right to publish on his Facebook page. Evaluate this claim ethically. Does the First Amendment trump professional loyalty in this case?
4. Do news organizations that promote their Web sites and encourage employees to use social media set themselves up for these sorts of conflicts? How might they be avoided?

CASE 4-B

What Would Socrates Have Done? The Disappearance of Hillary Clinton

LEE WILKINS
University of Missouri

Photographs are sometimes labeled iconic too soon. But the photograph of President Barack Obama surrounded by his cabinet watching the real-time video of the attack on the compound where Osama bin Laden had been in hiding was labeled iconic before it was 24 hours old. As you look at the picture, notice that the papers in front of Secretary of State Hillary Clinton and others are "blurred." The White House, before it released the photograph, distorted the image so that, it said, high-security information would not be revealed through a detailed examination of the photograph itself.

Official White House Photo by Pete Souza

The meaning of the photograph, generally through an analysis of the expressions on people's faces, has been debated. For example, many who viewed the photograph said Clinton was the only person in the room showing shock at the images. Clinton herself has countered that interpretation, saying she was merely covering her nose and mouth to block a sneeze. The photograph itself, as well as the raid on the bin Laden compound, also became of the subject of a political campaign commercial and the subtext for foreign policy discussions in the 2012 presidential election.

Numerous print publications and broadcast outlets reproduced the photo. One of those was a Brooklyn-based Hasidic newspaper *Der Zeitung,* a paper that is written in Yiddish and serves a small segment of the ultra-orthodox Jewish community in that city.

In the photograph of the bin Laden raid printed in *Der Zeitung,* the image of Hillary Clinton and White House staffer Audrey Tomason, director for counterterrorism for the U.S. Security Council, were literally Photoshopped out of the picture.

Editors claimed that Secretary Clinton was deleted from the photograph because the paper serves a readership that places a high value on female modesty.

Critics countered that *Der Zeitung,* which translates as "*The Time,*" has edited out other images of women because the publication itself has an ideological objection to women holding positions of power.

"Visit these links to read more about this story and see *Der Zeitung's* controversial photo:
http://www.washingtonpost.com/blogs/blogpost/post/hillary-clinton-audrey-tomason-go-missing-in-situation-room-photo-in-der-tzitung-newspaper/2011/05/09/AFfJbVYG_blog.html
http://www.npr.org/blogs/thetwo-way/2011/05/09/136143892/
hasidic-newspaper-removes-clinton-another-woman-from-iconic-photo"

Micro Issues

1. As you look at the two images, does how Hillary Clinton is dressed support the claim of editing for "female modesty"?
2. Would it have been appropriate for the paper to simply crop the picture on the right-hand side, thus cutting out the images of Clinton and several others and resulting in a photograph that focused more specifically on President Obama and Vice President Joe Biden?
3. Since this newspaper reached only a small group, and since the undoctored photograph was available from many other sources, is any of this really significant?

Midrange Issues

1. The doctored photograph was brought to the attention of the wider public when it was reported—critically—in other newspapers. What is the role of these other newspapers with regard to *Der Zeitung* and readers, viewers and listeners?
2. One commentator, quoted in the *Daily Mail* in the UK, noted, "This is a bit silly. Secretary of State Clinton was not dressed immodestly. There was no intent of objectification in the photo. Haven't the editors got something better to do?" How should the editor of *Der Zeitung* respond to this criticism? How might such a response emphasize the concept of loyalty?

Macro Issues

1. This same event—the death of Osama bin Laden—became controversial for another reason: The White House refused to provide photographs of bin Laden's corpse or his burial at sea? Some journalists—in many countries—supported this approach; others disputed it. How would you analyze the White House approach in your role as journalist? In your role as strategic communication professional?
2. What should be the role of ideology in journalism?
3. What should be the role of ideology in strategic communication?

CASE 4-C

Twitter Ethics for Journalists: Can You Scoop Yourself?

CHARLOTTE BELLIS
TVNZ—Christchurch, New Zealand

Journalists in every developed nation are experimenting with using Twitter as a reporting tool. The site allows members to post searchable updates of fewer than 140 characters at a time about themselves and the world around them in updates called "tweets." "In countries all around the world, people follow the sources most relevant to them and access information via Twitter as it happens—from breaking world news to updates from friends," reads Twitter.com. One blogger on CisionBlog headlines, "Social media is a virtual Rolodex for journalists and media relations people." ReadWriteWeb.com believes Twitter helps them with quality assurance, discovering breaking stories, conducting interviews and promoting their work. A columnist on Poynter believes Twitter's ability to search updates "could make it easier for journalists to track beats, trends or issues."

However, some have questioned whether the personal element Twitter invokes could result in a lack of vetting, unethical behavior or a blurring of traditional boundaries between journalist and citizen.

In January 2009, David Schlesinger, Editor-in-Chief at Reuters, published a blog entitled Full Disclosure: Twittering away standards or tweeting the future of journalism? after twittering from the World Economic Forum in Davos, Switzerland. Other journalists there joined @daschles in his Twitter experiment as they pushed to be the first to break developments, post comments on the behind-the-scenes experience and promote their stories. With '#davos' as the standard signoff for the attending journalists, any Twitterer could follow a continuous stream of comments from the ski resort.

However, the *Silicon Alley Insider* highlighted Schlesinger in a story headlined "Reuters Scoops Itself by Twittering from Davos." While at the meeting, Schlesinger—under his Twitter handle @Daschles—had tweeted comments like, "[Financial speculator George] Soros—financial industry has to shrink by half! #davos." And another: "Soros—new financial system needs to emerge before we can talk about length of recession." The *Insider* article asked Schlesinger "If a Reuters correspondent had done that, would you fire him/her?"

Schlesinger responded that Twitter is journalism and that it has the potential to be dangerous. He said he was not embarrassed that his tweets beat the Reuters newswire, adding he was not destroying Reuters standards by encouraging tweeting. "If great storytellers use [microblogging, macroblogging and social networking] platforms to display their knowledge, access, expertise and abilities, I think that is a marvelous advance."

In a follow-up interview Schlesinger said he encourages his reporters to experiment but understood how his tweets could stir debate, particularly because journalism is at an "inflection point" in history. ". . . A company like Reuters makes most of its money from being first, so by challenging our own systems and thus business model I became a legitimate target."

"Twitter is such a fast medium that it challenges our standards to always have, for example, two pairs of eyes on a story," said Schlesinger. "Do we have whole new standards for Twitter? Do we allow the unedited and unvetted?"

As journalism works to remodel itself for the 21st century, many believe the instantaneous nature of the Internet is a key element in the industry's viability. For journalists the problem becomes should they publish—via tweets—information as soon as it is known, even when the nature of the medium itself dictates that the information will lack context. Or should the journalist hold off and spend time getting the context of the story, vetting it through a more regular editorial process and publishing it in a more traditional, less instantaneous medium?

Another problem for journalists using Twitter is that the social networking site was built for instantaneous, personal thoughts. Twitter naturally lends itself to divulging information as if to a friend and results in tweets that have a personal tone. Twitter makes it easy to muddle the personal and the professional as Canada's *National Post* technology reporter David George-Cosh, known as @sirdavid on Twitter, learned. After declining an interview with reporter George-Cosh, a marketing professional twittered: "Reporter to me, 'When the media calls you, you jump,

OK!?' Why, when you called me and I'm not selling? Newspapers will get what they deserve."

The reporter saw the tweet and responded with six heated tweets that included multiple expletives directed toward the marketing professional. MediaStyle.ca characterized @sirdavid's response with this headline: "*National Post* reporter has total Twitter meltdown." Hours later, the *National Post* apologized on their Editor's blog for the reporter's conduct on Twitter.

Micro Issues

1. Do you think it is important for journalists to distinguish their professional roles from their personal ones on social network sites? If you do, how might that be accomplished?
2. If you were Schlesinger's editor, how would you have responded to him "scooping" his own organization on the story? Does it matter that the organization paid him a salary to do this work?
3. If Schlesinger were a freelancer, do you think the same rules should apply? Why or why not?

Midrange Issues

1. Has the advent of Twitter or the Internet changed the nature of the "scoop" or of objectivity?
2. Should news organizations, or individual journalists, develop policies outlining how they will and will not respond to things that are written about them or their work online?
3. Is promoting a story an appropriate use of Twitter? Who should do it? Why?

Macro Issues

1. Does the personal nature of a social networking site make it an inappropriate place for journalism? Does the fact that tweets are so brief? How might your answers be supported by concepts such as Ross's duties?
2. Ask your friends how much it matters to them that the news and/or entertainment media they use get something first. What do you think hard news journalists should make of these responses? Feature reporters?

CASE 4-D

Where Everybody Knows Your Name: Reporting and Relationships in a Small Market

GINNY WHITEHOUSE
Eastern Kentucky University

Everybody is a source when you're covering an agricultural town with a population under 12,000.

But Sunnyside Police Sergeant Phil Schenck had not been a source for Jessica Luce when he asked her out for a date during a Halloween party in 1999. Luce had worked as a general assignment reporter at the *Yakima Herald-Republic* for almost a year. Sunnyside, Washington, was one of four communities she covered in this first job out of college. The two spent time together infrequently over the next two months.

"I was interested in him, we had fun, but if I had been asked what was going on I would have said we were friends," Luce said.

Nonetheless, a co-worker was incredulous. Luce remembers him saying, "You can't go out on a date with a source. It's one of the biggest taboos in journalism!"

The *Herald-Republic*'s four-page code of ethics advises staff to avoid conflicts of interest but offered no specifics on personal relationships that might cause conflicts of interest.

Luce decided to keep her relationship with Schenck quiet. She had never needed Schenck as a source and never thought the occasion would arise.

Schenck's boss, however, was another matter. Sunnyside Police Chief Wallace Anderson had been accused of shooting a great blue heron outside the police station, storing explosives at the station house and of having a threatening temper. Following a lengthy and expensive investigation, Anderson resigned in November.

By New Year's Day, Luce and Schenck decided they were definitely dating. "I kept my relationship under wraps save for a few confidants at work. I felt the relationship would be perceived as something wrong," Luce said. "But I didn't see it interfering with my job. Phil and I didn't talk about work as much as normal couples might. We knew it wasn't fair to either one of us."

In mid-February, Schenck was named acting captain, the number two position in the Sunnyside police department and the official media spokesman. Luce realized she needed to be pulled off the Sunnyside police beat immediately. Her editors agreed.

"It was hard to talk with them about my private relationship and I was forced to define things about the relationship that I hadn't even done for myself," Luce said.

Craig Troianello, her city editor, sat her down for a long conversation. "Jessica made it easy because she was straightforward. We didn't ask intimate questions—that's irrelevant in this case," Troianello said. "By taking the proactive ethical stand that she did, it was easy for us to deal with this."

Luce said Troianello emphasized that he was not questioning her integrity. However, he had to make sure he hadn't overlooked something that could be perceived as a conflict by readers.

"This was a lesson on perception versus reality," Luce said. Luce's reporting did not affect Schenck's promotion, nor had Schenck ever implied that a story should or should not have been covered. Nonetheless, Schenck benefited from the chief's departure.

Troianello said he was never worried that Luce's reporting was compromised, but he wanted to make sure the newspaper was above suspicion. "Issues involving the police department were in the forefront of the news," Troianello said. "People could read anything into it—that she was protecting the chief that she was trying to bring the chief down. Those kinds of spins drove my concern."

On the other hand, Schenck questions whether a strict conflict-of-interest standard is realistic in a small town. "Everybody is a potential source—even the clerk at the grocery store. We eat food. If her husband or boyfriend is a farmer, you could say she is promoting eating. This is an ideal that might be somewhat impractical," Schenck said. "If you can't be a real person, how can you report on real people?"

Luce says if she had to do it all over again she would not have kept the relationship a secret as long as she did. Nonetheless, it would still be hard to talk to a supervisor about dating. Troianello said he understands the complexities of a journalist's personal life but would rather Luce had brought the relationship to the newspaper's attention by New Year's Day, when the two began dating.

However, he understands the dynamic of the situation. "She's in a small town where the number of people with four-year degrees and professionals is small," Troianello said. "It seems like there will be some mixing at some point. Relationships could occur as naturally as it does in the newsroom. I married a copy editor."

Once their relationship went public (they were later engaged), Luce was surprised at how supportive the community and city officials were, including the new police chief (someone other than Schenck). "What we as journalists see as an ethical problem and conflict of interest isn't necessarily going to be seen as an ethical problem by the public."

However, Luce never heard comments one way or another from the former chief or his supporters. On several occasions, city officials have questioned whether Schenck leaked information to Luce or *Herald-Republic* reporters. Schenck simply explained that he had not. "I deal with stuff every day that Jessica would love to get her hands on," Schenck said. "But we just don't talk about it."

Luce now covers education in the city of Yakima.

Micro Issues

1. Did Luce have a responsibility to tell her editors about her relationship with Schenck? If so, when should Luce have informed them?
2. What responsibility did the *Yakima Herald-Republic* editors have to explain expectations on conflicts of interest? Is spelling out those expectations necessary or appropriate in a code of ethics?
3. How would the ethical questions have changed if Schenck worked in another capacity for the city, such as being a teacher?
4. How would the ethical questions have changed if Luce and Schenck had remained only friends?

Midrange Issues

1. What aspects of their lives should journalists be able to keep private?
2. Is public perception of an ethical problem truly relevant?
3. Journalists spend most of their time with two groups: their sources and their co-workers. Considering those limitations, is dating possible or advisable?

Macro Issues

1. Can journalists cover communities effectively if they are expected to remain remote and removed?
2. How specific should codes of ethics be on conflicts of interest?

CASE 4-E

A Question of Role: Is a Documentary Filmmaker a Friend, a Journalist or An Entertainer?

NANCY MITCHELL
University of Nebraska–Lincoln

In 1998, independent filmmaker David Sutherland wrote, produced, directed and edited a story about a young Nebraska farm couple, Juanita and Darrel Buschkoetter and their three daughters. It is a riveting story of the family facing the dual hardships of trying to keep the family farm and the family intact. With more than 200 hours of film shot over three years, Sutherland painted a portrait of the impact of the economic struggles of family life.

Sutherland interviewed 40 families before picking the Buschkoetters. Sutherland showed the couple examples of his work so they knew what they were getting into. During filming, neither Sutherland nor his crew ever became friends with the family. However, he said he did develop a friendship after the project wrapped up.

The series won critical acclaim. The documentary was nominated for four Television Critics Association awards, including Program of the Year. The project also was included in many critics' list for Best of TV for 1998, including the *Chicago Tribune, TV Guide* and the *Boston Globe*. Steve Johnson, critic for the *Chicago Tribune,* called it: "One of the extraordinary television events of the decade. 'The Farmer's Wife' is a breathtaking piece of work, a harrowing intimate love story set against an unforgiving physical and cultural landscape."

David Bianculli, *New York Daily News* said: "Watching 'The Farmer's Wife' is time very well spent: This is an honest, haunting, unflinching instructive and intimate study of a family that seems doomed to fail, but refuses to give up easily." Ron Miller of *The Oregonian,* wrote, "Not until this week's 'The Farmer's Wife' has any filmmaker probed so deeply into the heart of an American family with such gut-wrenching results."

The film attracted 18 million PBS viewers when it first aired, making it one of the most watched series in PBS history. The six and one-half–hour documentary aired in three segments. The first segment introduced viewers to the Buschkoetters, who tell the story (without the intrusion of a narrator) of the troubles they face both in their marriage and the risk of losing the farm after years of drought.

The second segment chronicles family life and the relentless challenge to make ends meet and the danger of losing the farm. The loan officer, Hoy Bailey of the USDA, tells the Buschkoetters to ask all the creditors for an extension. In one scene Juanita drives at night to the office of one of the creditors, where she asks for a two-year extension. The creditor, Rich Kucera, listens to her and eventually agrees. The next scene finds Darrel in the kitchen of their home and Juanita arrives home to tell Darrel that Kucera has agreed, reluctantly, to extend their agreement. Darrel comments that he can't believe that Kucera was nice:

DARREL: "He wasn't even nasty?"
JUANITA: "No."
DARREL: "Richard, not nasty? That's a first. . . . I couldn't even imagine that guy being nice."

In the ensuing scene, Darrel calls Hoy Bailey. The loan officer tells Darrel that all of the extensions have been granted except for one for $100 and without that, they'll lose the farm in a buyout.

DARREL: "You mean $100 would cause a buyout?"
HOY: "Yep."
DARREL: "Don't you think that's a little bit ridiculous? I mean, if it had to be, I could go out and sweep a street and make $100 and eliminate a buyout."

The last episode depicts the resolution of their problems. Darrel harvests a bumper crop but suffers the stress of working his farm and another to make enough money to feed the family. After Darrel lashes out, Juanita takes their girls to her sister and leaves him, but they return after a week or so. Darrel seeks counseling and the couple seems to be saving their farm and their relationship.

Sutherland describes himself as "a portraitist," not an investigative reporter. He said he crafted the film in such a way as to let interactions tell the story without a narrator. Sutherland described the approach as "third person, close up." Sutherland said he had no agenda for the film but added that he was concerned about those being filmed trying to use him to promote their agenda.

In answer to the question of how far he would go to not interfere with the story he said: "If someone's life were in the balance, I'd have come up with the money." Sutherland said Darrel and Juanita's dream of saving the family farm was parallel with his own dreams of creating a documentary that was an intimate portrait with a social issue as a backdrop. To Sutherland, it was important to "talk to them [the subjects] from your heart and not taking advantage of them."

In the final episode, when Juanita left Darrel, Sutherland chose not to follow her even though Juanita gave him permission. Sutherland trusted the story could be told in another way at another time and he eventually captured a summary of the event after the family was reunited.

Response to the series and the publicity led to opportunities for the Buschkoetters. They testified before Congress on the plight of the family farm, traveled on publicity tours and gave speeches. Sutherland stated that the Buschkoetters' girls gained more self-esteem. Sutherland said the project "made me fall in love with America again. It was about people who tried their best. What more could you ask for?"

Micro Issues

1. If you were the producer, would you have lent the Buschkoetters the $100 if doing so meant they wouldn't lose the farm? What does it do to the story if you lend the money? What does it do to the story if you don't lend the money? What does it do to the family?
2. Would you answer the question differently if you were a news journalist working on an in-depth piece on the same subject?
3. Did Sutherland make the right decision about filming the marital breakup? By not following her, do you think Sutherland helped or hurt the situation, or was there no effect?

Midrange Issues

1. When asked if he thought the personal rewards of creating a documentary might be construed as using people for personal gain, Sutherland responded: "I'm as uptight about

them [subjects of his documentaries] using me." Evaluate this statement. Is this same tension prevalent in news journalism?

2. Sutherland describes himself as a portraitist, not an investigative reporter (e-mail to author, Sept. 7, 2003). Do you think this gives him freedom to make different choices than he would had he claimed to be an investigative reporter?

3. Does having a camera present change the story? Do you think filming the meeting when Juanita asks the creditor for the extension on the loan changed the creditor's behavior? Does that matter?

4. When, if ever, can a journalist or documentarian become friends with those he has written about?

Macro Issues

1. Is it possible to produce a documentary from an objective point of view? What should be a guiding principle in creating this type of work?

2. Does a documentary need to conform to different ethical understandings than other entertainment forms—for example, reality television or a prime-time magazine show? Why?

CASE 4-F

Conflicted Interests, Contested Terrain: The *New York Times* Code of Ethics

BONNIE BRENNEN
Marquette University

In January 2003, the *New York Times* broke a lengthy tradition and published its new ethics code on the Web. The *Times* decision was an important one, for ethics codes are often controversial in both their creation and their application. However, ethics codes can be an important marker of specific social practices created under particular social, economic and political conditions at distinct times in history.

For example, members of the American Newspaper Guild in 1933 crafted one of the first ethics codes developed by journalists rather than managers. That code suggested the "high calling" of journalism had been tarnished because news workers had been pressured by their employers to serve special interests rather than the public good. Conflict of interest was centered on the relationship between reporters and sources and the code made a particular point that business pressures were putting undue stress on newsrooms. The code recommended that to combat business pressures the news should be edited "exclusively in newsrooms."

Ethics codes in general are controversial among professionals and scholars. Some maintain that ethics codes are nothing more than generalized aspirations— too vague to be of any use when specific decisions must be made. Others insist codes can be helpful to beginning journalists, photographers and public relations practitioners; they provide some guidance in the form of rules that can be internalized as professional expertise and experience deepen. And still others see codes as a manifestation of the ideology of an era—more about power and politics than ethics.

The new *Times* code linked its creation to the public perception of the "professional reputations of its staff member(s)." The code was directed to "all members of the news and editorial departments whose work directly affects the content of the paper."

The code focused primarily on conflict of interest. In fact, the code did not mention accuracy and fairness and devoted only a single sentence to privacy. However, when addressing conflict of interest, the code was both specific and detailed. The *Times* code considered the impact that spousal relationships might have on news coverage. It also addressed whether journalists working abroad should abide by the ethics and mores of the countries in which they are stationed, most of which do not provide the equivalent of First Amendment protections.

The code required staff members to disclose yearly speaking fees in excess of $5,000 and prohibited staff members from accepting gifts, tickets, discounts or other "inducements" from organizations the *Times* covered. Staff members could not invest in companies they covered, and payment for favorable or altered coverage was specifically forbidden.

However, staff members were allowed to do certain sorts of unpaid work— for example, public relations for a child's school fund-raising event. But *Times* staffers were forbidden from giving money to candidates or causes, marching in support of public movements or appearing on radio and television shows to voice views that went beyond those of the paper. When family members, such as spouses, participated in such activities, *Times* staffers were required to disclose those activities to management and recuse themselves from certain sorts of coverage.

The *Times* code was protective of the newspaper's place in the marketplace. Staffers were prohibited from disclosing confidential information about the operations, plans or policies of the newspaper to other journalists. Such questions were to be referred to management. If readers asked such questions, *Times* staffers were encouraged to respond "openly and honestly." *Times* staff members also were prohibited from doing freelance work for any media outlet that competed with the *Times*. "Staff members may not appear on broadcasts that compete directly with the *Times'* own offerings on television or the Internet. . . . As the paper moves further into these new fields, its direct competitors and clients or potential clients will undoubtedly grow in number."

Micro Issues

1. Should managers and owners be subject to a code of ethics, particularly for publications as influential as the *Times*?
2. Why is the notion of perception—as opposed to action—important in considering the issue of conflict of interest?
3. Should the *Times* code have addressed a variety of common journalistic issues—such as accuracy, fairness and privacy?

Midrange Issues

1. Disclosure is often suggested as a remedy for conflict of interest. Evaluate this remedy.
2. Should conflict of interest rules be different at a small newspaper as opposed to the *Times*?

3. Does the *Times* code infringe on staffers' First Amendment rights? Do journalists give up some of their rights as citizens in order to do the work of journalism?
4. Are there instances when recusing oneself from an assignment is unsatisfactory? What should journalists do if such a case arises?
5. Should a conflict of interest extend as far as prohibitions against a journalist being an officer in the parent–teacher association (i.e., PTA or PTO) of his or her child's school? An officer in your local homeowners' association? Does the potential for those organizations to get involved in the news pages (i.e., teacher problems, zoning protests) influence your decision?

Macro Issues

1. What are the specific historical developments in the field of journalism that may have promoted the development of this particular version of *The New York Times* code?
2. Research indicates that codes that are developed by the newsroom have a much better chance of influencing behavior than codes that are superimposed by management. If the *Times* had used this approach, would it have "discovered" the actions of reporters such as Jayson Blair (details of the Blair case may be found on the Internet) and his falsified stories?
3. Does the *Times* code place the organization's financial health on equal footing with the public trust? Is that appropriate?

CASE 4-G

Quit, Blow the Whistle or Go with the Flow?

ROBERT D. WAKEFIELD
Brigham Young University

Anyone who spends sufficient years in public relations will face a crisis of conscience. Practitioners are trained for the tenuous task of balancing institutional advocacy with the "public interest" (Newsom, Turk and Kruckeberg 1996). Yet this role can lead to personal conflict, as it did in my case.

The setting was an urban school district with about 40 schools and more than 35,000 students. Its superintendent had a national reputation for innovative community outreach, and he was a media favorite. I worked with him for five years before he accepted a statewide position. His replacement was a quiet man with conservative views who, along with the administrative team he brought with him, believed that educators were trained to run the schools and could do so best with minimal interference.

Like most inner-city school districts, the system was losing students as people moved to the suburbs. In the previous decade, a student population that once filled four high schools could now fill only three.

The seven-member school board had approached—and then abandoned—the question of closing one of the schools because the proposal aroused such strong feelings among students, faculty and parents. However, the new administration, trying to balance those responses against the financial drain of supporting an additional high school on taxpayer dollars, decided to broach the question again.

Promised a tumultuous situation, the new administrators aggravated the problem by how they handled it. Rather than sharing the issue with the community or with school faculties to seek a mutually agreeable solution, they tried to resolve the entire problem behind closed doors.

I first learned about the closed-door approach at a "study meeting" with the school board. The new superintendent held these informal meetings during his earliest days in the district; they tended to be so boring and ambiguous that journalists seldom attended.

Before the meeting in question, the superintendent asked me whether any media would be present. I told him one reporter might come late. As the meeting began, I was surprised to hear him tell the board and the few staff members, "If any reporter shows up, I will change the subject—but today we're going to talk about closing a high school." He then outlined the results of meetings he had already held on the issue, discussed a proposal from a local community college to buy the building so it would not be abandoned and sought the support of the four high school principals.

Thus began my ethical conundrum. I agreed that the enrollment problem was serious and that closing a school was probably the best alternative, but I opposed the administration's method of resolving the issue. As public relations officer, I believed that public institutions must be open and that involving those affected by the closure in the actual decision-making process would eventually generate long-term support for whatever decision was made. I was appalled at the attempts to exclude the public; but I said nothing.

Closed doors can quickly swing ajar, and it took less than one day for news of the decision to leak. The school targeted for closure was one of the oldest in the state. It had recently received a U.S. Department of Education award as an exemplary inner-city school, but its community was the least affluent and arguably the least politically powerful.

The day after the "study session" and with a regular board meeting scheduled for the same evening, reporters called to verify what they were hearing. (Chief executives often forget that supervisors of individual units within the system have their own allegiances. In this case, one of the high school principals left the "study meeting" and informed his teaching staff that they would be receiving transfer students "from that inner-city school." The rumors began.)

After the phone calls, I asked the superintendent what he planned to say at the board meeting and was told, "We will discuss space utilization needs." I told him about the calls and that our jobs would be threatened if we were not truthful with the community. To his credit, he responded quickly and openly. The evening meeting unfolded as expected. The room was jammed with district patrons and with the media. The expected lines were drawn. Underlying the fervor was a common theme: closing a traditional high school was awful enough, but the secretive way in which the administration had reached its conclusions was unforgivable.

The next several weeks were an intense period of work for a young public relations officer. I did media interviews, talk shows and forums to explain the situation. I also met with dozens of teachers, parents and citizens, both to hear their comments and to take their suggestions. I had to be careful that my words represented the district instead of myself. I had worked with some local reporters for several years and felt comfortable giving them background so they could seek additional materials without revealing me as the original source. It was a personal risk, but the reporters never betrayed my trust.

Two additional incidents epitomized my ethical struggles. The first occurred after the initial board meeting, when a top administrator said the community misunderstood why decisions were made behind closed doors. I lobbied for openness. The administrator admonished me to remember who paid my salary, a rebuke that confirmed the new administration did not share my own values.

The second incident occurred when I was asked to meet with a man who had been chosen to speak on behalf of the community. I had taken only a few steps into his office when he said to me, "You don't agree with your administration, do you?" My response was silence while he explained his position.

For some reason, it was this encounter that forced my crisis of conscience: do I quit, blow the whistle or keep quiet? I had a wife and child to support; the employment picture at the time was not robust. Right or wrong, I surmised that the various relationships I had developed could appease many angry feelings. I also believed in the importance of education. So, I decided to stay through the crisis, then seek new employment.

About one month into the crisis, the board retained a consultant who, like me, believed in open communication. Two weeks later, four board members came to my office and requested a meeting. Because this constituted a majority of the board, such an assembly violated the law requiring the meeting be made public. I violated the law and invited them to stay. They said they were worn down by the constant tension and asked what I, as a public relations practitioner, thought they should do.

To me, the answer was straightforward. Relying on basic public relations formulas and common sense, I suggested that they could diffuse the tension by reverting to what should have been done in the first place: announce that selected representatives from throughout the city would form a committee to help review the situation and come to a decision that would then be discussed by the board.

To my surprise, the board members took this advice to the administration, and much of what I recommended was done. A few months later, the school was closed in a tearful farewell. And, five weeks after the school closed, I accepted a job with a local public relations firm.

Micro Issues

1. What sort of press releases or other talking points should Wakefield have prepared once the rumors began?
2. Should Wakefield have gone off the record with reporters he trusted?
3. Are there some sorts of decisions governmental bodies make that really should be kept from the media and hence the public? Is this one of them?
4. How should Wakefield have responded to the racial subtext of some of the protests about the closing of the school?

Midrange Issues

1. Should Wakefield have "blown the whistle" on the board members who requested an illegal meeting?
2. Was it appropriate for Wakefield to advise the board to take an approach different from that suggested by the superintendent?
3. How much does Wakefield's previous experience with a different superintendent influence his understanding of how the district works? How did this "workplace" socialization influence his ethical thinking?

Macro Issues

1. To whom should Wakefield be loyal?
2. Should he ever have told members of the community of his own personal views?
3. How does Wakefield's job compare with that of a press secretary for a political figure?
4. Is it ever appropriate to keep journalists in the dark about how political decisions are made?

5

Privacy: Looking for Solitude in the Global Village

By the end of this chapter, you should be able to:

- **appreciate the difference between the right to privacy and a need for privacy.**
- **distinguish between the law and ethics of privacy.**
- **understand the concepts of discretion, right to know, need to know, want to know and circles of intimacy.**
- **understand the contextual nature of privacy, particularly when social media are involved.**
- **understand and apply Rawls's veil of ignorance as a tool for ethical decision making.**

WHY PRIVACY IN THE NEW MILLENNIUM?

By any measure, 2011 was a terrible year to be a New Orleans Saints fan. Less than two years after winning the Super Bowl, the team, its coach and many of its players found themselves the subject of the most serious penalty the National Football League had ever levied. The reason: the team's defensive coordinator (who was subsequently suspended indefinitely from the league) had run a "bounty system" where Saints players were rewarded financially for "cart-offs" and exceptionally hard hits. Among the main targets were opposing players who had already sustained concussions.

Filmmaker Sean Pamphilon was working on a documentary about former Saint Steve Gleason, who has the neurological disorder ALS—Lou Gehrig's disease. In his research he discovered the bounty system among defensive players in the Saints locker room. Pamphilon recorded Defensive Coordinator Gregg Williams urging players to target an opponent with a history of concussions before a playoff game. Pamphilon released the audio recording during the NFL's investigation of the bounty system over the objections of Gleason and despite heavy public criticism. Gleason opposed releasing the speech because he did not want to violate the trust of the Saints who had cooperated in making the documentary.

The conflict between Gleason on the one hand and Pamphilon on the other illustrates the confounding nature of contemporary discussions about privacy. In earlier times, privacy was often binary—it was something you had or something you did not. Today, that binary world is full of grays—in fact, Helen Nissenbaum, one of the foremost scholars on the subject, argues that social media and many other forms of technology have erased the public–private dichotomy. Nissenbaum's sophisticated thesis is that privacy is neither a right to secrecy nor a right to control information but rather a right that individuals have to "control . . . the appropriate flow of personal information" in a variety of contexts (Nissenbaum 2010, 127).

The documentarian's decision making illustrates her point well. First, keeping the audio record of the speech "private" could be considered ethically appropriate, if maintaining the trust of essential sources is the primary goal. But, there were other interests to consider, something Nissenbaum notes when she says that contemporary thinking about privacy almost always acknowledges a conflict of interests.

One of those competing interests surely was the physical well-being of the football players who had unknowingly become the target of the cart-offs and hard/illegal hits. Another was the integrity of the documentary film itself. A third was certainly the NFL investigation, which had potential criminal overtones. And, then there's the average football fan, savvy enough to know that the games itself is potentially dangerous for players and informed enough to know that the long-term physical implications of repeated concussions is inevitably making its way from the football field into state statutes.

Gleason's desire to maintain trust—a central positive goal for protecting privacy—came into direct conflict with what philosophers call the "harm principle." People would be hurt if the audiotape remained private, something we saw happen at Penn State University when allegations of child abuse by a former coach were kept secret by administrators for up to 14 years while the victim count rose as well. Pamphilon could have been in another sort of trouble if the audio had remained private until the film was released.

In sum, the individual history and professional roles of the parties potentially affected by the decision to release the information illustrates what scholars call "context-relative informational norms." That analysis, as the above example illustrates, will seldom result in a rule that fits all cases and all eventualities. But, before you can begin to conduct such an analysis on a complicated issue, it's important to understand some of the history and vocabulary of the term "privacy" and some contemporary criticisms of how modern culture understands these important concepts.

PRIVACY AS A LEGAL CONSTRUCT

The modern-day legal notion of privacy began in the 1960s with a taxonomy worked out by the late William Prosser, dean of the University of California–Berkley law school. Prosser argued that the law of privacy had remained stagnant for several decades because the notion of "privacy" meant many things to different people. Because of the work done by Prosser, today the tort of privacy is manifest in four distinct ways:

1. Intrusion upon a person's seclusion or solitude, such as invading one's home or personal papers to get a story.
2. Public disclosure of embarrassing private facts, such as revealing someone's notorious past when it has no bearing on that person's present status.
3. Publicity that places a person in a false light, such as enhancing a subject's biography to sell additional books.
4. Misappropriation of a person's name or likeness for personal advantage, such as using Hollywood megastar Julia Roberts's image to sell a product without her permission.

While this four-part list is straightforward, problems exist. Not every state recognizes every tort—particularly "false light." Also, our notion of privacy is dynamic, subject to change. What once might have been an embarrassing, private fact—for example, that an unmarried woman is pregnant—is now commonplace knowledge and, quite often, cause for celebration. In the past, cancer was rarely mentioned in coverage of the famous. Today it is not only mentioned, it is often used to raise awareness of the disease. It even enters into the realm of public policy, as when cancer survivors Sens. John McCain or the late Arlen Spector referred to their own medical struggles in the very public debate on national health care reform. Similarly, one's sexual orientation has increasingly moved toward commonplace knowledge. But at the same time, information once available for the asking, such as a student's telephone number or the address of an individual based on driver's license registration, is now closed by a maze of privacy legislation enacted at the end of the last century.

To further cloud the issue, the claim to privacy is different for different categories of people. Public figures, for example, are subject to a different standard than are others. There are "limited" public figures and even "accidental" public figures thrown into the spotlight by chance. Just exactly who the courts will consider a public figure fluctuates, leaving a journalist doing a story in a vulnerable position. As the newspaper lawyer in *Absence of Malice* told the young reporter played by Sally Fields, "They never tell us until it's too late."

When the media invade privacy, a huge verdict can make a plaintiff rich, but it cannot return that sense of control the initial invasion takes away. And interestingly, the courts have never awarded the same mega-verdicts for invasion of privacy as for libel on the theory that one's reputation is more valuable than one's privacy. So the law provides an unsatisfactory solution both for journalists and victims. Ethical thinking prior to broadcast or publication is preferable to a court battle.

One of the major problems of thinking of privacy through this legal lens is what philosophers consider a misleading connection between privacy and money. Recall the discussion in Chapter 3 about the moral implications of a culture in which everything can be marketed or monetized. Marketing personal information— through social media and search engines—is an example of the reduction of ethical reasoning to a cost–benefit analysis lodged in the market. Philosophers assert that the commodification of private information erodes the core of both individual

---

The Need for Privacy

The so-called *right to privacy* has been widely debated and written about, but the arguments are made more problematic by the fact that the term never appears in the U.S. Constitution. Relatively little has been written about the "need for privacy." Philosopher Louis W. Hodges writes on the *need for privacy,* saying that "without some degree of privacy, civilized life would be impossible" (Hodges 1983).

Both a personal and societal need for privacy exists, Hodges claims. First, we need privacy to develop a sense of self. Constance T. Fischer (1980) states that people need privacy to "try out" new poses, future selves and so on, without fear of ridicule by outsiders. If we are to become the person we wish to be, we need a certain degree of privacy to develop that person apart from observation. Religious cults that seek cognitive control over their members do so in part by depriving the members of any real degree of privacy, restricting both growth and reflection.

Second, society needs privacy as a shield against the power of the state. As the state gains more information about its citizens, it is increasingly easy to influence, manipulate or control each one. Precisely because the state is feared, limitations on the power of the state, such as the Bill of Rights, were established to protect private life (Neville 1980). Throughout history, totalitarian regimes have used extensive government surveillance—the near absence of privacy—as a major component of any attempt to create a uniformly subservient citizenry, a subject that dominates Orwell's *1984.* Third, society needs privacy as a shield against Internet sites like Facebook and others who demand large sums of data about you to enter into site.

Therefore, while much of the debate focuses on the *right to* privacy, an equally compelling argument must be made for the *need for* privacy. *Privacy is not a luxury or even a gift of a benevolent government. It is a necessary component of a democracy.*

---

autonomy and authentic community. While the law may be a place to begin, it is hardly a satisfactory framework in which to make ethical choices.

Journalists have often been caught between what the law allows and what their consciences will permit. This confusion has led to ethical bungling on a scale that undermines the profession's credibility and feeds the stereotypical notions that journalists will do anything to get a story, and that audiences will willingly consume anything the journalist delivers. As Nissenbaum (2010) notes,

> Learning that privacy is not as interesting to most people as learning that it has been "threatened," "violated," or "invaded." In short, people want to identify the moral and political significance of any given instance of diminished privacy; they want to know in general terms when privacy claims are justified. Since a right to privacy imposes obligations and restrictions on others, it is important that the right be circumscribed in a non-arbitrary manner (p. 72).

Nonarbitrary is the key here—journalists, strategic communication professionals and their audiences need some systematic ways of making privacy decisions. For Americans, some of that systematic analysis begins with the law.

PRIVACY AS AN ETHICAL CONSTRUCT

The ethical basis for privacy is much older than the legal one and appears throughout literature, asserting that privacy is a "natural right" that we possess by being human. Privacy is considered a need, a way of protecting oneself against the actions of other people and institutions. Privacy carries with it the notions of control and limited access. The individual should be allowed to control who may have certain sorts of information and, sometimes, the context within which that information is presented.

Communitarian thinking links privacy and community instead of seeing them as competing forces. "A credible ethics or privacy needs to be rooted in the common good rather than individual rights" (Christians 2010). "Communitarians see the myth of the self-contained 'man' in a state of nature as politically misleading and dangerous. Persons are embedded in language, history, and culture, which are social creations; there can be no such thing as a person without society" (Radin 1982). In the communitarian view, the community itself—the larger society— benefits from maintaining individual privacy. That maintenance, however, is in some modest tension with the needs of the community. In communitarian thinking, corporate demands would be every bit as subject to restriction as government for the same reason—the health of the community which, in turn, supports the flourishing of individuals. Christians considers control over commercial data banks, along with government surveillance and invasive news coverage of victims of tragedy, as the most important privacy questions emerging in the 21st century. Although privacy is related to human experience, the concept itself is not relative. "Privacy's moral weight, it's importance and a value, does not shrink or swell in direct proportion to the numbers of people who want or like it or how much they want or like it," Nissenbaum 2010, 66). Perhaps the best example of this is Article 12 of the Universal Declaration of Human Rights.

European scholars have linked privacy with a capitalist market economy on the one hand and the interventions of the welfare state on the other. "What does privacy mean to the homeless and the unemployed? . . . Is there a point to privacy if people do not have the means and the power to enjoy freedom?" (Gutwirth 2002, 52).

The central role of technology also influences contemporary theory. Scholars note that individual control over the bits and bytes of private information is much more difficult to accomplish (some assert impossible) for the average individual, particularly if that person is coerced by economic or political necessity (Marx 1999). Some outside of academia have suggested that in modern society the very notion of privacy is impossible. "Privacy is dead" headlines have been appearing since the 1990s. In 1999, Scott McNealy, then CEO of technology developer Sun Microsystems, called consumer privacy issues a "red herring," according to *Wired* magazine. "You have zero privacy anyway," he said. "Get over it."

Donald Kerr, a former deputy director of the U. S. Office of National Intelligence concurs with McNealy's observations on privacy. In talking with a *Newsday* reporter in 2007, Kerr told the reporter that in an "interconnected and wireless world" that anonymity was quickly becoming a thing of the past.

In philosophy, the concept of privacy cannot stand apart from community. Responsibility for keeping things private is shared: individuals have to learn when to share or withhold information, while the community has to learn when to avert its eyes. Legal scholar Jeffrey Rosen notes that this attention to the role of the community in avoiding "the unwanted gaze" (the title of his book) stems from Talmudic law. He writes:

> Jewish law, for example, has developed a remarkable body of doctrine around the concept of *hezzek re'iyyah,* which means "the injury caused by seeing" or "the injury caused by being seen." This doctrine expands the right of privacy to protect individuals not only from physical intrusions into the home but also from surveillance by a neighbor who is outside the home, peering through a window in a common courtyard. Jewish law protects neighbors not only from unwanted observation, but also from the possibility of being observed. . . . From its earliest days, Jewish law has recognized that it is the uncertainty about whether or not we are being observed that forces us to lead more constricted lives and inhibits us from speaking and acting freely in public (Rosen 2000, 18–19).

The last sentence is important: fear of being observed causes us to partially shut down our lives where we are celebrating, mourning or just going about our daily pattern. The law is detailed and strict. If your window looks into your neighbor's private courtyard, you must seal your window shut.

Taken into a media context, the "injury caused by being seen" gets thorny. Part of the problem with a "shoot first, edit later" philosophy for photographers and videographers at the scene of a tragedy is that the "injury caused by being seen" has already been exacerbated by the camera. The injury is something the Facebook protestors understood intuitively—they wanted only their closest friends to know about their breakups, hookups, etc. Like the philosophical approach developed by the Greeks, privacy is linked to our ability to "become" human and retain some element of dignity while doing it. "Only citizens who respect one another's privacy are themselves dignified with divine respect" (Rosen 2000, 19).

THE CONTINUING CONFLICTS

But privacy is a complicated matter; it doesn't trump every other right in every context. In practice, protection of privacy or what constitutes invasion of privacy is not always clear.

Grcic (1986) asserts that privacy can be negated by more compelling rights. In simpler times, the right to invade privacy belonged almost exclusively to the government. For example, an individual must relinquish control of a substantial amount of private information to complete federal and state income tax forms, and failure to provide such information makes one legally liable.

For the survival of the entire political community, the government demands that its citizens provide it with certain information that is otherwise private. However, specific rules govern such disclosure. The government cannot legally give your tax return information to other interested parties. Such a check on government power theoretically allows the maintenance of some level of individual privacy.

However, the government is not the only institution today that can demand and receive private information. Banks, credit companies, doctors and attorneys all request (and usually receive) a variety of highly private information, the bulk of it willingly disclosed. Inevitably, such disclosure is one-directional. While you are expected to provide your physician with your medical history to ensure proper treatment, your physician might be surprised if you inquired about her success rate with a particular surgical procedure, and she certainly is not required to give it to you. Doctors in states where laws requiring such information be made available to patients have been debated usually go on record as being against disclosure, saying that the information devoid of context can be deceiving or outright wrong.

Computers and databases have become tools for gathering and storing private information. Huge industries have cropped up selling private information. When you buy a house or apply for a job, the information industry disgorges huge amounts of legal and financial information about you with about a 40 percent chance of some error, according to some industry figures. The tensions over what should or should not remain private are not resolved; they are merely accounted for in today's complex society. And even when consumers are given a free chance to look at and correct their credit information, only a small percentage do, despite the financial advantage to do so.

Thinking about privacy philosophically has prompted scholars to develop four different types of potential harms when privacy is invaded. They are:

- informational harm such as identity theft;
- informational inequality, such as governments and corporations amassing large amounts of data about individuals without their knowledge or consent;
- informational injustice for example, transferring data from your financial records to the local newspaper without appropriate contextual information; and
- encroachment on moral autonomy, "the capacity to shape our own moral biographies, to reflect on our moral careers, to evaluate and identify with our own moral choices, without the critical gaze and interference of others" (van den Hoven 200, 439).

Contrast these sorts of harms with those outlined in American constitutional law and see if you find the philosophical approach more or less satisfactory in our data-soaked information age.

DISTINGUISHING BETWEEN SECRECY AND PRIVACY

People tend to think of private information as something they would like to keep secret, but such thinking confounds the two related but separable concepts of privacy and secrecy.

Secrecy can be defined as blocking information intentionally to prevent others from learning, possessing, using or revealing it (Bok 1983). Secrecy ensures that information is kept from *any* public view. Privacy, however, is concerned with determining who will obtain access to the information. Privacy does not require that information never reach public view, but rather who has control over that information which becomes public.

Secrecy often carries a negative connotation. But secrecy is neither morally good nor bad. Privacy and secrecy can overlap but are not identical. "Privacy need not hide; and secrecy hides far more than what is private. A private garden need not be a secret garden, a private life is rarely a secret life" (Bok 1983, 11).

The law has given us an interesting metaphor for the ethics of privacy. In *Dietemann v. Time,* jurist Alan F. Westin viewed privacy as the ability to control one's own "circles of intimacy." In the case, two reporters for the former *Life* magazine lied to Dietemann to enter his California home and later expose him as a medical quack practicing medicine without a license. While the courts saw some social utility in exposing such behavior, Dietemann had a reasonable expectation of privacy in his own home, and ruled against the media in the civil suit that followed.

Philosopher Louis W. Hodges has used the concept of circles of intimacy to develop a working concept of privacy for journalists and other professionals. If you conceive of privacy as a series of concentric circles, as Figure 5.1 illustrates, in the innermost circle you are alone with your secrets, fantasies, hopes, reconstructed memories and the rest of the unique psychological "furniture" we bring to our lives.

The second circle you probably occupy with one other person, perhaps a sibling, a spouse, a parent, roommate or loved one. You might hold several "you plus one" circles simultaneously in life and the number and identity of these you plus

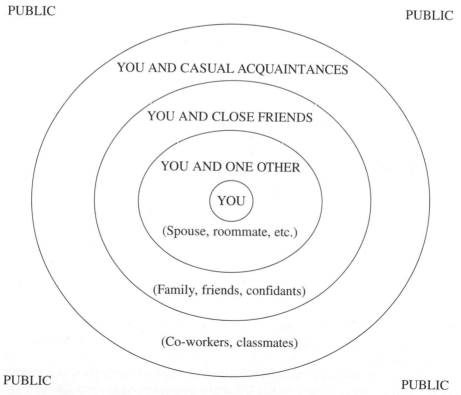

FIGURE 5.1 The concept of circles of intimacy

one circles might change at various times in your development. In that circle, you share your private information, and for that relationship to work well, it needs to be reciprocal—based on trust.

The third circle contains others to whom you are very close—probably family or friends, perhaps a lawyer or clergy member. Here, the basis of relationships is still one of trust, but control over the information gets trickier. This circle was probably the issue in the Facebook controversy—information the sender thought would be known by a few became known by many. It's the nature of information. As the ripples in the pond of intimacy continue to spread, what you reveal about yourself becomes progressively more public and less intimate, and you lose progressively more control over information about you.

Using this model, privacy can be considered control over who has access to your various circles of intimacy. Invasion of privacy occurs when your control over your own circles of intimacy is wrestled from you by people or institutions. Rape victims who unwillingly see their names in print or their pictures broadcast frequently speak of the loss of control they felt during the experience as being similar to the loss of control during the rape itself.

Journalists sometimes invade circles of intimacy either accidentally or purposefully. Awareness of the concept will allow you to consider the rights and needs of others as well as the demands of society, particularly when the issue is newsworthy. Under at least some circumstances, invasion can be justified, but under other circumstances it's not. Part of the ethical growth of a journalist is to know when the rule applies and when the exceptions should occur.

DISCRETION: WHETHER TO REVEAL PRIVATE INFORMATION

With the distinction between privacy and secrecy in mind, the next problem confronting the ethical journalist is "discretion"—a word not usually associated with journalism. Bok (1983, 41) defines discretion as "the intuitive ability to discern what is and is not intrusive and injurious."

We all decide at times to reveal private information, and doing so wisely is a mark of moral growth discussed in the final chapter of this book. Discretion demands moral reasoning. Once a source decides to reveal private information, a reporter's discretion remains the sole gatekeeper between that information and a public that might need the information or might merely want the information. Take, for instance, the journalist covering the scene of a tragedy who gets answers to the posed questions, but the interviewees are clearly in shock and in no condition to be making complex decisions like the cost and benefits of granting an interview. Indeed, within a few hours, the family has hired an attorney to do the talking for them and you, for the time being, have the only interview. In times like these, the journalist is forced to rely on discretion to decide if he is feeding the voyeur or the citizen in each of us.

What is a journalist to do with information resulting from another's indiscretion? Kantian theory would suggest that the journalist treat even the indiscreet source as the journalist herself would wish to be treated, making publication of the indiscretion less likely. Yet many journalists claim that, in practice, everything is "on the record" unless otherwise specified. In situations like these, a return to Ross's list of prima facie duties could be helpful. What is my duty to an often vulnerable and sometimes unwitting source? To a curious readership or viewership? To a media owner who wants (and pays for) my story?

Returning to the issue of Facebook, it seems that many 18- to 22-year-olds have yet to learn discretion in their postings. And the problem is even greater on MySpace, which draws an even younger crowd. Indiscreet postings have led to numerous problems including sexually predatory behavior by some adults and even stalking or cyberbullying by peers. And reality television—which is usually anything but real—is an almost textbook case of persons willing to endure or divulge almost anything to get a chance at fleeting fame.

WHEN THE RIGHT TO KNOW IS NOT ENOUGH

Just as the distinction between secrecy and privacy is easily confused, there is also a misconception on the part of both journalists and the public among the concepts of "right to know," "need to know" and "want to know." However, the three concepts are distinct and not interchangeable.

Right to know is a legal term often associated with open-meeting and open-record statutes. These laws are a legal, not ethical, construct. Journalists have a legal right to the same information that other members of the public may obtain—for example, the transportation of hazardous materials through their communities.

Ethical problems can emerge from right-to-know information. Is it ethical to print everything a journalist has a legal right to know? For instance, police reports routinely carry the names of suspects, victims and witnesses to a variety of crimes. If a reporter has information that might harm, on the local level, the right to a fair trial or, on the national level, national security, should it be withheld?

Need to know originates in the realm of philosophy. One function of the mass media is to provide information that will allow citizens to go about their daily lives in society, regardless of political outlook. Providing information the public needs to know includes within it the concept of journalistic tenacity and responsibility.

Too often, when journalists assert the public has a "right to know" what they mean is that citizens "need" the information to get along in their daily lives. For example, the average citizen cannot examine bank records—those records are specifically excluded from the Freedom of Information Act. But what happens when government fails? Consider the turmoil a few years ago in the financial sector. Investors lost billions in a New York–based Ponzi scheme. Major banks have written off billions of losses. Major investment banks have faltered. Enron became a synonym for bad corporate management. Because of "carnage" left behind when these events happen, journalists could reasonably argue that at least some information about the health of financial institutions and the character of those who run them is needed by the public to make informed economic decisions. Need to know requires a tenacious journalist, as the law is not a tool for such stories.

Need to know is the most ethically compelling argument of the three. Need to know demands that an ethical case be constructed for making known information that others wish to keep private. Need to know also means that a case be made that the journalism is not engaging in mere voyeurism. When an argument is framed in terms of right to know, it reduces the journalist to ethical legalism: I will do precisely what the law allows. When an argument is framed in terms of need to know, however, it means that counterbalancing forces have been weighed and that bringing the information to light is still the most ethical act.

Finally, there is the issue of **want to know,** which speaks to the curiosity in all of us. Want to know is the least ethically compelling rationale for acquiring and disseminating information. We all want to know a lot of things—what our neighbors do in the evening hours, how much money other people earn and who in Hollywood is sleeping with whom. While we may want that information, however, we don't really need it and most certainly have no right to it.

Journalists—especially bloggers—have become sources for much want-to-know information. A number of media outlets have been founded on the public's desire to know about celebrities, criminals and even common folk. Nearly a century ago, *Police Gazette* titillated its readers with information they wanted to know that no other media outlet provided. Today that function is filled by slick Web sites and syndicated television shows such as "TMZ." In the mainstream media, it is want-to-know print magazines and video magazines that are the only growth area in the entire industry.

Consider the world of YouTube, where anything you want to know is probably available. Have a blooper at your wedding? There's an entire category for that. In the world of YouTube and its competitors, everyone can get the 15 minutes of fame predicted by pop artist Andy Warhol. And if you need to be reminded what the want-to-know market is worth, in 2006, Google purchased YouTube for $1.6 billion.

WHAT THE AUDIENCE DOES ALSO MATTERS

Many of the most troubling individual cases that raise larger privacy issues are just like that described above—information brought to public notice not by strategic communication professionals or journalists but by average people who are computer literate and have something they believe is important to convey. Consider 30-year-old Matthew Creed of Shawnee, Kansas, who in May of 2012 developed the Web site blabbermouthkc.com. Creed said the Web site was a community service, but its content focused exclusively on the mug shots and addresses of people arrested in Johnson County.

Creed's site contained information about those who had been arrested; there was no information on whether formal charges had been filed or on convictions. Some of the photos were of people arrested for infractions such as a minor in possession of tobacco or driving a car with an expired registration.

Superficially, Creed was operating on the principle of public shaming. "That was the biggest thing, to make others aware of those that were living around them that were breaking the law and to try to get those breaking the law to think twice about their future actions," Creed said in an interview with the Associated Press. While numerous Web sites in the United States provide this sort of information, Creed added a new wrinkle. For $199.99 he would remove the listing immediately and for removal within a few days the fee was pegged at $149.99. "This guy is just a bottom-feeding vulture. The idea that he was trying to help the community is a total farce," said Jay Norton, a Johnson County attorney who represented some people featured on the Web site.

While Creed's approach to public shaming is perhaps uniquely market oriented, the fact that he is taking information made public by virtue of government (and hence paid for by taxpayers) and broadcasting it via the Web to a larger audience is not unique. For instance, any aggregator can choose to carve out a niche on the Web with Supreme Court opinions—free content thanks to the government. But, in the case of Creed and blabbermouthkc.com what he is doing is philosophically important.

Some scholars are suggesting that ethical standards, which were once the exclusive purview of professionals, should in this age of the Internet be open-sourced (Ward and Wasserman 2010). What that means is that ethical standards regarding important issues such as privacy would be arrived at through an open dialogue with audience members as well as journalists, public relations professionals and others. Whether open-sourced ethics is a good idea in philosophical terms, in practical terms, it may be the wave of the present where the consumer of information on the Web is just as likely to be providing information—knowingly or not—in the transaction. Thinking through the implications of these rapidly shifting roles requires pointed and philosophically informed thought. It's either that or accepting that Web sites such as blabbermouthkc.com reflect professional norms.

JOHN RAWLS AND THE VEIL OF IGNORANCE

Preserving human dignity in times of crisis is a difficult task. Political philosopher John Rawls, an articulate proponent of the social contract theory of government, has provided a helpful exercise to make decisions about particularly thorny privacy issues (Rawls 1971).

Rawls's theory of "distributive justice" takes the best from utilitarian theory while avoiding some of its problems. It begins with the premise that justice should be equated with fairness. In order to achieve fairness, Rawls suggests an exercise he calls the "veil of ignorance." In the exercise, before a community can make an ethical decision affecting its members, the community must consider the options behind a veil of ignorance. Behind the veil, everyone starts out in an "original position" as equals. Later, Rawls would define the "original position" as one where each member of the community making the decision is not aware of his or her status or lack thereof, financial or physical assets and even potential. Stripped of all this knowledge a person is now in his or her "original position."

Rawls suggests that, behind the veil, rational people would be willing to make and to follow decisions when individual distinctions such as gender or socioeconomic status are laid aside. For example, if the issue is whether to photograph or interview survivors at the scene of an airline crash, you could gather many people with diverse views behind the veil. Among them could be a reporter, a photographer, a survivor, a victim's family, an average reader or viewer, the management or owner of the media outlet, the owner of the airline, paramedics at the scene, the flying public and others. Behind the veil, in the original position, none of the participants would know what their status would be when they emerged. *Their arguments would then be free of bias that comes from points of view.* The participants would argue the pros and cons of the public's need to know and the victim's right to privacy without knowing whether they would emerge as a reporter, a reader or a victim.

When people begin their deliberations behind such a veil, Rawls suggests that two values emerge. We will first act so that *individual liberty is maximized;* however, we will also act so that *weaker parties will be protected.* We will look at each concept separately.

First, Rawls suggests the liberty of all will be valued equally. Behind the veil, freedom of the press (a liberty journalists cherish) becomes equal to freedom from intrusion into private life (a liberty readers cherish). How you retain both becomes a debate to be argued from all points of view, free of bias.

Second, behind the veil, the weaker party is usually protected. Few participants would make an ethical decision that might not be in the interest of the weaker party unless the evidence was overwhelming that it would better the lot of the entire group. Behind the veil participants would be forced to weigh the actual and potential harm that journalists, as powerful people representing powerful institutions, could inflict on people who are less powerful.

It is important to note that consensus is not required, and maybe even not expected, behind the veil. The veil of ignorance is designed to facilitate ethical discussions, not stymie them from lack of unanimity. Using the veil of ignorance, the ethical decision maker arrives at what Rawls calls "reflective equilibrium," where some inequalities are allowed. However, they will be the inequalities that contribute in some significant way to the betterment of most individuals in the social situation. For instance, the consensus of the group behind the veil might be to run a photo of a victim of tragedy if it might prevent a similar tragedy from occurring.

Reflective equilibrium summons what Rawls calls our "considered moral judgment." Balancing the liberties of various stakeholders, while protecting the weaker party, allows for an exploration of all of the issues involved, which utilitarianism sometimes fails to address.

Using the concepts of right to know, need to know, discretion and circles of intimacy, along with Rawls's concept of distributive justice, will provide you with the ethical tools to begin the work of balancing conflicting claims of privacy. These tools will enable you to better justify your choices, to make decisions systematically and to understand what went wrong when mistakes occur.

Suggested Readings

ALDERMAN, ELLEN, and CAROLINE KENNEDY. 1995. *The right to privacy.* New York: Alfred A. Knopf, Inc.

BOK, SISSELA. 1983. *Secrets: On the ethics of concealment and revelation.* New York: Vintage.

GRCIC, JOSEPH M. 1986. "The right to privacy: Behavior as property." *Journal of Values Inquiry,* 20, pp. 137–144.

HIXSON, RICHARD F. 1987. *Privacy in a public society.* New York: Oxford University Press.

HODGES, LOUIS W. 1983. "The journalist and privacy." *Social Responsibility: Journalism, Law, Medicine,* 9, pp. 5–19.

NISSENBAUM, HELEN. 2010. *Privacy on context: Technology, policy and the Integrity of Social Life.* Stanford, CA: Stanford Law Books.

ORWELL, GEORGE. 1949. *1984.* San Diego: Harcourt Brace Jovanovich.

RAWLS, JOHN. 1971. *A theory of justice.* Cambridge, MA: Harvard University Press.

ROSEN, JEFFREY. 2000. *The unwanted gaze: The destruction of privacy in America.* New York: Random House.

SCHOEMAN, FERDINAND D., ed. 1984. *Philosophical dimensions of privacy: An anthology.* New York: Cambridge University Press.

Cases on the Web

www.mhhe.com/mediaethics8e

"Naming names: Privacy and the public's right to know" by John B. Webster

"Public grief and the right to be left alone" by Philip Patterson

"A reporter's question: Propriety and punishment" by Stanley Cunningham

"Computers and the news: A complicated challenge" by Karon Reinboth Speckman

"Honor to die for: *Newsweek* and the Admiral Boorda case" by Philip Patterson

"Culture, law and privacy: Should ethics change in a cultural context?" by Lee Wilkins

"Arthur Ashe and the right to privacy" by Carol Oukrop

"A Person of Interest" by Cara DeMichele

"Blind Justice? On Naming Kobe Bryant's Accuser after the Rape Charge is Dropped" by Patrick Lee Plaisance

CHAPTER 5 CASES

CASE 5-A

Anderson Cooper's Not-So-Private Life

LEE WILKINS
University of Missouri

In July 2012, CNN's Anderson Cooper confirmed what was already known to many in the inner circles of the media elite: "The fact is, I'm gay, always have been, always will be, and I couldn't be any more happy, comfortable with myself, and proud," Cooper wrote to Andrew Sullivan, who published the statement on his Daily Beast blog.

The fact that Cooper confirmed that he is gay was news, perhaps, to the average CNN viewer. For those in the extended media world, the statement was—well—not news. As early as 2007, *Out* magazine had ranked Cooper as the second most influential gay man in the United States. His sexual orientation had been published in, among other places, the *New York Times,* but Cooper himself had refused to either confirm or deny the accuracy of the reports, saying that he wanted to do nothing that would cause others to question his neutrality as a journalist.

Cooper is what many would dub a celebrity broadcaster, but he has had more reason than most to consider the implications of privacy on himself as a person and on his professional career.

Cooper was born on June 3, 1967, to fashion designer and heiress Gloria Vanderbilt and her fourth husband, writer Wyatt Cooper. Gloria Vanderbilt was often the subject of media coverage and admittedly sought such attention through most of her life, including the publication of memoirs that detailed many of her affairs. Cooper's father died when he was 10.

Cooper became a Ford model when he was 11. The adult looked back on that initial employment as an attempt to be "financially independent" from his incredibly wealthy family. He graduated from Yale University in 1989, one year after his older brother committed suicide by jumping from the Vanderbilt's 14th-floor New York apartment, an event that received significant news coverage as well as first-person account of the event by his mother. Cooper credits his brother's suicide with initiating his interest in journalism.

In 1992, Cooper began to work as a fact checker with Channel One, a television channel that was (and still is) broadcast into many public school classrooms. Cooper covered the democracy movement in Burma on forged press credentials; his reports from there ultimately aired on Channel One. That effort was followed by reporting from Somalia, Bosnia and Rwanda.

In 1995, Cooper became a correspondent for ABC News, a post he left in 2000 to host a reality television program called "The Mole." He left that program after the terrorist attacks of 2001 to return to news.

Cooper's career moved to the next level during his coverage of Hurricane Katrina, when he confronted a number of political figures about the frequently incompetent response of the state and federal governments to the disaster. Cooper has been called the anchor of the future and the first and best known of a new breed of television news anchors who combine emotion with traditional reporting.

Micro Issues

1. Is Cooper's sexual orientation news? Should it be news?
2. Is Cooper a celebrity? A journalist?
3. Does his sexual orientation compromise his journalistic standards? In what ways? On what sorts of stories?
4. If you answered yes to the question above, does *your* sexual orientation compromise your journalistic standards? How would you know?
5. Would your answers be different if Cooper were elected to public office? The CEO of a Wall Street firm?

Midrange Issues

1. Journalists often work for organizations that require them to have a "Facebook presence." What sort of information should be on such a professional Facebook page?
2. Is Cooper's often emotional reporting from disaster-torn regions good journalism or just good television? Justify your answer.
3. Does such emotional coverage compromise objectivity?

4. Cooper has said that his mother's publicity seeking prompted him to consider another way to live an adult life. How would you connect this statement to the concept of privacy?
5. Is it possible to regain professional journalistic standing after hosting a reality television program?

Macro Issues

1. Reconcile the concepts of transparency and privacy, as you understand them.
2. Are the privacy standards for people like Cooper philosophically different from those for the people whose arrests are reporting on blabbermouthkc.com and similar Web sites?
3. What are some contexts, for example boarding an airplane, in which you are willing to give up some privacy? Why? How do these contexts fit the sorts of information-based privacy issues raised in the chapter?

CASE 5-B

Facebook: Should You Opt Out or In?

LEE WILKINS
University of Missouri

For most college students, on most college campuses, Facebook has become *the* social networking site—a place to meet people, talk to friends, form interest groups outside of geographical constraints and beyond the prying eyes of parents and teachers. Many college students access Facebook multiple times daily.

In September of 2006, Facebook made changes that automatically alerted everyone in a user's network anytime any other member of that person's network updated anything. Users were flooded with minutia. Even more objectionable was that messages intended for one person, or one part of a network, were directed to *everyone* in a network (Stanard 2006). The furor was immediate and passionate:

> If you don't want this information to be out there, don't put it on Facebook. How did the news feed work any differently than the real-world gossip chain? . . . Eh, maybe this will convince people that they shouldn't put their whole lives on the Internet.
>
> It's not the fact that they can see it, it is the fact that it is "broadcast" that makes it bad. I don't care that people I know find out that I break up with a girl, but I don't want it to be sent RSS style to everyone I know.

Facebook CEO Mark Zuckerberg apologized to Facebook users and relented on the policy change. In 2007, Facebook users protested again, this time over a feature called Beacon, which tracked user actions on dozens of outside Web sites and revealed information about users' actions and purchases to their Facebook friends. The Beacon feature was removed from Newsfeeds, and users now have opt-out control over whether their data are sent to third-party applications.

The protest of Beacon was significant because the tracking feature was similar to tracking tactics often employed by online advertising, though usually without user awareness. According to the Center for Democracy and Technology ("Privacy Implications of Online Advertising" 2008), a Harris Interactive/Alan F. Westin study found that "59% of respondents said they were not comfortable with online companies using their browsing behavior to tailor ads and content to their interests even when they were told that such advertising supports free services. A recent TRUSTe survey produced similar results. It is highly unlikely that these respondents understood that this type of ad targeting is already taking place online every day".

Because users are commonly unaware of this practice, they are unable to take action to protect their personal information if they wanted to. Although Web sites and advertisers sometimes offer opt-out options for users, few consumers "have been able to successfully navigate the confusing and complex opt-out process" (13). What all these discussions pointed out was that, once posted, Facebook owned the information about its users and was selling it for a variety of purposes. This ownership arrangement was spelled out in the terms and conditions on the site, but many of the sites almost 1 billion users didn't understand the ownership issue and its implications.

How confusing was thinking about privacy on Facebook? In 2009, the *New York Times* published a guide to Facebook privacy settings: users had to go through more than 100 different steps to alter their privacy profiles on the popular Web site. Facebook itself got the message. In the next year, it altered its software to make it much easier for users to change privacy settings. With two clicks, it was now possible to replicate what had taken more than 100 clicks a year earlier.

But, Facebook continued to push the privacy envelope. In 2011 the Web site adopted automatic facial recognition, making it easier—and even encouraging users—to tag new photos placed in the site by Facebook friends. Furthermore, the facial recognition feature was an opt-out option—users could say they wanted it only after the fact. Those who did not want it could opt out only after photos had been tagged.

That move proved controversial in Europe, where a group of privacy watchdogs, the Article 29 Data Protection Watch Party which has the power to punish firms that violate privacy, launched an investigation. That move was followed in Great Britain and Ireland. The Information Commissioner's Office of Britain is "speaking to Facebook" about the privacy aspects of the technology, said Greg Jones, a spokesperson for the group, telling reporters that he expected Facebook to be "upfront" with its consumers on how their personal information was being used.

In the United States, there continued to be what some considered unintended consequences. In 2009, one survey found that 45 percent of employers use Facebook and Twitter to screen job candidates. Two years later, a Microsoft survey found that the figure might be as high as 75 percent despite repeated and public cautions that using the social Web sites to screen job applicants raised real issues of discrimination by virtue of age, gender or ethnicity that might come with viewing wall posts. In 2011, the Library of Congress announced that it would archive and store all tweets since Twitter was founded in 2006—making the 144-character comments as long-lived as those in any book or in the *Congressional Record.*

But, the impact of Facebook and other devices, including mobile phones, was not merely informational: it was psychological and sometimes physical. One multinational study in Europe found that young people who were asked to withdraw from using their electronic devices for 24 hours began to show the physical, psychological and emotional signs of withdrawal normally associated with addiction.

And, in 2012, in response to a number of highly publicized cases of cyberbullying, including some that resulted in death or suicide of teenagers and young adults, Facebook augmented the power of its Family Safety Center and provided new tools to report cyberbullying. Meanwhile, just before Facebook's launch as a public company to offer stock to investors, General Motors withdrew its advertising from the site saying that Facebook ads had demonstrably little impact on sales. Some point to the General Motors decision as one of the factors of a lackluster launch of Facebook stock.

At the core of the debate over Facebook and many other, similar Web sites is the concept of privacy. Respond to the questions below based on your personal experience.

Micro Issues

1. Should journalists use information gathered on Facebook as part of the reporting process? If the answer is yes, are there guidelines?
2. Should strategic communication professionals use the information about individual consumers provided on sites such as Facebook for purposes of target marketing? If the answer is yes, are there guidelines?
3. Should the rules for professionals, such as journalists and strategic communication professionals, be different than those for average Facebook users?

Midrange Issues

1. Should the ownership of information on Facebook reside with the person who did the posting, with Facebook "friends" or with Facebook itself—a corporation? Use an ethical analysis to justify your answer.
2. Distinguish in ethical terms between an employer requiring a drug test and an employer vetting a potential employee on Facebook or Twitter.
3. Should it be possible to delete yourself from social networking sites?
4. Is there an ethical distinction between your information posted on social networks and the connections you make with friends—and their information—on those same networks, particularly in how networks sell that information to third parties?

Macro Issues

1. Privacy advocates have suggested that all systems such as Facebook should operate on an opt-in basis—in other words, the user would have to agree up front that certain information should be available to third parties. Critique this stance applying utilitarianism, the work of John Rawls and communitarianism.

2. What institution, if any, should regulate social networking site content, particularly for problems such as stalking, bullying and identity theft?
3. What are the potential ethical implications of government, as compared to corporations, archiving information posted on sites such as Facebook and Twitter?
4. Is Facebook's evolving privacy policy setting an example of open-sourced ethics? What, if any, are the problems with this approach?

CASE 5-C

Politics and Money—What's Private and What's Not

LEE WILKINS
University of Missouri

When the Supreme Court in 2011 decided that corporations and unions could contribute an unlimited amount of money to political campaigns—what is referred to as the Citizen's United Decision—most political pundits and scholars agreed that the opinion had the potential to alter the democratic election process.

The Supreme Court decision renewed journalistic emphasis on covering campaign finance. It was a story that had been around for at least 50 years but, with the new ruling, received new urgency. The journalistic reasoning was fairly straightforward: if wealthy individuals (who were not themselves candidates for public office) were willing to write checks to politicians they supported for millions of dollars, shouldn't the public know something about these donors?

Because of campaign finance laws that were not altered by the Supreme Court ruling, large and unlimited donations went to Super PACs, outsized political action committees that are not legally required to report the source or size of their donations as a candidate would have to, for instance. What happened nationally with campaign finance was also evident at the state and sometimes the local level. Even state Supreme Court justices were not immune from the attacks levied by outside interests on them. When a midlevel state elected official coming up for re-election encountered an opponent funded by a Super PAC, the resulting tsunami in cash overwhelmed these traditionally underfunded campaigns.

In the early months of the 2012 presidential campaign the *New York Times* reported the following:

- Billionaire Harold Simmons gave $1 million to Newt Gingrich's political action committee, another $1.1 million to Texas Gov. Rick Perry's Super PAC, and $10 million to American Crossroads, a Republican-oriented Super PAC advised by controversial GOP strategist Karl Rove.
- Peter Thiel, PayPal co-founder and a self-identified libertarian, gave U.S. Rep. Ron Paul's PAC $2.6 million.

Multiple news organizations reported that Gingrich's largest financial supporter, Sheldon Adelson, had donated more than $10 million to the Super PAC Winning Our Future.

- Millionaire Rex Sinquefield, of St. Louis, Mo., donated more than $1 million to various campaigns in the state, including campaigns focusing on public education and conservative political candidates.

While the bulk of million-dollar donations went to Republicans, President Barack Obama's campaign also received:

- at least $1 million in support from the Service Employees International Union; and
- $2 million from film industry executive Jeffrey Katzenberg.

The U.S. Chamber of Commerce, both nationally and locally, endorsed candidates, often accompanied by sizable donations from individual members.

Many of the large-dollar donors were on record with controversial political opinions or business decisions. Simmons, for example had clashed with the Environmental Protection Agency over compliance with regulations for a Texas radioactive waste dump, Thiel had blamed giving women the right to vote on the rise of the welfare state, and Freiss had said that aspirin was an effective contraceptive when women "put it between their knees."

When the Obama campaign placed a list of million-dollar GOP donors on its Web site, Frank VanderSloot, who had contributed more than $1 million to the Mitt Romney Super PAC, characterized Obama's list as an "enemies list" borrowing the term from the Nixon presidency when such a list did exist. Both VanderSloot and the billionaire brothers, Charles and David Koch, who had bankrolled many political campaigns, claimed that the publication of their names and their donations had made them subject to attacks and a loss of business.

On June 20, 2012, in a report by NPR's Andrea Seabrook, VanderSloot was quoted as saying that he had lost customers, received negative press and been the target of unsavory e-mails. VanderSloot refused to talk with NPR in its series on millionaire donors—not a single donor was willing to be interviewed on the record—but had spoken earlier with Fox News about the response to his donation after it became public.

As might be expected, the publicity and reporting surrounding these donations made its way to Congress. There, Republican Mitch McConnell (KY) said that the coverage was infringing on the donors' right to free speech. "This is nothing less than an effort by the government itself to expose its critics to harassment and intimidation. That's why it's critically important for all conservatives, and indeed all Americans, to stand up and unite in defense of the freedom to organize around the causes we believe in."

Democrats shot back quoting conservative Supreme Court Justice Antonin Scalia who was on record as saying that publicity is part of the price of getting involved in the game of politics as it is now played.

NPR, in its series on millionaire donors, also asked the large-dollar contributors why they were unwilling to be interviewed by NPR for the story. The question was met with universal silence.

Micro Issues

1. Most Americans think of money—how they earn it and how they spend it—as very private. Should campaign contributions be treated the same way as salary information or income tax returns for private citizens?
2. Can you justify using ethical theory in the current state of reporting campaign donations? Should those who give a great deal of money be treated differently? Why or why not?
3. Can you justify using ethical theory in the current state of reporting how much candidates contribute to their own political campaigns?

Midrange Issues

1. Apply Nissenbaum's concept of control over the contextual flow of information to the subject of covering campaign finance.
2. Does journalistic reporting on the individual political beliefs and agendas of donors—both large and small—make the ethical mistake of guilt by association?
3. Did NPR make the correct decision in broadcasting that no donors would speak on the record about their campaign contributions?

Macro Issues

1. Many news organizations, particularly broadcast networks and local affiliates, had very profitable years in 2012. Should news organizations be required to report the source of their income, particularly when it comes from airing campaign commercials?
2. How do you think Americans should define political speech? Connect your thinking to the privacy of the secret ballot, the notion of the marketplace of ideas, and your views about the relationship between money and politics.

CASE 5-D

Children, Privacy and Framing: The Use of Children's Images in an Anti-Same-Sex-Marriage Ad

YANG LIU
University of Wisconsin

The brief ballot measure read, "Only marriage between a man and a woman is valid or recognizable in California" (www.votergide.sos.ca.gov 2008) but it was packed with potential for conflict. So when the parents of some San Francisco first graders recognized their sons' and daughters' faces in an advertisement promoting California's controversial 2008 Proposition 8, which successfully sought to outlaw gay marriage in the state (www.protectmarriage.com 2008) they were shocked.

The ad picked up two scenes from a Web site news video clip originally produced by the San Francisco *Chronicle* for a news story that described 18 students attending their lesbian teacher Erin Carder's wedding. The newspaper story was a feature piece that took no position on Proposition 8. The story included an account of the wedding, which was held on October 10, 2008. In the newspaper piece, and on the 80-second accompanying video, the children's participation was described as "tossed rose petals and blowing bubbles . . . giggling and squealing as they mobbed their teacher with hugs." The story noted that it was a parent who suggested the trip and that because every student needed parental permission to attend, two students did not accompany their classmates to the wedding.

However, the central message of the advertisement was, "children will be taught gay marriage unless we vote Yes on Proposition 8" using two scenes with the children's images. The first showed the children in a group, and their faces are somewhat difficult to distinguish. The second showed a single child looking into the camera. The ad did not include the scenes of the children hugging their teacher that were part of the original news story. In addition, the creators of the ad altered the color tones in the scenes with children to be somewhat darker than the original news story as posted on the *Chronicle* Web site. The ad featuring the video clip of the wedding was one of several similar ads run in support of Proposition 8.

After viewing the ad, four of the parents of the children involved wrote a letter to the Yes-on-Proposition-8 campaign, demanding that the campaign stop running the ad. Their request was denied. The *Chronicle* did not question the use of the copyrighted material in the ad nor did it make a request that the ad be discontinued.

Micro Issues

1. How would you evaluate the truthfulness and accuracy of the video accompanying the political advertisement?
2. Three days after the ad began airing, law Professor Lawrence Lessig said in a National Public Radio interview that the law "should not stop the ability of people to use material that has been publicly distributed." Evaluate this statement using ethical theory.
3. Do children constitute a vulnerable audience when it comes to privacy?

Midrange Issues

1. All advertisements, by virtue of their brevity, engage in selective use of facts. Evaluate whether this ad is within that professional mainstream in an ethical sense.
2. What should the *Chronicle* do about the use of news material for the purpose of political persuasion, regardless of the specific issue?

Macro Issues

1. How would you evaluate the statement that this ad constitutes protected political speech?
2. It has been argued that the children do not have the ability to reason about the politics of same-sex marriage in this wedding, so they were not expressing consent to the same-sex marriage, but only expressing affection for their teacher. Is their participation in the wedding a private matter without political meaning, or not? Justify your answer.

6

Mass Media in a Democratic Society: Keeping a Promise

By the end of this chapter, you should be familiar with:

- many of the criticisms leveled at the way the U.S. media cover government and elections.
- the special problems of reporting on terrorism and hate.
- why the media should be concerned with social justice for the powerful and the powerless alike.
- evaluating all forms of political communication through a single, ethically based framework.

INTRODUCTION

Americans view the written word as essential to political society. The First Amendment to the U.S. Constitution states:

> Congress shall make no law respecting an establishment of religion, or prohibiting the free exercise thereof; or abridging the freedom of speech, or of the press; or the right of the people peaceably to assemble, and to petition the government for a redress of grievances.

Scholars such as John C. Merrill (1974) assert that the First Amendment should be interpreted purely as a restriction on government, emphasizing freedom of expression and downplaying any notion of reciprocal journalistic responsibility. *In other words, freedom of speech extends not only to speech written or uttered by "mainstream" media but also to minority voices, even those who are decidedly unpopular.*

But others, including Alexis de Tocqueville, who studied our democracy nearly two centuries ago, viewed the press of the day as an essential antidote to a culture that valued liberty over community. The press, de Tocqueville said, was an

130

MOTHER GOOSE&GRIMM © 1999 Grimmy, Inc. King Features Syndicate.

incubator of civilization, an idea that political philosopher John Dewey would further for the mass media of his day just under a century later.

Madison, Hamilton and Jay in the *Federalist Papers* expected citizens to be informed and to participate in politics. They knew that political debate, including what was printed in the press, would be partisan and biased rather than objective, but they also believed that from this "noisy" information the rational being would find the truth. Unfettered communication was essential to building a new nation. Citizens had an obligation to read such information; the press had an obligation to provide it.

Tucked within all of this, we believe, is a promise that the mass media, both in 1791 and now nearly 225 years ago, will provide citizens with what they need to know to get along in political society, an analysis now called the "social responsibility theory" of the press. However, assuming such a responsibility is becoming progressively more difficult because of the increasingly complex structure of the contemporary American political system.

EVALUATING POLITICAL COMMUNICATION

For the Greeks, where democracy was born, the art of politics was considered a gift from the gods, who provided men with *adios,* a sense of concern for the good opinion of others, and *dike,* a sense of justice that makes civic peace possible. In the ancient myth, these gifts were bestowed on everyone, not just some elite. All men were able to exercise the art of politics through rhetoric and argument in the assembly, a form of direct democracy that survived for only a few years in Athens. No newspapers, no television, just in-person debate. The Greeks called it *polity,* which translates as community, one of the Greeks' highest ethical constructs.

Greece was also the last place that direct democracy was practiced, and considering the contemporary cacophony, that's not such a big surprise. It's not just the negative campaign commercials. It's the barrage of opinion masquerading as analysis on cable television. It's the thousands of blogs available on the Internet, the candidate campaign Web sites. It's entries into domains such as Facebook, and it's the late-night comedians.

Comedy Central and all the rest. One study by the Pew Charitable Trusts in the past decade found that more than half of Americans under age 50 get their news about politics "regularly" or "sometimes" from late night comedians and subsequent research showed that to be the case more recently in both of the elections of Barak Obama. But these respondents were also among the least likely to know basic facts about candidates. Even on the lowest level, politics, for most, is a mass-mediated event.

Evaluating all this political information is a problem for both media consumers and journalists. Furthermore, as news blends into entertainment and persuasion leaches into both genres, providing a consistent way of examining every political message becomes essential in ethical analysis. Political scientist Bruce A. Williams (2009) has begun this process with a four-part test he believes will help you determine when information has political relevance:

- First, is the information **useful**—does it provide citizens with the kind of information that helps individual and collective decision making?
- Second, is the information **sufficient**—is there enough of it and at enough depth to allow people to make informed choices?
- Third, is the information **trustworthy?**
- Fourth, **who is the "audience"**—the political "we" on which the ancient Greeks placed so much emphasis?

Information that meets these criteria should be considered politically relevant, mediated information regardless of genre or source, Williams says. Under this test, a Jon Stewart show or a Stephen Colbert monologue would be considered politically relevant communication every bit as much as a campaign ad or an investigative piece. Under this sort of analysis, cable news programming, which often features dueling opinions by talking heads talking over each other (often unsubstantiated by evidence), *would actually fare less well* than the comedy monologue.

In a famous dustup between cable news personality (now CATO Institute fellow) Tucker Carlson and Comedy Central comedian Jon Stewart took on the entire genre of punditry with Stewart suggesting that his show was more truthful and politically relevant. Interestingly, Stewart has made that claim in other arenas—that Comedy Central actually has political clout, adding that it personally frightens him—which gets a good laugh but makes a poignant point.

Putting all political communication into the same arena also has another virtue: every message can be evaluated along the same standard. Here, again, Williams (2009) suggests four criteria.

- **Transparency**—Does the audience know who is speaking? This has become a major problem in recent elections with the rise of PACs and groups not bound by campaign finance rules and rarely bothered with the total accuracy of their claims, something seen on both sides in the 2009 debate over health care reform.
- **Pluralism**—Does the media environment provide an opportunity for diverse points of view, either in different messages that are equally accessible or within a single message? Does every side have access to the engines of information that are now the modern equivalent of the face-to-face rhetoric of ancient Greece?

- **Verisimilitude**—Do the sources of the messages take responsibility for the truth claims they explicitly and implicitly make, even if these claims are not strictly verifiable in any formal sense?
- **Practice**—Does the message encourage modeling, rehearsing, preparing and learning for civic engagement? Does it encourage activities like voting or less direct forms of political activity like thinking about issues, looking at Web sites, blogging or talking to neighbors face-to-face? Is the ad or article empowering or does it contribute to the cacophony that has dominated recent political campaigns?

Williams's framework is applicable at the individual story/ad level. However, the role of the media also may be evaluated at the institutional level—what most scholars refer to as institutional role. At this level, it is not the individual story or single ad but the aggregation of all of them that matters. In most scholarship, media role is analyzed in terms of the media's relationship to the state and specifically to the political system (Christians, Glasser, McQuail, Nordenstreng & White 2009). When thinking about role, it is important to understand that all institutions in a specific society influence one another. Authoritarian political regimes need methods of communicating with citizens to maintain order and control. Therefore, in authoritarian regimes, the media need to obey the strictures of the state in order to continue to function at the organizational level. At the individual level, promoting the goals of the state keeps individual journalists out of jail at the most extreme or allows them to maintain a license to continue to practice professionally.

Recent scholarship outlines four normative roles for the media in democratic political systems. Normative used in this way means a description of how the media ought to behave. In real life, and in real theory, individual organizations can fulfill multiple roles simultaneously. These roles are:

- The *radical role* operates when the media provide an alternate vision to the current political and social situation in a country;
- The *monitorial role* is what citizens most often think of when they speak of the watchdog function of the news media;
- The *facilitative role* is perhaps best captured by news coverage of elections and political advertising about candidates and public issues. Both news and ads can facilitate governing, although how well that role is accomplished is the source of much analysis and debate;
- The *collaborative role,* where the media promote the views of the state. Broadcasting weather forecasts can serve this role as can much less benign forms of collaboration.

The way a nation governs is reflected in its media. How a democracy develops depends, in part, on the conversation the media have with other, important institutions in that democracy. How citizens, professionals and scholars evaluate media performance depends significantly on the role expectations of a particular media system. Thinking about role provides a somewhat abstract but certainly achievable set of standards. Those standards will vary from democracy to democracy, but they persist across counties, cultures and languages.

While this puts all political messages on a level and ethically based playing field, contemporary democratic politics still produces some morally relevant variations—at least when it comes to news and persuasion. We will review some of the most commonly acknowledged issues now.

GETTING ELECTED

For any politician to enact change, he or she must first be elected, and in our mass society, that means turning to the mass media to reach the electorate. In one classic study, voters admitted learning more about candidates' stands on issues from advertising than they did from news (Patterson 1980). And considering that modern presidential campaigns place ads only in contested states, many voters get little exposure to even the limited and one-sided information coming from ads unless they access them online. For voters in non-"battleground" states, much of their exposure to negative ads comes only if a cable or network news outlet does a story on the ad.

In the past few presidential campaigns, Web sites have become increasingly important. But since they are under the control of the candidate and not bound by any constraints of objectivity or completeness, they too qualify as advertising. So today, more than 30 years after the first studies indicated it to be true, advertising is still the leading source of information for most people in most campaigns.

Because ads are a leading source of campaign information, factual accuracy, therefore, must be the starting point for ethical political advertising. As philosopher Hannah Arendt has noted, "Freedom of information is a farce unless factual information is guaranteed and the facts themselves are not in dispute" (Arendt 1970).

News stories about elections emphasize strategy and tactics rather than stands on issues, forcing voters who want to become informed about the candidate's policy choices to get their information from ads, often "negative" or "attack" ads framed by the other side. They do this in part because policy information is largely missing from news stories which tend to focus on polls, who's hot and who's not, electability and character, but usually only the search for flaws.

Contemporary voters can discern the various types of political ads, according to election studies. Comparative ads, ones that contrast candidate positions on specific issues, were viewed as information rich, and voters view them as an appropriate part of political discourse. Attack ads, ones that are personal and negative, that contain no "positive" or "issue-oriented" information, were disliked and distrusted in the studies. A few years ago, a majority of political ads were either positive or contrasted stances of the candidates (Benoit 1999). Another study from the same time showed that voters were able to distinguish among negative, comparative and positive or biographical ads (Jamieson 2000).

At the time between the Patterson study (1980) and the Jamieson study (2000), survey results provided ample evidence that it is possible to create ethical political advertising on the local, state and national levels and win. However, in just a decade, the tide has turned, and "going negative" is now seen as the only route to victory for candidates at all levels. And as an added inducement to create negative

Ed Stein © 1992 Reprinted with permission of UNIVERSAL UCLICK. All rights reserved.

ads, candidates see them run repeatedly, for free, as the negativity of the ads are debated endlessly on cable news, feeding the media's voracious appetite for anything new from the campaign trail.

Today, "ad watches" put the claims in political ads to the tests of truthfulness and context. Anecdotal evidence suggests that aggressive journalism focusing on attack ads and negative campaigning can have an impact on the voters' knowledge of particular candidates. Under the social responsibility of the press, it is the responsibility of journalists to evaluate political advertising as legitimate news and to hold candidates publicly accountable for the advertising sponsored by a campaign or, in the grayer areas, advertising paid for by political action groups, even those disavowed by the candidate.

Ideally, political advertising would be factual and rational. The use of emotional arguments designed to stir listeners or viewers "to set aside reason" is a "violation of democratic ethics" (Haiman 1958, 388). There may, however, be times when valid issues have strong emotional content, such as the ongoing debate over abortion or immigration. The melding of emotion and issue in such cases is not unethical. Totalitarian regimes have historically used emotional rather than rational appeals to either gain or retain power.

However, such ads usually lack any evidence to support the claims. Seeking the evidence behind political assertions has historically been the role of the news media. When this sort of journalism is lacking, it begins a cycle that was foreseen by Walter Lippmann: "In the absence of debate, restricted utterance leads to the degradation of opinion . . . the more rational is overcome by the less rational, and the opinions that will prevail will be those which are held most ardently by those with the most passionate will" (Lippmann 1982, 196).

If political advertising is indeed a "special case" (Kaid 1992), then journalists and their audiences should demand higher standards, more regulations or both. While some of the solutions to the current problems have both First Amendment and financial ramifications, they are worthy of discussion. They include the following:

- Allot limited amounts of free time to qualified candidates for major office to level the playing field for candidates;
- Strengthen state regulations against corrupt campaign practices and find ways to enforce those regulations;
- Encourage journalists to stop covering the "horse race" aspect of campaigns and focus on problems and solutions;
- Hold candidates accountable for their ads and for the ads of political action committees or other groups such as MoveOn.org;
- Teach journalists to read and report on the visual imagery of a campaign, and to ask candidates questions about it;
- Allow attack ads only if they include the image of the candidate directing the attack;
- Reject unfair or inaccurate ads created by political action committees;
- Conduct ad watches as part of media coverage of a campaign, analyzing the ads for omissions, inconsistencies and inaccuracies.

It takes money to buy ads, and in contemporary democratic societies that means the candidate with the most money often has the loudest voice. Many argue the influence of money in the political system is pervasive and corrosive. Bills have been introduced in Congress to limit the power of money in politics only to see the bill die in the political process, be ignored in the real world by substituting "soft money" for restricted money or rendered moot by recent Supreme Court decisions.

In the 2012 election cycle, following the *Citizens United v. Federal Election Committee* decision, the Supreme Court essentially allowed supporters of candidates—including corporations and unions—to collect and spend unlimited amounts of campaign funds. While the impact was most noticeable at the presidential level, Senate and House races and even state legislative races also were influenced by an influx of campaign cash, much of it from supporters outside the geographic boundaries of specific legislative districts. It can be argued that money buys elections, especially in the light of evidence that the most heavily funded campaign wins more often than not. However, it can also be argued that monetary gifts are merely precursors to votes and the most popular candidate in gifts is often the most popular in votes as well. Whether the money brings the votes or popularity brings the money, one thing that is constant is that, the lower level the race (state legislators, judges, etc.), the more impactful these outside gifts can be.

How to deal with the influence of money in elections is an important policy question, but there seem to be few answers. Politicians are too tied to the existing system to be objective, and the media that could presumably investigate political money and its negative influence are compromised by the act of receiving so much of the cash. The problem cannot be "solved" in this brief chapter, but it is worth considering whether a media system in a democracy might not be able to be a part of the solution rather than a part of the problem.

LEARNING ABOUT LEADERS AND THEIR CHARACTER

Today, a pressing political issue is whether people can become acquainted well enough and deeply enough with any candidate to acquire an opinion. After all, a representative democracy rests on the Greek concept of *adios,* a concern for the good opinion of others. Except for a small group of insiders, the mass media have become the primary source of political information, including information about character. In addition to providing voters with facts, something that is generally assumed to be the role of news, the media also provide citizens with a framework to understand those facts.

Candidates have been quick to utilize a variety of media outlets. Former California Gov. Arnold Schwarzenegger announced his candidacy on the "Tonight Show." Because journalists cover national campaigns in a pack, there is seldom any really distinctive political reporting during elections (Crouse 1974; Sabato 1992). However, for journalists, campaign assignments hold the opportunity for personal prestige. The person who covers the winning candidate for a network will almost assuredly become the White House correspondent for the next four years, a guarantee of celebrity status, increased income and real political power by setting the agenda of White House coverage. Journalists covering a national election have almost as much at stake as the candidates they cover.

Further, journalists treat front-runners differently than they do the remainder of the candidate pack (Robinson and Sheehan 1984). Front-runners are the subject of closer scrutiny, but those examinations are seldom about issues. When Secretary of State Hillary Clinton was running for president in 2008, her front-runner status resulted in coverage that nearly everyone, including the journalists producing it, felt was subtly sexist. Clinton maintained that she had to campaign as much against the stereotype as she did against her opponents.

Candidates and their paid consultants have developed strategies that will allow them either to capitalize on front-runner status and image or to compensate for a lack of it. In the movie *The Adjustment Bureau,* Matt Damon portrays a young and good-looking candidate who uses his concession speech early in the film to poke fun at the absurd amounts his staff paid to test his shoes, his ties, etc. But the movie makes a good point: TV-friendly candidates are more likely to receive free media—the Sunday morning programs, the 5:00 p.m. news, the higher-rated cable news shows, etc. Candidates have mastered the "photo opportunity" and, for incumbents, the "Rose Garden strategy" designed to thwart anything but the most carefully scripted candidate contact with the voting public.

At the same time candidates try to script their every move, the media have the right, and the responsibility, to get "behind the curtain" (Molotch and Lester 1974) to the real candidate. What happens after the curtain is down often makes news in ways the candidates could not have foreseen. Often it is sexual scandal or financial wrongdoing that brings down the carefully crafted veil that major politicians erect. Journalists face a number of questions in cases such as these. Just because the information is available and even accurate does not automatically mean that it is relevant and ethical to broadcast or print it.

Conceptualizations of character have changed significantly since the founding of the republic, when character was defined in Aristotelian terms—an observable collection of habits, virtues and vices. Freudian psychology has altered that definition to include motivation, the subconscious and relationships that help form all of us as people. What journalists cover is "political character," the intersection of personality and public performance within the cultural and historical context. Character is dynamic—the synergy of a person within an environment (Davies 1963). Journalists who explore character often do so for an ethical reason, despite apparent invasions of privacy.

Political figures are powerful people. Ethicist Sissela Bok (1978) has noted that when an unequal power relationship is involved, it is possible to justify what would otherwise be considered an unethical act. To paraphrase Bok, investigation of the private character of public people is validated if the person investigated is also in the position to do harm. In those cases, invading privacy in an attempt to counter that threat is justified. However, that invasion also needs to meet some tests (Schoeman 1984):

- The invasion must be placed in a larger context of facts and history and must include context to provide meaning;
- The revelation of private facts about political figures should meet the traditional tests of journalism and needs to be linked to public, political behaviors before publication or broadcast becomes ethically justifiable;
- The invasion of privacy must further the larger political discourse and must meet the most demanding ethical test: the "need to know."

Careful reporting on character can pass these tests. However, journalists must also weigh the harm done to others, particularly family members, who have not sought the public limelight. In the campaign of 2008, one of the ethical quandaries reporters faced is whether the pregnancy of former vice presidential candidate Sarah Palin's unmarried daughter was news. Arguments can be made for both sides of the controversy, but eventually, however, virtually every media outlet ran the story, including many who did so using faulty logic after determining that the story was already "out there."

Even reporting that passes the three tests above must be filtered through discretion—a word usually used in moral development theory. In ethics, discretion means having the practical wisdom not to reveal everything one is told, even if facts or events would be of casual interest to many. Journalists have the difficult problem of being discreet in their news coverage, even when candidates, their handlers or supporters and opponents have been indiscreet—sometimes deliberately so. Discretion prevents mainstream media from slipping into "tabloid journalism" or the domain of gossipy blogs that cast doubt on our journalistic motives and credibility.

Reporters covering political character should be aware that there are several building blocks of character, including the:

- politician's development of a sense of trust;
- politician's own sense of self-worth and self-esteem;
- development of a politician's relationship to power and authority;
- early influences on adult policy outlook;
- way a politician establishes contact with people;
- flexibility, adaptability and purposefulness of mature adulthood;
- historical moment.

The media's current emphasis on covering political character provides the best illustration of the need to balance the demands of governing with privacy. No culture has ever expected its leaders to be saints; in fact, some cultures have prized leadership that is decidedly unsaintly. In American culture, the concept of public servant—which is the work of politics—has been replaced by the epithet "politician"—synonymous with "crook," or "liar," a caricature reinforced in popular culture by iconic films such as *Mr. Smith Goes to Washington* or *All the King's Men*. However, Americans were reminded that public service can be a high calling, as shown by the first responders to the 9/11 tragedy, many of whom lost their lives. The late Senator Edward Kennedy described his job as public service. Such service, dating as far back as Athens, was considered the mark of a life well lived.

THE PROPER ROLE OF THE MEDIA— GUARD DOG OR LAP DOG?

One of the ironies of democratic politics is that, in order to accomplish something, you first have to get elected, but it is accomplishing something, not getting elected, that is the major work of politics. Journalists fuel the irony by covering politicians more at the time of their elections or re-elections and paying much less attention to their policymaking in between elections. Regulatory agencies, cabinet offices and the courts are not considered glamour beats by the national press corps. Annual surveys by journalism watchdog groups show a dwindling number of reporters on the regulatory beat, which accounts for the late start the media had on a story like global warming until it was forced to the forefront by former Vice President Al Gore in his award-winning documentary. A similar decline in coverage has been noted for years in state legislatures as well.

Yet the national press corps, particularly, is often a player in the policy process by reporting "leaks" and granting "off-the-record" interviews. Political scientist Martin Linsky (1986) describes how leaks have become part of the Washington policymaking process. Government officials, both elected and appointed, use the mass media to leak a story to find out how others will react to it—floating a "trial balloon" in the press. Other times, policymakers will leak a story because they wish to mount support for or oppose a cause.

Sometimes leaks take the form of whistle-blowing when a government employee honestly believes the public good is not being served by the system.

Watergate's famed (and now named) source, "Deep Throat," apparently was so motivated when he leaked key parts of the government investigation into the Watergate break-in to *Washington Post* reporters Bob Woodward and Carl Bernstein, who wrote a set of stories that ended in the resignation of President Richard Nixon. More recently, the initial information about the Abu Ghraib prison abuse scandal in Iraq came to journalists in e-mails from service men and women who were alarmed at the treatment of Iraqis held at the prison and of the military command's unwillingness or inability to change the system.

More than two decades ago, Linsky (1986) wrote about the role of the media in the policymaking process and raised two important points regarding ethical journalistic practice still relevant today. First, leaks are an acceptable way of doing government business and policymakers are using them skillfully. Second, leaks can alter the outcome of the policy process itself, and much anecdotal evidence exists to support this conclusion. Of fundamental importance for journalists is the question of whether reporters, editors and their news organizations should become consciously involved in the process of governing by participating in the leaking process, and if so, in what manner. Recent scandals involving faked stories have caused most national media to tighten their regulations on when they grant off-the-record requests and when they use the information. But still the practice is common.

Most ethicists agree that the media's primary function is to provide citizens with information that will allow them to make informed political choices (Elliott 1986; Hodges 1986). Media organizations are expected to act as a watchdog on government. Edmund Burke, in a speech in Britain's House of Commons during the late 1700s, first called the media the "Fourth Estate" (Ward 2004). In the United States, the Founders protected the press in the Bill of Rights. Thomas Jefferson saw the press as the guardian of the public's interest despite the bitter, partisan nature of the press of his day.

The watchdog media, set apart by custom and by law, also have a "guide dog" function to help citizens make their way through the political process. However, when the press covers politics as a constant "food fight" by competing interests, both journalists and citizens are soured to the process. Political reporter E. J. Dionne in *Why Americans Hate Politics* (1991) argues that defining news as conflict (as virtually every journalism text does) inevitably reduces political debate into a shouting match. And, post-9/11 there is always the chance that critical coverage of government, especially the Pentagon, will be labeled "unpatriotic" by critics, including many in political power. This is not a problem exclusively confined to the U.S. system, as documentaries such as *Control Room*—in an in-depth look at the al-Jazeera news gathering operation— make clear.

Dionne agrees with Plato, who said that democratic politics, while a "degenerative" form of government, was probably the best available system considering that human beings were its primary components. And the same can be said of the humans who cover the governing process. Media critic James Fallows (1996, 7) goes one step further. He holds journalism directly responsible for voter apathy, congressional gridlock and government via opinion polls rather than political leadership. In a quote that rings just as true today as it did when he made it before the turn of the century, Fallows claims:

> The harm actually goes much further than that, to threaten the long-term health of our political system. Step by step, mainstream journalism has fallen into the habit of portraying public life in America as a race to the bottom, in which one group of conniving, insincere politicians ceaselessly tries to outmaneuver another. The great problem for American democracy in the 1990s is that people barely trust elected leaders or the entire legislative system to accomplish anything of value. . . . Deep forces in America's political, social and economic structures account for most of the frustration of today's politics, but the media's attitudes have played a surprisingly important and destructive role.

Media critic Katherine Hall Jamieson (1992) has suggested that, when it comes to politics, journalists should get themselves a new definition of news. Instead of emphasizing events and conflict, Jamieson believes news stories could equally revolve around issues and multiple policy perspectives. Fallows and others insist that implicit in the right to report on politics is that successful governing is an outcome for which the media are partially responsible. The cynical assumptions that government can never act for the public good, and that journalists and the media are somehow outside and perhaps even above the political system, are almost nihilistic. Ethical practice allows journalists and their media consumers to become more conscientiously involved in the American democratic political system.

MODERN PROBLEMS: TERRORISM AND HATE

Terrorism is, at its most fundamental level, an act of communication; it communicates hatred toward the target. Scholars suggest that terrorism was not possible (or effective) before the modern mass media were capable of amplifying the message of hate. Terrorists and the media have a symbiotic relationship: terrorists need the media to communicate their messages, and the media garner ratings and increased readership when terrorism is in the news, even while deploring the violence. Simultaneously, the media must perform a dual role: acting as filters of the terrorists' message and as watchdogs of government response.

Terrorism presents journalists with what philosophers call "hard questions." Terrorism is news, but news coverage furthers terrorists' ends and makes more terrorism likely. How to break that cycle has been the subject of much professional anguish throughout the world, with some governments resorting to censorship of news. And objectivity is often antithetical to the situation. In the face of some forms of terrorism such as genocide, journalists must take the side of humanity, even if it means abandoning objectivity. CNN correspondent Christiane Amanpour argued on air with former president Bill Clinton about America's reluctance to get involved in the racial and civil war after the former Yugoslavia disintegrated. Amanpour was not alone in her views, and after extensive debate the United States and NATO did engage in the conflict.

Terrorism also presents nation-states with hard problems. Nations under attack almost reflexively clamp down on their citizens—particularly those who question or dissent. Democracies pass laws, for example the PATRIOT Act, that enhance

government's powers over its citizens. The PATRIOT Act not only increased the government's powers of search and seizure (unchecked by the courts), but also allowed incarceration of suspected terrorists without bail or public notification. What made the act more devastating was the inclusion of a provision that made it impossible for journalists to get information needed to evaluate the effectiveness of the act. If truth is the first casualty of war, then independence of thought and action is the first casualty of terrorism.

Journalists perform another role in such historic times—that of moral witness. Ethicist Patrick Plaisance (2002) suggests that when journalists report on such events as terrorism, its causes, its execution and its results, the journalist functions as a "moral witness" because such news stories cannot be understood or reported outside of a moral framework. Plaisance and others assert that to be detached and objective about genocide and hate is to condone it. When journalists write the first draft of history of the early part of this century, they must deal with competing claims about justice, community, truth and power. Such reporting requires excellence in both ethical reflection and professional technique. It has seldom been more difficult—or more important—to do both well.

SOCIAL JUSTICE IN A DEMOCRATIC SOCIETY

Just as there are members of a power elite, there also are those who feel excluded from political society. One popular interpretation of U.S. history has been to track the gradual extension of power to ever more diverse publics. But the process has been uneven and contentious. All minority groups seek access to the political process and, since the mass media have become major players in that process, they seek access to media as well.

Media ethicists suggest these political and social "outgroups" provide the mass media with a further set of responsibilities. They assert that the mass media, and individual journalists, need to become advocates for the politically homeless. Media ethicist Clifford Christians suggests that "justice for the powerless stands at the centerpiece of a socially responsible press. Or, in other terms, the litmus test of whether or not the news profession fulfills its mission over the long term is its advocacy for those outside the socioeconomic establishment" (Christians 1986, 110).

This socially responsible view of the media suggests that journalists have a duty to promote community and the individuals within it. Those who are in significant ways outside the community—economically, socially or culturally—need a voice.

Christians's argument can be amplified beyond democracy's racial, ethnic and economic outgroups. In contemporary democratic society, clearly some "things" also are without political voice. The environment, ethnic issues, poverty and human rights violations beyond American shores all have difficulty finding a powerful spokesperson. These issues cross traditional political boundaries. Those who will be affected by them also need a voice.

Communitarian thinking takes social responsibility to the next level. It urges that justice is the ethical linchpin of journalistic decision making. If justice becomes the fundamental value of American journalism, then the media have the goal of transforming society, of empowering individual citizens to act in ways that promote political discussion, debate and change (Christians et al. 1993).

What makes journalists uneasy about either the communitarian or social responsibility approaches is that they smack of a kind of benevolent paternalism. If individual human beings carry moral stature, then assigning one institution—in this case the mass media—the role of social and political arbiter diminishes the moral worth of the individual citizen. The mass media become a kind parent and the citizen a sort of wayward child in need of guidance. Such a relationship does not promote political maturity.

While the weight of recent scholarly opinion sides with Christians, the view is not without risk. If accepted, it means a thorough change for the mass media in the U.S. political system. That change would bring about other changes, some of them not easy to anticipate. But whether change is what's needed, or merely a return to the strict libertarian view, both call for some sophisticated ethical reasoning.

As Thomas Jefferson said, being a citizen of a democracy is not easy—to which journalists might well add, neither is covering one.

Suggested Readings

CHRISTIANS, C., T. GLASSER, D. MCQUAIL, and K. NORDENSTRENG. 2009. *Normative theories of the media: Journalism in democratic societies.* Champagne: University of Illinois Press.

DIONNE, E. J., JR. 1991. *Why Americans hate politics.* New York: Simon & Schuster.

FALLOWS, JAMES. 1996. *Breaking the news: How the media undermine American democracy.* New York: Pantheon.

FRY, DON, ed. 1983. *The adversary press.* St. Petersburg, FL: The Modern Media Institute.

JAMIESON, K. H. 2000. *Everything you think you know about politics . . . and why you're wrong.* New York: Basic Books.

LINSKY, MARTIN. 1986. *Impact: How the press affects federal policymaking.* New York: W. W. Norton.

MADISON, JAMES S., ALEXANDER HAMILTON, and JOHN JAY. *The Federalist papers.*

WARD, STEPHEN. 2004. *The invention of journalism ethics.* Montreal: McGill-Queen's University Press.

Cases on the Web

www.mhhe.com/mediaethics8e

"The David Duke candidacy: Fairness and the Klansman" by Keith Woods
"Whose abuse of power: The *Seattle Times* and Brock Adams" by Lee Wilkins
"Denver's Rocky Flats: The role of the alternative press" by Lee Wilkins
"Terrorist use of the news media: News media use of terrorists" by Jack Lule
"Singapore: Balancing democracy, globalization and the Internet" by Seow Ting Lee

CHAPTER 6 CASES

CASE 6-A

The Truth about the Facts: PolitiFact.com

LEE WILKINS
University of Missouri

You would think journalists—the folks who write the "first draft of history"—would have better memories about accepting political claims at face value. But, early in 1950 when Wisconsin Republican senator Eugene McCarthy stood at a podium in Wheeling, West Virginia, and claimed to have a list of 205 state department employees who were members of the Communist Party, news organizations reprinted the statement without further corroboration. The news coverage destroyed lives and reputations, despite the fact that McCarthy had no such list nor was he ever able to produce one. Journalists learned that facts, what people say, and truth are not always closely connected. From that point forward, political journalists emphatically did not want to repeat the mistake.

Washington, D.C., Bureau Chief Bill Adair, *Tampa Bay Times,* who came to the nations' capitol in 1997 during the era when acid political rhetoric and partisan shilling were gaining a national platform on cable television and becoming more and more common in Congress, did have a journalist's instinct for truth. More than that, he felt professionally compelled to help his readers distinguish among political claims, no matter who was making them, and discoverable facts. It was in this context that he developed the Web site PolitiFact.com, which was initially supported by his newspaper, the *Tampa Bay Times* (formerly the *St. Petersburg Times*) and produced in conjunction with *Congressional Quarterly.*

Fact checking itself is not new. The *New Yorker* magazine earned much of its journalistic reputation for its fact checking: a not-always-perfect process where a separate group of journalists checked the facts in *New Yorker* stories before they were printed. What made PolitiFact distinct—and memorable and marketable, according to Adair (personal communication 2012)—was the invention of the Truth-O-Meter, a visual representation of whether a statement was completely true to "pants on fire," a reference to the chant many Americans grow up with: "liar, liar, pants on fire."

When PolitiFact.com researched the truth behind political statements, it ranked them, from truthful, to mostly true, to mostly false, to whoppers. Adair believes it was the Truth-O-Meter that separated his fact checking site from many others. His own research shows that most readers look at the Truth-O-Meter first; many do not investigate further into the actual reporting and analysis that fuels the individual ranking.

Other elements also separated PolitiFact.com from its competitors. Beginning in 2009, the site awarded the "Lie of the Year" which, that year, went to former Alaska governor Sarah Palin for her utterly mendacious statement that the Patient Protection and Affordable Care Act would lead to death panels deciding whether elderly Americans would live or die. In 2011, the "Lie of the Year" went to the Democratic National Committee for its statement—carried in political ads as well as new stories—that the Republican budget approved by the U.S. House of Representatives would repeal Medicare. The Web site has fact-checked sketch comedy (*Saturday Night Live*) and Jon Stewart—himself a fact checker of some repute. Adair says that he does not pay attention to whether one political party or the other is found to be lying more often (as some studies have shown), but that the site is even-handed in selecting claims to be checked. PolitiFact.com is potent enough that those who are accused of lying—or even not telling the complete truth—contest its claims in the media, often vociferously.

And, in an era when Web site hits matter in terms of revenue, Adair is also forthright about the impact of Truth-O-Meter on the site's popularity and hence profitability. When this book went to press, PolitiFact.com was carried by nine different newspapers, and it had imitators as prominent as the *Washington Post*'s Fact Checker which uses a graphic of Pinocchio's nose to visually illustrate the extent of the lie involved.

The *St. Petersburg Times* and PolitiFact.com were awarded the Pulitzer Prize for national reporting in 2009, for "its fact-checking initiative during the 2008 presidential campaign that used probing reporters and the power of the World Wide Web to examine more than 750 political claims, separating rhetoric from truth to enlighten voters."

Micro Issues

1. Is what PolitiFact.com does reporting? Is it objective reporting?
2. How would you evaluate the truthfulness of the Truth-O-Meter?
3. Why is the truthfulness of a statement examined in a separate news story instead of becoming part of continuing coverage? Is this approach ethically defensible?

Midrange Issues

1. Should individual journalists be responsible for checking the political claims of public officials, or is that job best left to "fact checkers" and Web sites such as PolitiFact.com?
2. Should there be a parallel Web site to check the claims of commercial messages? What would be the ethical rationale for such a site?
3. Adair has said that he believes the site would not be as successful without the Truth-O-Meter, even though he acknowledges that truth is often more subtle than a simple rating would indicate. Do such sites need a gimmick to cut through the clutter of political speech today? Can such gimmicks be ethically justified?

Macro Issues

1. Based on the theories of truth outlined in Chapter 2, what is the standard of truth PolitiFact.com employs? What are the dangers and benefits of employing this standard as opposed to others?
2. Evaluate this statement by James W. Carey in light of the efforts of PolitiFact.com: "There is no such thing as a fact without context."
3. Provide an ethical rationale for "fact checking" *Saturday Night Live* or *The Daily Show.*

CASE 6-B

WikiLeaks

LEE WILKINS
University of Missouri

In her book about secrets, ethicist Sissela Bok maintains that there are only two professions that regard keeping secrets as morally questionable at the outset: psychiatrists and journalists. Had she written the book about three decades later, Bok would at least have had to consider one additional, if nontraditional profession: computer hackers.

Australian-native Julian Assange, who describes his profession as hacker, has made the assertion multiple times that secret keeping, when done by nation-states, is bad. Assange means this characterization in a moral/ethical sense. Thus, in 2005 and 2006, he created an organization—his title there was CEO and editor—that had the goal of releasing of state secrets that were leaked to the nonprofit group.

While Assange was interested in all secrets, he was particularly interested in those kept by the most powerful nation on earth and its allies: the United States. In those early years, Assange began e-mailing the British publication *the Guardian* with unsolicited tips that led *the Guardian* to some remarkable stories, among them the Kroll report which detailed how former Kenyan president Danile Arap Moi had stashed hundreds of thousands of pounds in foreign bank accounts—a story of political corruption most news organizations would have been proud to publish.

Assange first came to media attention in the United States in 2010 when WikiLeaks published the video footage of Iranian civilians, including journalists working for Reuters, being gunned down by a United States Apache helicopter. The U.S. military had denied this version of events, and continued to do so until the video emerged. The resulting news coverage, coming as it did when the U.S. was bogged down in what became a decade-long conflict, catapulted Assange to international media attention.

But, Assange had a great deal more information to offer. In 2010, WikiLeaks published more than 400,000 documents—everything from raw reports of foreign service officers to military accounts of specific incidents—about the U.S. prosecution of war in Iran and Afghanistan. Collectively called the war logs, these documents and their release raised central ethical questions for news organizations.

Those questions began with how individual news organizations cooperated with Assange in the release and verification of the documents. In addition to *the Guardian,* the *New York Times* and the German publication *Der Spiegel* entered into collaborative arrangements with Assange that allowed the individual news organizations to verify the facts in the documents and, when necessary—for example, when life might be at stake—to redact elements of the documents (most often names and locations) in news accounts.

These collaborative arrangements were unprecedented, in part because they involved multiple news organizations and were international in scope, and, in part, because these documents—unlike the Pentagon Papers which had set the standard for leaks that questioned the U.S. government's international political policies— were about events that were ongoing and had the potential to upset or even end decades of diplomatic efforts. In addition, Assange himself proved exceptionally difficult to work with (Leigh and Harding 2011). He was often impossible to contact, unreliable in terms of keeping agreements and, by 2011, was embroiled in a criminal sex scandal in Sweden.

The various collaborative arrangements Assange developed with news organizations, particularly the *New York Times,* fell apart in the months after the publication of the war logs. Ultimately, Assange placed the documents—unredacted and unverified—on the Web. In April 2011, WikiLeaks began publishing secret files about the prisoners in the notorious Guantanamo Bay prison camp. How journalists treated all these files became the focus of one element of the ethical debate surrounding this complicated series of events.

A second focus of ethical debate was how WikiLeaks obtained its information. WikiLeaks did no independent reporting. Instead it relied on others to provide "leaked" information. In the case of the war logs, that source was 23-year-old Bradley Manning, an army private who, as of this writing, is on trial in a military court on a variety of charges, one of which carries the death penalty although prosecutors did not seek it.

After Manning's arrest, it was widely reported that the private had an access to classified information in his role as a communications specialist, that he was bright, interested in technology and computers from an early age, and gay at a time when the U.S. military still operated under the policy of "don't ask, don't tell." Service men and women who "came out" were dishonorably discharged. As more details about Manning emerged, WikiLeaks critics questioned whether Assange had taken advantage of a vulnerable young man who did not understand the magnitude of the charges that could be leveled against him and would lack the personal resources to amount a vigorous defense if his role in the war logs were discovered.

Finally, there was Assange himself, a complex, mercurial figure even before the war logs were released. Assange was concerned about whether powerful governments—particularly the United States—would extradite him to the United States to face a multiplicity of charges emerging from his role in the release of classified documents.

Micro Issues

1. Is Assange a journalist? A hacker? An information intermediary? A whistle-blower? In an ethical sense, does his occupation matter?
2. Sophisticated news organizations entered into agreements with Assange before they published documents. Based on an ethical analysis, what should those agreements have focused on? Why?
3. When presented with documents such as those in the war logs, what specific steps should news organizations take to confirm them? Does this include asking government officials to verify or explain the contents?
4. How should news organizations treat both WikiLeaks and Manning? After you have reviewed coverage, how would you evaluate the journalists' relationship with these two sources?

Midrange Issues

1. At one point, Assange hid in *Guardian* reporter David Leigh's house. Is this an appropriate thing for a journalist deeply involved in the story to do for a source? Does your answer change if Leigh were a documentary filmmaker?
2. How would you respond to the previous questions if the leaked documents came not from government but from a private, for-profit organization such as a chemical or pharmaceutical firm?
3. In an ethical sense, contrast the process of "going under cover" from publishing leaks.
4. Strategic communication professionals often have access to corporate strategy documents and similar sorts of information. Evaluate whether strategic communication professionals have the same sort of whistle-blower responsibility as those who uncover government wrongdoing.
5. Does Assange's personal character matter in how a journalist or new organization should evaluate his actions?

Macro Issues

1. What role do organizations like WikiLeaks fulfill in democratic societies? How is that role like and unlike that of news organizations?
2. Governments frequently claim that some of what they do needs to remain secret to be effective. Evaluate this claim from the perspective of a citizen, a journalist and, a diplomat.

CASE 6-C

Control Room: Do Culture and History Matter in Reporting News?

LEE WILKINS
University of Missouri

Almost a decade before the 2011 Arab Spring, there was al-Jazeera, a fledgling Middle Eastern television network with 40 million viewers predominantly in that region. (In the current day, al-Jazeera includes a staff in Washington, D.C., and the network itself is available worldwide including a strong cable and Internet presence.)

Journalists routinely cite the expression that "Truth is the first casualty of war", but those in charge of al-Jazeera also know that modern war cannot be waged without an intense propaganda effort on all sides of the conflict. Thus, when the United States was getting ready to invade Baghdad, director Jehane Noujaim requested and received permission to film the work of al-Jazeera journalists as they covered the conflict. The 86-minute film entitled *Control Room* won numerous awards.

Noujaim said that his goal was to produce a documentary about how truth is gathered, delivered and ultimately created by those who deliver it. By telling the story of the coverage of the Iraqi invasion through the eyes of Arab journalists— many of whom had worked for news organizations such as the BBC before they worked for al-Jazeera—the documentary provides an insider's view of how journalists report a complicated story, often questioning the conventional wisdom of one or both sides involved.

One focus of the film is Captain Josh Rushing, a military public information officer, who is shown trying to explain the American side of the story to the al-Jazeera journalists. Rushing maintains that Iraq has weapons of mass destruction, that the Iraq invasion was not an attempt by the United States to capture oil resources and to—from his point of view—provide a truthful account of these early days of the conflict. The film also shows the journalists questioning Rushing's facts, asking him to provide proof of what he says. For his part, Rushing says that he believes that the al-Jazeera journalists are biased toward the regime of Saddam Hussein and uses as evidence to support that view, noting that al-Jazeera did not document the atrocities that regime perpetrated on Iraqi citizens.

Other element of the film are tough to watch. They include footage of injured and dead Iraqis who died as the result of U.S. bombing as it invaded the country. Also included are images of U.S. prisoners of war as they are questioned by Iraqi troops. Journalists working for al-Jazeera are shown debating what they should show in terms of gory images. And, the journalists from al-Jazeera are also shown discussing their personal opinions of American foreign policy that led to the invasion—they opposed it—and their belief that the American public will demand that the U.S. government embark on a course other than invasion. The impact of images is also debated in the film—particularly the colliding of images about Israel with public opinion in the Middle East and how the images of Israeli aggression are linked to U.S. foreign policy and this particular decision to invade Iraq.

The film also shows U.S. officials, from the Secretary of Defense Donald Rumsfeld to former Vice President Dick Cheney, claiming that al-Jazeera journalists were lying and their network's coverage was entirely propagandistic. These segments are juxtaposed against al-Jazeera journalists saying that they define their role as showing the human side of war. Interspersed are actual images from al-Jazeera broadcasts that include interviews and press conference footage from former President George W. Bush—coverage the network broadcast that was vociferously criticized by Middle Eastern governments. The network was equally harshly criticized—predominantly by American officials—for broadcasting the images of American POW's. Journalists from al-Jazeera are asked if they can be objective about the conflict; those same journalists ask American correspondents the same question. Rushing himself notes that al-Jazeera's coverage is powerful precisely because U.S. news organizations were not showing these images domestically.

The film also shows the shock of the al-Jazeera journalists as Bagdad is overthrown. And, the biggest emotional punch of the film comes when one al-Jazeera journalist who elected to stay in Bagdad to report on the invasion is killed in a U.S. airstrike on the hotel in which hundreds of journalists were staying. The United States says the airstrike was a mistake; journalists from many nations disputed this claim. Through it all, the film documents the journalists doing what they believe is their job under difficult physical and emotional conditions.

After you have seen the film, respond to the following questions:

Micro Issues

1. How do you think the journalists working for al-Jazeera define their jobs? Is their definition of journalism different from your own?
2. How do you think the public information office for the military defines his role? How do you see his role as supporting or impeding the work of gathering the news? Would you say the same thing about the public information officer for your local police department or public health department?
3. Contrast the public statements by government officials about al-Jazeera during this era of history with the statements made about the network during the Arab Spring. What do you think has led to this change in public perception about the network?

Midrange Issues

1. Should U.S. television networks have shown the same sort of footage about the invasion as al-Jazeera? Justify your decision in terms of the institutional role of the media in a democracy.
2. Al-Jazeera journalists were not embedded with U.S. troops during the invasion. How might the process of embedding have changed coverage, both for embedded and nonembedded journalists?
3. The head of al-Jazeera says, "I have plans for my children. I will send them to America to study, and they will stay there." Rushing says that he believes his role is to promote understanding between the Western and the Arab cultures. Evaluate both these statements in light of ethical theory.

Macro Issues

1. What is the difference between propaganda and news in wartime?
2. Are there certain journalistic values that cross culture and language?
3. What are common frustrations—regardless of employer—that the journalists in the film appear to share?
4. You are being asked to evaluate this film about a decade after it was first produced. Knowing what you now know about recent political history, evaluate the job that al-Jazeera did in covering the Iraq invasion. Evaluate the job that American journalists did.

CASE 6-D

Victims and the Press

ROBERT LOGAN
National Institute of Medicine, Washington, D.C.

Alice Waters' daughter, Julie, seven, has leukemia. Her illness was diagnosed in its early stages in March 2000. Julie's physicians believe her condition can be successfully treated.

Ms. Waters, 37, lives in a mobile home in an unincorporated area a few miles from Metroplex, a city of 1.5 million. Ms. Waters' street is the only residential section in the area. At the north end of the street—which has 12 mobile homes on each side facing one another—are four large gas stations that catch traffic off the interstate that runs a quarter mile away to the west. At the south end of the street (about a quarter mile away) are two large tanks that are a relatively small storage facility for Big Oil, Inc. Next to this—starting almost in her backyard—is the boundary of a successful, 700-acre grapefruit orchard, which borders on a municipal landfill. About a quarter mile away are large well fields that are the principal source of drinking water for Metroplex.

In July 1999, a 6-year-old boy in the household two doors down from Ms. Waters was diagnosed as having leukemia. He was not as lucky as Julie; his diagnosis was late in the progression of his disease, and he died in December 2000. In 2001, an infant girl became the second baby born with birth defects in the neighborhood within seven years. Both families moved before Ms. Waters came to the neighborhood in 1999. Internal medicine specialists Dr. Earnest and Dr. Sincere met Julie soon after she was admitted to the hospital in October 2000. They were instrumental in getting funding for Julie's care when her mother was unable to pay. They are members of Worried M.D.s for Social Responsibility, a self-proclaimed liberal, national public interest group that gets actively involved in national political issues.

The physicians told Ms. Waters that they were suspicious about the causes of Julie's illness. Three cancer and birth-defect incidents on the same street, the physicians said, were not a coincidence.

In November 2001, they began to collect water samples from the wellhead at Ms. Waters' house. They sent the samples to a well-regarded testing lab in another city. Since then, they have tested the water at a professional lab every four months.

Every test revealed traces of more than 10 human-made and natural chemicals often associated with oil storage tanks, pesticides, grapefruit orchards, gas station leaks, lead from automobile emissions and a large landfill.

However, each chemical occurs consistently at 6 to 15 parts per billion, which is considered safe for drinking water based on standards set by the U.S. Environmental Protection Agency (EPA). At higher levels these chemicals are associated with carcinogenic risks or increases in birth defects, but the levels found at Ms. Waters' wellhead are within safety thresholds set by the EPA. There is no evidence the chemicals are associated directly with the health problems found in Ms. Waters' neighborhood.

At a fund-raising party last night for mayoral candidate Sam Clean, Drs. Earnest and Sincere privately told Clean what they had found. Clean is a well-known public figure, has a reputation as an environmentalist, owns a successful health food restaurant chain, is media wise and looks good on television. He is a long shot to become mayor and needs fresh issues to draw attention to his candidacy.

At 11:00 a.m. today, KAOS news radio begins running as the top story in its 20-minute news rotation "Clean Attacks City Lack of Cleanup." In the story, Clean gives a sound bite attacking city officials for "ignoring cancer-causing agents in water in a neighborhood where children have died, which is next door to the city's water supply." He describes the neighborhood's medical problems and describes (without naming) Julie and Alice Waters. The news report explains that water from the neighborhood has several "toxic agents believed to cause cancer at higher levels" and points out that the city's water wells are within a quarter mile of oil tanks, gas stations, a grapefruit orchard, a landfill and septic tanks. County officials are said to be unavailable for comment. The report runs throughout the day at 20-minute intervals.

By 2:30 p.m., calls to the switchboard have jammed the newsroom. The callers who get through are frightened about their drinking water. City Hall's switchboards are jammed. The callers sound upset and ask whether their water is safe to drink.

By 4:00 p.m., reporters from the local ABC affiliate are already knocking on doors in the trailer park and sending live reports from the scene. Neighbors tell them where Alice and Julie Waters live.

At 4:15 p.m., your managing editor gives you the story. You are an ambitious reporter for *Metroplex Today*, the only morning newspaper in Metroplex. Both of you realize this is clearly Page 1 potential, but you have only a few hours before deadline for the next morning's edition. After a few phone calls, you discover that the mayor, the city council and most city and county officials are all out of town at a retreat and are unavailable for comment. The regional EPA office is not answering the phone.

A trusted spokesperson for Regional Hospital tells you that Drs. Sincere and Earnest are furious at Clean for releasing the story and have no comment. She fills you in with all of the above information. The same Regional Hospital spokesperson says Ms. Waters does not want to be interviewed. She suddenly realizes that her husband, whom she walked out on several years before, might see the story and return to town.

Sam Clean is more than happy to talk to you.

Micro Issues

1. Is Clean a reliable enough source for KAOS radio to base its reports on?
2. Should KAOS have broadcast the story?
3. Should you respect Ms. Waters's wishes and leave her and her daughter out of the story?
4. Are Dr. Earnest and Dr. Sincere reliable sources?
5. What do you tell the public about whether the water supply is safe?

Midrange Issues

1. Would you be working on the story if KAOS and ABC had ignored it?
2. Would you be working on the story if there was little public reaction after the KAOS broadcast?
3. If Ms. Waters decides to do an interview on ABC later today, do you then include her in your story?
4. If city and county officials remain unavailable, how do you handle their side of the story? Does that delay publication until you can get more information, or do you go with what is available?
5. Are there unbiased sources you can contact about risk assessment? Who?

Macro Issues

1. How do you handle the discrepancy between the information from the EPA and the skeptical scientists and environmentalists?
2. What is the public's probable reaction to reporting this story? Should your newspaper take any precautions to prevent public panic? If so, what should they be?
3. How risky is the water compared to risks we take for granted, such as traveling by car? Can you think of a relevant comparison for your article comparing the relative risk of the water to a well-known risk?
4. Is it the media's role to speak for a society that is averse to many risks? How might the media accomplish this function?

CASE 6-E

For God and Country: The Media and National Security

JEREMY LITTAU
Lehigh University

MARK SLAGLE
University of North Carolina–Chapel Hill

The ethical issues involving the intersection of the media and national security typically revolve around the question of duties and loyalties. Those questions, as the following three-part case demonstrates, are long standing. They also allow journalists to evaluate the consistency of their reasoning over time—something good ethical thinking is supposed to promote. How journalists respond to these cases also may depend on the differing philosophies individual journalists and their news organizations adhere to.

With this introduction, decide each of the following three cases, all of which have an important role in the history of journalism ethics. As you resolve the various issues in each case, ask yourself whether you have been consistent in your decision making and what philosophical approach or approaches best supports your thinking.

Case Study 1: The Bay of Pigs

In 1961, an anti-communist paramilitary force trained and supplied by the CIA was preparing to invade Cuba and topple Fidel Castro. Although the desire of the American government to overthrow Castro was no secret, the specifics of the invasion plan were not known to the public. On April 6, a *New York Times* reporter filed a story with his editors that declared the invasion was "imminent." The paper prepared to run the story with a page-one, four-column slot using the word "imminent" in the text and the headline.

After much discussion, *Times* managing editor Turner Catledge and publisher Orvil Dryfoos decided to remove the word "imminent" from the story and shrink the headline to a single column. These changes were made, in part, in response to a phone call from President John F. Kennedy, asking the paper to kill the story. On April 17, the anti-Castro forces landed at Cuba's Bay of Pigs, where all group members were either taken prisoner or killed. The botched invasion was a major embarrassment for Kennedy, who later told Catledge that if the *Times* had run the story as planned it might have prevented the disastrous invasion (Hickey 2001).

Micro Issue

1. Did the *Times* act ethically in downsizing and downplaying the story?

Midrange Issue

1. Are there certain categories of information, for example troop movements or the development of new weapons, that journalists as a matter of policy should either downplay or not publish as all?

Macro Issue

1. How should journalists respond if government officials request that specific "facts" (that are not true) be printed as part of a disinformation campaign to confuse our enemies?

Case Study 2: Osama Bin Laden

Since the attacks of Sept. 11, 2001 until his death at the hands of the U.S. military in 2012, Osama bin Laden and his deputies released a series of video and audio tapes containing speeches about their ongoing operations. Many of them have first aired on al-Jazeera, the Arab-language news channel that broadcasts in the Middle East but also can be received in many American and European markets. The U.S. government, specifically President George W. Bush, urged the U.S. media not to rebroadcast these tapes, arguing that they might contain coded messages to al-Quaeda "sleeper cells" and could result in more attacks. Most broadcast networks acquiesced to the request, although it was never made clear whether any of the tapes, in fact, contained such messages (Spencer 2001).

Micro Issue

1. How is this request like and unlike President Kennedy's request to the *New York Times?*

Midrange Issues

1. Does the fact that other news agencies in other countries broadcast the tapes have any bearing on what U.S. broadcasters should do?
2. Should U.S. broadcasters have agreed to this request in October of 2001? Should they agree to the request today? Why or why not?

Macro Issue

1. How would you respond to a viewer who says that broadcasting the tapes is unpatriotic and puts American lives at risk?

Case Study 3: Make News, Not War?

In 1991 CNN correspondent Christiane Amanpour arrived in the Balkans to cover the breakaway of Slovenia and Croatia from Yugoslavia. After witnessing several brutal battles, including the siege of Dubrovnik, she moved on to Bosnia to cover the hostilities there for almost two years. Troubled by the lack of coverage the war was receiving, Amanpour encouraged her editors to devote more time to the issue. In 1994, Amanpour appeared via satellite on a live television broadcast with President Bill Clinton. She asked the president if "the constant flip-flops of your administration on the issue of Bosnia set a very dangerous precedent." Amanpour's pointed questions embarrassed the administration and generated more coverage of the war and of American foreign policy. Amanpour later admitted she wanted to draw more attention to the plight of the Bosnian Muslims (Halberstam 2001).

Micro Issues

1. Should Amanpour consciously have tried to influence U.S. foreign policy in this way?
2. If she had not tried to influence U.S. policy, would she have been complicit in the genocide that followed?

Midrange Issues

1. Are some issues, such as genocide, so ethically reprehensible that journalists should speak out as citizens in addition to fulfilling their professional responsibilities?
2. Is it appropriate for journalists to testify at war crimes trials when they have witnessed and reported on atrocities?

Macro Issues

1. Is it naive for journalists to continue to say that "we just let readers make up their minds" on these issues? If you answer yes, what does that say about the ethical dilemmas that come with the power we have as journalists?
2. Media theorist Marshall McLuhan predicted more than a half-century ago that wars of the future would be fought with images rather than bullets. How true has that prediction become in the ongoing war on terror?

CASE 6-F

Mayor Jim West's Computer

GINNY WHITEHOUSE
Eastern Kentucky University

The quiet, conservative city of Spokane, Wash., woke up to a surprise on Thursday, May 5, 2005, as residents opened their newspapers. They discovered that Mayor Jim West had used his city computer to solicit young men in gay chat rooms and that two men claimed West had sexually molested them as children.

In the months prior, West had been e-chatting on Gay.com with someone he believed to be an 18-year-old recent high school graduate, and offered him a city hall internship, sports memorabilia, help getting into college and excursions around the country. In reality, he had been corresponding with a forensic computer expert hired by the *Spokesman-Review.*

Reporter Bill Morlin had spent two years along with Reporter Karen Dorn Steele tracking down allegations from the 1970s that West had sexually molested boys while he was a county sheriff's deputy and a Boy Scout leader. West had been close friends with fellow deputy David Hahn and fellow Scout leader George Robey, who both committed suicide after sexual abuse allegations were brought against them in the early 1980s.

In 2002, the reporters discovered links to West while investigating abuse by local Catholic priests. West was at that time Republican majority leader in the Washington state senate and was considering running for what he called his "dream job"—being mayor of his hometown, Spokane. During the campaign, the reporters did not believe they had enough information to confirm any allegations. Eventually, they received tips from both anonymous sources and sources who would later go on the record and swear in depositions that West had abused them. One man, Robert Galliher, said West molested him at least four times as a child and that he was assaulted repeatedly by Hahn. Galliher, who says he has struggled with drug addiction as a result of the molestations, said he was in prison in 2003 when West visited him and sent him a message to keep his mouth shut. In addition, other young men reported that they had had sex with West after meeting him on gay chat lines and had been offered favors and rewards.

Spokesman-Review Editor Steven Smith and his staff spent days agonizing over creating a fictional character to go online at Gay.com and consulted with ethics experts at the Poynter Institute and elsewhere as they considered options. Smith told Spokane readers that the newspaper would not ordinarily go to such lengths or use deception, "But the seriousness of the allegations and the need for specific computer forensic skills overrode our general reluctance." Most important, Smith said the *Spokesman-Review*'s decisions were based on concerns about abuse of power and pedophilia, and not whether the mayor was homosexual.

The forensic expert, who previously worked for the U.S. Customs Office, followed strict guidelines. The expert posed online as a 17-year-old Spokane high school student and waited for West to approach him. The expert did not initiate conversations about sex, sexuality or the mayor's office. In the months that followed, the high school student supposedly had an 18th birthday. West then requested meetings with the fictional young man and arrived in a new Lexus at an agreed-upon spot—a golf course. His picture was taken secretly and the forensic expert broke off contact.

West was told about the forensic investigator in an interview with *Spokesman-Review* staff the day before the story broke. He admitted to the offers made within the chat room but denied abusing or having sex with anyone under age 18. When asked about the abuse allegations from the two men, West told the *Spokesman-Review* editors and reporters, "I didn't abuse them. I don't know these people. I didn't abuse anybody, and I didn't have sex with anybody under 18—ever—woman or man."

West insisted that he had not abused his office and that he was not gay. After the story broke, local gay rights advocate Ryan Oelrich, a former member of the city's Human Rights Commission, told the newspaper that he had resigned after coming to the conclusion West appointed him in an effort to pursue a sexual relationship. Oelrich said West offered him at one point $300 to swim naked with him in his swimming pool. Oelrich declined.

A conservative Republican, West blocked antidiscrimination provisions in housing for homosexuals, and voted against health benefits for gay couples while he served in the Washington state legislature and as mayor. He supported legislation barring homosexuals from working in schools or day care centers and called for bans on gay marriage. He told "The Today Show" that he was merely representing his constituents' views.

West asserted a message that he would repeat eventually on CNN, MSNBC and in a host of other national broadcasts: "There is a strong wall between my public and my private life."

Many political scientists disagreed with West's interpretation. Washington State University Political Science Professor Lance LeLoup said using an elected position for personal benefit is both unethical and "a misuse of power." Gonzaga University Political Science Professor Blaine Garvin told the *Spokesman-Review*, "I think it's a pretty bright line that you don't use your command over public resources to earn personal favors. That's not what those resources are for."

At the same time, some media critics criticized the newspaper's choice to use deception. The public cannot be expected to believe journalists and the veracity of their stories if lies are told to get at information, said Jane Kirtley, director of the Silha Center for Media Ethics and Law at the University of Minnesota. Speaking at a Washington News Council Forum on the *Spokesman-Review*'s coverage, Kirtley asserted that police officers can practice deception as part of their jobs, but journalists should not.

"It's one thing for the police or the FBI to pose as a 17-year-old boy," William Babcock, journalism department chair at California State University–Long Beach, told the *Seattle Post-Intelligencer.* "It's another for a journalist to take on the role of junior G-man and do something that essentially is considered police work." Babcock insists that the *Spokesman-Review* should have gotten the information through traditional reporting methods, but he agreed that no one, particularly a city mayor, should expect privacy in an online chat room.

Poytner Ethicist Kelly McBride, who previously was a reporter at the *Spokesman-Review,* said deception should not be normal practice but that the newspaper considered key ethical obligations: that the issue is grave and in the public interest, alternatives are explored, the decision and practice are openly shared with readers and the mayor is given the opportunity to share his story.

Jeffrey Weiss, a religion reporter for the *Dallas Morning News,* said he rarely believes the ends should justify the means, "but some do."

The FBI investigated West on federal corruption charges but did not find his actions warranted prosecution. Special Counsel Mark Barlett said in a media conference, "Our investigation did not address whether Jim West's activities were ethical, moral, or appropriate. . . . We did not attempt to determine whether Jim West should be the mayor of Spokane."

In December 2005, Spokane voters ousted the mayor in a special recall election. West later said the newspaper had created a "mob mentality" and that considering the accusations, even he would have voted against himself. On July 22, 2006, West died following surgery for colon cancer, a disease he had been fighting for three years. He was 55.

Micro Issues

1. Do you agree that police officers are ethically permitted to use deception but journalists are not?
2. Was the *Spokesman-Review* justified in using deception? Under other what extreme circumstances do you believe deception might be justified?

Midrange Issues

1. Some critics claimed that West's story would come out only in a provincial, conservative community, and that his story would not have been news had he been the mayor of Chicago or Miami. Do you agree?
2. Sissela Bok says deception might be permitted if the act passes the test of publicity. Does the *Spokesman-Review* meet that standard?
3. Should the use of a forensic computer expert in this case be characterized as the ends justifying the means? Why or why not?

Macro Issues

1. Should there be a wall between the public and private lives of public officials? At what point do public officials' private lives become public concern? Is public officials' sexuality always part of their private lives?

2. The *Spokesman-Review* is locally owned by the Cowles Publishing Company. The family business includes a downtown mall with a parking garage, which was developed in financial partnership with the city of Spokane. The garage has been subject to repeated lawsuits and controversy. Some critics believed that the *Spokesman-Review*'s delay in reporting about the mayor was due to a conflict of interest. Editor Steve Smith insists that the story was reported as the facts became evident. How do locally owned media companies manage covering their own communities without incurring conflicts of interest?

7

Media Economics: The Deadline Meets the Bottom Line

By the end of this chapter, you should be familiar with:

- the economic realities of the social responsibility theory of the press.
- the economic and legislative initiatives that have combined to place control of information in the hands of fewer and larger corporations.
- how various mediums have coped with the current economic and technological realities of media.
- the "stakeholder" theory of economic success.

INTRODUCTION

"I think the biggest challenge my generation is going to face is to convince people my own age that news is worth paying for. We've never done it."
STUDENT, UNIVERSITY OF MISSOURI SCHOOL OF JOURNALISM

In the summer of 2009, one of the nation's leading media companies, the *Washington Post,* tarnished its reputation with an idea quickly labeled "pay for play" by critics. In a story broken by Politico.com., the *Post* printed a brochure advertising a series of *Washington Post* "salons" where for the price of $25,000 interested parties could spend an evening with lobbyists, lawmakers and White House officials, along with *Post* reporters. The salons—which were canceled within days of the revelation of the idea—were to be held in the home of *Post* publisher Katharine Weymouth and the conversations led by the editor of the *Post.* The first proposed session was to be on health care.

Critics came from everywhere. White House press secretary Robert Gibbs joked at a press conference that he might not be able to afford to take a question from a *Post* reporter. Weymouth, who had been on the job for only 17 months with no prior newsroom experience, took the blame after initial releases blamed the marketing department for issuing an unapproved brochure. She wrote a front-page apology.

The media firestorm was reminiscent of the *L.A. Times*/Staples Center scandal (see the case study later in this book) where that paper became a financial partner of the new downtown arena at the same time it was covering the opening with a special section. Reporters for that paper were taken by surprise by the financial arrangement, just as the *Post* newsroom knew nothing of the proposed salons until the story broke on a Web site founded by ex-*Post* writers. Another similarity in the two scandals is that in each case the problem arose on the watch of a new publisher with no formal journalism background.

Within a week, the salon affair became just one more anecdote to be added to newspaper closings and mass layoffs to reveal an industry in peril. About a decade earlier, newspapers had jumped to the Web with no real financial model other than the hope that advertising would eventually catch up, and customers were resisting any retroactive attempt to pay for news content they were habituated to enjoying for free. Only the *Wall Street Journal* seemed capable of holding the line on charging readers for content. In one of the ironies of the situation, industry surveys have shown that more readers than ever before were going to a "newspaper" for information, but most of them were Web readers paying nothing for the service. And since most newspapers were part of chains and those chains part of media conglomerates, the perils of the daily paper threatened even the few healthy parts of the media economy.

The *Post* controversy is a microcosm of the problems facing the industry today, but the issue, in some form or another has been around since the "payola" scandals of the 1950s that resulted in congressional hearings and fines for subsequent offenders who took money to put recordings on the air.

Today's media are in a financial meltdown, a problem that began with the newspaper industry but in many ways it has migrated to television and to the advertising industry. In 2009, the magazine industry appeared to be taking the brunt of the financial changes with industry standards such as *Newsweek* shedding both pages and staff while other venerable publications, such as *Gourmet* and *PC Magazine,* closed entirely. Indeed, the only circulation growth in the magazine industry was in celebrity and gossip magazines.

But whether the communications channel was newspapers, magazines or television, the financial strain affected and is affected by the government's news organizations cover, the stockholders those same organizations answer to and the bureaucracies that makes the rules. In this chapter we will look at one theory that has guided the press for more than half a century and then look at how individual media are fulfilling their promise envisioned by the theorists. We will then conclude with an alternate view of accountability in the new millennium.

A LEGACY OF RESPONSIBILITY

The *social responsibility theory of the press* was developed in the 1940s by a panel of scholars, the Hutchins Commission, with funding from Henry Luce, the conservative founder of *Time* magazine. The social responsibility theory envisioned a day when an active recipient of news and information was satisfied by a socially responsible press. According to the Hutchins Commission, media have the following five functions in society:

1. To provide a truthful, comprehensive and intelligent account of the day's events in a context that gives them meaning.
2. To serve as a forum for exchange of comment and criticism.
3. To provide a representative picture of constituent groups in society.
4. To present and clarify the goals and values of society.
5. To provide citizens with full access to the day's intelligence.

But social responsibility theory has a fundamental flaw: it gives little attention to modern media economics. This omission occurred in part because multinational corporations and chain ownership were still on the horizon when the Hutchins Commission worked. Because the theory was developed early in the McCarthy period, there was also an unwillingness to link economic and political power for fear of being labeled Marxist. This omission means that *the social responsibility theory does not deal with the realities of concentrated economic power,* particularly in an era when information has become a valuable commodity.

As the mass media became enormous, economically powerful institutions, they joined what political scientist C. Wright Mills (1956) called the "power elite," a ruling class within a democratic society. Time has proved Mills right. Power is found not only in the halls of government but also on Wall Street. And power is found not only in money or armies, it is also found in information. Media organizations, precisely because they have become multinational corporations engaged in the information business, are deeply involved in this power shift.

Today the media are predominantly corporate owned and publicly traded, with media conglomerates among the largest (and until recently, the most profitable) of the world's corporations. The corporate owners of the average news operation are more insulated from contact with news consumers than virtually any other business owner in America. And, there are fewer of them. Most local media outlets in the world are owned by six multinational corporations and each has become increasingly large in an attempt to gain market efficiencies.

This emergence of media as economic and political power brokers leads to the question of how a powerful institution such as the mass media, which traditionally has had the political role of checking other powerful institutions, can be checked. Can the watchdog be trusted when it is inexorably entwined with the institutions it is watching? For instance, when a media outlet is owned by a corporation such as General Electric, can it cover the health care debate objectively when the parent company might have a stake in the outcome through inventions and patents?

Similarly, what news organization can be trusted to take a critical look at the Federal Communications Commission's consideration of loosening the ownership rules when the conglomerate that owns individual outlets stands to profit from the changes? As media corporations expand in the pursuit of profit, who will watch the watchdog? Perhaps as important, who will watch the new kids on the block, Google and Facebook, both of which have "projects" that include news and both of which also attempt to monetize every hit.

When the social responsibility theory was framed in the 1940s, the primary informational concern was scarcity: people might not get the information they needed for citizenship, and until recently, government agencies such as the FCC were still basing policy decisions on the scarcity argument when any consumer with cable or a satellite dish knew otherwise. Today, however, the primary informational concern is an overabundance of raw data: people might not filter out what they need through all the clutter. Media and their distribution systems changed, but the theory remained silent, especially about the role of profit.

The clash of large, well-financed institutions for control of information is a modern phenomenon. Classical ethical theory, which speaks to individual acts, is of little help in sorting out the duties and responsibilities of corporations larger than most nations that control the currency of the day: information. Americans are unwilling to accept government as the solution to counter the concentrated economic power of the media, and government has been hesitant to break up the large media conglomerates. Europeans have taken a different view, in many cases using tax dollars to support a government-controlled broadcast system. In some cases, such as the Scandinavian countries, tax dollars also support newspapers—with the goal of sustaining multiple, distinct voices in the public sphere (Picard 1988).

HYPER-COMPETITION AND ITS IMPACT ON NEWS

Legacy journalists, those journalists who did not come of age as "digital natives," and the news organizations that employ them face a huge shift in the assumptions about what makes news media profitable and praiseworthy. Legacy journalism emerged from an era of low-to-moderate economic competition. Even though specific rivalries were often intense, they were local and definitely not across media platforms. Individual organizations competed for consumer satisfaction and time, consumer spending, content, advertisers and employees. More than 15 years ago, media scholar Steve Lacy (1989) predicted these low-to-moderate competitive environments would produce a quality news product based on individual organizations' financial commitment to news, which in turn was perceived useful by audience members and sustained by a journalistic culture that valued excellence and public service.

But, low-to-moderate competition no longer exists in the contemporary media marketplace. Instead, you now live in an era of hyper-competition, much of it provided by Web access. In hyper-competition, *supply substantially exceeds demand so that a large percentage of the producers in the market operate at a financial loss.* Classical economic theory holds that hyper-competition cannot exist permanently. However, news and information are not traditional economic commodities; they are called "experience and credence" commodities, meaning that a consumer cannot judge whether the product actually meets his or her individual needs until he or she has invested in and spent time with the product. News also is linked to social welfare, a category of products with significant external values not readily captured by price point or profit margin.

Media economists Ann Hollifield and Lee Becker, based on evidence collected in multiple nations as well as the United States, suggest that the current media marketplace is a hyper-competitive one (Hollifield and Becker 2009). The results are predictable.

First, markets fragment. Just a look at the titles of magazines that have recently closed gives you a glimpse of how fragmented the market can get in the chase for just the right demographic. Recent examples include *Travel and Leisure Golf, Domino,* a home magazine named "Launch of the Year" by *Ad Age* just three years before magazine conglomerate Condé Naste closed it, *Plenty,* a magazine for those interested in green living that lasted five years, and finally *SI Latino,* a product of *Sports Illustrated* that had a circulation of 500,000 at the time of its close. What all these magazines had in common was a large parent company trying to find success in smaller, more targeted issues.

Fragmenting markets drive down profits because access to everything from advertisers to readers/viewers to workers declines. As profits decline, content quality also declines. News organizations will increasingly implement low-cost strategies. These low-cost strategies will drive down wages for professionals, journalists will have to produce more in less time and with fewer resources and news organizations will begin to rely on unpaid nonprofessionals to provide some content. As competition intensity reaches hyper-competition, profits for most media organization will disappear or nearly disappear.

Hollifield and Becker note that as a result of the financial stress, both news organizations and individual journalists will become more susceptible to influence peddling from such activities as bribery, monetary subsidies, information subsidies and the trading of editorial content for advertising or other sources of revenue. "Hyper-competition unchecked will create conditions that increase the likelihood that journalism ethics will be violated at both the organizations and individual levels" (Hollifield and Becker 2009, 67).

However, industry thinking has traveled in some entirely new directions. From the level of the individual journalist or strategic communication professional to the organizations that employ them, today there are multiple experiments with "new" business models. While it is difficult to categorize them, they share is an attempt to shift the costs of producing and distributing content to the individual listener/reader/viewer rather than to advertisers. New business models are producing some efforts that, just a few decades ago, were seen as an unprofitable backwater or completely ethically forbidden. Documentary films were once a staple of art film houses attracting small audiences. Today, they take on issues of public importance, combining traditional newsgathering efforts with Hollywood-style cinematic techniques. Some are financially successful, and some, such as Josh Fox's *Gasland,* have influenced public policy. Audio documentaries thrive as well in outlets such as NPR, where consumer suggestions are sometimes the starting point for NPR documentaries, a polar opposite of the "agenda setting" role of the press that media theorists wrote about in the latter part of the 20th century.

Other examples are all across the media landscape. The *New York Times* now has an "op doc" section attached to the more traditional opinion page. Some blogs, the home of the amateur opinionator, have become successful enough that they have been purchased by mainstream news organizations, often with little change to content, frequency, etc. from the days before they found financial security. Alternative publications thank advertisers in the body of their news copy. And almost everyone, from the folks who sell you household products to the stodgiest of the "old guard" newsrooms, is experimenting with reader/viewer/listener engagement. From allowing consumers to comment on stories, to pretesting news programming, or developing ad messages, the public now has a say in what "content" is.

The result is what at least one scholar has called "liquid journalism" where "traditional role perceptions of journalism influenced by its occupational ideology—providing a general audience with information of general interest in a balanced, objective and ethical way—do not seem to fit all that well with the lived realities of reporters and editors, nor with the communities they are supposed to serve" (Deuze 2008, 848).

Before you dismiss this as mere theory, think back to the anecdote that opened this chapter. When news organizations, and even individual journalists, worry about their "brand" rather than the public they serve, something essential has changed. Perhaps the most troubling element in this strand of research in media economics is that the public appears not to value—or even sometimes recognize—that quality is declining. In hyper-competitive situations, ethics takes a back seat to survival and the common good becomes the loser in the process.

TELEVISION: CONGLOMERATION, CONSOLIDATION AND SURVIVAL

Television, a medium that began its existence as a free service brought to the public by willing advertisers, has morphed into something that 9 out of 10 Americans now pay for twice—once with their cable or satellite bills and, for most, twice with their attention to advertising. Yet television, particularly at the network or cable level where programming is produced, is always in search of more efficiency and revenue streams.

Take the two entities that are the original television networks: NBC and CBS. In the past decade, both have acquired more assets from publishing houses to cable networks to content distributors. The goal of all this financial activity is not only to find profit centers but also to create vertically integrated companies with diverse sources of income. Consider this scenario:

- By acquiring production facilities, networks can now own the shows they broadcast, a new phenomenon cutting deeply into the old system of buying programs from independent producers who took the risks in order to reap the possible rewards if shows were picked up.
- By acquiring cable stations such as Bravo, networks control outlets for their shows as they go into the lucrative phases of syndication, taking advantage of legislation that ended the FCC's old "fin-syn" rule prohibiting networks from being syndicators.
- By acquiring the maximum number of local television stations owned by law, networks have a built-in advantage for uploading news when it happens in a market where they own a station, something that Rupert Murdoch's Fox brand has perfected even after getting a late start in the market.
- By acquiring the rights to broadcast major and minor sports, amateur and professional alike, both of the traditional two, NBC and CBS, launched their own 24/7 cable sports networks to rival EPSN, which is owned by another traditional network, ABC.
- By acquiring aftermarket distributors, networks make money on rentals and sales of boxed DVD sets of popular series after their original airing. Even series that were closed after two or three seasons find an afterlife in boxed sets.

The result is a pair of companies that have survived in the broadcasting industry for nearly a century and that can now control a product from the filming of the pilot episode to the last airing of the syndicated show or personal download, sometime decades from now. And it must be emphasized that much of what is now possible in the bullet points above has only recently been made possible by FCC and court rulings as well as generous antitrust rulings. And NBC and CBS are but two "legacy" media corporations to have acquired their way to financial success.

Media consolidation allows for a diversification of income. In the case of NBC, after the acquisition of Universal, revenues went from 90 percent advertising-based to 50 percent, with the remainder coming from subscriptions, admissions, licensing and other ancillary income. By weaning away from advertising, media companies have hedged against the vagaries of recession.

Conglomeration, consolidation and the aftermarket added more revenue streams and made things more predictable for stockholders. But not everyone is happy with the direction media ownership is taking. Groups as diverse as the National Organization for Women and the National Rifle Association criticized and challenged recent changes in ownership limits proposed by the FCC. FCC commissioner Michael Copps, in a minority dissent to the loosening of ownership restrictions, called the changes another step in the "Clear Channelization" of American media, a reference to Clear Channel, a media company that had benefited from earlier relaxation of ownership limits in radio, only to become a lightning rod for consumer complaints about nonlocal ownership of radio stations.

Columbia Journalism Review Editor at Large Neil Hickey (2003) summed up the fears of many when he concluded,

> What we risk over the long haul is ownership creep that may eventually see the end of the few remaining rules, and with them, the public's right to the widest possible array of news and opinion—at which point, robust, independent, antagonistic, many-voiced journalism may be only a memory.

Soon after the new ownership rules were proposed, they were challenged in court and in Congress. Consumers—organized on the Internet—objected so vigorously that Congress ultimately rejected the changes. One particularly contentious proposal would have allowed newspapers to own local television stations in the market where they published. Critics claimed that when the local newspaper is allowed to own two or more television stations and up to eight radio stations in the nation's largest markets (the number allowed by FCC regulations), competition in news would no longer exist and the public would lose important viewpoints.

Ironically, the critics got their way and newspapers were enjoined (again) from owning television stations in their local market based largely on the argument that the ban would ensure more diversity in the market. The irony is that the net result might be that the critics of newspaper ownership of television outlets might have hastened the death of the local paper in several communities where readership was drastically declining.

MOVIES AND MUSIC: BLOCKBUSTERS AND PIRATES

While digital technology sent shock waves throughout all media industries, the strongest tremors were felt in the entertainment business. There, digital technology arrived at the same time a handful of global companies took control of about 85 percent of the record industry. The rationale for the consolidation in the music industry was that profits from established labels and artists would be used to promote new talent. However, the corporate approach meant that managers now focused on quarterly profits and selling records rather than making music and promoting art.

Corporations wanted blockbuster hits. They were difficult and expensive to make and promote and impossible to predict. Walmart, the largest retailer of music in America, wanted to make its profits from the industry while carrying only about 2 percent of all releases available in a single year (Anderson 2006).

Chris Blackwell, who began a small record label in the 1970s and sold it to PolyGram in 1989, said:

> I don't think the music business lends itself very well to being a Wall Street business. You're always working with individuals, with creative people, and the people you are trying to reach, by and large, don't view music as a commodity but as a relationship with a band. It takes time to expand that relationship but most people who work for the corporations have three-year contracts, some five, and most of them are expected to produce. What an artist really needs is a champion, not a numbers guy who in another year is going to leave (Seabrook 2003, 46).

Other industries are affected by the new economic realities as well. Major studios no longer want to make medium-budget films—from $40 million to $80 million. Instead, they prefer smaller films for $10 million or less and "blockbuster" films with budgets of $100 million or more. Films in the middle—particularly the $40 to $60 million range—are now considered too risky to make by many producers and some studios.

Plus, investors want films with a built-in audience, so a huge percentage of the nation's screens are filled with sequels, comic book heroes and action-adventure movies known to be big in foreign distribution. For instance, in 2011, 9 of the top 10 grossing movies were either sequels of a previous movie or tie-ins with a fictional book or comic book character. Most of these top 10 will eventually see yet another sequel as long as audiences are willing to pay. So *The Hangover* (grosses of $277 million) becomes *The Hangover 2* (grosses of more than $255 million) and its premise is the foundation for *The Bridesmaids* (grosses of $169 million). The urge to create a sequel is irresistible for Hollywood. Such movies, regardless of their merit, consume a huge proportion of available screens leaving art films, indies and the like pushed aside. In addition, promotion budgets for potential blockbusters have become so bloated that smaller films with more modest budgets tended to get lost in the noise. These promotions created large opening weekends typically followed by drop-offs in attendance of up to 70 percent as the word of mouth got out that some films were not that good.

The effect of this trend was that midpriced, independent films, with fewer explosions and with no-name actors, have less chance of being made than ever before. True, there was the occasional medium budget breakout but the entertainment industry, focused as it was on the "blockbuster" business model, continued to play it safe. The same mentality is true of music and book publishing as well, where fewer producers meant fewer outlets for artists and a dumbing down of content to please a mainstream audience.

Meanwhile, another threat to the digital entertainment industries emerged. Piracy and sharing of digital files sent music CD sales plummeting and threatened movies as download speeds and storage space allowed for the transfer of very large files. Those who did buy their music legally through iTunes, Rhapsody or some other source opted to pay less than a dollar for a tune they like instead of nearly twenty dollars for the corresponding CD. In 2002, the industry shipped 33.5 million copies of the year's 10 best-selling CDs, barely half the number it had shipped in 2000. Today, that number has been halved again, with a "best-selling" CD often registering sales in the tens of thousands compared to chart-topping "albums" in the early rock era that routinely sold half a million copies.

The music industry—from producers to radio station owners—was slow to realize that consumers had forever changed the way they would buy and listen to their music. Sir Howard Stringer, the chair of the Sony Corporation of America, called downloaders "thieves" and compared them to those who shoplift from stores. The recording industry initially filed suit against some select downloaders and was successful in shutting down the very popular, but ultimately illegal, file-sharing site Napster. But, eventually, a pricing structure that made downloading inexpensive, combined with the emergence of popular devices to play it on such as the iPod, seemed a more effective—and more profitable—remedy. Recording's gain was radio's loss, though as iPods became the equipment of choice for the under-40 audience to access music. A look at the top 10 formats in radio, available at several industry Web sites, validates the fact that it is a medium with an aging audience.

Meanwhile the movie industry, not yet hurt as deeply as the music industry, raced to find its own equivalents of the dollar download, especially after the DVR made high-quality copying easy. By making legal movies readily available through retail kiosks at as low as a dollar per night or easily available through the mail with services like Netflix, the industry got at least some money from the movie aftermarket at the same time that domestic and foreign box office held strong.

The ethical implications are obvious. As you read this section, ask yourself these questions:

- When was the last time you bought a CD or DVD as opposed to burning one belonging to a friend?
- Have you ever loaned out a CD or DVD to be copied by a friend?
- Do you agree that person-to-person music sharing or video sharing constitutes theft?
- Is file sharing a good way to register a protest about the impact of profit?
- Is Sir Howard Stringer right that it is equivalent to shoplifting?
- Would you feel the same way if someone shared *your* work?

On an industry-wide level, new artists, especially those who don't fit the corporate view, will find the Internet to be a two-edged sword. It will give them the publicity they need at an affordable cost, but it will allow for file sharing or dollar downloads that make it virtually impossible to make significant sums of money. As is often the case in the mass media, the development and adoption of a new medium or delivery technology has unanticipated consequences for existing media and formats. For music, the solutions are elusive and the stakes are high. Will creative people, who find their energies unusable in the music industry, turn to other mediums, or will the industry—and most importantly—consumers find a way to reward the creators of this most personal of medium?

NEWSPAPERS: LOSING THE PENNY PRESS REVOLUTION

Financing the American media through advertising is so deeply ingrained in the system that it is hard to imagine any other way. Yet newspapers in America were supported solely by their readers for more than a century. Incidentally, in 1920, then-Secretary of Commerce Herbert Hoover argued for commercial-free radio, a funding formula that would have likely failed or at the least, changed the medium entirely.

The legacy funding formula for most newspapers was created more than 170 years ago when Benjamin Day, publisher of the *New York Sun,* started the "penny press" revolution by lowering the price of his newspaper to a penny at a time when his competition was selling newspapers for a nickel. He gambled that he could overcome the printing losses with additional advertising revenue—if circulation increased. When his gamble paid off, virtually every publisher in town followed his lead.

What Day did was farsighted. By pricing their products at or below the cost of printing, publishers cast their economic future with their advertisers. But advertisers demand "eyeballs" and paid circulation, guaranteed by the Audit Bureau of Circulation, was the standard. The system worked as long as circulation increased to cover the increasing costs of covering the news. But readership peaked more than two decades ago, and newspapers began shedding costs. Some sold to chains. Others combined with rivals in "joint operating agreements"(JOAs) which were, in effect, a congressionally approved exception to antitrust laws. Under a JOA, rival papers could combine press operations, billing operations, etc. but act as rival newspapers in their quest for news. However, with more than 30 years of history to evaluate the impact of the JOA legislation, what scholars and stockholders now know is that no joint operating agreement has allowed both newspapers to survive under the new financial arrangement for longer than a decade.

Such consolidation efforts were not nearly enough to survive the onslaught of the Web and a business model that provided news—an expensive commodity to produce—for free online. Layoffs and hiring freezes became a fact of life at large and award-winning papers such as the *Los Angeles Times,* the *Chicago Tribune* and the *New York Times* and smaller community papers as well. No one has found a way to "monetize" the Internet operation, and an attempt to gain more readers by being more convenient eventually had become a way for many to not pay for news content at all. Although ads were possible and even populous on newspaper Web sites, advertisers were loath to pay the same amount that audited readership had commanded. Major newspapers such as the *Rocky Mountain News* in Denver folded. Some, like the *Wall Street Journal,* decreased their page size while most decreased their page count beginning a cycle where smaller "news hole" required fewer journalists. Other papers, most recently the *New Orleans Times Picaynne,* went to less-than-daily circulation in an attempt to survive.

But no other good ideas emerged, and at the time this book went to press, newspapering remained in serious trouble. The local newspaper in most communities had long been a monopoly operation with returns of greater than 20 percent annually common before the bleeding of circulation and advertising. Even after cutbacks, newspapers still boast a "name brand" in most communities and the largest reporting staff in any given local market. Economically, small market dailies are actually thriving financially. However, with readers decreasing, some newspapers are increasingly putting video segments on their Web sites in an attempt to siphon viewers from local nightly newscasts. How this even more expensive use of the Web will play out is unknown, but it does demand that journalists be cross-trained for the new media reality as newspapers add video and sound and television stations add print stories to their Web sites.

THE MODERN DILEMMA:
STAKEHOLDERS VS. STOCKHOLDERS

The current state of media financial affairs can be summarized as an emphasis on corporate responsibility to the stockholders of publicly traded corporations—including the six media behemoths. In stockholder theory, corporations and their leaders have a single, overriding and legally binding promise to those who purchase stock: increase the share price. Milton Friedman, who first articulated the theory, suggests that increasing the share price is *the* promise that managers make. Whatever is legally done to promote that end is ethically right.

In every key media format—radio, television, newspapers, magazines, cable television and motion pictures—more than half of the gross revenues are concentrated in a handful of corporations—what media economics researcher Ben Bagdikian (1990, 5) has called "a de facto ministry of information within a democracy." If decisions are made to release only CDs that have a chance to go platinum, the will of one stakeholder—new or emerging artists—bends to the will of the corporation that can scarcely afford to foster unknown talent on the shareholder's dollar. The same can be said of new filmmakers, authors or any other would-be artist wanting to reach mass audiences.

Business ethicist Patricia H. Werhane (2006) has a different vision of the traditional stakeholder map. She says that some sorts of businesses—such as health care—have a public responsibility that extends beyond individual stockholders. These companies, she says, should operate from an "enriched stakeholder" model as opposed to a "profit-driven stockholder" model. The enriched stakeholder model puts something other than the corporation at the center of the "stakeholder" map (for health care, she suggests the patient) and rings that central stakeholder with government, investors, the court system, medical professionals, insurance companies, managed care plans and others. By changing the stakeholder map, Werhane suggests that other "promises" surface and that other measures of success emerge. Recent suggestions for fixing the nation's health care crisis have included paying doctors for outcomes rather than procedures—a form of practicing stakeholder ethics.

Werhane says that this way of thinking can result in some extraordinary outcomes. The Grameen Bank model pioneered the concept of "micro loans" to fight poverty in Bangladesh. The notion of lending very small amounts of money to individuals with good ideas was a way to leverage the "borrowers" (more than 90 percent of them women) and their families out of poverty. The micro loan concept and its inventor, Muhummad Yunnus, were awarded the Nobel Peace Prize in 2006. And, the bank itself remains both solvent and profitable, but criticisms of the approach have included that the model does not seem to transfer well to other poor nations.

The stakeholder model of media economics has much to recommend it. At the center of the map are citizens and community. Around the center is a ring including audiences, creative artists, stockholders, governments, nongovernmental organizations, journalists, strategic communication professionals, corporate managers and employees. By asking what benefits citizens living in communities the most, media corporate managers would begin to use a different gauge of success that does not place profit first in every situation. Media corporations would no longer search for a one-time "hit" that can be packaged, imitated (think reality television) and mass reproduced (think movie sequels). Instead, they would make smaller investments in a variety of experiments, allowing creativity and connection to community to help determine what works for both stakeholders and stockholders and what does not.

SOCIAL RESPONSIBILITY IN THE NEW MILLENNIUM

But stakeholder theory is far from a reality in the media universe. Good journalism is expensive, and in an era of declining subscriptions and ad revenues, few newsrooms enjoy budgets as large as in past years. The television networks have closed entire bureaus, and many newspapers have pulled back on overseas correspondents, leaving coverage of foreign news to the wires and CNN. The current era of cutbacks and consolidations has been noted by media researcher Robert McChesney (1997), who makes this analogy:

> Imagine if the federal government demanded that newspaper and broadcast journalism staffs be cut in half, that foreign bureaus be closed, and that news be tailored to suit the government's self-interest. There would be an outcry that would make the Alien and Sedition Acts, the Red Scares and Watergate seem like child's play. Yet when corporate America aggressively pursues the exact same policies, scarcely a murmur of dissent can be detected in the political culture.

The effect of cutbacks is lost news for the consumer. One photojournalist, Brad Clift, told the authors that he went to Somalia months before U.S. troops were dispatched, using his own money because he felt the starvation there was an underreported story. Only an occasional network crew and a handful of newspapers pursued the Somalia story before former President George H. W. Bush committed U.S. troops to the region in December 1992. Most news organizations, like this photojournalist's employer, declined to cover the emerging story, pleading that they had depleted their international budgets by covering Operation Desert Storm. But, other approaches and organizations are emerging—funded by cooperative agreements among news organizations and sometimes foundations. They have produced excellent journalism. Some, such as ProPublica, have won prestigious awards, including the Pulitzer Prize.

In reading the code of ethics of the Society of Professional Journalists, two of the "guiding principles" of journalism speak directly to the ethics of media economics: (1) seek truth and report it as fully as possible and (2) act independently. Seeking the truth can be personally and financially expensive, something that stakeholder theory demands and stockholder theory avoids.

Some media companies *have* learned the lesson. McKinsey and Company (National Association of Broadcasters 1985) studied 11 of the nation's great radio stations, such as WGN in Chicago and reported what made an excellent radio station. Their findings were:

- The great radio stations were audience oriented in their programming; and
- The great radio stations were community-oriented in their promotions.

Great radio stations had a knack for becoming synonymous in their communities with charitable events and community festivities even without an immediate return on investment. The attitude is summed up by WMMS (Cleveland) General Manager Bill Smith:

> If you want a car to last forever, you've got to throw some money back into that car and make sure that it's serviced properly on a continual basis. Otherwise, it's going to break down and fall apart. We know that we're constantly rebuilding the station one way or another. We throw the profit to the listening audience . . . to charities, to several nonprofit organizations, to free concerts or anything to affect the listeners of Cleveland as a whole . . . because they identify us as being community-minded.

Uplifting examples are far too rare. Entry-level salaries for journalists in both print and broadcast are far too low—under $30,000 in one survey, draining the industry of the talent that might solve some of the seemingly insoluble problems. But a strong democracy requires a strong media and valid solutions must be found. The stakes could not be higher.

Suggested Readings

AULETTA, KEN. 1991. *Three blind mice: How the TV networks lost their way.* New York: Random House.

BAGDIKIAN, BEN H. 2000. *The media monopoly.* 6th ed. Boston: Beacon Press.

CRANBERG, GILBERT, RANDALL BEZANSON, and JOHN SOLOSKI. 2001. *Taking stock.* Ames: Iowa State University Press.

MILLS, C. WRIGHT. 1956. *The power elite.* New York: Oxford University Press.

MCCHESNEY, ROBERT W. 1991. *Rich media, poor democracy: Communication politics in dubious times.* Urbana: University of Illinois Press.

PICARD, ROBERT G. 2010. *The economics of financing media companies.* New York: Fordham University Press.

SPENCE, EDWARD A., ANDREW, ALEXANDRA, AARON QUINN and ANNE. DUNN, 2011. *Media, markets and morals.* London: Wiley-Blackwell.

Cases on the Web

www.mhhe.com/mediaethics8e

"Union activism and the broadcast personality" by Stanley Cunningham

"A salesperson's dilemma: Whose interests come first?" by Charles H. Warner

"Turning on the *Light:* The San Antonio newspaper war" by Fred Blevins

"Calvin Klein's kiddie porn ads prick our tolerances" by Valerie Lilley

"*Ms.* magazine—No more ads!" by Philip Patterson

CHAPTER 7 CASES

CASE 7-A

Who Needs Advertising?

LEE WILKINS
University of Missouri

Everybody loves a bargain, and in 2008 at the onset of the American Great Recession, Andrew Mason decided he could capitalize on it. He founded a Web-based firm called Groupon, which in the years since its founding has been controversial in a number of ways.

Mason's business model was simple. He would ask local merchants in individual cities—he began in Chicago—to provide an electronic "coupon" for their services. The discount on goods and services: 50 percent. When the coupon was redeemed, the merchant retained 25 percent of the proceeds with the remainder going to Groupon. Merchants thus paid no upfront costs.

The initial coupon deal was offered to a certain number of people, and if a target threshold was reached, then everyone who signed up on the Web site got the coupon and the discount. If not enough people were interested, then the entire deal was off. Groupon avoided all forms of traditional advertising by working on a social media model, and a financial juggernaut was born. Today, Groupon is in about 500 markets in 44 countries. The corporation has gone public and, at one point, was expected to be the fastest-growing Web-based company ever, achieving $1 billion in revenues in record time.

Consumers generally loved the possibilities, but because Groupon targeted local businesses in individual cities, its results for merchants were mixed. Offering 50 percent off services could result in small businesses being literally overwhelmed, particularly if those services were things like massages which required a set amount of time and employee effort regardless of price. One small English bakery that normally produced about 100 cupcakes per month was slammed after a Groupon offer, having to produce 102,000 cupcakes in the same amount of time. Many merchants discovered that their Groupon-inspired customers came for the bargain only; the bargains did not result in repeat business. The Groupon offers meant that merchants could keep only 25 percent of the sale price for goods and services; for some, this meant a loss-leader of significant, and sometimes crippling, proportions.

Groupon also faced other troubles, including criticism for a Super Bowl commercial the firm ran and some problems in the United States with state regulators for goods such as alcohol. At least one consumer sued Groupon, claiming that there was no expiration date on Groupon deals but that merchants were unwilling to honor them past a certain point.

In 2012, Groupon also launched a VIP club where, for a $30 subscription fee, consumers would get a 12-hour jump on the latest offerings.

Initially, there were no serious competitors to Groupon, but about two years after the firm took off, Living Social became the Web site's first national competition.

In addition, media organizations—which saw potential advertisers either walking out the door or failing to buy ads—got into the business of acquiring Groupon-like firms in an effort to recapture at least part of the revenue stream.

Micro Issues

1. For most of the past 20 years, news organizations have been under enormous economic pressure to justify their product. Groupon and its imitators are providing similar pressures on traditional strategic communication. What does strategic communication have to offer that firms like Groupon do not? Is there an ethical base for what strategic communication professionals do?
2. Groupon hires many people to write copy for coupon announcements. Analyze this role in terms of ethical obligations—to the firm, to consumers, to other strategic communication professionals

Midrange Issues

1. Working with Groupon had some expected consequences for some merchants. Ethically, was Groupon in any way responsible for these problems? Does the concept of let the buyer beware help you justify your response?
2. Groupon relies on a community of sorts to make its business model work. Critique what Groupon thinks of consumers.

Macro Issues

1. Does Groupon pass the expanded TARES test?
2. If you had to outline a business model for a Groupon-like service that your news organization or advertising agency is developing, what would be the central elements of that model? How does ethical theory inform, or fail to inform, your thinking?
3. How would you respond to the following: The biggest challenge my generation of strategic communication professionals is going to face is convincing businesses, nonprofits and consumers that advertising and public relations have something to offer beyond the cheapest prices for goods and services.

CASE 7-B

Netflix: Not So Fast . . . A Response to Customer Furor

LEE WILKINS
University of Missouri

In 1997, Marc Randolph and Reed Hastings came up with an idea that is now so common in the United States that it has become a verb. What the two men invented was the beginnings of Netflix, a subscription-based movie rental service that allows consumers, depending on how much they were willing to pay, to rent an unlimited number of DVDs without fear of late fees or other penalties that were part of the film-rental market in previous decades. Unlike Blockbuster and other video rental stores, Netflix was a mail-order firm that had no traditional stores, avoiding the large overhead of its older rivals.

To say that Netflix was successful is an understatement. The company went "public"—meaning it allowed consumers to purchase stock—in June of 2002. Financial success was only one measure; Netflix, which had more than 100,000 titles available, is also credited with helping spur the growth in the "Indie" film market. The Netflix Web site also experimented with computerized evaluations to predict what films—and later television shows—subscribers would most enjoy. The firm signed exclusive deals with a number of content providers, and its founders made a concerted effort to keep up with technological change.

As technology improved and bandwidth expanded, it became possible to download films to personal computers, and Netflix was in the forefront of that effort. Televisions now come preprogrammed to received Netflix offerings, and as the first decade of the new century closed, Netflix managers realized that the core of their business had moved from the snail-mail delivery of DVDs to instant streaming to a variety of devices owned by the consumer, among them personal computers, mobile phones and tablets.

As the firm grew, problems developed. Netflix was successfully sued over claims about how rapidly DVDs would arrive at subscriber households, which resulted in a change in how the firm promoted the service. But, Netflix was extraordinarily popular. For less than it would cost two people to see a single first-run film at the local cinema, subscribers could watch almost unlimited films in their homes for a month. At the beginning of the service, most new releases were available on Netflix within six months of opening at theaters.

It was not uncommon for consumers, and even movie reviewers, to suggest that a particular movie was worthy only of Netflix viewing. Consumers could, and did, save themselves money this way. And, if you missed a first-run film due to work, travel or family issues, never fear: within a few weeks, you could Netflix it. By early 2011, Netflix announced it had about 23.6 million subscribers, most of them in the United States although there also were many in Canada. Netflix also took an interest in politics. Its political action committee was particularly concerned about intellectual property regulation and enforcement.

So, it seemed to CEO Marc Randolph and his staff that the local extension of the brand in September 2011 was to split Netflix into two companies, the first retaining the original name and specializing in "instant viewing" and the second to be called Qwikster, which was designed to carry video games but also would retain the original DVD, snail-mail business. A two-tiered pricing structure was also announced. Subscribers could have "instant-view" only for about $8 per month or retain both services for about $15 per month. Subscribers were notified of the changes via e-mail; news reports, beginning first in the tech industry, followed rapidly.

And then, all heck broke loose.

Consumers were incensed. They didn't like the separation of the DVD portion of the business from the streaming portion of Netflix. They didn't like the new pricing structure, which was an increase at a time when individuals and families were still trying to recover from the Great Recession. And, consumers really didn't like being informed about the changes via e-mail in a way that indicated they were going to be given very limited choices about their Netflix service.

So the consumers quit. In the month after the Qwikster announcement more than 800,000 U.S. subscribers canceled their Netflix subscriptions. Netflix stock dipped.

Management reconsidered and walked the changes back. An unusual public apology followed that said, in part: "Consumers value the simplicity Netflix has always offered and we respect that," said Netflix co-founder and CEO Reed Hastings. "There is a difference between moving quickly—which Netflix has done very well for years—and moving too fast, which is what we did in this case."

In January of the following year, Netflix subscriptions had risen by about 600,000 from the October lows.

Micro Issues

1. Using ethical theory as a guide, what is an appropriate relationship between a company such as Netflix and its subscribers?
2. Netflix stays within the boundaries of U.S. and international copyright laws. As a consumer, do you think it's important to support firms such as Netflix, Hulu and others—or do you still download media content for free?
3. Netflix has been given credit for making independent films and documentaries much more widely available. Using stakeholder theory, evaluate this somewhat unexpected consequence of the movie rental business.

Midrange Issues

1. Some strategic communication professionals suggested that what Netflix needed was better public relations. Evaluate this claim. What might that campaign have looked like?
2. Did Netflix as a corporation do the ethical thing by withdrawing from its new business model? Evaluate this from the perspective of the consumer, the stockholders and the stakeholders.

Macro Issues

1. How does the concept of "content on demand" influence the business of news and entertainment programming? What are some potential ethical "pitfalls" this approach highlights?
2. Evaluate the Netflix program that rates how well a particular consumer might like specific content in terms of privacy, target marketing and content production.

CASE 7-C

Outsourcing the News

LEE WILKINS
University of Missouri

It's not news to anyone that newspaper budgets and staffing have been slashed in the past decade. It's also not news to anyone that one response to the contraction of the newspaper industry has been an emphasis on hyper-local coverage. Hyper-local coverage attempts to compete with Web-based news by supplying the sort of information that Google News or the Huffington Post simply would be unable to collect.

Hyper-local coverage—reports from the police blotter; box scores of high school sports; filing of permits for businesses, construction, bankruptcy and the like—was once the work of traditional reporters. As one editor told the staff of the Boulder *Daily Camera,* "if there's a traffic jam, I want people to be able to look in the paper and know what caused it and how long it lasted."

Hyper-local news clashes with the staffing economics of the contemporary newspaper newsroom.

Enter Journatic, a service that began in Chicago in 2006. CEO Brian Timpone told news organizations that his firm would collect such hyper-local information, much of it available electronically, and package it for publication. The fee structure for this work—that is, what was paid by the newspapers for this sort of information—has never been made public nor, with certain exceptions, have the newspapers that subscribed to the service. The longstanding exception is the real estate section of the San Francisco *Chronicle.*

Timpone said that he got the idea for Journatic when, as a 24-year-old television reporter, he found himself in Duluth, Minn., a community he knew nothing about. Timpone's insight was hardly novel; indeed, much of the criticism of television journalism has focused on the fact that most young reporters spend from 18 months to three years in a market before they move on. Newspapers, particularly as they became financially squeezed, often downsized by letting older, more experienced journalists "go" in favor of newer, less expensive replacements. Those young journalists seldom knew their communities as well as the more experienced reporters.

So, what Journatic did was to take over the "scut work" of covering these routine but very localized events and business and legal transactions. Timpone maintained that it was not important to have reporters stationed in the communities they were writing about to get this sort of coverage.

What Timpone had not counted on was the qualms of a new hire, Ryan Smith, who began working for Journatic in January of 2011 for $10 per hour with no benefits. Initially, when Smith worked primarily for Journatic's sister organization BlockShopper.com, he noticed that information was often taken entirely from LinkedIn, that story writing was done by people outside the United States, including the Philippines, and that bylines were sometimes falsified. When Smith moved formally to Journatic, he said he noticed that the bylines of Journatic-produced pieces included news organizations such as the Houston *Chronicle* and New York's *Newsday.*

"I felt like the company I was working for was accelerating the death of the newspaper, luring many members of the industry into their own demise with the promise of short-term savings," Smith told the Poynter Institute. Ultimately Smith decided to contact Michael Miner, the *Chicago Reader*'s media reporter, to discuss his concerns. Miner wrote a story, which circulated on some blogs, but Smith remained unsatisfied. In the spring of 2012, he contacted Ira Glass at Public Radio International's "This American Life," which reported and broadcast the Journatic story in June of that year under the headline "Switcheroo."

"People didn't think much about the beef they were eating until someone exposed the practice of putting so-called 'pink slime' into ground beef. . . . I feel like companies like Journatic are providing the public 'pink slime' journalism" Smith told the Poynter Institute after the "This American Life" episode aired.

National Public Radio is a big platform, and journalists, including those who manage the newspapers that worked with Journatic, heard the story. One of those was the *Chicago Tribune,* which not only worked with Journatic but was in the midst of negotiating a deal of purchase the privately held company. Brad Moor, vice president of Targeted Media for the Tribune Company, spoke on the record to "This American Life" and noted a team of 40 *Tribune* staff members had been unable to generate enough content to drive the Web traffic the *Tribune* sought. So the paper hired Journatic, laid off 20 staffers, and had three times the amount of content than had been produced before.

But, after the story ran nationally, the *Tribune* took a deeper look at some of the Journatic content. It discovered that a local sports story had been fabricated. There were other problems as well. On July 13, 2012, the *Tribune* suspended indefinitely its relationship with the organization. As part of the investigation of Journatic's practices, the Tribune learned that some copy was being written by workers in the Philippines who were paid the equivalent of 35 cents for every story they produced.

Journatic, in turn, fired its head of editing, Mike Fourcher.

And, the grass roots media advocacy group Free Press has posted a petition on its Web site that allows signers to contact news organizations so they can weigh in on how they feel about local news being reported from remote locations—some of them out of the country.

Micro Issues

1. Using ethical theory as well as the concept of hyper-competition, explain why you believe news organizations were willing to work with Journatic. Is this justifiable?
2. Was Ryan Smith right to go public with his concerns? How would you evaluate his role?
3. The "scut work" of journalism is routine. Is there an ethical justification for leaving it in the hands of regular staffers, even though that means news organizations may not make as much money?

Midrange Issues

1. Contrast the ethical implications of the approach of Journatic with that of Patch, Gawker or other similar models. Are there ethical distinctions?
2. Examine your own thinking regarding Journatic's wage and salary structure.
3. How should news organizations that subscribe to services like Journatic ensure quality content? Should they make this effort, even though it might be costly?

Macro Issues

1. Would you go to work for Journatic or a similar organization?
2. How is the work of Journatic like and how is it unlike other forms of citizen journalism where users create content?

CASE 7-D

Transparency in Fund Raising: The Corporation for Public Broadcasting Standard

LEE WILKINS
University of Missouri

In Chapter 2, we asked you to consider the implications of transparency as a guiding ethical standard in collecting and disseminating news. This case links that principle to the Corporation of Public Broadcasting and its new code of ethics.

When the Corporation for Public Broadcasting (CPB) developed a code of ethics they decided to apply the concept of transparency to the entire organization, both newsgathering and fundraising. What was ground breaking about the effort was CPB's attempt to apply a single ethical standard to its fundraising actvities, and within that, the relationship the corporation has between its donors and its news and entertainment content.

The transparency in funding document opened with this general statement of principles:

> That trust is the foundation of the relationship between the public and public media. Every year, thousands of Americans support their local public radio and television stations. These donors don't require a contract and rarely even make specific requests about how their money is to be used they simply have faith in the integrity, expertise, and goodwill of their local station. The importance of this trust is magnified whenever a station takes on a journalistic role.

The standard notes that the relationship between public broadcasting stations and donors should not be merely financial—that donors represent a significant element of political support and social capital in their own communities. The transparency standard emphasizes that transparency should not apply only to donors—stations themselves need to become more transparent about their financial operations, obligations and potential entanglements. But, the standard also called for a "firewall" between donors and the various local news organizations associated with public broadcasting, most often National Public Radio and local NPR programming.

The standard also suggests that stations make fund-raising information available and publicly accessible, including gift acceptance policies, guidelines governing the use of challenge grants, donor rights, appropriate donor acknowledgment, conditions of acceptance of anonymous gifts, and guidelines for seeking and accepting foundation grants. The policy also includes sections that outline the rules public broadcasting must comply with promulgated by the Federal Communications Commission and the Internal Revenue Service.

CPB's transparency fund-raising standard is probably the most radical attempt by a media organization to rethink, and to make public, what is a non–advertising based business model. It is unique because it is based on an ethical concept. Keeping all of this in mind, respond to the following questions.

Micro Issues

1. In an ethical sense, distinguish between advertising and CPB sponsorship.
2. Do newspaper display ads provide a kind of transparency of financial support for a specific publication? Is such advertising ethically distinct from the CBP transparency standard?
3. If you were a CPB or NPR donor, would you be willing to have your name announced on the air? Placed on a Web site? Why or why not?
4. If you helped run a foundation, do you think you would be willing to provide funds to a news organization knowing that your support would become public in this way?

Midrange Issues

1. CPB receives about 2 percent of its budget from taxpayers in the form of a congressional allocation. Should the transparency standard also speak to taxpayer support?
2. CPB is a nonprofit organization. Discuss the ethical implications of a transparency standard for for-profit news and entertainment organizations.
3. Compare the transparency standard with the published guidelines for personal or foundation support of organizations such as Investigative Reporters and Editors, the Pulitzer Center, or ProPublica. Which do you find the most ethically justifiable?

Macro Issues

1. Using the concepts of stakeholder and stockholder theory, evaluate the transparency fund-raising standard.
2. Public broadcasting television and radio stations have on-air fund-raising drives during the year. How would you compare these fund drives with traditional advertising placed in newspapers, magazines or on television and commercial radio?
3. One ethically based justification of paid advertising is that many advertisers dilute the influence of any single advertiser. Evaluate this claim ethically. Do you believe the same evaluation applies to public broadcasting sponsors?
4. In an age when media finances are difficult, are firewalls a luxury that can no longer be afforded?

CASE 7-E

Crossing the Line? The *L.A. Times* and the Staples Affair

MEREDITH BRADFORD AND PHILIP PATTERSON
Oklahoma Christian University

The *Los Angeles Times,* in a "special report" on December 20, 1999, called attention to an event its editors perceived as a breach of journalism ethics. The multistory report was entitled "Crossing the Line." What made this report extraordinary is that it was the *Times* itself that had crossed the line that triggered this journalistic exposé.

A few weeks earlier, the Staples Center, a $400 million sports and entertainment arena in downtown Los Angeles, had opened to great fanfare. Most observers shared the hope that the facility, which would house two basketball franchises and one hockey team, would spark a revitalization of downtown. Staples Inc. had won the naming rights to the arena by paying $116 million.

Tim Leiweke, president of the Staples Center, left with $284 million more to raise, had initiated talks with McDonald's, Anheuser-Busch, United Airlines, Bank of America and others to become "founding partners." He was eager to have the *Los Angeles Times* as a founding partner because of previous joint successes and because he thought the paper could contribute value beyond cash.

The Staples arena already had a promotional arrangement with the *Los Angeles Times* in exchange for cash payments from the *Times* and free advertising in the paper. "The arrangement is similar to that many big-city papers have with their local professional sports teams," said David Shaw, the *L.A. Times* Pulitzer Prize–winning media critic, in an investigative piece on the controversy (Shaw 1999). "But for the Staples Center, Leiweke wanted more. He wanted the *Times* as a founding partner."

Since the Staples Center could be a major contributor to the revitalization of downtown Los Angeles, *Times* executives were "eager to participate," Shaw said. The price for founding partners ranged from $2 million to $3 million per year for five years. Jeffrey S. Klein, then senior vice president of the *Times,* who supervised early negotiations on the Staples deal, "didn't think it was worth what they were asking." Negotiations stalled for several months in 1998 until a "Founding Partner Agreement" was accepted on December 17, 1998, between the L.A. Arena Company and the *Los Angeles Times.* Part of the language in the agreement stated the two companies "agree to cooperate in the development and implementation of joint revenue opportunities."

"Although all of the principals in the negotiations say that the precise terms of the Staples deal are confidential," Shaw reported, "information from a variety of sources shows that in effect the *Times* agreed to pay Staples Center about $1.6 million a year for five years—$800,000 of that in cash, $500,000 in profits and an estimated $300,000 in profits from what Leiweke had called 'ideas that would generate revenue for us.'"

This latter part of the deal was clarified in a clause of the final contract that said, in part, that the *Times* and the L.A. Arena Company would agree to cooperate in the development and implementation of joint revenue opportunities such as a special section in the *Los Angeles Times* in connection with the opening of the arena, or a jointly published commemorative yearbook, Shaw said.

These "joint opportunities" were to create $300,000 of net revenue for each party annually. According to the contract, these opportunities would be subject to the mutual agreement of both parties.

On Oct. 10, 1999, the *Times* published a special issue of its Sunday magazine dedicated to the new Staples Center sports and entertainment arena.

Only after the section was published did most of the paper's journalists learn that the *Times* had split the advertising profits from the magazine with the Staples Center. Feeling that the arrangement constituted a conflict of interest and a violation of the journalistic principle of editorial independence, more than 300 *Times* reporters and editors signed a petition demanding that publisher Kathryn Downing apologize and undertake a thorough review of all other financial relationships that may compromise the *Times'* editorial heritage.

The petition, in part, stated "As journalists at the *L.A. Times,* we are appalled by the paper entering into hidden financial partnerships with the subjects we are writing about. The editorial credibility of the *Times* has been fundamentally undermined."

Less than two years before the episode, Downing had been named publisher by Mark Willes, the new chief executive of Times Mirror Corporation, parent company of the *Los Angeles Times,* despite having no newsroom background. Her previous experience had been as a legal publicist. Willes had moved from General Mills to Times Mirror in 1995. Willes had made no secret of his desire to "blow up the wall between business and editorial" (Rieder 1999). He was also on record as telling *American Journalism Review* in 1997 that "[the] notion that you have to be in journalism 30 years to understand what's important, I find rather quaint" (Rieder 1999).

Downing did apologize, calling it a "major, major mistake." After taking questions at a two-hour staff meeting on October 28, she admitted that she and her staff "failed to understand the ethics involved" (Booth 1999). Downing meanwhile canceled all future revenue-sharing deals with Staples, promised to review all contracts with advertisers and ordered up awareness training for the ad side.

For his part, Willes seemed to reverse his earlier stance when he said, "This is exactly the consequence of having people in the publisher's job who don't have experience in newspapers" (Rieder 1999).

On the business side of the paper the arrangement was widely known and discussed openly for most of 1999. Downing says she deliberately withheld the information from Michael Parks, the paper's editor, but did not direct her subordinates on the business side not to talk about it to him or to anyone else in editorial, according to several reports.

Shaw reports that Willes argued that the absence of such discussion only shows the need for "more communications, not less. . . . The profit-sharing deal happened not because the wall came down," Willes says, "but because people didn't talk to one another when they should have."

In an interesting argument, Downing claimed if the editorial side of the paper did not know about the profit-sharing deal with the Staples Center before printing, then the Sunday magazine devoted to the Staples Center would be unbiased. The un-informed editorial staff would have no reason to be biased.

Many critics from inside and outside the newspaper agree with Shaw that "readers have no reason to trust anything the *Times* wrote about Staples Center, or any of its tenants or attractions, anywhere in the paper, now or in the future, if the *Times* and Staples Center were business partners." He adds that readers will wonder whether other improper arrangements, formal or informal, might also exist or be created in the future with other entities, agencies and individuals covered by the *Times.*

Whether connected to the Staples affair or not, massive changes were in store for Willes, Downing, Parks and the *Times.* The newspaper was bought by the Tribune Company, publisher of the *Chicago Tribune,* in March 2000. All three employees were gone within a year.

Micro Issues

1. Critique Willes's early and late statements about journalistic experience in newspaper management positions.
2. Is the actual loss of credibility as disastrous as the reporters felt, or does the public really have the same sensibilities as those in the profession?
3. How does entering into the contract with the Staples Center differ from the sports department accepting press passes for the events held in the arena?

Midrange Issues

1. If one acknowledges that "the wall" is good and necessary, how does that affect media engaged in advocacy journalism?
2. Shaw entitled his article "Journalism Is a Very Different Business." In what ways do you think journalism differs from other businesses?

Macro Issues

1. In the new information age, where so many competing views can be found on most issues, is "the wall" still relevant?
2. When a newspaper is a publicly traded company, do the loyalties of the paper shift from the public to the shareholders? If not, how can you justify a move that might be counterproductive to profits?
3. After you read the next case, determine if the episode above is a factor in the recent decline in circulation of the *Los Angeles Times.*

CASE 7-F

Profit Versus News: The Case of the *L.A. Times* and the Tribune Company

LEE WILKINS
University of Missouri

Editor's Note: *In April 2007, the entire Tribune Company was sold to entrepreneur Sam Zell for a reported $8.2 billion. He reported he will break up the media conglomerate, including selling off the Chicago Cubs to help pay for the acquisition. The case below is still an excellent example of what publicly owned newspapers across America face in an era of rising costs and declining revenue sources.*

In October 2006, management of the Chicago-based Tribune Company, the relatively new owners of the *Los Angeles Times,* fired Jeff Johnson, publisher of the newspaper. The reason: Johnson had objected publicly to newsroom staff cuts ordered by the parent corporation.

"Jeff and I agreed that this change is best at this time because *Tribune* and *Times* executives need to be aligned on how to shape our futures," said Scott Smith, president of Tribune Publishing, a subsidiary of the Tribune Company

(Seelye 2006). A memo to the staff distributed at the paper added: "Sorry to tell you that we are told that Jeff Johnson is out as publisher of the *Los Angeles Times*."

Johnson had not gone quietly. Faced with corporate instructions to boost earnings by 7 percent, which was to be accomplished in part by cutting newsroom staff as well as utilizing increased technological efficiency, Johnson went to the community for support and got it. Twenty Los Angeles civic leaders, among them former U.S. Secretary of State Warren Christopher, the Los Angeles County Federation of Labor chief Maria Elena Durazo, L.A. Police Commission Chairman John Mack and Geoffrey Cowan, dean of the University of Southern California's Annenberg School of Communication, protested, noting, "All newspapers serve an important civic role, but as a community voice in the metropolitan region, the *Los Angeles Times* is irreplaceable" (Rainey 2006).

Instead, they urged the parent corporation to put more money into the paper, not less. In the six years of *Tribune* ownership, the paper had lost more than 200 journalists, moving from a staff of about 1,200 to about 940.

At issue was one central question with a multitude of implications: was the *Los Angeles Times* contributing enough to the bottom line of its parent corporation—a contribution that was reflected in the price of *Tribune* stock? In the 21st century, with chains and conglomerates, media finances are complicated, and those affecting newspapers are no exception.

The Tribune Corporation purchased the paper and its other substantial holdings from the Chandler family in 1999, an indirect result of the turmoil at the paper that erupted after the Staples Center problems (detailed in the previous case). The *Tribune* owned additional newspapers, 26 television stations (including Los Angeles' KTLA) and the Chicago Cubs baseball team. Despite this diversity of holdings, the stock price of the Tribune Company had remained relatively stagnant. In the same month as the firing, the Tribune Company announced that its third quarter operating revenues for the entire conglomerate were down 2 percent from the previous year, but publishing profits were off 17 percent. This was attributed to declines of both advertising (down 2 percent from 2005) and circulation (down 8 percent in a year).

In order to boost the price, the corporation had engineered a $2 billion buyback of company stock. The *Tribune* also set a target of $200 million in company-wide cost cutting over a two-year period. The company was also selling some of its media holdings but had no plans to sell the baseball team because it would have adversely affected the corporation's synergistic media strategy in its hometown, Chicago.

However, Tribune Corporation stockholders, including the Chandler family—with multiple seats on the Tribune Board of Directors—remained unsettled about their investment. This was despite the fact that the *Times* continued to make a substantial profit. Its operating profit margins were at about 20 percent—ahead of most big metropolitan newspapers. However, its cash flow had declined, according to sources inside the paper (Rainey 2006).

During the same time period, the *Times*' photo department staff had decreased by about a third and the graphics and design department had lost about 40 percent of its staff. Large daily operations in Ventura County and the San Fernando Valley, which had been scaled back previously, had shrunk again to just a handful of reporters. The paper had won 13 Pulitzer Prizes in the previous five years but had lost former editor John S. Carroll, who resigned about a year before Johnson was fired. The pressure to slash newsroom staff had played a role in his decision to leave (Rainey 2006).

"This newspaper does so many things well," Dean Baquet, the news editor said. "It is one of only three or four papers in the country with really robust foreign bureaus and that cover the war in Iraq in depth. . . . We have a D.C. bureau that competes on every big story. We cover the most complicated urban and suburban region in America. We do a lot of other things. You can't continue to do that if [staff reductions] keep up" (Rainey 2006).

In response to the newsroom turmoil, Smith affirmed the national stature of the paper but added, "There is a misperception that counting numbers of people is the right way to measure the quality of a great newspaper. You are mixing quality and quantity" (Rainey 2006).

Micro Issues

1. What should individual reporters and editors at the paper do? Should they cooperate with the new editor? Strike?
2. Assuming some cuts will have to be made, which of the activities outlined in Banquet's quote—or others you might think of—do you think the editors should relinquish?

Midrange Issues

1. Was it appropriate that this dispute go public? Who should cover the news of large media organizations?
2. Is the *Los Angeles Times* a national media resource? Should that make any difference—to the staff? To the corporate owners?
3. How might someone like John Stuart Mill, in light of his essay "On Liberty," evaluate this situation?

Macro Issues

1. Several Los Angeles billionaires, including David Geffen, expressed an interest in buying the *Times*. What might local ownership mean to the paper? Are there downsides to local ownership?
2. Would an owner like Geffen, with deep financial and creative ties in the entertainment industry, present important conflicts of interest for any staff? If so, how might they be handled?
3. What is the impact of a "synergistic media strategy" on the way a local newspaper covers its community?
4. Ask your parents about their retirement accounts. Would they be willing to take a lower return on investment in a situation like this to ensure a robust local newspaper? If you have a retirement account, would you?

8

Picture This: The Ethics of Photo and Video Journalism

By the end of this chapter, you should be familiar with:

- **the legal and ethical issues involved in photojournalism in the area of privacy.**
- **the legal and ethical problems of file footage and "eyewash."**
- **the conundrum of open source journalism.**

INTRODUCTION

In the years leading up to the American Revolution, many of the main figures worked with words. They were press owners, postmasters, pamphleteers, etc. They controlled the words that filtered down to the people where the notion of being for or against the impending war would be made. In the decades that followed, the currency of persuasion was the written word.

But by the time of the Civil War, photography, literally "writing with light," had left the studio and had entered the battlefield. The haunting images of that war by Matthew Brady had an effect on a nation raised on words. Although it would take more decades to develop, one of the earliest notions of privacy was the freedom from having one's image "stolen." In 1901, a preteen, Abigail Roberson, found her image on posters and even painted on barns, advertising a brand of flour—all without her permission. Although she didn't win her case—because there was no law against what happened—New York was quick to pass the nation's first privacy law a year later focusing specifically on the unwarranted use of one's image.

There is something personal about images. They are intimate; they are subjective. What some see as obscene, others see as artistic. Images have power—from personal to commercial to political. The iconic images of Sept. 11, 2001, capture both emotion and information for Americans. So do images of the fall of Baghdad several years later, only these images mean something quite different depending on whether the viewer is Americans or Iraqi.

Marshall McLuhan said more than half a century ago, there will come a time when wars are fought not only with bullets, but also with images. The power of images is so overwhelming that the George W. Bush administration banned the presence of press photographers at the Air Force base where flag-draped coffins containing the remains of soldiers killed in action in Iraq and Afghanistan came in almost daily. Today, the battle for the lasting image of any armed conflict is an important one with enormous stakes. So, the lone man facing down a tank in the middle of China's Tiananmen Square may not have won the war (and indeed he didn't) but the image of that man did win a major battle, so much so that today any totalitarian government has to control a nation's images as well as its missiles.

THE CITIZEN AS PHOTOJOURNALIST

Nowhere is the concept of citizen journalist more accepted than in photography, where devices like cell phones have made virtually everybody a photographer and most a videographer. Add in the hundreds of thousands of video cameras that businesses employ for security, and virtually no event—from one child stomping on another in a soccer match to a would-be terrorist buying household chemicals to make a bomb—falls outside the realm of cameras. Today's editorial question is rarely "Do we have art?" It's more likely "Do we use this photo or that one?" often from sources whose day job is not journalism.

Decades of technological developments have dramatically shortened the time between the occurrence of a news event and the dissemination of photos or video of it to the public. Digital photos can be posted to the Web almost instantaneously. Video is routinely beamed live into television homes across America and posted to the Web in seconds. Once, the most instantaneous ethical decision in photography was: "Shoot or don't shoot?" Today the question has added layers: "Post or don't post?" Or: "Go live or not?" Or: "Do we use this amateur video?"

Decisions that once could be made in the relative calm of the newsroom after a dramatic tragedy now must be made in the field in an increasingly competitive media environment. And making the right decision can be the difference in being applauded for ingenuity or being criticized for insensitivity.

PROBLEMS IN THE PROCESS

Your grandparents had sayings such as "the camera never lies" and "seeing is believing." Yet as Arthur Berger (1989) points out in *Seeing Is Believing,* because of the many variables in photography—camera angles, use of light, texture and focus—a picture is always an *interpretation* of reality, not reality itself. He adds that a dozen photographers taking pictures of the same scene would produce different views of the reality of it. The story below illustrates that.

Only one photographer, Nat Fein, won the Pulitzer Prize for photography while taking a picture that dozens of other photographers were shooting—the retirement of Babe Ruth's number by the New York Yankees. Notice that by moving

© *The Estate of Nat Fein.*

to the rear of his subject, Fein captured a different angle and told a different and more dramatic story with his photo. Not only did the photo win journalism's top prize, it has been called the iconic sports photograph of the 20th century—all by manipulating the angle of the photo and capturing not only Babe Ruth, but, off to the right of the photo, all the photographers who had shot the cliché shot for their newspapers.

Not only does the camera differ from the eye in its ability to manipulate angle, light and focus, but cameras also capture an isolated reality by presenting us with a slice of life, free from context. In *About Looking,* John Berger (1980, 14) says:

> What the camera does, and what the eye can never do, is to fix the appearance of that event. The camera saves a set of appearances from the otherwise inevitable supersession of further appearances. It holds them unchanging. And before the invention of the camera nothing could do this, except in the mind's eye, the faculty of memory.

The role of journalism is to place context back into the ubiquitous images created by professionals and amateurs alike. It's not enough, from an ethical stand-point, to say, "Here's what happened" to an audience who probably knows the news before the newscast airs or the newspaper hits the street. They also know that photos are easily manipulated on any laptop computer and video is only marginally harder to change, but not by any means impossible. Because of those two facts, journalism must say: "Here's why we believe this happened the way you are seeing it." Otherwise, the nightly news does nothing for the consumer that YouTube can't do better.

TO SHOOT OR NOT TO SHOOT?

Arriving on the scene of a newsworthy event, the photographer must make several decisions. The most basic is whether or not to shoot the photo of a subject who is in no position to deny the photographer access to the event. Often these vulnerable subjects are wounded, in shock or grief-stricken. In that newsworthy moment, the subject loses a measure of control over his or her circles of intimacy (see Chapter 5 for a description of this concept). That control passes to the photographer, who must make a decision.

Goffman (1959) claims people possess several "territories" they have a right to control. Included in Goffman's list are the right to a personal space free from intrusion (i.e., by a camera lens) and the right to preserve one's "information," such as a state of joy, or grief, from public view.

By its very nature, photojournalism is intrusive and revealing—two violations of Goffman's sense of self. Someone else's misfortune is often good fortune for the photojournalist. In the last century, more than half of the winning images in top photography contests were pictures of violence and tragedy. And most of the amateur images that make the news are of violence and tragedy. So eventually every photojournalist happens on an assignment that intrudes on a subject's privacy. Garry Bryant (1987), a staff photographer with the *Deseret News* of Salt Lake City, offers this checklist he goes through "in hundredths of a second" when he reaches the scene of tragedy:

1. Should this moment be made public?
2. Will being photographed send the subjects into further trauma?
3. Am I at the least obtrusive distance possible?
4. Am I acting with compassion and sensitivity?

To this list Bryant adds the following disclaimer (1987, 34):

What society needs to understand is that photographers act and shoot instinctively. We are not journalists gathering facts. We are merely photographers snapping pictures. A general rule for most photojournalists is "Shoot. You can always edit later."

The line between newsworthiness and intrusiveness, between good pictures and bad taste, is often blurry. Donald Gormley, the general manager of the *Spokane Spokesman-Review,* offers some insight into the difference between photos that are universally offensive and photos that are simply tough to view:

Compassion is not the same as good taste. If a reader knows the person pictured in a very dramatic photograph, he may find it offensive. That's a sin against compassion. If he is offended whether he knows the person or not, the sin is probably one against good taste (1984, 58).

Editors argue that decisions cannot be made concerning photos that do not exist. Not every picture of grief needs to be ruled out just because the subject is vulnerable or grieving. Where to draw the line is a decision best made in the newsroom rather than at the scene. The photographer who attempts to perform a type of ethical triage at the scene of a tragedy might find his career in jeopardy if the assignment fails to capture the pathos of the event when all other photographers succeeded. In addition, the photographer who fails to capture some of the event, for whatever reason, fails to capture some of the truth for the reader or viewer.

However, the window of time for deciding later is closing. Today's technology means that television is often live at the scene of a tragedy, broadcasting footage even before the immediate family is alerted. Scenes that might once have been edited now go straight on the air. An important stage in the ethical decision-making process is bypassed. And with the advent of camera phones, even more events are being captured and offered to the media to illustrate stories.

How can the victims of tragedy come to life as vulnerable humans with feelings to a professional who sees the world most of the time through a lens? A few years ago, at a conference entitled "Crime Victims and the News Media," victims of violent crime met the journalists who covered their stories. One participant noted at the end of the conference, "Once a journalist hears their simple, eloquent stories of what happened to them, he will never approach the story of a human tragedy in quite the same way."

Essentially, the photographer who is deciding whether and how to photograph a tragedy is wrestling with the dilemma of treating every subject as an end and not merely a means to an end. We can agree that powerful images of accident victims may cause some drivers to proceed more safely, but if that message often comes at the expense of an accident victim's privacy, is it a message that needs to be told?

Warren Bovée (1991), in an essay entitled "The Ends Can Justify the Means— But Rarely," offers this set of questions to help the photographer find the answer.

1. Are the means truly morally evil or merely distasteful, unpopular, etc.?
2. Is the end a *real* good or something that merely *appears* to be good?
3. Is it probable that the means will achieve the end?
4. Is the same good possible using other means? Is the bad means being used as a shortcut to a good end when other methods would do?
5. Is the good end clearly greater than any evil means used to attain it?
6. Will the means used to achieve the end withstand the test of publicity?

TO ACCEPT OR NOT ACCEPT

It goes by a number of names—open source journalism and citizen journalism being among the most popular. But regardless of the label, the process is essentially the same: citizens, acting as amateur journalists without pay, submit both words and images to various Web sites. Some, such as YouTube, were established by entrepreneurs. But others are established and managed by news organizations. And, even if your local television station or newspaper doesn't have an open source site, increasingly citizens are trying to contribute their efforts to professional news organizations.

Some of those contributions have changed history. For example, amateur video aired first on local and then on national television news of African-American Rodney King being beaten by a uniformed, Caucasian police officer is credited with both riots and racial tensions in Los Angeles. Amateur video first uploaded to the Internet, and then later picked up by traditional news organizations, of Republican Sen. George Allen of Virginia uttering an apparently racist remark is one of the elements credited with his electoral defeat in 2006. And then, there's the recurrent video of midwestern tornados—taken at great personal risk by amateurs who aren't paid for their efforts and accepted by media outlets well aware that the weather garners the highest ratings during the traditional local television news show.

Before the Internet opened the possibility of open source journalism to thousands of bloggers and videographers, the government could and did exercise control over the media by denying access to information or battlefields or by selectively granting access or leaks to those in favor with the administration. But the Web changed all that, as *Newsweek*'s David Ansen writes in his review of the 2006 film about World War II propaganda, *"Flags of our Fathers"* (Ansen 2006, 71):

> What the Pentagon didn't foresee, and couldn't control was, the rise of new media—the unfiltered images popping up on the Web, the mini-TV cams put in the hands of soldiers that emerge in the recent documentary, *The War Tapes*. We don't see much of the real war on network TV, but the unauthorized documentaries—*The Ground Truth, Gunner Palace* and many more—come pouring out. Just as many people think they get a straighter story from Jon Stewart's mock news reports than from traditional outlets, it's been the "unofficial media" that have sabotaged the PR wizards in the Pentagon. The sophistication of the spinners has been matched by the sophistication of a media-savvy public.

Governments also use the images of amateurs when they help. The men charged with the 2005 subway bombings in London were identified in part through the use of images passengers on the city's underground captured with their cell phones. Those images, together with sophisticated face recognition technology, became a tool of law enforcement.

The emerging ethic of open source journalism has forced some interesting compromises with the emerging ethic of the blogosphere. (For a more detailed discussion, see Chapter 10.) But, open source journalism—particularly if it is managed by a more traditional news organization—faces the same ethical tests as more traditional photography. The premiums are accuracy, fairness and originality. Editors at open source cites realize that they must subject amateur content to the same journalistic standards—although not necessarily the same creative and aesthetic standards—as work by professionals. For instance, contributed video cannot be staged or re-enacted and then presented as news. Editors must be able to verify the accuracy, and sometimes the context, of citizen contributions.

STAGING PHOTOGRAPHS AND VIDEO

During a sweeps week, NBC's magazine show "Dateline" aired an 18-minute segment on a faulty design of General Motors pickup trucks that concluded with video of a truck exploding into flames immediately after a side-impact collision. More than 300 people had died in such collisions and the story included gripping still photographs

Calvin and Hobbes

by Bill Watterson

> "Your work sounds interesting." Francesca said. She felt a need to keep neutral conversation going.
>
> "It is. I like it a lot. I like the road, and I like making pictures."
>
> She noticed he'd said "making" pictures. "You make pictures, not take them?"
>
> "Yes. At least that's how I think of it." That's the difference between Sunday snap-shooters and someone who does it for a living. When I'm finished with that bridge we saw today, it won't look quite like you expect. I'll have made it into something of my own, by lens choice, or camera angle, or general composition or all of those.
>
> "I don't just take things as given; I try to make them into something that reflects my personal consciousness, my spirit. I try to find the poetry in the image."
>
> Robert James Waller, *The Bridges of Madison County*

of charred bodies pulled from accident scenes. They also produced court documents from the many suits filed against GM, including videotaped testimony from independent auto safety experts and a former GM engineer, all saying that the corporation had known about the design flaw yet had chosen to do nothing.

However, NBC did not inform viewers that, in order to ensure fire in the closing video, "sparking devices" had been mounted on the test cars by the independent testing agency the network had hired. General Motors filed a libel suit against the network, charging that the network had staged its dramatic video. In an unprecedented move, the "Dateline" anchors read a three-minute retraction of the original "Dateline" story, admitting that the network had aired the concluding video even though it was staged. The NBC–General Motors confrontation proved to be the end for network news president Michael Gartner who resigned less than a month later.

The NBC incident raises several questions. Is there a place for reenactment in the news? If so, when? How should such photos and video be labeled? The issues are not trivial, nor are they resolved. In a poll conducted by the National Press Photographers Association, the *number one ethical problem* reported by photojournalists was setup shots.

Photographer John Szarkowski (1978) writes of "mirror" and "window" photographs and his 1978 Museum of Modern Art show was entitled "Mirrors and Windows." The two types of photos are also roughly analogous to realistic and romantic photography. According to Szarkowski, window photographs should be as objective a picture of reality as the medium will allow, untouched by the bias of the lens or the photographer. On the other hand, the mirror photograph attempts to subjectively re-create the world in whatever image suits the photographer. Anything can be manipulated: light, proportion, setting, even subject.

Each type of photography has a function. A large percentage of the government-commissioned Dust Bowl–era photographs that have seared our memories of the Depression would fit into the mirror category. Photographers searched for settings, posed people and shifted props to achieve the maximum effect. On the other hand, the photos that show us the horrors of war and famine, and arouse public opinion, are windows, where the photographer captures the moment with no attempts to alter it. *The problem comes in the substitution of one for the other.* When a photograph mirrors a photographer's bias, yet is passed off as a window on reality, the viewer has been deceived.

ELECTRONIC MANIPULATION

Those who get their news from the Internet could hardly have missed it. The day after the 2005 Madrid train bombings the same photograph appeared on the front pages of a number of European newspapers—sort of. One front page displayed a photograph of the bombing with a bloody, detached limb in the foreground. Another paper displayed the same photograph, but the limb wasn't in it. Other papers cropped the photo so that only a part of the limb could be seen. Still others printed the photo in color, and some of those intensified the color of the blood with color saturation. It was the same photograph, but the electronic alternations were too obvious to ignore.

The history of photo manipulation is long, beginning with such crude drawing-board techniques as cropping with scissors and paste, darkroom techniques such as "burning" and "dodging," and, more recently, airbrushing. Today, technology allows increasingly sophisticated changes to be made to an image after it has been captured. Any person familiar with InDesign or any of many other software packages is keenly aware of how photos can be manipulated.

Technology has, in fact, made the word "photography"—literally "light writing"—obsolete, as a lighted reality no longer need exist in order for a "photograph" to be created. Photos and video are now what photography researcher Sheila Reaves (1987) has called a "controlled liquid." Writing more than two decades ago, in the infancy of computer manipulation of photography, Reaves foresaw a time photos would lose their "moral authority" while Tomlinson (1987) wrote that photos could lose their legal authority as well. As a more sophisticated audience visual media, viewers will bring with them a skepticism not present in previous generations of consumers.

Most editors and photographers agree that manipulation or staging of news photos is generally more culpable than manipulation or staging of feature photos. During the 2003 war in Iraq, a photojournalist for the *Los Angeles Times* was fired for combining two similar photographs into one more aesthetically pleasing one. While the resulting photo was so similar to the "real" ones that the difference escaped the eye of the photo editor, a line had been crossed, and the photographer was dismissed.

The reason for the different standard for news photography is a presupposition that *while art may be manipulated, information may not* (Martin 1991). The problem for audiences is compounded by the fact that both advertising and non-news sections of the newspaper make frequent use of these techniques. Confusion over what is appropriate in one context and not another is bound to occur, but we suggest that the same standard of visual truth telling can and should be applied to advertising as well.

SELECTIVE EDITING

Another ethical question centers on the video editing process: whether editing itself renders a story untrue or unfair. Actually, the term "selective editing" is redundant. *All* editing is selective. The issue is who does the selecting, and what predispositions they bring to the process.

A dual standard has emerged between words and photos. The writer is allowed to reorder facts and rearrange details into an inverted-pyramid story on the rationale that the reader wants the most important facts taken out of sequence, and even out of context, and placed first in the story for more efficient reading. The result is praised as good writing and is taught in every journalism program.

However, should a photographer attempt to do the same thing with a camera—rearrange reality to make a more interesting photo or videotape—the result is called "staged." Our unwillingness to allow visual journalists the same conventions as print journalists says something fundamental about the role of visuals in the news. When a writer edits, it makes for a more readable story, and the act is applauded. When a photographer or video editor does the same thing, he or she is open to accusations of distortion.

That is because we evaluate news photos according to print standards: linear and logical. Yet video and photographs are neither. They have a quality Marshall McLuhan called "allatonceness" that we are not quite comfortable with as a technology. Just what the photographer can do with the visual truth the camera uncovers is still a topic of debate.

However, as long as readers hold the view that "seeing is believing," that view—whether based in reality or not—becomes a promise between the media and their audiences that photographers and videographers should be hesitant to break. While many photojournalists argue that "seeing is believing" should have never been a cultural truism (see Lester 1992), others argue that we must work within our readers' or viewers' predispositions about the truth of what they see. Steve Larson (quoted in Reaves 1991, 181) director of photography for *U.S. News & World Report,* summarized this viewer-based rationale:

> The photo is a record of a moment in time. We're on shaky ground when we start changing that. We must maintain this pact. Catching a moment in time has history. When you look at a Matthew Brady photo there is that sense "this really happened." I believe strongly that's where photography draws its power.

EYEWASH

Imagine a new government study that is released on compulsive gamblers that you are told to make into a video package for tonight's news. You might show a woman enjoying herself on a sunny afternoon at the races. While her action is taking place in public view, she might or might not be a victim of the syndrome addressed in the article, although the casual reader might infer that she is, indeed, a compulsive gambler. In this context, the photo is serving the purpose of "eyewash," decoration for a story that bears no genuine relationship to it.

Eyewash has had a brief history in the courts. A Washington, D.C., television station used a tight shot on a pedestrian facing the camera, chosen at random, to illustrate the "twenty million Americans who have herpes." The court ruled that the combination of the film and the commentary was sufficient to support an inference that the plaintiff was a victim of herpes, which she contended was not true. But in another case, a young couple photographed in a public embrace in the Los

Angeles Farmer's Market had "waived their right of privacy" by their voluntary actions according to the California Supreme Court, which said that publication of their photograph merely increased the public who could have viewed the plaintiffs in their romantic pose.

While the courts have been ambiguous on the matter of eyewash, the media have created divergent policies to cover the issue. Some newspapers and television stations, for instance, will use no picture not directly related to the story. Others limit the use of file or stock footage to that which is clearly labeled. Others limit the shooting of eyewash only by insisting that it occur in public view.

The issue is exacerbated by the voracious appetite that both television and the print media have for visuals. Virtually all surveys have shown that the presence of a photo adds to the number of readers for a newspaper story, while television news consultants insist that viewers will watch "talking heads" for only a few seconds before diverting their attention elsewhere. The answer to the question "Have you got art?" often means the difference in running or killing a story. Good visuals can get a story in the coveted first slot on the nightly news or the front page of the newspaper.

Given the importance of visuals, it is not surprising that ethical lines blur. Coleman (1987) tells the story of his young son falling off a horse and breaking his arm. A photographer friend took a picture of the boy "dirty, tear-stained, in great pain, slumped in a wheelchair with his arm in a makeshift sling" on his way to the operating room. About a year later, a textbook publisher ran across the photo and wanted it as an illustration for a book on child abuse. Coleman denied the request but added that the photo could have easily been selected if he had not been easily available for the publisher to ask. The public would have been deceived by a photograph of a boy who had been a victim of nothing more than a childhood accident.

AESTHETICS AND ETHICS

Many newspapers and morning news shows have used the "Post Toasties Test" to determine the photos or video that accompanies early morning news stories. The test gets its name from a popular breakfast cereal and is a sensitivity test for media that might be at the breakfast table from newspapers to television and even Web sites. The test asked the question, "Does this need to be shown at breakfast?" Or in another iteration, "Should children see this over their morning breakfast?" According to Hodges (1997), no photographer or photo editor has identified "what exactly what we mean by 'in bad taste' The closest they come is to note that people do not want bloody pictures at the breakfast table."

Hodges argues that many issues in visual journalism that appear to be lapses in ethics are actually differences in opinion over matters of aesthetics—the ancient Greek branch of philosophy that considered beauty and what is beautiful and also whether beauty could be objectified or codified so that everyone could agree on its qualities. He also states that the ethics questions are more easily identified and solved than the aesthetic ones.

The question is central to the plot of *Mona Lisa Smile,* a 2003 film set in the 1950s at Wellesley College. When a first-year art history teacher (Julia Roberts) went off the syllabus (which all the students had read) and asked if a seemingly grotesque slide of a carcass was art, the reactions were quick and deep. "Aren't there standards?" asked one student. "Of course there are," said another, and the clamor started that would continue throughout the year as a determined teacher introduced the young ladies to Jackson Pollock and other contemporary artists despite the warnings of her dean.

On the issue of how rational humans could differ on the aesthetics, or beauty, of an image, Hodges states: "The mushroom cloud from the atomic bomb, for example, has always appeared beautiful to me. Those pictures led to moral rejoicing that the war was about over and my father would soon be coming home. For others, the cloud is symbolic of human evil, power and inhumanity."

An agreement on aesthetics is one of the most difficult in all of philosophy. Hodges states; "Philosophers, whose function is inquiry into the good (ethics), the true (epistemology) and the beautiful (aesthetics) have been far more successful and helpful in uncovering standards for the true and the good than for the beautiful."

Often, editors are required to consider both the good, the true and the beautiful simultaneously when looking at a photo that may or may not offend, that may or may not be "ugly" or may or may not be altered or doctored in any way.

CONCLUSION

The debate over visual ethics is emotionally charged and constantly changing with technology. Simultaneously, the consumer of news photography is sometimes presented with a product too raw to be watched and at other times too polished to be believable.

The problem lies in the nature of the photojournalist's job. On a day-to-day basis, photography can be a mundane and poor-paying job. One daily newspaper made waves in the summer of 2009 when it fired its entire photography staff, hired back a few at reduced salaries and opted for reader-submitted photos to replace the rest. So when an opportunity for a gripping photo does arise the desire to break out of the daily grind can lead to excess.

Photojournalists should operate under this version of Kant's categorical imperative: *Don't deceive a trusting audience with manipulated reality and don't offend an unsuspecting audience with your gritty reality.* Fortunately, only a small percentage of photos offend, and only a small percentage of photos are staged or electronically manipulated. However, photographers are dealing with a trust that readers and viewers have placed in them. If that trust is betrayed, it will be slow to return.

Suggested Readings

BERGER, ARTHUR ASA. 1989. *Seeing is believing.* Mountain View, CA: Mayfield Publishing Co.
BERGER, JOHN. 1980. *About looking.* New York: Pantheon Books.
Journal of Mass Media Ethics. 1987, Spring–Summer. Special Issue on Photojournalism.

LESTER, PAUL. 1991. *Photojournalism: An ethical approach.* Hillsdale, NJ: Lawrence Erlbaum Associates.

_____. 2003. *Images that injure.* 2nd ed. Westport, CT: Greenwoood Press.

NEWTON, JULIANNE. 2000. *The burden of visual truth: The role of photojournalism in mediating reality.* Hillsdale, NJ: Lawrence Erlbaum Associates.

Cases on the Web

www.mhhe.com/mediaethics8e

"Film at 10: Handling graphic video in the news" by Sonya Forte Duhé
"Looking at race and sex: When do photographs go too far?" by Beverly Horvitt
"Faking photos: Is it ever justified?" by James Van Meter

CHAPTER 8 CASES

CASE 8-A

The Case of the Well-Documented Suicide

PHILIP PATTERSON
Oklahoma Christian University

On August 19, 2012, filmmaker Tony Scott, director of such popular hits as *Top Gun, The Taking of Pelham 123* and *Day of Thunder,* leapt to his death off the Vincent Thomas Bridge in San Pedro, Calif. Tony and his brother, Ridley Scott, were both directors and had formed a production company together. According to his family, Tony Scott had no health issues that might have precipitated his act. He left suicide notes in his car and in his office prior to the jump.

What made this suicide notable, besides the high profile of the victim, was the number of witnesses—and photos—that documented the death both from the perspective of the bridge and from the perspective of the water below where day cruisers watched the event unfold.

Several people who were driving over the bridge when Scott jumped described witnessing what happened. According to the *Los Angeles Times,* the reactions varied from those who thought they were seeing a suicide to those who thought perhaps it was an extreme sports stunt.

"He was on the roadway close to the fence looking around. He was looking around and fumbling with something at his feet. He looked nervous," David Silva told the *Times.* Silva said Scott "paused a couple of seconds and then began to climb the fence. He put his foot on the top of the fence and paused again. And then he threw himself off. I immediately thought, that guy is dead."

Eric Brill, 59, said to the *Times,* "I could very, very clearly see his face. He was very determined. He was not crying, he didn't look upset, he didn't look sad. He just looked very resolute."

According to a staff report on the "TMZ" Web site, a video of that fatal leap "was captured on tape by multiple cameras . . . one showing Tony crouched the moment he began to jump . . . and "TMZ" has learned the shots are being vigorously shopped around . . . for a price."

"TMZ" reported that many people had used their cell phones for video and photos of the suicide. They added that the footage was also captured by a surveillance camera from a nearby business. "TMZ" declined to buy the footage but said that it was being shopped around to other sites.

One spectator called 911 and LA Port Police fished Scott's body out of the water soon after. An autopsy revealed no sign of cancer—a rumor that circulated in the hours after news of his death was broadcast.

Micro Issues

1. Are the photos and video of the suicide newsworthy? If the jumper had been a noncelebrity, is it still news?
2. Did the availability of photos or video make this an "above the fold" newspaper story or a television news package before the first break?

Midrange Issues

1. One of the photos that was shown to "TMZ" was reportedly of Scott at the moment he crouched to jump. Does that photo pass the breakfast table test? Are children a factor in the decision you make?
2. Do you see a difference in a photo of the jump as opposed to video of the entire jump? If so, what?
3. Using ethical theory, make a case for either including video of the suicide on your news program and/or Web site or not.

Macro Issues

1. Should there be a law prohibiting any bystander from profiting from an event like this? Does your answer change if the photographer could have rendered aid but chose to shoot pictures?
2. Best practices suggest that news organizations run coverage of suicide that includes the "warning signs" of suicidal behavior and local crisis counseling numbers to help forestall cluster suicides that have been documented in a number of cultures over several decades. The Scott stories ran with none of this information. Critique this approach, using ethical theory. What is the ethical obligation of the news media in situations like this?

CASE 8-B

What Do I Do First?

LEE WILKINS
University of Missouri

On Thursday, August 16, 2012, Associated Press photographer Gerald Herbert was on his way to an assignment in Biloxi, Miss., when he saw a sport utility vehicle that had slammed into trees along the side of a rural road. Two women were trapped inside.

The car was on fire in the engine compartment and the fire was increasing, getting to the point where it was fully involved.

She was crying and screaming for help and nobody could help. People were yelling "fire extinguishers" so I ran out on to the highway where all the traffic had stopped. I was running between all the parked cars looking for 18-wheelers because I know they carry fire extinguishers.

I would up running probably a half-mile to three-quarters of a mile, jumping on the cabs of all these 18-wheelers, telling them a woman was burning to death in a car, and to please get up there with their fire extinguishers.

I directed them onto the emergency lane. In time, I got about six tractor-trailers going down the breakdown lane. They all got out and started putting the fire out.

Simultaneously a cement mixer had shown up, and he had a hose and he probably made the biggest difference because I'm told that while I was marshaling the trucks to get their fire extinguishers up there, the flames were coming through the engine wall. He put his hose on her and he doused her and made sure the flames didn't get on her.

It was a really horrific feeling to hear her screaming and seeing those flames grow to high and get so close. You knew she was going to perish and there was nothing you could do about it. It sent a horrible chill through your spine.

AP Photo/Gerald Herbert.

Ultimately, the flames got knocked down. Someone hooked a cable to the car and a pickup truck pulled the car out of the trees. At this point, they were able to pry the door open and get her out as the fire was finally extinguished.

It never occurred to me to go into journalistic mode until the fire was knocked down. I knew she was safe so I went and got the cameras. The car accident is not news to the AP, but this clearly was an amazing heroic effort by all these people, and I wanted to document it. . . .

It was really powerful to see all these people saving someone from dying. It was amazing.

Micro Issues

1. Analyze Herbert's decision using the philosophical theories of utilitarianism, W. D. Ross, and feminist ethics. What elements do you find in common?
2. This incident had a happy ending. Do you think Herbert's response should have changed if the two women (they were sisters) had died, either at the scene or later? How might the photographs have changed?
3. This story ran nationwide. Was this an appropriate choice for news editors at papers thousands of miles away?
4. Contrast the coverage of this story with the many other stories about passersby helping those trapped in car wrecks. How does a journalist being involved change coverage? Is this appropriate?

Midrange Issues

1. Please read the fact situation in Case 8-G and then contrast the ethical decision making in this case with that made by the photographer in that case. What are the morally relevant differences?
2. How does Herbert's thinking match or not match the steps for photographers described in this chapter on deciding when to shoot?
3. Evaluate the composition and aesthetics of this photograph. Does it constitute a "good" photograph in terms of craft?

Macro Issues

1. Should the AP reward Herbert for his actions?
2. Please look at the fact situation of Case 8-F. How do Herbert's choices contrast to those of Greg Marinovich, the photographer in that case? How do you evaluate the impact of context—both in terms of country and in terms of the involvement of others—on the photographers' ability to help?
3. Can you develop a set of guidelines for photographers that outlines when it would not be appropriate to abandon the journalistic role for the helping one?
4. Compare the actions of this photographer with the onlookers at the suicide in the previous case. Is it reasonable to expect more from the onlookers on that bridge? Would it have been unreasonable to approve of Herbert's action if he had gone "into journalistic mode"?

CASE 8-C

Problem Photos and Public Outcry

JON ROOSENRAAD
University of Florida

Campus police at the University of Florida were called on a Saturday to a dorm to investigate "a large amount of blood on the floor of a women's bathroom," according to police reports. They determined that the blood "appeared to have been from a pregnancy miscarriage" and began searching the dorm area. Some time later a police investigator searching through a trash dumpster behind the dorm found bloody towels, plastic gloves, and a large plastic bag containing more towels and the body of a 6- to 7-pound female infant.

Police discovered no pulse. Rigor mortis had set in. After removing the body from the bag, the police briefly placed the body on a towel on the ground next to the dumpster. The photographer for the student paper, the *Independent Florida Alligator,* arrived at this time and photographed the body and dumpster.

Photo courtesy of the Independent Florida Alligator. *Used with permission.*

Later on Saturday, the 18-year-old mother was found in her dorm bed and taken to the university's hospital. The hospital exam revealed "placenta parts and the umbilical cord in her" and she was released later in good health. A local obstetrician contacted about the case said that judging by the size of the infant, it was likely a miscarriage and not an abortion. The infant was determined to be about seven months developed.

The story began on the front page of the Monday issue, across the bottom of the page, under the headline "UF police investigate baby's death at dorm." It jumped inside to page 3 and was accompanied by the photo.

It was a dramatic photo, contrasting two well-dressed detectives and one uniformed policeman with the naked body and contrasting the fragile human form with the harsh metal dumpster filled with pizza and liquor boxes. The photo was played 7 by 5 inches.

The story was well written and the photo dramatic but likely offensive to many—potentially so offensive that the newspaper's staff debated most of Sunday about how to use it. The editor decided to run it, but in an unusual move she wrote an editor's column explaining why that appeared on the opinion page of the same issue. It showed a scene one might visualize in a ghetto but not on a college campus. It showed that supposedly sexually educated and sophisticated college students still need help. The editor wrote:

> Even with these legitimate reasons we did not run the picture on the front page. This is partially in response to our concern that we do not appear to be exploiting this picture to attract readers. . . . We also examined the photographer's negatives to see if there were any less graphic prints. . . . Is the message perceived by the reader worth the shock he or she experiences? After pondering what we feel is a very profound photo, we decided there is. This was a desperate act in an area of society where it is not expected. The picture shows it.

The local daily covered the story Monday in a police brief. No photo ran. It was determined that the body was from a miscarriage. The woman involved left school. The campus paper got several letters critiquing its coverage of the story. Many chose to criticize the editors for running the photo, while some praised the staff for pointing out the problem and for listing places on campus where sex and pregnancy counseling was available. Some letters did both.

An example of some of the outrage over the running of the photo by the *Alligator* came from a female student who called the coverage "the most unnecessary, tactless piece of journalism I've ever encountered." Another letter from a male student called the photo "in poor taste and extremely insensitive." The writer added, "There are times when good, sound judgment must override 'hot' copy."

Perhaps the most pointed comment came from a female writer who added 24 other names to her letter. The letter stated:

> The incident *could* have been used to remind people that they need to take responsibility for their own sexuality. The story *could* have been used as a painful reminder that there are many un-educated, naïve people out there who need help. But, unfortunately, the *Alligator* chose to sensationalize the story with a picture, completely nullifying any lesson whatsoever that might have been learned.

Micro Issues

1. Should the photographer have taken the picture? Justify your answer.
2. Is this a legitimate story, and if so, does it belong on page 1?
3. If this was the only photo available, did the paper then have to run it?
4. Various letters to the editor called the photo "unnecessary," "tactless" and "insensitive." What would you say to those charges if you were on the staff?

Midrange Issues

1. Does running the photo inside lessen any criticism of poor taste? Did its placement mitigate any ethical criticism?
2. If the staff was so unsure, was the editor correct in writing a same-day rationale for its publication?
3. Critique the reasoning stated by the editor in running the photo. What moral philosophy, if any, would lead one to agree with the action?

Macro Issues

1. Should a paper play a story and photo like this to crusade about a problem?
2. Is the perceived social value of such a picture worth more than the shock and criticism?
3. Was the writer correct in her assessment that the shock of the photo negated any good that might have been done by the story?
4. Should a campus newspaper have a different standard—of taste, play, news value—than a "regular" daily?

CASE 8-D

Manipulating News Photos: Is It Ever Justified?

LEE WILKINS
University of Missouri

Author's Note; *By the decision of the* Los Angeles Times, *the photos in question in this case are not available. However, various Web sites have covered this controversy and some include the photos.*

The visual images of the 2003 war in Iraq were extraordinarily controversial. Photo editors, particularly at large media outlets, had to make decisions about hundreds of photographs every day. Sunday, March 30, was no exception. That night, *Los Angeles Times* director of photography Colin Crawford had edited about 500 photos of the war when he saw a picture from staff photographer Brian Walski. The photo depicts a group of Iraqi citizens sitting on the ground as an American soldier, armed with a rifle, stands in the foreground.

The *Times* ran the photo on Page 1, and so did sister publications the *Hartford Courant* and the *Chicago Tribune*. Thom McGuire, the *Courant*'s assistant managing editor of photography and graphics, said, "It was a great image."

But a *Courant* employee, who was looking through the images for a friend, thought he noticed a problem—what appeared to be a duplication of the Iraqi citizens in the background of the picture. He brought the problem to the attention of a copyeditor, who alerted McGuire. "After about a 600 percent magnification in Photoshop, I called Colin to ask for an investigation," McGuire said.

In Los Angeles, Crawford was disbelieving. He thought the apparent duplication of the background crowd was probably due to some sort of technical, satellite-related glitch. "He sent us 13 very good images Sunday," Crawford recalled. "We had to get information and give him the benefit of the doubt."

As it turned out, Walski had used his computer to combine elements of two photographs, taken moments apart, in order to improve the composition. Once that admission was made, Crawford fired him. All the publications that ran the composite photo ran corrections.

In his apology, Walski told other *Times* employees, "I deeply regret that I have tarnished the reputation of the *Los Angeles Times,* a newspaper with the highest standards of journalism . . . and especially the very talented and extremely dedicated photographers and picture editors and friends . . . . I have always maintained the highest ethical standards through my career and cannot truly explain my complete breakdown in judgment at this time."

Another *Times* staff photographer, Don Barletti, told the Poynter Institute's online discussion group that he recalled seeing Walski after he returned. Walski told him, "Now no one will touch me. I went from the front line of the greatest newspaper in the world, and now I have nothing. No cameras, no car, nothing."

Barletti also said he understood how the alteration might have happened. Walski had been in the desert for days under harsh conditions with little sleep and food and under enormous pressure. "He got into a zone," Barletti said. "He was on a head roll, making fantastic images, and it got out of hand. He told me that he did not plan to send the image and was just messing around. He sent it anyway . . . didn't know what he was doing, but he did it. With all that he was facing, how did he have the presence of mind? It just got out of hand."

When asked about the issue, *New York Times* photographer Vincent LaForet agreed that the breach was serious. "There is not ever a good time for such manipulation, but this is the worst time. What really differentiates us from other photographers and media is our credibility. We have a history of getting it right, accurately. . . . Our credibility is all that we have."

Micro Issues

1. How should the newspapers that ran the original photo have corrected the error?
2. Should Walski have been fired? Why or why not?
3. Many journalists who examined the photo did not notice the problem until it was pointed out to them. Is the minor nature of the alteration relevant in the ethical discussion? Why or why not?

Midrange Issues

1. Suzanne Lainson, also commenting on the issue on the Poynter Web site, said, "Why is the culture of the photojournalist supposed to be different than that for the print, audio or video editor . . . rather than condone editing photos, perhaps we should not condone editing print, audio and video data." Evaluate this comment.
2. What should be the role of editors—in an ethical sense—in the newsroom?
3. Should employees blow the whistle on colleagues when they think there has been an ethical breach? If not, why not? If so, how should they do it?
4. How does the electronic manipulation of the persons in the background differ from the photographer simply asking the people to move to a certain location before the photo is taken? Are they equally culpable from an ethical sense?

Macro Issues

1. "People do not expect 'truth' or 'reality' from their media—today's media audience is much more aware of the doctored nature of everything they read, see and hear than we like to think. I'm sure this *LA Times* story did not come as a surprise to most people," wrote Mark Deuze. Analyze this statement. How might media organizations assure viewers and readers of the veracity of the information they publish?
2. Eric Meyer, who commented about the issue on the Poynter Web site, said, "A photo is like a direct quote. You chose what to quote or what to photograph. But, when you run a direct quote or a photograph, you don't alter it to 'make it better.'" Evaluate this statement.

CASE 8-E

"Above the Fold": Balancing Newsworthy Photos with Community Standards

JIM GODBOLD, MANAGING EDITOR
Eugene Register-Guard, Eugene, Oregon

JANELLE HARTMAN, REPORTER
Eugene Register-Guard, Eugene, Oregon

Author's Note: *On Nov. 10, 1993, a nightmare unfolded in Springfield, Oregon, a quiet town adjoining the university community of Eugene, as Alan McGuire held his 2-year-old daughter, Shelby, hostage in their house. By the end of the standoff both were dead and the media had captured some horrific photos.*

Seven children had died as a result of child abuse in Lane County, Oregon, in the 20 months prior to that day, and the media had just witnessed the eighth. Jim Godbold was the assistant managing editor of the Eugene Register-Guard *at the time. The remarks in this case are from an interview with him months after the event.*

Godbold: The call came over the police scanner shortly after noon. We responded to a hostage situation, a man holding someone at knifepoint in a Springfield neighborhood. We knew it was probably 20 minutes from the *Register-Guard* in the best of possible circumstances so we really scrambled. Photographer Andy Nelson and police reporter Janelle Hartman went as fast as they could to the area.

We got there when the police were trying to set up a perimeter to get people away from the area. It was real pandemonium right when Andy arrived. The situation didn't unfold for more than a few minutes before there was a burst of flame inside the house that caught the attention of the police officers, and they immediately made the decision that they were going to have to go inside.

A group of officers ran at the door, and then all of a sudden Alan McGuire, the man who was in the house, came hurtling through the front window on fire. I am not even sure if police officers knew how many people were in the house at the time. His wife had escaped from the home. She had been held at knifepoint and bound, and she had somehow gotten out and she let police know that their 2-year-old daughter, Shelby McGuire, was in the house.

Shelby was a hostage and being held at knifepoint. Police saw her and tried to set up a telephone line so they could negotiate with McGuire, but the events unfolded rapidly, and after Alan McGuire jumped through the front window, police broke down the door. Two officers hauled McGuire's flaming body to the ground and tried to douse the flames with a garden hose. Inside the house one of the officers saw Shelby McGuire sitting upright on the couch. She had a plastic grocery produce bag over her head, and it apparently had been duct-taped in some fashion, maybe around the neck.

They immediately tore the bag away. A detective picked Shelby up and sprinted out of the house with her. It was at that moment that Andy Nelson snapped his picture of one of the officers with Shelby's body in his arms, running out, two other officers standing on the side of the doorstep, another officer with a hose near Alan McGuire, and Alan lying on the ground. The flame's now out, but the charred and still smoking body was present in the viewfinder as Andy snapped the picture.

At that moment the officer with Shelby McGuire, the 2-year-old, began mouth-to-mouth resuscitation on the front lawn. Andy subsequently took a photograph of that. Then they rushed both Alan and Shelby McGuire to the hospital. We did not know Shelby's condition. The police didn't respond about whether she was able to be resuscitated.

We have a standing policy at the newspaper that as a general rule we don't run photographs of dead bodies of children. That immediately triggered the kind of review that we would go through to determine where this particular incident was going to stand up on our policy, whether or not anyone was going to argue for publication or against publication.

We began to talk about the policy and the potential community reaction that we might face. The discussion was pretty brief. The photo was so compelling and the situation that it sprang from so horrifying that we began looking at the photograph and saying,

"Well, I don't know, but look at what the photo has captured." "People are going to be upset." "This is potentially a photograph of a dead 2-year-old child."

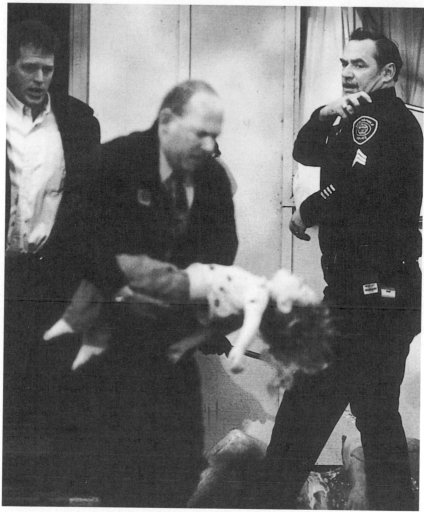

Photo courtesy of the Eugene Register-Guard. *Used by permission.*

"Look at the concern and the expression on the police officers' faces. This is an example of what they deal with day in and day out. They are up against this kind of domestic violence hostage situation and people don't realize that."

So, the debate was intense, and yet pretty short. We prepared a selection of pictures, and we brought those to the then-managing editor Patrick Yak and made the case that this is going to be a tough photograph for us to run. This is going to be one that we are going to have to be prepared to defend. But we believe it's that kind of exception to the rule that we look for.

The public response to the publication of the Shelby McGuire photograph was unprecedented in my 22 years in journalism and unprecedented at this newspaper. I have not come across a case, having been shown a number of them subsequently,

Photo courtesy of the Eugene Register-Guard. *Used by permission.*

that is of the magnitude per capita of reader response to a single photographic image. We received on the order of 450 telephone calls that began the moment people got the newspaper, which started at 6:00 a.m. First they came into our circulation department. The circulation department switchboard became overloaded and gave them the main newsroom switchboard, which didn't open until 7:30. At 7:30 when they threw the switch, all 20 of our incoming phone lines lit up, and the calls began to roll over into a holding pattern that had never been utilized by our switchboard before.

I was called at home by Al Gimmell, the corporate controller, who said, "We are inundated with telephone calls. We need some help." So I immediately came in to try to handle telephone calls, and I tried to find the time in between phone calls to call other editors in, but the calls were coming so rapidly that every time I hung up it rang again. When I picked up my voice mail messages, I had 31 unanswered messages, and that was probably 7:45 in the morning.

The range of responses weren't monolithic, except in their anger. But the anger came from different places. For some people the anger came from a belief that we had simply stooped to a tremendously sensational graphic crime picture trying to sell newspapers. For others the anger came from the terrible sense of violation that the surviving mother and brother of Shelby McGuire would have to wake up to the morning after their ordeal and see this on the front page of the hometown newspaper.

Another component argued that this was wholly inappropriate for the kind of newspaper the *Register-Guard* has been and continues to be. That 5-year-olds and 6-year-olds were sharing the newspaper at the breakfast table, and parents were finding themselves in a position of having to explain this horrifying incident and having the question "How is the little girl?" asked again. And there was also a range of response from people who were themselves victims of domestic violence or spouses of victims or had family members who were involved in it. For them it was a combination of anger and pain.

I spoke with literally dozens of people through tears. It was an emotional response that was overwhelming and people were extremely upset by the picture.

Most asked the question "Why? I need to understand why the newspaper published this picture."

We were really, I think, at a loss initially to respond to that question. I think a lot of that had to do with being in a very real sense out of touch with a substantial number of readers. The kind of reaction that we had was not anticipated by anyone in the news department.

If we were presented with a similar situation and a similar photograph today, we would absolutely not do it the way that we did it in the Shelby McGuire case. Thousands of our readers have defined for us a boundary in this community and for this newspaper that I don't think until we began to see it materialize we had any sense of exactly where it was.

Micro Issues

1. Look at the photos that accompany this text. The photo of the officer carrying out Shelby McGuire ran in full color above the fold, two-thirds of the page wide and 6 inches tall. Does a photo of that size oversensationalize the story?
2. The photo of Sergeant Swenson's attempts to resuscitate Shelby ran below the fold in a small two-column photo. Why do you think the decision was made to run this photo smaller and lower?

Midrange Issues

1. Does the fact that Shelby died influence your decision on whether to run the photos? If so, in what way?
2. Does the fact that at least one television station and the local Springfield newspaper were there with photographers influence your decision to run the photos? If so, in what way?
3. Does the fact that seven other children had died in Lane County in less than two years affect your decision to run the photos? If so, in what way?
4. The biweekly *Springfield News* chose to run a front-page photo of Alan McGuire falling out of the front window of his home, his badly burned flesh still in flames. However, they covered the front page with a wrapper that read "Caution to Readers" and explained the content of the stories and photos underneath the wrapper. Critique that approach to handling the story.
5. A local television station showed a few seconds of the scene described above after warning viewers of the violent nature of the video that followed. The station got fewer than 20 complaints. How do you explain the vast difference in the reaction to the broadcast and print photos?

Macro Issues

1. What are the privacy rights of:
    a. Shelby McGuire?
    b. Shelby McGuire's mother and 4-year-old brother?
    c. Sergeant Swenson?
2. Critique the argument that these photos should be shown because they illustrate the type of tragedy that law enforcement officers are often called upon to handle.

3. Critique the argument that these photos should be shown because they illustrate the horror of domestic violence.

4. Critique the statement that "If we were presented with a similar situation and a similar photograph today, we would absolutely not do it the way that we did it in the Shelby McGuire case." In your opinion is that based on sensitivity to reader concern or caving in to reader pressure?

CASE 8-F

Horror in Soweto

SUE O'BRIEN, FORMER EDITORIAL PAGE EDITOR
The Denver Post

On September 15, 1990, freelance photographer Gregory Marinovich documented the killing, by a mob of African National Congress supporters, of a man they believed to be a Zulu spy.

Marinovich and Associated Press reporter Tom Cohen spotted the man being led from a Soweto, South Africa, train-station platform by a group armed with machetes and crude spears. Marinovich and Cohen continued to witness and report as the man was stoned, bludgeoned, stabbed, doused with gasoline and set afire.

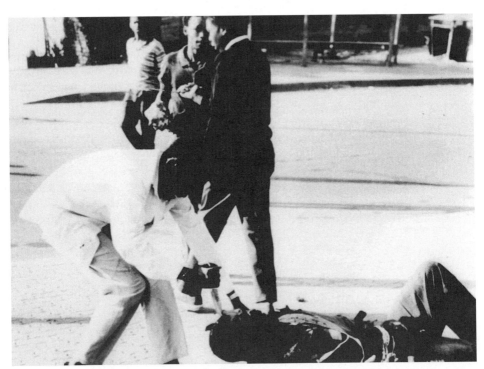

AP Photo/Greg Marinovich.

It was one of 800 deaths in two months of factional fighting among blacks as rival organizations vied for influence in the declining days of apartheid.

The graphic photos stirred intense debate among editors. In one, the victim, conscious but stoic, lies on his back as a grinning attacker poises to plunge a knife into his forehead. In the final photo of the series, the victim crouches, engulfed in fire.

As the series was transmitted, several member editors called up to question what the photographer was doing at the scene—could he in any way have stopped the attack? In response, an advisory went out on the photo wire, saying Marinovich had tried to intervene and then, when told to stop taking pictures, had told mob leaders he would stop shooting only when they "stopped hurting that man."

Decisions on what to do with the photos varied across the country, according to a survey. If any pattern emerged, it was that newspapers in competitive markets such as Denver, Minneapolis–St. Paul and New York were more likely to go with the harsh graphics.

The burning photo was the most widely used, the stabbing the least. Several editors said they specifically rejected the stabbing as too extreme. "It showed violence and animalistic hatred," said Roman Lyskowski, graphics editor for the *Miami Herald.* Another editor, who agreed that the stabbing was much more disturbing than the burning, said he recalled immolation pictures from the Vietnam era. "That's not as unusual an image as that knife sticking right out of the skull."

When the Soweto series cleared at the *Miami Herald,* the burning photo was sent to Executive Editor Janet Chusmir's home for her approval. At her direction, the immolation picture ran on the front page, but below the fold and in black and white. The detail revealed in color reproduction, Chusmir and her editors agreed, was too graphic.

At the *Los Angeles Times* and *Dallas Morning News,* however, the burning photo ran above the front-page fold–and in color.

The *St. Paul Pioneer Press* chose the stabbing for front-page color. "I look at the moment that the photo freezes on film," said News Editor Joe Sevick. "Rarely do you see a photo where a knife is about to go into somebody." The photo ran in color on the *Pioneer Press* front page, accompanied by the story Cohen had written on the attack and a longer story on the South African government's attempt, announced that day, to crack down on black-on-black violence.

In Denver, at the *Rocky Mountain News,* Managing Editor Mike Madigan wanted to run a comprehensive package on the Soweto story. The tabloid's only open page was deep in the paper, but a page 3 box referred readers to the story with a warning the photos were "horrific and disturbing." Inside, stories on the attack and government crackdown and an editor's note on Marinovich's intervention accompanied three photos: the victim being led away from the train station, the stabbing and the burning.

Most papers that ran the more challenging photos involved top management in the decision. Frequently, top editors were contacted by telephone, or came in from home, to give the photos a final go-ahead.

In most newsrooms, the burning or stabbing photos made it to the news desk for approval or rejection. But there, they sometimes were killed abruptly. "The editors at that point said no," one picture editor reported. "They would not take the heat."

Several editors deferred to the so-called breakfast test. "The question is 'Which of those photos would help tell the story without ruining everyone's breakfast?" asked Rod Deckert, managing editor of the *Albuquerque Journal.* One editor said his paper is especially likely to deemphasize disturbing material in the Sunday paper, which children often read with their parents. But many editors who rejected the more brutal pictures said the "breakfast test" is irrelevant. "If you're putting out a paper in New York and don't have something that's going to cause some discomfort over breakfast, then you're probably not putting out the full paper you should," said Jeff Jarvis, Sunday editor at the *New York Daily News.* "I don't think the breakfast test works for [today]."

Others cited distance tests. Some newspapers, in deference to victims' families, are less likely to use death photos from within their own circulation areas. Another editor, however, said his paper is *less* likely to run violent photos unless they are local and have a "more immediate impact on our readership."

Newspapers also differed widely on how they packaged the Soweto story. Some accompanied a photo series with the Cohen and crackdown stories, and a note on Marinovich's intervention. Some ran a single photo, often the burning, with only a cutline and a brief reference to the train-station incident in the "crackdown" story. Two respected big-city dailies, which omitted any reference to the Soweto attack in their accompanying stories, ran cursory cutlines such as "Violence continues: A boy runs away as an ANC supporter clubs a Zulu foe who was beaten, stabbed and set ablaze."

Although 41 papers used at least one of the Marinovich photos, only four—the *Charlotte Observer, Akron Beacon-Journal, Rocky Mountain News* (Denver) and *USA Today*—told the story of Marinovich's attempt to halt the attack.

Among collateral considerations at many news desks was the coverage of South African troubles that had gone before. At least one editor said the Soweto photos, which followed several other beating and killing photographs from South Africa that had been used earlier in the week, were "just too, too much."

With only three exceptions, editors said race did not figure in their considerations. One white editor said the fact that both attackers and victim were black deprived the series of clarity: "You don't have a sense of one side against another. You don't have a sense of right or wrong." Two editors who identified themselves as African-American, however, argued for aggressive use of the photos. Both work in communities with significant black populations. "I think black readers should be more informed about this," one said. "Across the board, black Americans don't realize what's going on with the black-on-black violence."

Front-page placement and the use of color frequently triggered reader objections, but the adequacy of cutline information and accompanying copy also appear significant. The *Albany Times Union* was flooded by phone protests and subscription cancellations. Two other papers perceiving significant reader unrest—the *Dallas Morning News* and *Los Angeles Times*—ran the burning photo in color on their front pages. But each of the three papers also ran the front-page photos with only cutline accompaniment, referring readers inside to the stories that placed the images in context.

In retrospect, *Rocky Mountain News'* Madigan said he was very pleased with the final Soweto package and readers' reaction to it.

AP Photo/Greg Marinovich.

It wasn't so much the idea that, "Yeah, we ran these really horrific pictures and, boy, it knocked people's socks off." I don't think that was the point. I think it was more the way we handled it. Just one word or the other can make a terrific difference in whether the public starts screaming "sensationalize, sensationalize," or takes it as a thoughtful, important piece of work, which is what we were after.

Micro Issues

1. In all but the most important stories, would you support a ban on dead-body photos in your newspaper or newscast?
2. Some editors believe it is their ethical duty to avoid violating readers' sense of taste or compassion. Others argue that it is their duty to force society to face unpleasant truths, even if it means risking reader anger and rejection. Whose side would you support?
3. Many readers suspect that sensational photos are chosen to sell newspapers or capture rating points by appealing to morbid tastes. Do you believe they're right?

Midrange Issues

1. Editors sometimes justify running graphic photos by saying they can provide a "warning bell," alerting people to preventable dangers in society. What values might the Soweto photographs offer readers?
2. Is the desire to avoid offending readers an ethical consideration or a marketing consideration?

3. Is it appropriate to base editorial decisions on what readers are likely to be doing at home: to edit newspapers differently, for instance, if they are likely to be read at the breakfast table, or present newscasts differently if they are to air during the dinner hour rather than later in the evening?

4. As an editor, would you be more likely to run a photograph of someone being murdered if the event happened in your own community, or if it happened thousands of miles away and none of your readers would be likely to know the victim or his family?

5. Do you see any distinction in:
   a. whether a violent photo is run in color or black and white, or
   b. whether it is run on the front page or on an inside page?

Macro Issues

1. Is aesthetic, dramatic or photographic value ever reason enough to run a picture, regardless of how intrusive it may be or how it may violate readers' sensitivities?

2. Is it your responsibility as an editor to find out if a photographer could have saved a life by intervening in a situation rather than taking pictures of it? Is that information you need to share with your readers?

3. Is it your responsibility as an editor to find out if the presence of the camera at the scene in any way helped incite or distort an event? Is that information you need to share with your readers?

4. When dramatic photographs are printed, how important is it for readers or viewers to be told all the background of the story or situation?

CASE 8-G

Death in Print: Publication of Hurricane Katrina Photographs

ABIGAIL M. PHEIFFER
University of Missouri–Columbia

"Do we publish this photograph of a dead body?" This is one of the most difficult questions newspaper editors can face. Editors at newspapers across the nation faced this question repeatedly as they reviewed wire photographs from the coverage of hurricane Katrina destruction in Louisiana and Mississippi. This case examines the Sept. 2nd photographic coverage of this event in three newspapers—the *Los Angeles Times, Chicago Tribune,* and *St. Louis Post-Dispatch.* Specifically, the study examines whether or not they published James Nielsen's photograph provided by Getty Images. The image depicts a woman standing on a bridge, feeding her dog as a corpse floats in the water underneath her. Sept. 2nd was the fifth day of the Katrina disaster.

All of the newspapers employ a similar process for choosing wire photographs on the day prior to publication of each issue. The first step is for a few wire editors to review the entire collection of photographs provided to them by Getty Images, the Associated Press and other wire services. These editors view hundreds of photographs and narrow the options down to those that they believe have the strongest visual impact.

The second step is to have a morning or early afternoon review of this initial edit. This takes place in the form of a formal meeting of all photo editors, an informal discussion of the photos among the photo editors or a full newsroom staff meeting. At this time the photo editors consider the merits of each photograph and learn the subject matter of the stories for which they must choose photographs. Based on this analysis the initial wire photo edit is narrowed to a smaller group of photos. One editor, often the director of photography or an assistant managing editor, reviews this narrowed edit and decides which photographs he or she believes should be on the front page, also known as A1. This editor then attends an afternoon A1 meeting and makes a pitch to the top editors, usually the executive and managing editors. This pitch includes the photo representative's opinions on where a photo should run in the newspaper and why it should run there. Detailed discussions of each possible A1 photo occur and final decisions are made regarding where photos will run.

St. Louis Post-Dispatch

The *St. Louis Post-Dispatch,* a newspaper that ranks 21st nationally in circulation among American newspapers with 271,386 daily circulation and 428,601 circulation on Sunday, published six Katrina photographs. The Nielsen photograph was published on page A10 and was stripped across the top of the page at roughly 4 inches tall and 11½ inches wide. The photograph was cropped from the top and bottom, cutting out some of the water, bridge and what appears to be the base of a light post. This puts greater visual emphasis on the corpse, woman and the bag of trash in the water. The front-page photograph for Sept. 2nd by Dave Martin of the Associated Press showed thousands of people boarding buses in Metairie, La., a suburb of New Orleans.

Larry Coyne, Director of Photography for the *St. Louis Post-Dispatch,* presents the photographic options for each day's edition in the A1 meeting. Coyne argued for the Nielsen photo to run on A1 but was in the minority. According to Coyne, the newspaper received many wire photographs that included dead bodies, but the publication was taking a cautious approach to running one, waiting for a photograph that was worthy of such a strong subject matter. Coyne advocated that this photograph run on the front page because it showed not only the tragedy of Katrina, but also how people were attempting to continue with their everyday lives. For him the juxtaposition of these two visual statements summarized the event and the destructive results of Katrina's power. "To get a full understanding you have to see it," Coyne said. "Until you see it, it is a figment of your imagination."

Coyne noted that there was a lively conversation in the A1 meeting regarding the Nielsen photograph, including a focus on whether or not the photograph trivialized the events of Katrina. There was concern that the photograph could offend readers because it included a corpse, but in the end the majority supported running the bus photo as the lead image because they felt it was more relevant to the stories planned for the Sept. 2nd edition.

James Nielsen /AFP/Getty Images.

Los Angeles Times

The *Los Angeles Times,* a newspaper that ranks 4th nationally with 843,432 daily circulation and 1,247,569 circulation on Sundays, published 15 Katrina photographs. The Nielsen photograph was published on the middle of the front page, just below the lead photo. The Nielsen photograph ran at approximately 3¼ inches tall and 5½ inches wide. The lead photograph, shot by Michael Ainsworth of the *Dallas Morning News,* showed a mob of evacuees arguing outside of the Superdome as they were boarding buses. The photo editors do work with a page designer early in the photo selection process, before a final decision is made, to determine where each photo will run. Although deference is given to the photo editor, the page designer's opinion is considered regarding where and how large the photographs will run in the publication.

Steve Stroud, the Deputy Director of Photography, represents the national, foreign and often the metro photo desks in the A1 meeting and makes the pitch for the A1 photos. Stroud states that the photo editors did consider not running the Nielsen photograph because of its graphic nature. However, the driving factor in the decision to run the image on the front page was that at the time the staff knew that at least several hundred people had died in New Orleans and there were predictions that the final body count could be in the thousands. Nielsen's work accurately represented one of the major stories that was coming out of the event on that day.

As Stroud stated, "Our role is to inform people and remind people in a way that is appropriate to the event." The Ainsworth photo was selected as the lead image because it is more active, better represents chaos and affects more people.

Chicago Tribune

The *Chicago Tribune,* a newspaper that ranks 6th nationally with 586,122 daily circulation and 950,582 circulation on Sunday, ran 17 Katrina photographs in the Sept. 2nd issue. The Nielsen photograph did not run on Sept. 2nd, but did run in a special section entitled "Special Report: Hurricane Katrina" on Sept. 4th. The image appeared on the bottom of page seven of the special section at roughly 4½ inches tall and 8½ inches wide. The image was cropped slightly from the top. The lead photograph on Sept. 2nd was a Getty Image photo by Mark Wilson that depicted crying women trying to help a relative who appeared to be fighting death outside of the New Orleans Convention Center.

Rob Kozloff, the Metro Picture Editor, was the substitute A section photo editor the week the Sept. 2nd edition was published. Kozloff believed that the Nielsen photograph was probably considered for publication in the Sept. 2nd edition, but was not one of the 15 photos that received serious consideration for A1. He stated that there were many photographs that dramatically depicted the emotion of the day. Some of these images were a better fit than the Nielsen photograph to the storylines planned for the Sept. 2nd edition. However, Kozloff felt that the image provided an accurate perspective once it was placed among many other photographs in the special section. When these images were viewed as a group they accurately represented the entirety of the Katrina disaster. According to Kozloff, Nielsen's work was intriguing because it is not clear to the viewer if the woman is aware of the body.

In all three cases these newspapers made it clear that an extensive discussion involving multiple management members is expected when an image is controversial. Each of the following questions was raised by one or more of the newspapers when deciding whether or not a photo will run and where it will run. Even though none of the newspapers had specific policies that covered the tragedy of Katrina, collectively, these questions form a set of criteria.

1. Is the image relevant to the stories that will run in the issue?
2. Is the photograph in good taste or is it too graphic?
3. Is there a compelling reason for challenging the reader with a controversial image?
4. Is the content of the image newsworthy? Does it educate the reader?
5. Does the image revictimize or embarrass the photo subjects or family members of the subjects?
6. What is the most important news story of that day?
7. Can readers tolerate the image when eating their cereal in the morning?
8. What is the tolerance level of our specific readership?
9. How technically strong is the image?
10. Is it likely that there will be a stronger image for the same topic in the future?
11. Is the image properly stating the case or is it overstating it? Is the image emblematic or gratuitous?
12. Does the event warrant use of a graphic photograph?

None of these editors mentioned selling newspapers as a criterion for deciding which image to use. The editors do consider not running controversial images or placing them inside the newspaper at a smaller size where they are not as startling to a reader.

When discussing controversial images the editors said the discussion often includes weighing the "good" of educating the public versus the "bad" of violating the privacy of the subjects in the photograph. Most of the editors indicated that they felt it was necessary to use a picture that forced the reader to confront death in order to understand the gravity of the situation in New Orleans.

The bottom line was best stated by Greg Peters of the *Kansas City Star,* when he said: "As a picture editor you learn every day and try to get smarter every day. We try to get better every day."

Micro Issues

1. Is the Nielsen photo a page 1 photo on the fifth day of the tragedy? Why or why not?
2. What story does the Nielsen photo tell?

Midrange Issues

1. Does moving a controversial photo to the inside pages of a newspaper allow the editors more latitude in what they show? Why or why not?
2. Does a warning before graphic video is shown on a local newscast give the station more latitude in what it shows? Why or why not?
3. If the body had been recognizable, would that change your opinion of running the photo? If the body had been unrecognizable but naked, would that change your opinion?

Macro Issues

1. Is it important that photos pass the "breakfast test" of acceptability before being run in the paper?
2. In weighing the "good" of educating the public to the horrors of the Katrina tragedy versus the "bad" of shocking the readership, where do you stand on running this photo? When the "bad" is the invasion of privacy of the dead individuals, where do you stand on running this photo?

CASE 8-H

Manipulating Feature Photos: The Case of a *Redbook* Magazine Cover

ELIZABETH HENDRICKSON
University of Tennessee–Knoxville

The June 2003 issue of *Redbook* magazine looked at first glance like many other popular magazines on the newsstand: It featured a cover photo of a popular actress surrounded by multiple cover lines. This particular cover starred actress Jennifer Aniston, wearing a red tee shirt and blue jeans, with hands on hips. The accompanying cover line touted:

> **Jennifer's Secret Passion:**
> She opens up about making babies, Brad's beard, and the tough time that tested—strengthened—their love
>   Plus: The key to her relaxed American Style.

A look inside the magazine credits the Aniston photograph to Barbara Green, for Image Direct/Getty Images, which indicates the cover image was not from a studio photo shoot, but rather, the photo was purchased from a stock photo agency.

While it is not uncommon for a popular magazine to utilize celebrity stock photos within its pages, it is somewhat unusual for a mainstream women's magazine to feature a stock photo of an A-list celebrity on its cover. However, what truly sets this cover apart from other competing women's titles was the public dispute between Aniston's publicist and magazine representatives that followed in the cover's newsstand wake.

According to Aniston's publicist, Stephen Huvane, the cover was procured without his consent, a tacit misstep when booking celebrities for magazine covers. But perhaps more significantly, Huvane claimed the cover photo was not one image but three different photos pieced together to make a composite photo. "The pants and her left hand with the wedding band are from one picture, her right arm, which is thicker and discolored is another, her head is from a paparazzi shot, her shirt is painted on, they changed her hair," said Huvane (Rush and Molloy 2003).

Additionally, Huvane complained that the inside photo credit gave a makeup credit, "as if she posed for a photo shoot."

A *Redbook* spokeswoman defended the cover, saying, "The only things that were altered in the cover photo were the color of her shirt and the length of her hair, very slightly, in order to reflect her current length." Moreover, *Redbook*'s then Editor-in-Chief Ellen Kunes, responded, "It's 100% her" (Rush and Molloy 2003).

While Huvane reportedly considered legal action against *Redbook* for "blatant manipulation of her [Aniston's] image," none was ultimately pursued. However, Huvane issued a statement perhaps even more damning to the magazine: that Aniston would never pose for *Redbook*. In 2003, the magazine industry considered Jennifer Aniston newsstand gold, with covers featuring the actress often being a title's top-selling newsstand issue for the year. The publicist's declaration was particularly salient given *Redbook*'s somewhat dire newsstand situation at that time. From 2002 to 2003, *Redbook*'s single copy sales had dropped 15.2 percent to an average of 471,930 copies sold per month. It may thus seem logical to assume that the magazine was hoping to boost single copy sales with an Aniston cover.

So why did *Redbook* editors seemingly feel compelled to bypass Huvane's approval in lieu of stock photos of the star? It was likely a matter of access. Aniston's publicist manages her image, so in an effort to restrain access to his client and control exclusivity, Huvane was approving very few publicity requests in 2003. The only June 2003 magazine cover Aniston posed for was *Harper's Bazaar.*

While the case of Aniston versus *Redbook* is a recent and palpable example of digital manipulation, the matter has been lurking within the publishing industry for nearly 25 years. The February 1982 cover of *National Geographic* was perhaps the first and most infamous example, done in a pre-PhotoShop age. In order to make a photograph of the Egyptian pyramids fit onto a vertical layout, editors digitally manipulated one of the pyramids closer to another without revealing the manipulation to their readers. Another notorious instance was a 1989 cover of *TV Guide,* featuring Oprah Winfrey. In the image, Winfrey's body was superimposed onto the body of actress AnnMargret (Kim and Paddon 1999). The reason given was that no photos were available of the newly-slim Oprah for the *TV Guide* cover, so they manufactured one.

Such cases raise ethical issues within the industry as to what can and should be done with the newly evolving technology. When the tools exist to create an image that appears more attractive, more flawless and possibly, more sellable, are there ethical constraints on publishing a relatively harmless but digitally created image?

Photographic manipulation is commonly considered to be altering or tampering with a photograph, thus shifting it from its truthful, natural state. But there is no general consensus on how much manipulation is allowable before the "truth" of the photo is compromised. For instance, while certain magazine editors do not feel it is wrong to digitally take out wrinkles, under eye bags or stray hairs from a photo image, others feel it is unethical to remove background images from a photo image.

According to sources within the magazine industry, Kunes' decision was not one existing in the industry mainstream, but rather one found on the professional fringes. However, the criticism centered more on professional need for continued access to celebrities, and less on truth or on duty to the reader. As one magazine art director (Hemmel 2006) said:

> It's a perception thing, if you do that you'll never get another cover. Certain people will talk to you but you can't get a shoot with them. It's considered within the industry that if you don't shoot them they shouldn't be on your cover. A lot of times they put them on their cover because they sell. But it's just looked down upon.

Micro Issues

1. Did *Redbook* cross an ethical line when it chose to put Aniston on the cover using a stock photo?
2. If it did, indeed, piece together a photograph from more than one source as Huvane claims, did *Redbook* cross an ethical line?
3. Since an increasing number of readers know how to manipulate digital photos and likely do so on their home computers, is it still deception to manipulate photos in this more media-savvy time?

Midrange Issues

1. Are the ethical standards of photography for *Redbook* different from a news magazine such as *Time* or *Newsweek?* If so, in what way?
2. Does *Redbook* have a duty to not alter photos that occur in a news story within the magazine on a topic such as women's health? Do the rules differ for news stories and features within the same magazine or newspaper?

Macro Issues

1. Who owns the image of Jennifer Aniston? Her? Her publicist contracted to manage her image? A photographer who has a signed contract with her? A medium that buys an authorized photo of her? All of the above?
2. Write a policy that addresses photo manipulation for a magazine such as *Redbook*.

CASE 8-I

Photographing Funerals of Fallen Soldiers

PHILIP PATTERSON
Oklahoma Christian University

Editor's Note: *In 2012, the war in Afghanistan became the longest-running war in U.S. history. And August of that year was one of the bloodiest months in the history of that conflict. With American soldiers dying weekly, the case below about their funerals is repeated across the nation.*

On May 11, 2004, an improvised explosive device struck the vehicle in which Army Spc. Kyle Adam Brinlee, 21, was riding in Iraq. He was killed in the explosion, the first combat-related death of an Oklahoma National Guard member since the Korean War. On May 19, more than 1,000 people gathered in the Pryor, Oklahoma, High School Auditorium for his funeral. Guests included the governor of Oklahoma, who spoke at the ceremony. Members of the media were allowed to attend but confined to a sectioned-off area. Most of the media were reporters from Oklahoma City and Tulsa media outlets.

In attendance also was photographer Peter Turnley who was shooting a photo essay for *Harper's Magazine.* It was to be the first of four "major eight-page photo essays" of Turnley's work that *Harper's Magazine* would showcase in the coming year (2004) according to a press release on the National Press Photographers Web site (www.npa.org). Turnley was a well-known photographer whose work had been on the cover of *Newsweek* more than 40 times according to Turnley's own Web site (www.peterturnley.com). He also had photos appear in such publications as *Life, National Geographic, Le Monde* and *The London Sunday Times* among others. He had also covered wars in such locations as Rwanda, South Africa, Chechnya, Haiti, Afghanistan and Iraq.

In August 2004, three photos from Brinlee's funeral appeared in *Harper's* in a photo essay entitled "The Bereaved: Mourning the Dead in America and Iraq." The essay focused on both American and Iraqi funerals with several pictures of grieving families, a photo of doctors unable to save a 10-year-old Iraqi boy and a stark scene of Iraqis passing by a corpse lying on the street in Baghdad. In an interview given before the essay was published (Winslow 2004), Turnley said, "This first essay speaks in images about a very important theme touching our world today in a way that I don't think has been seen much before elsewhere."

One of the photos shows Brinlee in an open casket at the rear of the auditorium with several mourners still seated in the background. As of the fall of 2006, this photo does not appear on a Web site of all the Turnley photo essays for *Harper's Magazine.* It was not available for printing in this book, but can be found on page 47 of the August 2004 edition of the magazine.

Brinlee's family filed suit against Turnley and the magazine claiming a variety of torts including intentional infliction of emotional distress, invasion of privacy and unjustly profiting from the photos. In their filing, the family claims that despite the large crowds in a public school, the funeral was a "private religious ceremony." They added that the photos went "beyond all bounds of decency."

The family claimed that Turnley had been told by the funeral director to abstain from photographing the body of the soldier. In a response to the court, Turnley denied he had received the instructions, and claimed the body was placed near the media section for access. In a later interview with CNN, Turnley claimed: "It seems to me that the responsibility of a journalist today is to tell as much as possible about the true realities of what is taking place in the world. My desire is to simply try to dignify the reality of what people experience in war by showing the public what does happen there."

"The casket was open for friends and family—not to gawk at and take pictures and publish them. Not for economic gain," the lawyer for the family argued in an interview with the Associated Press.

The family sought $75,000 in actual damages on complaints including publication of private facts, appropriation of Brinlee's photo for commercial purposes and intrusion. In December 2005 a federal judge ruled that the family privacy was not invaded by the photos. "[P]laintiffs appear to have put the death of their loved one in the public eye intentionally to draw attention to his death and burial," Judge Frank Seay ruled in granting summary judgment to the media defendants. Elsewhere in the ruling, Seay pointed out that the plaintiffs lost their right to privacy during the funeral by choosing to publicize the event.

Harper's Magazine publisher John R. MacArthur echoed the ruling of the judge. "For me, from the beginning, it was a First Amendment issue and it was also a matter of our integrity. I have not met anyone yet who thought that photograph was disrespectful in any way."

Micro Issues

1. Can a funeral that is held in a public place be considered a private event?
2. Does it make a difference that Turnley and other media were given permission to attend the funeral?
3. Does it make a difference that the photos taken were of images in plain view of those attending the funeral?

Midrange Issues

1. Is newsworthiness a legal defense to the claim of invasion of privacy? Is it an ethical defense?
2. Does the fact that the family allowed media coverage of the funeral prevent them from suing for the distress that the Turnley photos allegedly caused? If the family had not allowed media coverage of the funeral, would your opinion of Turnley's photos be different?
3. In what way, if any, would video of the funeral differ from the still photographs of Turnley?
4. Are open-casket photos of soldiers a reality that journalists should be covering as Turnley contends or "beyond all bounds of decency" as the family contends? Can the two sides be reconciled?

Macro Issues

1. Is this a First Amendment issue as the judge and the media maintain? When other rights, such as the right to privacy, come into conflict with the First Amendment, how is the conflict best resolved?
2. What is the role of the media in covering conflicts such as the war in Afghanistan or the Arab Spring, which turned genocidal in Syria? Do wounded soldiers or civilians have any privacy rights that trump the public's right to know?

9

New Media: Continuing Questions and New Roles

By the end of this chapter, you should be able to:

- **separate the first informer from the information verification role in journalism.**
- **develop professional strategies for using the Internet as a reporting and advertising tool.**
- **delineate important policy issues the Internet raises for journalists and citizens.**

The original journalists in America were citizens who stepped into the role of pamphleteers or publishers based on a desire to shape an emerging nation. Most of them, like Benjamin Franklin or Thomas Paine, had sources of income outside of their role as citizen journalists, and many lost money in their publishing pursuits. During the next 100 years, the role of professional journalist emerged in the new democracy and for the next century, the delivery of information was primarily considered the role of the full-time professional.

However, no formal education or license is required to be a journalist. Toward the end of the 20th century—propelled by the Internet—it became evident that the role of "journalist" no longer belonged exclusively to the trained writer working at a recognizable institutional media outlet.

And even institutionally employed journalists today often step out of their institutional roles through their tweets and blogs—some out of passion, others by contract with their employers. Citizen journalists who have never been in a newsroom now create Web sites, write blogs and gain twitter followings whose readers rival in numbers the readers of the mainstream press and whose stories often break important national and international news. Videos on YouTube often receive a number of "hits" that would rank them among the top-rated television programs if they had been measured by the Nielsen ratings. While the delivery methods are new, the concept is old: citizen journalists as the eyes and ears of the public. And as they point their cameras at increasingly serious topics, the results are often dramatic.

226

The most dramatic of these events was the 2011 Arab Spring, a country-by-country revolution in the Middle East that owed its emergence to social media and the ability of cell phone users to congregate to protest dictatorships that, in the ensuing months, collapsed, sometimes peacefully but often through the use of military force. New York University Professor Clay Shirky predicted something like the Arab Spring in his 2009 book *Here Come's Everybody* when he noted that the Internet gave individuals the power to organize as never before. While Shirky was prescient in his analysis of one kind of organizational capacity the Internet makes more possible, he and many others failed to grapple with the specific kind of organizational tool the Internet itself constitutes.

The Web is very good for getting people together in a common cause, whether it's overthrowing a government or tracking down a stolen bicycle by asking "friends" to keep an eye out for it. Social media is particularly adept—it appears—in separating people into groups. In fact, as the film *The Social Network* makes clear, the original impetus for the site was all about what sociologists call in-groups and out-groups—a way of giving everyone access to the sort of social status as "cool kids" that too many geeks and brainiacs were denied in high school and college. Getting rich in the process didn't hurt, either.

But, social media does not appear to be an effective organizing tool in the sort of activities, like forming a government after a revolution, that require face-to-face interaction over a long period of time with people who are like and unlike "you" in significant ways. The Internet is great for that initial burst of energy; the sustained commitment to building a "new" social and political structure of almost any sort demands time and face-to-face interaction. While social media can promote some of that effort, the technology itself appears to make some sorts of human activity no more possible than has been the case in other eras.

In-groups and out-groups are also ethically problematic. Indeed, if philosophical theory is taken seriously, then one of the intellectual goals of ethical thinking is trying to lessen and where possible eliminate the in-group, out-group divide. In a democracy, listening only to "friends" can lead to the sort of political structures that the Arab Spring successfully overcame. Professionally, some of the best journalism and advertising emerges not when you are thinking "just like" everyone else, but when you succeed in making others take a look at things for a point of view that is unlike their individual experiences.

In the early 21st century, social media seems to be separating two roles that about 400 years of media history had previously blended. The role of information provider and collector—what some scholars and professionals now refer to as the "first informer" role—can be done by citizens as well as journalists. But citizen journalism lacks one important component that traditional media had: information verification. It is this second role—verifying information and placing it in a social, political and cultural context—that is becoming more and more the work of journalism.

The first informer role values speed. The information verification role is what makes the initial fact into something reliable and accessible to all. The information verification role values truth, context and equality. It can and does employ social media as a corrective—and sometimes an essential one. But, it is the ethical values of truth and inclusive access that will continue to fund professional performance in this Internet age. Indeed, if professionals lose their adherence to these values, there will be little to separate them from first informers and less to separate the institution of the mass media from its role as check and balance on the other powerful actors such as the modern nation-state and the multinational market.

THE VIRTUE OF ORGINALITY

How would you ethically use the following information: first take a photograph of a camel and electronically cut it into pixels. Then change the individual pixels' colors and reorganize them into an elephant. Next, download the resulting image, which now looks a great deal like an elephant and lacks a negative to indicate that it was once a camel, onto a Web site that belongs to your news organization or strategic communications firm, and link it to an article about natural history or a public relations release for a local wild animal shelter. Have your actions constituted some form of copyright infringement? Is it like using "freelance" work in a publication? Could the links or the original image constitute unjust enrichment? Are you cheating in some fundamental way?

Is the execution of the idea that the photograph represents the property of the photographer who shot the original image, the property of the multimedia author who took the photograph of the camel and changed it to an elephant, or the property

Ed Stein ©1996 Reprinted with permission of UNIVERSAL UCLICK. All rights reserved.

of the news organization that ultimately distributed it on a Web site? How about the designer or the content creator of the page? Is there an express or implied contract in any of these actions? Does the creator of the elephant image owe royalties or acknowledgment to the creator of the camel?

The ability to digitize information also challenges our intuitive assumptions about a variety of things—everything from the "reality" that a picture represents to the external symbol systems that words and images together create. Digitization enables media designers to confound the external referent as never before. Students at the turn of the century will recognize that Audrey Hepburn's image has been digitized and electronically inserted into a Gap ad. But students now or in the future may not recognize the original Audrey Hepburn, may not know that she was a film star and may not be aware that she has been dead more than half a century at that point. They will have lost the external referent to the image and much of the ad's potency with it.

Ethical thinking combined with sound professional practice can provide some paths out of this virtual swamp. The first, and probably the most basic, maxim arises from the habits of sound professional performance. Cite the source of your information—or your electronic bytes. After all, journalists are required to note the originators of their information when reporting on documents or interviews. Multimedia designers should be subject to the same standard, just as music arrangers (as opposed to composers) or screenwriters currently are. Just as important, source needs to be credible—even accurate. Newspapers and broadcast outlets are loathe to publish rumors. Internet news—if it is to succeed as a genuine information medium—needs to consider the same standard. Just as in the days of the film *The Front Page*, scoops for the sake of scoops are ethically suspect.

If noting the originators of your information creates problems, then be willing to accept those problems as the price of using the information. Many publications require that journalists avoid sourcing their stories exclusively from the Internet; some demand confirmation of an independent source with additional verification from nonvirtual documents and in-person interviews. In an ethical sense, such professional standards allow news organizations and those who work for them to achieve two results. In the Judeo-Christian tradition, you have avoided information theft, an ethically culpable act, and fulfilled the ethical duty of beneficence, sharing credit with the originator of your information, whether that is a particular author or the source of a quote in a feature story.

In addition, you've also done your best to uphold the professional standards of accuracy and truth. In this world of bits and bytes, application of a maxim of "Cite the source of your bytes" will prejudice you to the development of original and creative work, including multiple sources. And, using your own stuff, and not someone else's, improves performance.

The second maxim that emerges from a discussion of deception is this: information that has the capacity to deceive the rational audience member as to its origin, original referent or source must be regarded as suspect. While journalistic discussion of deception has generally focused on practices used to obtain stories, we believe the concept also applies to the relationship between the journalist and his audience.

The issue is whether using digitized information is intended to mislead the audience. Thus, an October 1996 cover of *Life* magazine that combined more than 400 previous covers into an image of Marilyn Monroe does not intend to deceive the audience because the editors clearly explained what they did. But lifting an image from one Web site, downloading sentences from another and combining them for your own news story without citing your original sources is a theft of other's work and an attempt to deceive both your editors and your audience.

While both plagiarism and forgery are clearly deceptive practices (Bok 1983, 218), the Web, with its nearly infinite possibilities as a source of information, has highlighted the need for journalists to take care. Even in a new era of pixels and bytes, journalists must maintain old-fashioned credibility with our audiences about the sources of our information and the means and methods of gathering that information.

MASS MEDIA AS AN INSTRUMENT OF FRAGMENTATION

If there was a single basic tenet of American mass media for most of our 200-plus years of existence, it would be the belief that the shared experience of consuming the daily news was crucial to informed participation in a democracy. But more than 30 years ago, Nicholas Negroponte, head of MIT's Media Lab and an early Internet guru, created a unique publication he called the *Daily Me*. Negroponte programmed his computer to develop a daily newspaper based on his information needs and desires as well as past information preferences, an experience he wrote about in the important early work *Being Digital* (1995). In a day when news was typically delivered for the masses on a prearranged schedule convenient to the sender, Negroponte's invention was a landmark one for its time.

Today, all of us now have the capacity to develop a *Daily Me* from the vast collection of information now on the World Wide Web. If every member of a society has access to personalized news, the implications for democracy are enormous. According to Cass Sunstein (2001), democracy demands two imperatives. First, people must be exposed to materials that they would not have chosen in advance and come across views that they would not have previously selected or even agree with. Second, many, or at least most, citizens should have a range of common experiences. In the absence of shared experiences, society will have a much harder time addressing social problems, Sunstein contends. Shared experience and the societal benefits of common knowledge were also at the core of the Cultural Literacy movement late in the last century.

Philosopher Jürgen Habermas is another advocate of this approach, arguing that one of the preconditions of a deliberative democracy is a large number of public forums where people meet by chance and begin a dialogue—none of which is possible in a society where everyone subscribes only to the *Daily Me*. Sunstein concludes that "The imagined world of the 'Daily Me' is the farthest thing from a utopian dream, and it would create serious problems from a democratic point of view."

SOURCES: NEW TECHNOLOGY
BUT CONTINUING ISSUES

New technology often raises old ethical issues with additional permutations, and the subtleties of sourcing on the Internet don't all focus on accuracy and speed. Journalists accept that readers and viewers may better understand and evaluate news if those stories identify information sources. Identification often goes beyond a mere name and address: journalists may provide background information so audience members understand why a person or document is cited. The professional standard is that sources should be named and that journalists must have compelling reasons for withholding a source's identity. Implicit in this standard is that sources are aware that they are talking to a journalist, or that a specific document has been requested for a journalistic purpose. The Internet can confound these implicit assumptions.

First, granting anonymity requires a mutual agreement between reporter and source, not a unilateral understanding imposed on one party by the other. Anonymous sources are expected to be the exception rather than the journalistic rule. Professional mores dictate that, should a reporter decide to grant anonymity, she does not have to divulge the source's identity to editors, other supervisors or, in rare instances, the courts.

Even the traditional practice of interviewing, now considered commonplace, was controversial at its inception. The critics claimed that interviewing would destroy reporting and that only first-person observation was worthy of making the newspaper. The critics of interviewing argued that if journalists adapted this reporting technique, they would slip into a moral morass, fall prey to aggressive exploitation and manipulation and would no longer serve the public. Reporters' power grew with the use of the interview because they could select which persons to question and determine which comments to include. As the journalistic practice of the interview developed concurrently with the rise of the professional ideal of objectivity, identifying news sources became accepted professional practice (Schudson 1995, 1978).

The role sourcing plays with readers and viewers has also been questioned in mass-communication research. One of the most widely accepted findings in the field is that audience members tend to disassociate the source from the message, what is known as the "sleeper" effect (Lowery and DeFleur 1988). Studies confirm that most people tend to retain the fact of what is said while forgetting the context in which they heard it. Practitioners, from Nazi master propagandist Joseph Goebbels through contemporary political consultants, have intuitively understood this human tendency to disassociate the source from the message. But readers and viewers are morally autonomous actors. Identifying news sources allows audiences to evaluate reports in terms of both content and a source's motives for divulging information. And with a recent Supreme Court decision allowing political action committees (PACs in popular vernacular) to spend unlimited money to benefit a political candidate with only small type on the television screen and a two-second disclaimer that this message did not come from the candidate, the stakes are high indeed to know who is funding the messages they see during a political season. Some of the most pointed negative advertising has come from these PACs, allowing the candidate to disavow any knowledge of a particular ad and even to lament its message if he or she wishes.

The motives for providing and withholding information are sometimes central to political coverage, and political reporters have added an element of elasticity to the practice of anonymous sourcing. The phrase "not for attribution" means journalists may quote what is said but agree to veil the source. Thus, the attribution "a high-level White House source" may mean anyone from the president himself to cabinet officers to other, well-connected administrative appointees. The phrase "on background" means journalists should consider the information given as an aid in placing facts in context. Background information also may be used as part of a sourcing trail: journalists in possession of background information may use their knowledge to try to get other sources to provide them with the same information on the record.

Journalists continue to debate allowing sources to go "off the record" or "on deep background." A strict interpretation of these synonymous phrases means that the journalist who accepts such information may not quote the specific source and, in addition, may not use his knowledge to pry the same information from other sources. This stringent interpretation has meant that editors have instructed reporters to literally leave the room when a source asks for such anonymity. Journalists have spent time in jail rather than reveal a source's identity. Less stringent interpretations suggest that journalists who accept information off the record may not name or in any way reveal the identity of the source but may use the information itself to leverage similar or related information from other sources.

Until quite recently such agreements were arrived at through face-to-face conversation and negotiation. However, the advent of the Internet and the ability of journalists to lurk at many places on the Web have changed these dynamics. Journalists surfing for story sources or leads must be careful to identify themselves professionally on the Internet when they begin "conversing" with another Internet user. Concepts such as citizen journalism have also changed the journalist–source relationship. Citizen journalists essentially function as reporters who are most often edited by professionals. But most citizen journalism projects do not attempt to either confirm or police how citizen journalists acquire their information. In some cases, citizen journalists appear to be subject to a different set of rules than are the professionals.

Some publications, for example the *Wall Street Journal,* maintain an informal policy that requires reporters to identify themselves as reporters when they begin their Internet conversations. The reasoning behind such requirements is that people, in this instance people who are "telepresent," need to know that they are dealing with a journalist working in a professional capacity. Since journalists are well aware of the pitfalls of being deceived by a source, "wired" reporters should be more than sensitive to these problems when they become the party to the conversation with the power to deceive.

Such professional identification—the Internet version of identifying yourself at the beginning of a telephone conversation—also raises additional professional issues. For example, it is possible for competitors, who also may be surfing the

Net, to learn about the direction of a story or even of its specific content during the reporting process. This increases the chance that other news organizations will learn about stories or angles they have missed sometime before actual publication. While this sort of competitive consideration has always influenced journalism, the Internet makes it easier and faster to learn what other news organizations are doing.

Whether in person or through fiber optics, journalists who cover police, the courts and other areas of public life often develop informal agreements with frequent sources about when and how information may be attributed. Such relationships are necessary but risky. Many journalists have had to decide whether they will "burn a source," that is, to reveal the identity of a source who has been allowed to remain veiled in earlier stories for a particularly important story.

Burning a source means terminating a relationship that worked well for both parties. It is considered a form of promise breaking. Historically, such promise keeping has been more of a one-way street. However, the capacity of sources to manipulate journalists—and hence news coverage—particularly on issues such as national security, raises important ethical questions, ones we ask you to consider in several cases in this book.

Keeping the trust between reporter and source intact is one reason that larger news organizations will often send an investigative reporter to cover a particularly sensitive story that arises on another reporter's beat. Sending an investigative reporter allows the beat reporter's sourcing agreements to remain undisturbed, ensuring a continuing flow of routine information while the investigation continues. There are significant ethical justifications for using anonymous sources. They are:

- Preventing either physical or emotional harm to a source.
- Protecting the privacy of a source, particularly children and crime victims.
- Encouraging coverage of institutions, such as the U.S. Supreme Court or the military, which might otherwise remain closed to journalistic and hence public scrutiny.

It is this final justification that is used most frequently by journalists. Reporters maintain that only when sources are allowed to remain anonymous will they provide newsworthy information that would otherwise place their careers or their physical safety at risk. While using the Internet as a reporting tool does not alter these justifications, it emphasizes the need for disclosure when working with sources in ways that nonvirtual journalists seldom encounter. The thinking may be the same, but the situation that prompts such reflection may look very different at first glance.

The Internet also had added new layers to sourcing—allowing readers/viewers to comment on published pieces and embedding links to allow readers and viewers to follow up for additional information. The impetus for reader commentary was at least twofold: first, it would promote reader/listener/viewer engagement, perhaps making stories more accurate and adding interest. Second, managers theorized that engagement would build an audience base that would be willing to pay for the project. The rationale for links was even more straightforward: the Web had unlimited space and providing links allowed for expansive coverage, providing the reader was willing to follow up.

But, like many such efforts, when readers or viewers were allowed to publish their comments on a story, there were some unexpected consequences. Reader comments were sometimes inaccurate—they spread unfounded rumors and promoted wild conspiracies. Sometimes they were vitriolic; readers indulged in personal attacks that, had they been done by a journalist, would have resulted in libel suits. News organizations had to develop policies that promoted civil and on-topic commentary—something that is not as easy as it sounds. For instance, in coverage of the drought and subsequent wildfires in the summer of 2012, a story by an urban newspaper about the loss of more than 40 nearly homes in the county attracted comments to a newspaper Website that called the county-dwellers "hicks" while others questioned their parentage in no uncertain ways. Others said that city resources such as firefighters should not be used to help people living outside the city limits. A comments section that should have been deluged with sympathy for the families, instead created a chance for some readers to anonymously ridicule nonurban residents whose mobile homes had been destroyed. Because of instances like this, many news organizations moved away from anonymous commentary, although some allowed readers to assume a "nome de plume," these "handles" still had to be registered by a real person providing real identification information.

Other organizations have developed and promoted an online commentary rating system which, over time, lets the readers of the comments relegate the sillier and more antagonistic comments to a much less prominent place on the Web site, often buried several "pages" down. And, some publications decided that, on certain sorts of stories, there would be no public commentary allowed. This online winnowing in many ways resembled the less technologically enhanced activity that professionals call "source verification"—a professional skill that involves learning who to trust and in what context so that information can be verified and credible before it is passed on.

Links proved equally problematic, in part because the drive to provide additional information sometimes converged with a profit motive. In a *Columbia Journalism Review* (*CJR*) study, the Web site Gawker was found to be a particularly heavy user of borrowed material, often with little credit or links to the original source. One Gawker posting on the Church of Scientology allegedly borrowed heavily from work done by the staff of the *St. Petersburg Times* according to *CJR*'s Bill Grueskin. In an article entitled "Gawker's Link Etiquette (or Lack Thereof)," Grueskin found that most of the links in the Gawker article were actually to other Gawker works and the ones that did lead to the original journalism of the *Times* were buried late in the article. Grueskin noted that his own earlier research while he was at WSJ.com indicated that if a link is buried in a story where the reader has scrolled two or more screens there is a 95 percent chance they would not leave the article for the link.

To counter the perceived lack of rules, some mainstream media news organizations, in late 2009, began efforts to make specific news items "ungoogleable"—that is, unreachable by a search engine other than the proprietary one offered for a fee by the medium. It was an effort that addressed revenue streams without full consideration of the ethical questions involved. Will locking up information behind a pay site allow news providers to roll back the clock and stop the free flow of information to the Web that began at the end of the last century? Or will it just send would-be readers looking elsewhere for the same information—assuming it is available at all?

In an exchange that provokes both laughter and tears, a reporter at the now-defunct *Rocky Mountain News* was told by a neighbor, "Well, I'm sorry the paper is going away, but I'll still read you on the Internet." The delusional Denver resident was not the only reader to fail to understand—and appreciate—the connection between the expensive process of newsgathering, including information verification and contextualization, and the apparently free access to its result through blogs and search engines.

Finally, there was the whole Kevin Bacon thing: how many links of separation were enough? If clicking through multiple links that began with a story about a local mosque landed readers and viewers on a hate Web site, who was responsible? What constituted due diligence when news organizations placed links in their stories?

POLICY OPTIONS: THE ROLE OF THE PROFESSION

Unlike some media technologies such as the printing press, the Information Superhighway was initially developed by the government for political reasons. The original Internet was a computer network designed first to support the military and then, in the 1960s, reorganized to allow scientists working primarily at universities and government laboratories worldwide to communicate quickly and easily among each other. This system remained confined to the intellectual and military elite until the early 1980s, when the Internet, as we now know it, began to take shape.

This unusual history—a mass medium that was "invented" to support government policy—has made the Internet a difficult fit for both academic study and journalistic necessity. Unlike the printing press, which began as a private invention and remained private property, the Internet has historically owed a great deal to the government in both conceptual and financial terms. Because journalists never were part of the early history of Internet development, the notion of using the Internet as a profit-oriented mass medium is a very recent invention. Grafting a concept of mass communication onto a system designed for government-supported communication is fraught with the potential to raise some difficult questions.

The political aspects of the Internet are fairly straightforward: by linking schools, hospitals and libraries, the government is supporting an infrastructure that will promote education and learning and thus strengthen the economy by providing a better-educated workforce. A better-educated workforce is also generally considered a more efficient one, thus making U.S. workers more competitive worldwide as well as driving down production costs domestically.

A better-educated populace, of course, also has military implications: it enables the military to draw from a more qualified pool of recruits who are being asked to operate increasingly more complicated weapons. Thus, the reasoning goes, the federal government fulfills its constitutional responsibility to protect Americans from international as well as domestic threats by supporting a system that will promote the country's growth and development in many obvious and subtle ways.

This conceptualization of the Internet is also founded in ethical theory. As you may remember from the discussion of utilitarianism in Chapter 1, the notion of the greatest good for the greatest number has profound democratic implications. Wiring schools and libraries should, in theory, provide access to the Internet for every American. Indeed, some libraries have experimented with e-mail addresses and Internet access for the homeless. Universal access to the Internet would follow Rawls's theory—it would allow the maximization of freedom (access) while protecting weaker parties (people of color, the poor) who might not have access to many other goods in U.S. society but can use the Internet as a way to better their individual and potentially collective lots in life.

Of course, journalists and journalism have not been included in this conceptualization. Yet many journalists have argued that access is only part of the picture—it does people little good to access information if they can't make sense of it. Some scholars have suggested that, as the Internet develops, journalism itself will change from a profession that primarily gathers facts—something anyone can now do, to a profession that places those facts within a context and makes them meaningful.

There is precedent for such a switch. News magazines went to contextual reporting and analysis rather than strict factual reporting in order to survive the death of the general interest magazines, as television penetrated America and delivered advertisers more cheaply than magazines. If the development of the Internet does indeed encourage newspaper development along these lines, then ethical thinking would demand that access to news coverage be distributed as widely as possible among the population and that it remain economically affordable.

That stance, of course, puts journalists at odds with all those segments of U.S. society that view the Internet as another potential profit center, including the multinational corporations for which increasing numbers of journalists now work. Insisting that affordable news become part of the policymaking that is currently swirling around the Information Superhighway would challenge the long-standing U.S. tradition of regarding journalism and government as irreconcilable adversaries.

Yet ethical (and in some ways political) thinking would seem to suggest that making news coverage accessible to every American via the Internet has significant potential benefits for the individual and society at large. It also would make journalists and the government partners—a true philosophical shift in the conceptualization of a "free" press.

Finally, such a partnership would demand that journalists themselves take an active part in developing and implementing legislation that will affect their working lives. Such a change in attitude also would require a philosophical shift, one that places journalistic responsibility to political society on a plane with worker responsibility to profitable media industries.

THE MEANING OF PROFESSIONALISM

At the turn of this century, "citizen journalism" was embraced by the traditional news media. It was viewed as a way to "catch up" and "latch on" to the generation of digital natives who were leaving newspaper readership. Citizen journalism was also cost-effective. Citizen journalists essentially function as reporters who may or may not be edited by professionals. But while citizen journalists often have a passionate interest in a particular public policy initiative or problem and are willing to write or blog about that single issue in great depth, they don't blog or seemingly have an interest in some of the most basic civic functions in American democracy—education, roads and highways, city councils and county commissions. Citizen journalists, in general, don't do investigative reporting. If the news agenda is to be left strictly to citizen journalists, by almost any measure, it will be not only lopsided, but also full of gaps and lacking in objectivity.

Proponents call this approach the "fifth estate," claiming that it parallels the Fourth Estate title that traditional news and opinion has carried as it served as a balance to government power. But an Internet-based fifth estate sometimes functions as an unchecked mob. The blogosphere raises questions of exactly who is a professional that extends far beyond who gets a pay check and speaks to whom and to what ideals one is loyal.

As the case studies through this book indicate, journalism and strategic communication have become so convergent in terms of message purpose and channel that it is no longer possible to segregate ethical questions by channel—newspaper or television—or by purpose—information or persuasion. But, the ethical questions this converged reality raises are seldom entirely novel. What we believe the Internet does is to promote some much better thinking about the boundaries between and among roles—both of individual professionals and of individual citizens.

In this century, it is irrational to think that every individual can perform every role with equal results. Some things really are better left to the experts, whether that is your physician, your accountant or your local or online editor. At its most basic, what defines a profession is not specialized knowledge—look at all the medical information you can find on the Web—or licensure—you don't need an attorney to craft a simple will or many other sorts of documents. You can download them and fill in the blanks. What separates the professionals from the amateurs at core is values and the ability to think ethically within a professional domain. The Web has not changed that; it has merely demanded that we get better at it.

Suggested Readings

ANDERSON, CHRIS. 2006. *The long tail: How the future of business is selling less of more.* New York: Hyperion.

BUGEJA, MICHAEL. 2005. *Interpersonal divide: The search for community in a technological age.* Oxford: Oxford University Press.

GODWIN, MIKE. 1998. *Defending free speech in the digital age.* New York: Times Books.

HALBERT, DEBORA J. 1999. *Intellectual property in the information age.* Westport, CT: Quorum Books.

NEGROPONTE, NICHOLAS. 1995. *Being digital.* New York: Alfred A. Knopf.

SHIRKY, CLAY. 2009. *Here comes everybody: The power of organizing without organizations.* New York: Penguin.

Cases on the Web

www.mhhe.com/mediaethics8e

"The witch and the woods mystery: Fact or fiction?" by Karon Reinboth Speckman
"The Napster debate: When does sharing become thievery?" by Laura Riethmiller
"Digital sound sampling: Sampling the options" by Don Tomlinson

"Cry Wolf: *Time* magazine and the cyberporn story" by Karon Reinboth Speckman
"Filmmaking: Looking through the lens for truth" by Kathy Brittain McKee
"The Madonna and the Web site: Good taste in newspaper online forums" by Philip Patterson
"The case of Banjo Jones and his blog" by Chris Heisel

CHAPTER 9 CASES

CASE 9-A

News Now, Facts Later

LEE WILKINS
University of Missouri

Supreme Court decisions are always eagerly awaited, but none more so than the Court's summer 2012 ruling on the constitutionality of the Patient Protection and Affordable Care Act. The facts of this case are taken from Tom Goldstein, publisher, of SCOTUSblog, a Web site that covers the U.S. Supreme Court and is sponsored by Bloomberg Law. The blog post is used with permission of the author.

News organizations prepared for the release of the Court's decision in a variety of ways. CNN worked for weeks on ways to make certain that the decision, as reported by CNN, reached as many Americans as possible through as many portals at the network has access to. It had spent a great deal of time thinking through its Internet strategy with an emphasis on getting the story first. Fox News has made a similar effort, although its Internet strategy is not as well honed. Megyn Kelly, a former lawyer turned television personality is assigned to the story for Fox. CNN is using an established team including a producer and on-air reporter.

The Supreme Court also has been active on the Internet front. The Court's technical staff is prepared to load the eagerly anticipated opinion on to the Court's Web site where it will be accessible to everyone from average Americans to the White House. Before 2012, the Court routinely e-mailed copies of opinions to parties involved in litigation, but in 2012 it began to rely only on the Web site. One week before the opinion was handed down, the Court denied a request from SCOTUSblog to e-mail the decision to that organization. In practical terms, what this meant was that the only people with access to the decision itself would be those in the courtroom when the decision was announced and those accessing the Web site. The Court made every effort to ensure that the site itself would remain in working order on this important day.

But, in the face of unprecedented demand for information, the Court's site crashed. That meant that the entire country relied on the news media for the story with no way to independently confirm news accounts.

The first reports of the decision, as carried by CNN and Fox, were that the Supreme Court had ruled the act unconstitutional. Those accounts were broadcast about seven minutes after the decision was handed down. In the case of CNN, the initial account of the ruling was broadcast even while its onsite producer was on a conference call with the network executives. The CNN social media team published tweets and RSS feeds stating unequivocally that the Supreme Court had struck down the act.

Fox, just a few seconds later, published a banner on the network saying "Supreme Court finds health care individual mandate unconstitutional." Bill Hammer, one of the network's most experienced journalists, was assigned to lead the coverage. A few seconds before 10:08, he stated on air that the individual health care insurance mandate has been overturned. Fox commentators began to discuss the impact of the ruling on the 2012 presidential election.

President Barack Obama saw both reports. He also had access to the SCOTUSblog conference call on speaker phone and SCOTUSblog on his computer. NPR picked up the CNN and Fox reports, saying the law had been struck down, as did the Huffington Post. The Huffington Post's social media team also ran with the story, neglecting to note the source of its information.

Tom Goldstein, SCOTUSblog publisher, is in charge of the coverage for the Web site, which is highly respected within the D.C. Beltway, including the journalistic community, for its Court coverage but little known to the average American. Goldstein, who was in the Supreme Court chambers when the decision was handed down, filed an initial post that merely said the Court had produced the decision.

About 90 seconds later, Goldstein skimmed the decision by reading the first sentence of every paragraph in the opinion and then conferred with colleague Lyle Denniston, who wrote the majority of the blog's coverage. Denniston and Goldstein agreed: the Court had upheld the act based on the tax clause of the U.S. Constitution. SCOTUSblog then reported that the law had been upheld. That information was picked up by the NPR News Blog, which attributed it to the Web site. At about 10:20 a.m.—less than 20 minutes after journalists received the decision—CBS also accurately reported that the law had been upheld.

At the White House, the president's advisers, after conferring with Goldstein about the focus of the ruling, concluded they needed to tell the president that his signature legislative act had been ruled constitutional.

Soon after SCOTUSblog published its version of events, CNN and Fox had the unenviable job of walking back their initial reports. Because it had put such effort into social media as part of the reporting process, the false reports broadcast by CNN reached many more people than had the Fox news coverage. CNN's seamless news network had, in this instance, become a serious disadvantage.

Goldstein, in his own blog about the events, said that CNN and Fox made three mistakes: first, they treated a complex decision as a breaking news story, even though the law itself would not have taken effect until 2014; second, the networks did not put "sufficiently sounds procedures in place" to deal with what many believed was going to be a complicated decision; and third, the networks appear to have failed to look at the consensus view of the wire reports which, in this instance, were accurate.

Micro Issues

1. Should this have been considered a breaking news story?
2. What should the journalists with access to the opinion have told their editor?
3. What should the editors have asked the journalists who were reporting the story?

Midrange Issues

1. What sort of stories should CNN and Fox have broadcast once they discovered that their initial reports were incorrect?
2. Is this the sort of story that general assignment reporters should not be assigned to? In other words, should only journalists with serious expertise be assigned to report stories such as this?
3. Evaluate Goldstein's statement that all journalists should have put more faith in the accuracy of the wires on this story. How would you—or would you—distinguish this from pack journalism?
4. If you were a manager, how would you—or would you—discipline the on-scene reporters whose initial reports were inaccurate?

Macro Issues

1. Fox News leans to the political right. Many said they believed the initial reports because they coincided with Fox's political ideology. Critique this statement.
2. Less than two months after the event, the head of CNN resigned. Is a mistake of this sort a resigning offense?
3. How do you think the Web site crash of the Supreme Court itself influenced these events, if at all? Do you think the Court itself bears some responsibility for the inaccurate reporting?
4. Contrast the conflicting values of speed, profit and accuracy in this case. Using ethical theory, construct a policy for your local television station on the reporting of breaking news that accounts for all three—speed, profit and accuracy.

CASE 9-B

What's Yours Is Mine: The Ethics of News Aggregation

CHAD PAINTER
Eastern New Mexico University

In June of 2008, The *Hartford Courant* cut 95 jobs from its news department, roughly half of its news staff, in two rounds of layoffs. But within a few months, with an online news hole to fill and a reduced staff, the paper started aggregating local news from surrounding dailies.

In a search of the publication's Web site for Aug. 29–30, 2009, *Journal Inquirer* reporter Christine McCluskey counted 112 stories that were written by the *Courant*'s Connecticut competitors *Bristol Press, New Britain Herald, Torrington Register-Citizen, Waterbury Republican American* and her own paper (McCluskey 2009). The stories were often—but not always—attributed to the original source, a practice Michael E. Schroeder, publisher of the *Bristol Press* and *New Britain Herald* called, "at best plagiarism, at worst outright theft" (McCluskey 2009).

Jeffrey S. Levine, the *Hartford Courant*'s director of content, explained his paper's position. "Aggregation is the process of synopsizing information from other news sources, most commonly by placing a portion of the information on your web site and linking to the original story" (McCluskey 2009). He cited a mistake in his paper's editing process that "inappropriately dropped the attribution or proper credit and in some cases credited ourselves with a byline to a *Courant* reporter" as the basis for the plagiarism claims.

The Society of Professional Journalists' code of conduct states "Never plagiarize" and the Associated Press code warns its writers: "don't plagiarize." Similarly, an ethics primer in online journalism from the University of Southern California's Annenberg School of Journalism states "Don't steal others' work. Such theft is plagiarism" (Niles 2009). Kovach and Rosenstiel call it a "deceptively simple but powerful idea in the discipline for pursuing truth: do your own work" (2007, 99).

However, aggregation is not a black-and-white issue. Is it acceptable to disseminate another news organization's work as long as that work is properly credited? Should the rules be the same for newspapers, broadcast outlets and online journalism? What about content-sharing organizations such as the Associated Press?

One of the core principles of journalism is the discipline of verification (Kovach and Rosenstiel 2007, 79). Aggregation violates that principle because it might not discriminate between rumor, fact and speculation (Kovach and Rosenstiel 2007) and because it doesn't allow for independent confirmation of facts. Falsehoods and rumor go unchecked even if the original source issues a retraction if the aggregators fail to correct or pull the offending story.

However, aggregation isn't a new concept in the news business.

Time magazine was a notorious aggregator. First published March 3, 1923, Henry Luce's flagship magazine aimed to summarize the news quickly, but few of its busy readers would have guessed that *Time* was digested entirely from the dozens of newspapers it subscribed to, "gaining its greatest free lunch from the opulent tables of the *New York Times* and *New York World*" (Swanberg 1972, 58).

Radio, at least in its infancy, relied heavily on newspapers for a steady supply of news reports. For their part, newspapers at first either cooperated with radio for increased exposure or completely ignored the new medium (Chester 1949). That changed with the rise of the CBS and NBC chain radio broadcasting networks, and increased advertising competition from radio. On April 24, 1933, the members of the Associated Press "passed a resolution directing the AP Board of Directors to refuse to give AP news to any radio chain" (Chester 1949, 255). State and national press associations "busied themselves with resolutions attempting to restrict news broadcasting, mostly because it was incongruous for newspapers to furnish free news" to their competitors in radio (Hammargren 1936, 93). Eventually the courts weighed in, punishing the most egregious uses of newspaper content on the radio airwaves as an unfair practice.

Currently, the Associated Press is battling aggregating Web sites such as Google News over use of unauthorized content. The Associated Press announced plans in July 2009 to create "a news registry that will tag and track all AP content online to assure compliance with terms of use." The proposed tracking system "will register key identifying information about each piece of content that AP distributes as well as the terms of use of that content, and employ a built-in beacon to notify AP about how the content is used" (AP.org 2009).

The Associated Press itself is a cooperative that supplies around-the-clock news content to its 1,500 U.S. daily newspaper members, as well as international subscribers and commercial customers (AP.org 2009). There is also a recent trend among formerly rival papers to form localized content-sharing arrangements (Ricchiardi 2009). The newspapers cite budgetary constraints and the cost of Associated Press content as the major reasons for the arrangements.

But Alan Mutter, a former editor in Chicago and San Francisco who currently writes the blog *Reflections of a Newsosaur,* speaks for those who regret the loss of diversity when he says: "Where there are multiple reporters covering the same beat or same event, you're going to get multiple views and everybody is going to try harder to go to a higher level of reporting. It's a fact of human nature that competition inspires better work" (Ricchiardi 2009).

Micro Issues

1. Does proper attribution solve the ethical problem of aggregation? If not, do you have an alternative idea?
2. If news organizations voluntarily agree to offer their content to be aggregated under specific conditions, does that eliminate the ethical issues?

Midrange Issues

1. Evaluate the following statement: Credibility, one of the foundations of journalism, is predicated on "The notion that those who report the news are not obstructed from digging up and telling the truth" and that the journalists can tell "the news not only accurately but also persuasively" (Kovach and Rosenstiel 2007, 53). Can an aggregator be expected to be a watchdog over information that their media outlet did not create?
2. How are content aggregators such as the Huffington Post distinct, in an ethical sense, from long-standing cooperatives such as the Associated Press?

Macro Issues

1. Is aggregation an issue primarily of economics or ethics? If aggregators such as Google News paid for content, would that solve the problem?
2. Who "owns" the news? Does a media outlet have the right to require that a consumer pay for information that he or she needs to be a participant in a democratic society? Did the framers of the Bill of Rights give any clues in this area?

CASE 9-C

The Information Sleazeway: Robust Comment Meets the Data Robots

FRED VULTEE
Wayne State University

In detailing the *Washington Post*'s reporting of a congressional lobbying scandal that exploded in 2006, the paper's ombudsman, Deborah Howell, touched off a cyber firestorm. Writing in her weekly column on Jan. 15, Howell noted that Republicans contended that "the *Post* purposely hasn't nailed any Democrats." On the contrary, she wrote, several stories "have mentioned that a number of Democrats . . . have gotten Abramoff campaign money." The *Post* hadn't found any Democrats in the "first tier of people being investigated," she added. "But stay tuned. This story is nowhere near over."

She was wrong. No Democrats had gotten campaign money from Jack Abramoff, the lobbyist at the center of the scandal, although he had told some of his clients to aim contributions to Democrats as well as Republicans. It was not until a week after her original column that Howell acknowledged her error and stated that the Abramoff matter, far from being bipartisan, was "a Republican scandal."

The *Washington Post* was caught flat-footed by a barrage of postings (which could only be charitably described as obscene). The postings overwhelmed one of the Web logs set up to foster public comment. In navigating the familiar journalistic terrain of correcting an error, the *Post* found itself in an unfamiliar situation where the Internet had taken the error far beyond the circulation barriers of the *Post*.

As critics on public discussion boards at washingtonpost.com took Howell to task for the error, she wrote a comment for the Web site that satisfied few and angered many: "I've heard from lots of angry readers about the remark . . . that lobbyist Jack Abramoff gave money to both parties. A better way to have said it would be that Abramoff 'directed' contributions to both parties."

Those who thought the matter was worth a more forthright admission of error were not satisfied. A torrent of comments poured in—enough of them obscenely and viciously personal that the *Post* closed the site to public comment on Thursday. When it reopened, with a much larger investment of staff time, public comments were much more carefully monitored.

The economic and social pressures on the *Post* are hardly unique. Like most metropolitan newspapers, it is losing circulation and advertisers at an alarming rate—more than three times the industry average for one accounting period a few years back (Smolkin 2005). Younger readers know its reputation but are intimidated by its bulk and more at ease with finding information they want elsewhere.

Like many other papers, the *Post* is aggressively exploring ways to put its journalistic expertise—whether in sports, business, government or international coverage—into play in interactive ways, involving almost half of *Post* staffers, with the number rising.

The ethical issue for the *Post* centers on the fact that one of the roles of a newspaper in a community is to foster public debate. Knowing that journalism is shielded by legal decisions that support the importance of uninhibited debate, how can a media outlet act as a forum for debate without exposing its own writers to scurrilous attacks?

The *Post*'s answer to the dilemma angered a number of vocal critics. The *Post*'s online editor, Jim Brady, summed up the criticism in a Feb. 12, 2006 article: "My career as a nitwitted, emasculated fascist began the afternoon of Jan. 19 when, as executive editor of the *Post*'s Web site, washingtonpost.com, I closed down the comments area of one of our many blogs" (Brady 2006). After Howell's first column, editors had removed about a hundred postings that violated the ban on profanity and personal attacks. Howell's midweek clarification only triggered a larger torrent, leading to Brady's decision to close the blog to comments—and to yet another flood of comments, this time directed at Brady.

Howell told a *Post* reporter that she had not asked for the site to be closed to commenting, saying, "I'm a First Amendment freak" (Farhi 2006). And Brady pointed to some irony in the conflict: "It was largely the reporting of the *Washington Post* that brought the Abramoff scandal to light in the first place—an inconvenient fact if one is attempting to assert that the *Post* takes its orders from the Republican White House."

Still, the string of comments on Howell's columns was closed. When comments on Post.blog resumed in February, it was with "minimal but firm rules." These rules included no personal attacks, no profanity and no posing as another writer. A profanity filter was installed, and staffers were assigned to read incoming messages, with the idea that "offensive or inappropriate" ones would be removed at once (Chandrasekaran 2006).

Micro Issues

1. Did the *Post* err in allowing readers to post uncensored messages prior to this problem?
2. Did the *Post* err in instituting profanity filters and staffers to read incoming messages after the problem?
3. How would you have handled the *Post*'s problem?

Midrange Issues

1. Should the original story of the ombudsman have been fact-checked to prevent the mistaken wording or is the copy of an ombudsman "out of bounds" for editorial control?
2. After the error was discovered and the deluge of messages began, was this a news story the *Post* should have covered?

Macro Issues

1. Is the Web site of a newspaper a forum that should be open to everyone without fear of censorship?
2. In the "marketplace of ideas" that is the modern Web log, do the normal rules of libel apply? Is a newspaper more culpable or less culpable for the content of its Web log if it fails to censor the posts?

CASE 9-D

Death Underneath the Media Radar: The Anuak Genocide in Ethiopia

DOUG MCGILL, EDITOR
The McGill Report

I first learned about the Anuak people while working as a volunteer teacher of English as a Second Language at a school in Rochester, Minn. I had a half dozen Sudanese immigrants in my ESL class, all of them refugees of the Sudan civil war and several of them "lost boys," young men separated from their families who had made their way to safe havens in the Midwest.

One of my students, a man in his late 20s named Obang Cham, was originally iden-tified to me by the ESL school as a Sudanese refugee. But when Obang's English began to improve, and we chatted over coffee, he told me a different story. He was a member of a small tribe called the Anuak who lived primarily in remote western Ethiopia. He said that more than 1,000 Anuak lived in Minnesota, and when I asked him why they had moved here, he gave me an answer I spent another nine months working to verify before committing it to print: "The Ethiopian government is trying to kill my people."

The first thing that I discovered was the Anuak were an invisible people not only in Minnesota but in the world. Although Anuak had been immigrating to Minnesota from the early 1990s, not a single major metropolitan or local paper in the United States had written anything about them. Was it possible that not a single reporter had ever met and chatted with an Anuak before? And if they had done so, and learned the story—of an unreported African genocide no less—why had they not published anything?

According to Obang, he had fled his Ethiopian village of Dimma on foot in 1992 after Ethiopian soldiers surrounded the village and began shooting Anuak. Two dozen died in that attack, he said. Many similar attacks during the early and middle 1990s are why so many Anuak now live in Minnesota. Yet the state had absorbed the cream of the crop of the young, strong male leadership of an entire Ethiopian tribe, and their wives, without notice or knowing. The Anuak were invis-ible in Minnesota and the world.

On December 13, 2003, my telephone started ringing in the afternoon. One after another, Anuak men whom I'd met in the previous months told me a chilling story—that one of the periodic massacres of Anuak men, women and children was underway at that very moment.

They were having cellular telephone conversations with friends and family in their home villages and were hearing, through their cell phone connections, the sounds of the massacre—shouting and screaming, gunshots, soldiers yelling and people sobbing and crying. Some of my sources described hearing soldiers bashing down doors, yelling "Put down that phone!" followed by gunshots and then silence. I spent hours on the phone that day, gathering every detail I could.

Through the cell phone connections, dozens of Anuak had heard essentially the same story over and over—that two troop trucks containing uniformed Ethiopian soldiers had arrived in town and disgorged soldiers who went from hut to hut and home to home in the village, calling out the Anuak men and boys and shooting them dead in the street. Occasionally, the soldiers were joined by non-Anuak citizens, or lighter-skinned Ethiopian "highlanders," who shouted "Today is the day of killing Anuak!" and killed their victims, usually with long spears, knives or machetes.

That evening and for several days following, I checked the wire services and the Web sites of the major daily newspapers in the United States, Europe and Africa. Not a word on the alleged massacre was published. On the Web sites of the Ethiopian embassy, the major Ethiopian newspapers and the U.S. Embassy in Addis Ababa: nothing. Finally, around Dec. 17, a small press release from the Ethiopian government came out reporting that "tribal violence" in western Ethio-pia had caused up to a dozen deaths. This was nowhere near what the Anuak in Minnesota were claiming based on their knowledge from hundreds of eyewitness accounts, and the Ethiopian government was placing blame in its press releases not on the Ethiopian Army but on tribes fighting each other. I placed a call to the press spokesman at the Ethiopian embassy in Washington, Mesfin Andreas. "The deaths occurred as troops tried to stop people from killing each other," Andreas said.

On the weekend after the first phone calls came in, Anuak refugees from all over the Midwest gathered at a church in St. Paul, Minn. to discuss the crisis. I attended the meeting where I met several hundred Anuak, and interviewed maybe three dozen, only talking to people who said they had spoken directly to people on cell phones who were eyewitnesses as the massacre was happening. The stories that I heard that day were identical to the ones that I'd gotten over the telephone a week earlier. Uniformed Ethiopian soldiers had done the killing with automatic rifles, targeting Anuak men and boys for killing and Anuak women for raping, and they'd gone house to house, sometimes with a list of names in their hands, calling out specific Anuak men by name.

Hundreds—not dozens—had died.

Back at home, I called an Anuak survivor in Ethiopia. He lived in Gambella, the town where the massacre occurred. He told of seeing uniformed Ethiopian soldiers killing Anuak men on the street from the window of his home. He'd hidden under his bed as soldiers marched by his home. His own son had died in the attack. While speaking to me, he said he could still see some bodies in the streets of Gambella, and that at a mass grave on one side of the town, several hundred corpses were strewn in piles. He and other Anuak survivors had counted the corpses and noted how they had died, he said. The total was some 425 killed either by gunshots to the head or back, or by spear thrusts and machete blows.

As a former reporter for the *New York Times* for a decade, I knew I would probably have been unable to publish the story in the *Times* even with all the material I'd gathered. The main problem was, I had not actually been in Ethiopia, nor talked face-to-face with any actual eyewitnesses to the killing. Instead, my sources were a strange new breed of witness—"earwitnesses" to the sounds of a massacre and to direct eyewitness accounts of the massacre, listened to over cell phones. I was not then aware, nor am I aware today, of any report of a massacre or other crime in the media based on witness accounts of this nature. They are the creation of our present strange new world of hyper-communication.

In the end, my decision finally to publish what I'd heard, pointing a finger directly at the Ethiopian army, boiled down to my gut feelings as a journalist and my conscience as a citizen. After a week of solid reporting, interviewing dozens of Anuak in Minnesota, as well as one eyewitness in Ethiopia and the Ethiopian embassy spokesman, I felt that I knew something close enough to the truth to publish. And my conscience told me it was my duty to publish, because even up to Dec. 22, the day I finally did publish an account of the massacre, not a single news publication had done so—anywhere in the world. If I didn't publish, who would?

Within days of my story appearing on the Internet, the leaders of Genocide Watch, a nongovernmental watchdog who investigate new cases of genocide wherever they happen in the world had made enough phone calls to justify hiring an investigator and sending him to Ethiopia to check out the claims made in my article. On Feb. 25, 2004, Genocide Watch published the investigator's report, "Today is the Day of Killing Anuak," based on interviews with dozens of eyewitnesses to the massacre in Gambella (Genocide Watch 2004). The report verified all of the key claims of *The McGill Report* article, including the number of Anuak killed and the fact that uniformed Ethiopian soldiers had carried out most of the killings.

Micro Issues

1. Using a search engine, how much can you find about the genocide of the Anuak that has appeared since McGill's Web site first published the story?
2. Is it fair to say that the international attention being given to the genocide in Darfur distracted the media and the relief organizations from the situation in Ethiopia?

Midrange Issues

1. Following a trip to Ethiopia, McGill still had problems getting the mainstream media to accept the story. What does that say about how mainstream news organizations operate?
2. Is acceptance of this story by a mainstream media outlet such as the Associated Press needed to somehow "validate" the reporting done by McGill?
3. McGill has had a long career in journalism, including the *New York Times* and *Bloomberg News*. However, many "bloggers" have not had any journalism experience or training at all. Are traditional media rightfully skeptical about stories that originate in blogs? Should citizens be skeptical?

Macro Issues

1. What does this case tell you about who is a journalist in the Internet era?
2. Why do you think that a massacre of 425 people in Ethiopia wasn't reported in the mainstream media for several months after it happened? Why was it a blogger in southern Minnesota who broke the story?
3. Members of the dispersed tribal communities of Anuak e-mailed the story by McGill all over the world within days of its publication. Is the Internet a more efficient outlet for international stories such as this one?

CASE 9-E

Born Just Right

LEE WILKINS
University of Missouri

Missouri School of Journalism broadcast news Professors Jennifer and Randy Reeves could not have been more excited about the birth of their second child. All the pre-natal checks were great, brother "Cam" was excited and the birth process itself went as expected. Baby girl Jordan was born happy and healthy—almost without flaw. However, sometime during Jen's pregnancy, the baby's umbilical chord had become wrapped around her right arm, choking off the blood supply to the developing limb. When she was born, Jordan's right arm did not extend as far as her elbow. The problem was an unexpected one; ultrasound had not picked it up prior to her birth. Jordan's "defect" was an unusual one. Very few infants are born needing a prosthetic limb.

Jenn Reeves is a talented and caring teacher who embraced new technology and did her best to incorporate it into her classes. But with the new baby less than three months old, Jenn applied her journalistic and new media skills to the newest problem in her life. She started the blog Born Just Right (http://www.bornjustright. com/), an effort that required learning some programming and a bit of technology to try to provide parents of kids with similar challenges to share experiences, learn from each other and build a community.

As Jenn learned, blogging is a complicated and time-consuming process, something she had to work around her already demanding teaching job and her equally demanding life as a wife and parent. Among the most popular kinds of blogs are "mom blogs" where mothers share their insights about parenting, children and family life. Originating and maintaining such a blog required daily effort. Frequent updates are mandatory—multiple times a day is best—if a blog is to appear high on a search engine list. Some mom blogs have become profitable; those blogs usually contain endorsements for particular products aimed at kids or their parents. Finding a computer program that would allow for the sort of interaction Jenn required also was work; during the blog's life, she's changed its computer architecture at least twice, always with the goal of making it easier for her to post and for others to comment.

What Jenn had in mind was not the typical mom blog. She was seeking other parents who faced the sort of challenges she did—everything from getting some state help with the expenses of paying and continuing Jordan's therapy, to finding people willing to construct prosthetic limbs for children who were going to outgrow them, an expensive proposition and, as the Reeves learned, one that was not well covered by insurance.

But, slowly, the blog and its audience grew. Jenn says her "blog" voice is distinct from her journalistic one—it's more personal, more emotional and very much more focused on the single issue of helping Jordan. It also chronicles the daily events in Jordan's life as well as the milestones, including photos. The first ballet lesson, the first dance recital, getting the first prosthesis, finding those who could and would help, all became blog entries. But, it's also journalistic; there's a wealth of information presented impartially from the point of view of someone who both needs and values the facts about government programs, private support and facing the problems that every child who is born just right encounters.

As of this writing, the blog itself has about 3,200 unique visitors. In the blog world, this is more than enough to interest sponsors—in other words, Jenn could monetize her blog should she choose. The blog has also resulted in some professional rewards for Jenn—she is invited to present at blogging conferences to talk about creating and sustaining a blog. She also uses the blog in her classes; in fact, in many of her classes, Professor Reeves requires her students to blog multiple times a week. She notes that blogging is really writing practice and that it can, in rare instances, move a student to the head of the applicant line for jobs after graduation.

In addition, the blog also has given the entire Reeves family some terrific opportunities. Disney, after it became aware of the blog, invited the entire family to visit Winter, the dolphin who was born without a fully developed tail and needed her own Dolphin prosthesis, when the film *The Dolphin Tale* was released. Jordan and Winter got to compare their "artificial" limbs. You can find photos of all of this on the blog itself.

Jenn herself says the blog has taught her a lot that she's been able to pass along in the classroom. But, it's also given her and her daughter a community. Jenn is not sure whether what she has created is point-of-view journalism, a non-money-seeking nonprofit, or a multiyear-long set of persuasive messages. But, as long as Jordan continues to approve, she will continue the effort.

Micro Issues

1. Take a look at the blog. Do you think it invades the privacy of the Reeves family?
2. How do you think Kant and Aristotle would evaluate this blog?
3. Do you think a blog such as this could have succeeded as well if its creator had not had some journalistic training and experience? Why or why not?

Midrange Issues

1. Do you think monetizing the blog would change its character? Evaluate your response in terms of loyalty and truthtelling.
2. Before this case study was written, Jenn Reeves reviewed it. Was this an appropriate approach? Evaluate your answer in light of the recent controversies about reporters clearing quotes with sources in the case in Chapter 2. If your answer in these instances is different, explain why, using ethical theory.
3. From the point of view of a strategic communication professional, how could or should Jenn ethically market her blog to, for example, help pay for Jordan's college expenses? Justify your response.
4. Should this blog become the subject of news stories?

Macro Issues

1. Is this blog journalism? Strategic communication? Link your answer to craft standards.
2. Evaluate the idea behind Born Just Right and its content according to ethical principles.

CASE 9-F

Sending the Wrong Message about Doing the Right Thing

NAOMI WEISBROOK
University of Missouri

On July 20, 2007, Black Entertainment Television (BET) introduced a short cartoon video entitled *Read a Book*. The cartoon encourages life skills including reading, maintaining good hygiene, responsible parenting and wise use of money in what appears to be a public service announcement. These messages are incorporated into the lyrics and sung by the cartoon rapper D'Mite. D'Mite bears a striking resemblance to Lil' Jon, at the time the reigning king of crunk, a subgenre of hip hop. Keeping with the style of crunk music, the video's lyrics are repetitive and filled with obscenities and the N-word. An uncensored version circulated on YouTube while a cleaner version was shown on BET.

The song was the brainchild of Bomani D'Mite Armah, an educator who works with young people in the Washington, D.C., area. He composed the song "Read a Book" because, "If crunk is what's in, I'll do crunk" (Harris 2007). After Armah circulated his song on MySpace for a while, it made it to BET's President of Entertainment Reginald Hudlin, who contacted Armah about making the song into a video (Martin 2007).

In addition to the obscenities, the video contains potentially offensive images, including women shaking their behinds with the word "BOOK" stamped across their pants. There is also an image of a book being loaded as a cartridge in an automatic weapon.

The video immediately created buzz on the Internet, generating more than one million hits and 4,000 comments on YouTube. Some comments praised the video: "[This video is] satirically presenting how the rap has degenerated into nothing but violent and sexual messages when it originally it [sic] was meant to convey important messages of black culture. So while the video shows both violent and sexual images it paradoxically is trying to send a positive message of how to lead a better life" (ROBOFISH).

Others were critical. When CNN anchor Tony Harris interviewed Tyree Dillihay, the video's director, Harris pointedly began the interview by asking, "You proud of this?" (Harris 2007). On his Rainbow PUSH coalition Web site, Jesse Jackson (2007) released a statement condemning "Read a Book," saying, "'Read a Book' heaps scorn on positive values and (un)intentionally celebrates ignorance. The narrator is obviously illiterate, unkempt and disrespectful. So who takes his advice seriously?"

Much of the controversy centers on exactly what the video is trying to say. According to Armah, "The message behind the song was secondary to the idea of parodying this style of music." In the same interview, Armah jokes that a friend told him that to write a crunk song the authors must be repetitive, aggressive and "curse as often as possible" (Martin 2007).

However, to someone unfamiliar with crunk music, the satire might be lost. Greg Forde, a African-American parent featured in CNN coverage of "Read a Book," points out that "the thing with satire, really clever satire, is that it speaks to a point, but you still realize it's satire. People who are not in our community are not going to see this as satire" (Harris 2007).

To those who don't recognize the satire, the video just appears to be methodically cataloging negative perceptions of African-Americans. In fact, according to the *Los Angeles Times,* "Most of the discussion centers on the negative stereotypes of African-Americans, rather than the language" (Braxton 2007). The negative stereotypes include gun use, men sitting on the porch drinking "40s" (40 oz. bottles of alcohol), drive-bys, irresponsible spending on decorative tire rims, negligent parenting and poor hygiene.

But, the video contains positive references to African-American history: There are images of historical figures such as Martin Luther King and the covers of several books such as *The Color Purple* and Maya Angelou's *I Know Why the Caged Bird Sings.*

Bomani Armah said he hopes people will get two messages from his song: that crunk music is ridiculous and that kids should read books. Armah says that he gets e-mails from kids thanking him for validating that getting an education is cool. Parents have told him that their kid picked up a book after listening to his song.

Micro Issues

1. BET claims on its Web site to provide "contemporary entertainment that speaks to young Black adults from an authentic, unapologetic viewpoint of the Black experience." Is it fulfilling that promise with *Read a Book?* Why or why not?
2. Critique the specific words and images used in this video, finding it on the Web if possible. What ethical values are dominant in *Read a Book?* Does it succeed in promoting those values?

Midrange Issues

1. Promoting literacy is a "good" cause. In fact, it's a noncontentious good cause; there is no pro-ignorance lobby to counter the message. Given the universal approval of the idea of literacy, does a campaign promoting it have greater creative latitude or must it take greater caution?
2. For satire to work it must have a reference point, which often means dealing in stereotypes to make a point. Should satire be used in a pro-social way such as a public service announcement? How would your answer change if the cause were Planned Parenthood? A ballot issue that has deeply divided the community?

Macro Issues

1. The *Read a Book* campaign is an example of strategic communication for a cause. When Yoplait puts pink tops on its product to support breast cancer research, this is another example of "cause-related marketing." Critique the concept of cause-related marketing.
2. How does the fact that this message was intended for children change the rules about what is allowable and what is ethically questionable? Do the responsibilities and duties of the message creators change for this particular audience?

CASE 9-G

Looking for Truth Behind the Walmart Blogs

PHILIP PATTERSON
Oklahoma Christian University

When you think of blogging, the image of a lone person passionately pounding out a late-night journal hoping to gain a few loyal readers comes to mind. But if you're Walmart, the largest retailing chain in the world, you can afford a little professional help, and that's precisely what the corporation did on at least two blogs until Walmart's public relations firm was forced to reveal the ruse.

Before the admission, rumors had been circulating about the authenticity of the blogs. In an article on cnnmoney.com entitled "Corporate Blogging: Walmart's

Fumbles," *Fortune* senior writer Marc Gunther (2006) broke the story in the mainstream press with this posting:

> A blog praising Walmart called "Walmarting Across America," ostensibly created by a man and a woman traveling the country in an RV and staying in Walmart parking lots, turned out to be underwritten by Working Families for Walmart, a company-sponsored group organized by the Edelman public relations firm. Not cool.

The couple, it turns out, were Laura St. Claire, a freelance writer and an employee at the U.S. Treasury Department, and Jim Thresher, a staff photographer at the *Washington Post.* And Walmart, far from being the lucky beneficiary of a blog that found happy Walmart employees at every stop, was shown to be behind the trip and was paying for the couple's support, including money for renting the RV, gas and fees for writing the blog (Gogoi 2006). And behind Walmart was Edelman, a nationally recognized PR firm as a part of their "Working Families for Walmart" campaign.

As bloggers expressed their outrage at the ruse, Edelman CEO Richard Edelman issued an apology on his personal blog. "I want to acknowledge our error in failing to be transparent about the identity of the two bloggers from the outset. This is 100 percent our responsibility and our error, not the client's" he wrote (Gogoi 2006).

But the happy RVing couple was not the only phony Walmart blog. Two days after Gunther's article, cnnmoney.com exposed the practice on its Web site, in an unsigned article entitled "PR Firm Admits It's Behind PR Blogs." In that article, the following information was posted:

> A public relations firm has revealed that it is behind two blogs that previously appeared to be created by independent supporters of Walmart. The blogs Working Families for Walmart and subsidiary site Paid Critics are written by three employees of PR firm Edelman, for whom Walmart is a paid client, according to information posted on the sites Thursday. Before Thursday, the authors of the blogs were not disclosed. But Web critics had been skeptical of claims that the blogs were grassroots efforts, and pushed for greater transparency.

Employees of the Edelman public relations firm were eventually revealed as the source of blogs on two more sites that produced favorable stories about Walmart and sought to debunk its critics. In mid-October of 2006, the following message appeared on www.forwalmart.com:

> In response to comments and emails, we've added author bylines to blog posts here at forwalmart.com. The site has been updated, but readers may have to refresh the page for the new information.

By clicking on the single name byline of "Miranda," the reader would find the following information: "Miranda Grill works for Edelman. One of her clients is Working Families for Walmart." The same message appeared on the www.paidcritics.com site, whose tagline is ironically, "Exposing the Paid Critics" in a posting entitled "A CHANGE TO PAIDCRITICS.COM" written by "Brian." A click on Brian's byline yielded the following information: "Brian McNeill works for Edelman. One of his clients is Working Families for Walmart."

According to its Web site (www.edelman.com), the Edelman public relations firm claims 2,220 employees in 46 offices worldwide and billed $305 million in fees in fiscal year 2006. It was named "Large PR Agency of the Year" by *PR Week US* in 2006. The "welcome" page on the Edelman Web site contains the following description over the signature of Daniel J. Edelman, founder and chairman, and Richard Edelman, president and CEO:

> We were the first firm to apply public relations to building consumer brands. We invented the media tour, created litigation and environmental PR, were the first to use a toll-free consumer hotline and the first to employ the Web in crisis management. That's just the beginning. Today we're on a mission: to make public relations the lead discipline in the communications mix, because only public relations has the immediacy and transparency to build credibility and trust.

There was no mention of the Walmart incident under "Latest Headlines" on the Edelman Web site in the week after the story broke.

Micro Issues

1. Should Edelman have acknowledged the problem on its Web site before the *Fortune* magazine reporter broke the story? Should it have responded afterward?
2. How common do you think Walmart's actions are? Is it possible that "grassroots" fan sites are actually paid for by celebrities or their publicists, for instance?
3. If Walmart is right that its critics are "paid," does that justify paying a public relations firm to say good things about Walmart?

Midrange Issue

1. In the "marketplace of ideas" is there any place for this type of "stealth" public relations?
2. How does this differ from "viral marketing," where companies try to generate "buzz" about products to bypass traditional advertising media to reach the public with a message, often paying agents in the process?
3. How does this differ from "product placement" in television or movies, where the audience is not informed if a product manufacturer paid to be on the screen?

Macro Issues

1. Upon hearing of Thresher's involvement, the *Post*'s executive editor demanded that he pay back any money he received for the trip and remove his photographs from the blog (Gogoi 2006). Should there be any other penalties for his actions? Does it make a difference if he is on his own time during the trip? Does it make any difference if every posting represents his true opinion?
2. Critics called for greater transparency in the blogs. Edelman claims to use "transparency to build credibility and trust." What does transparency mean in public relations? Is it different from transparency in journalism? Was Edelman transparent in its dealings on these two Web sites?
3. Barbara Ehrenreich in her book *Nickel and Dimed* writes a very different story about the plight of Walmart workers. To get the story, she took a job in a Walmart and attempted to live on the income it paid. Her best-selling book was highly critical of the way Walmart treats its employees. Is her work, for which she received royalties, any different than the paid Walmart bloggers? If so, in what way? Is Ehrenreich a journalist? Is it the role of journalists to put pressure on corporations such as Walmart?

10

The Ethical Dimensions of Art and Entertainment

By the end of this chapter, you should be able to:

- **understand the link between aesthetics and excellent professional performance.**
- **explain Tolstoy's rationale for art and apply it to issues such as stereotyping.**
- **understand the debate over the role of truth in popular art.**

In the last century, the primary use of media shifted from distributing information to providing entertainment and popularizing culture. In this chapter, we examine the ethical issues from the field of aesthetics. We will apply these principles, plus some findings from social science, to the art and entertainment industries, focusing on the responsibilities of both creators and consumers of entertainment.

AN ANCIENT MISUNDERSTANDING

Plato didn't like poets. His reasoning was straightforward: poets, the people who dream, were the potential undoing of the philosopher king. They were rebels of the first order, insurrectionists on the hoof, and he banned them from the Republic.

Plato's skepticism is alive today. Few weeks elapse without a news story about an artist or entertainment program that has offended. You are probably familiar with at least some of the following:

- The successful demand by British censors that the film *The Hunger Games* be shortened by seven seconds due to violent content. The deletion meant that children 12 and over could see the film in the UK.
- Jon Stewart's decision to criticize his own network, Comedy Central, for bleeping out dialogue in a "South Park" episode that included Muhammad as a character.

- Attempts to ban books, even classics such as *Catcher in the Rye* or *Lady Chatterley's Lover,* from public or school libraries for being too sexually explicit. Recently, *Harry Potter* books were the focus of the most successful and the most unsuccessful attempts to ban a book, a move led largely by conservative Christians.
- The controversy over government funding of art that some claim is obscene.
- Calls by conservatives and liberals to boycott television networks and their advertisers over allegedly objectionable content.
- The furor over rappers, television producers and filmmakers whose homophobic, misogynistic and sometimes clever content offend many while earning nominations for the industry's top awards.
- While these examples come from the West, other cultures and political systems show the same tendencies. In 2012, the Russian punk band Pussy Riot received a two-year jail term for its criticism of Russian President Vladimir Putin's policies.
- In China, architect and sculptor Ai Weiwei, a member of the team that designed the 2008 Olympic stadium nicknamed The Bird's Nest, was arrested and held without charge for more than two months in 2011 in response to his protests about the Chinese government's lack of action after devastating earthquakes and his allegations of government corruption.

Like Plato long ago, those who would restrict the arts do so because they mistrust the power of the artist or even the audience to link emotion and logic in a way that stimulates a new vision of society, culture or individuals.

OF TOLSTOY AND TELEVISION

Tolstoy was the sort of artist Plato would have feared. In his famous essay "What Is Art?" Tolstoy (1960) argued that good art had one dominant characteristic: it communicated the feelings of the artist to the masses in the way in which the artist intended.

> To evoke in oneself a feeling one has once experienced and having evoked it in oneself then by means of movements, lines, colors, sounds or forms expressed in words, so to transmit that feeling that others experience the same feeling—that is the activity of art. . . . Art is a human activity consisting in this, that one may consciously by means of certain external signs, hand on to others feelings he has lived through, and that others are infected by these feelings and also experience them.

Tolstoy's standard was so demanding that he rejected the works of both Shakespeare and Beethoven as being incapable of being understood by the masses. Tolstoy's rationale is particularly pertinent to photographers and videographers who, through their visual images, seek to arouse emotion as well as inform. Haunting pictures of starvation from the Third World have launched international relief efforts. Televised images of Katrina's victims spurred the resignation of some of FEMA's top officials—and affected the 2006 election. Award-winning dramas such as the play *Angels in America,* the AIDS quilt, movies such as *Philadelphia* (in which Tom Hanks won an Academy Award for his portrayal of an AIDS victim) and obituaries of famous artists who have succumbed to AIDS have all aroused both our intellects and our emotions about the disease. They invite action. Television and film documentaries have made viewers more aware of the plight of persons who are mentally disabled or homeless, raised important public policy questions and occasionally made us laugh, through a unity of purpose and craft.

Such work reminds readers and viewers of the moral power of art by putting us in touch with characters and situations sometimes more complex than our own lives. By thinking about these fictional characters, we enlarge our moral imaginations.

Unfortunately, Tolstoy's assertion that great art is defined by how it is understood by an audience also includes a genuine dilemma. Even if given Tolstoy's life experiences, many readers could not articulate the deep truths about human nature Tolstoy wrote about in *War and Peace*. Worse yet, it is nearly impossible to sell those insights to a sometimes lukewarm public, or to produce them on demand for

Calvin and Hobbes

by Bill Watterson

CALVIN AND HOBBES © 1992 Watterson. Dist. By UNIVERSAL UCLICK. Reprinted with permission. All rights reserved.

an hour a week, 36 weeks a year. The result is popular art that loses its critical edge and takes shortcuts to commonplace insight. In fact, some mass-communication scholars have argued that the unstated goal of popular art is to reinforce the status quo; popular culture, they say, blunts our critical-thinking abilities.

Today, mass media have become the primary cultural storytellers of the era. Nearly half a century ago, Ellul (1965) argued that in a modern society storytelling is an inevitable and desirable tool to stabilize the culture. This "propaganda of integration" is not the deliberate lie commonly associated with propaganda but the dissemination of widely held beliefs to the culture at large. Aesop's fables and the early *McGuffey Readers* influenced generations of Americans with subtle (or not) messages that reinforced the social structure. This is precisely where the entertainment media get their power—not in the overt messages but in the underlying assumptions that

---

What Is Art?

Philosophers, sociologists and artists have debated the meaning of art for hundreds of years. Prior to the Industrial Revolution, art was something only the well educated paid for, produced and understood. Mozart had to capture the ear of the Emperor to get a subsidy to write opera. Such "high" or "elite art" provided society with a new way to look at itself. Picasso's drawings of people with three eyes or rearranged body parts literally provided Western culture with a new way of seeing. Michelangelo's paintings and sculpture did the same thing in the Renaissance. But patronage had disadvantages. The patron could restrict both subject matter and form, a reality depicted in the film *Amadeus* where the Emperor informed Mozart that his work, *The Marriage of Figaro,* had "too many notes." Gradually artists discovered that if they could find a way to get more than one person to "pay" for the creation of art, artistic control returned to the artist. The concept of "popular art" was born. Scholars disagree about many of the qualities of elite and popular art; some even assert that popular art cannot truly be considered art. While both kinds of art are difficult to define, the following list outlines the major differences between popular and elite art and culture:

1. Popular art is consciously adjusted to the median taste by the artist; elite art reflects the individual artist's vision.
2. Popular art is neither abstruse, complicated nor profound; elite art has these characteristics.
3. Popular art conforms to majority experience; elite art explores the new.
4. Popular art conforms to less clearly defined standards of excellence, most often linked to commercial success; elite art is much less commercially oriented, and its standards of excellence are consistent and integrated.
5. Popular artists know that the audience expects entertainment and instruction; elite artists seek an aesthetic experience.
6. The popular artist cannot afford to offend its target audience; the elite artist functions as a critic of society, and his or her work challenges and sometimes offends the status quo.
7. Popular art often arises from folk art; elite art more often emerges from a culture's dominant intellectual tradition.

(if unchallenged) will become widely held societal values. For instance, entertainment content can reinforce the status quo by constantly depicting certain social groups in an unflattering and unrepresentative way, presenting a distorted picture of reality. Groups as disparate as Muslims and evangelicals have chafed under depictions (or omissions) that reinforce cultural stereotypes despite evidence to the contrary.

At least some such distortion is the natural outcome of compression. Just as substances such as rubber change form when compressed, so do media messages. Given only 15 seconds to register a message in a commercial, an advertising copywriter will resort to showing us the presumed stereotype of a librarian, a mechanic or a pharmacist. Using stereotypes as a form of mental shorthand is a natural way media work and was noted as early as 1922 by Walter Lippmann in *Public Opinion*. Lippmann said that we are all guilty of "defining first and seeing second."

Soon, we expect reality to imitate art. Mass communicators know the power of stereotypes and deeply held notions and use them. According to Tony Schwartz (1973), advertising messages are often constructed backward. The communicator actually starts with what the receiver knows—or believes he knows—and then constructs a message that fits within that reality. Schwartz calls it hitting a "responsive chord." Time is saved in plucking the chords already deeply held by the public rather than challenging stereotypes. So pimps are African-American, terrorists are Middle Eastern and no one challenges the unstated assumptions. The audience gets the idea of a pimp or a terrorist, but notions of racism and worse have been planted as well. While these images suit the artist's purposes, they are problematic.

TRUTH IN ART AND ENTERTAINMENT

No question in the field of aesthetics is more thoroughly debated with less resolution than the role of truth in art. Most philosophers seem to agree that artists are not restricted to telling the literal truth. Often artists can reveal a previously hidden or veiled truth, providing a new way of looking at the world or understanding human nature that rings deeply true.

But just how much truth should the audience expect from entertainment? And how entertaining should the audience expect truth to be? There are several opinions. At one point on the continuum is the argument that there is no truth requirement at all in art. At another point on the continuum is the belief that there must be one accepted truth for all.

Compounding the problem is that often the audience doesn't care when the lines of truth and entertainment are blurred. Jon Stewart and Stephen Colbert each host nightly satirical newscasts aired on the Comedy Central network. Surveys show that these fake news shows are actually a main source of news content for young people in the 18 to 30 age bracket. The fact that the shows feature interviews with real political figures, include "real" news footage of actual events and have the license to be satirical rather than fair and balanced seems to be of no consequence to the demographic attracted to the shows. An exchange between Stewart and Tucker Carlson, host of CNN's "Crossfire," during the 2004 campaign shows the tension between traditional news and satirical news in the box that follows.

When "Fake News" Calls out "Journalism"

Jon Stewart, host of Comedy Central's "The Daily Show," has always insisted that he is a comedian and that he reports "fake news." Stewart follows a long tradition of news being incorporated into entertainment programming, beginning with Orson Wells's 1939 radio play *War of the Worlds* and continuing through today's "Saturday Night Live" newscast.

What makes Stewart unique is that his "fake news" programs often incorporate actual news video and direct quotes from authors, newsmakers and political officials. Multiple polls have documented that young people between the ages of 18 to 30 get "some" or "most" of their public affairs information from Stewart. He has won both an Emmy and a Peabody Award, given for programming that raises important public issues.

At the same time, Stewart continues to work as a comedian and has hosted the Academy Awards, a night that perennially yields television's highest ratings. So, when Stewart appeared on "Crossfire," Carlson, his bosses and his audience believed they were booking a comedian. But Stewart was far from funny. Instead, Stewart lambasted Carlson, "Crossfire" and the television news media in general for doing bad political theater rather than their jobs. In a curious way, the media's reduction of the complexities of a presidential campaign to a "horserace" complete with each party and hundreds of journalists for both old and new media alike playing a daily game of "gotcha" with the candidates, had made a show like Stewart's which ridiculed the process not only popular but quite possibly necessary. Among the comments on the night in question were the following (transcript found at: transcripts.cnn.com accessed on October 27, 2006):

STEWART: "But the thing is that this—you're doing theater, when you should be doing debate, which would be great."

CARLSON: "You had John Kerry on your show and you sniff his throne and you're accusing us of partisan hackery?"

STEWART: "Absolutely. . . . What is wrong with you? . . . You know, the interesting thing I have is, you have a responsibility to the public discourse, and you fail miserably."

CARLSON: "You need to get a job at a journalism school, I think."

STEWART: "You need to go to one. The thing that I want to say is, when you have people on for just knee-jerk, reactionary talk . . ."

CARLSON: "Wait. I thought you were going to be funny. Come on. Be funny."

STEWART: "No. No. I'm not going to be your monkey. . . . I watch your show every day. And it kills me."

CARLSON: "I can tell you love it."

STEWART: "It's so—oh, it's so painful to watch. You know, because we need what you do. This is such a great opportunity you have here to actually get politicians off of their marketing and strategy."

CARLSON: "Is this really Jon Stewart? What is this, anyway?"

STEWART: "Yes, it's someone who watches your show and cannot take it anymore. I just can't. And come work for us, because we, as the people . . ."

CARLSON: "How do you pay?"

STEWART: "The people—not well. . . . But you can sleep at night."

Should there be a truth standard in art? The tendency of the status quo to impose a specific moral "truth" on the masses has been common to many cultures and political systems across the ages. In *The Republic* Plato had Socrates argue against allowing children to hear "casual tales . . . devised by casual persons." The Third Reich burned books deemed unsuitable for reading. In the United States, the battle historically has raged over library books. Classics such as *Huckleberry Finn, Of Mice and Men, The Grapes of Wrath* and *The Merchant of Venice* are but some of the long-revered and award-winning works that now face censorship by various school systems. The American Library Association reports that incidents of book banning now reach more than 1,000 instances annually, with little legal intervention. The U.S. Supreme Court has not heard another book-banning case since allowing a lower court ruling to stand in 1982.

Protests began early in the history of television. The 1951 show "Amos 'n' Andy" was condemned by the National Association for the Advancement of Colored People for depicting "Negroes in a stereotyped and derogatory manner." In the 1960s the United Church of Christ successfully challenged the license renewal of WLBT in Jackson, Miss., on the grounds that the owners had blatantly discriminated against African-Americans.

In the latter half of the 20th century, a variety of special-interest groups used more subtle methods to influence entertainment programming. Some, such as the Hispanic advocacy group Nosotros, worked closely with network bureaucracies, previewing potentially problematic episodes of entertainment programs, often altering program content before it reached the airwaves. Not all protests involve censoring a program. Some want to make sure that programming airs, such as advocacy groups who lobby advertisers and affiliates to ensure the airing of certain shows or inclusion of certain controversial characters in prime time.

New York Times television critic Jack Gould framed the problem of artistic accountability in the early days of these advocacy groups arguing that such agreements held

> latent dangers for the well-being of television as a whole. An outside group not professionally engaged in theatre production has succeeded in imposing its will with respect to naming of fictional characters, altering the importance of a leading characterization and in other particulars changing the story line (Montgomery 1989, 21).

And for the artist trying to create in the medium, network attempts to "balance" competing advocacy-group interests had come close to recreating the patronage system, albeit a far more sophisticated one with government as the patron.

The struggle over content becomes even more acute when governmental sponsorship is at stake. Some argue that because tax dollars are extracted from all, the programs they fund should be acceptable to all. Federal support for programs such as the National Endowment for the Arts (NEA) has been repeatedly questioned in Congress. Conservatives objected to funding artists such as photographer Robert Mapplethorpe, whose blend of homoerotic photos and traditional Judeo-Christian symbols offended many. Eventually, the criticism was a factor in the resignation of one of the NEA's directors, John E. Frohnmayer.

The government also censors directly. On multiple occasions Infinity Broadcasting was fined several hundred thousand dollars for disc jockey Howard Stern's on-air profanity and offensive racial slurs. Stern protested that the FCC's action amounted to an enforcement of political correctness. But others noted that Stern most often castigated disadvantaged people and groups. By 2006, Stern had left terrestrial radio and its rules for satellite radio, where he found a fat payday, artistic freedom and a much smaller audience.

In 2006 with the Broadcast Decency Enforcement Act, Congress raised the fine for a single count of indecency from $27,500 to $325,000. Because of the potential liability for crippling fines, producers of live programming such as the Grammy Awards and the Oscars were forced to put a delay on the broadcast to bleep out what the courts called "fleeting expletives" or nudity.

COP TV: ENTERTAINMENT, INFOTAINMENT OR NEWS?

In his ingenious Academy Award–winning script, *Network,* the late writer-director Paddy Chayefsky envisioned a time when the lines would be blurred between entertainment and news, rendering them indistinguishable. However, Chayefsky was wrong in one detail. News did begin to take on the look of entertainment (as he predicted it would, to great satirical effect) but he did not predict that entertainment would also begin to look like news with the two meeting somewhere in the middle.

Consider these television shows: "America's Most Wanted," in which the audience is encouraged to help by calling in tips for police; "Unsolved Mysteries," with its focus on the criminal and the paranormal; "Inside Edition," a voyeuristic look at stories dubbed "too hot to handle" for traditional network news; and others of the same breed, including "A Current Affair," "Hard Copy," "COPS," "Rescue 911" and any number of other spin-offs. Or consider "Dateline," which blurred the lines of entertainment programming and the apprehension of would-be child molesters duped on to the show's set—all for our entertainment including seeing them led off in cuffs.

And then came YouTube, where virtually no event was outside the range of cameras and videos shot by amateurs often found their way on to the mainstream media.

In what genre do these shows belong? When "America's Most Wanted" follows a bounty hunter on an illegal trip into Mexico to bring home a nationally known fugitive is it news or entertainment?

Currently, dozens of such pseudo-news, pseudo-cop, pseudo-court shows are in production simultaneously. Very little escapes our fascination. Dubbed "infotainment" by critics, these shows are hot with television programming executives and audiences alike. Producers love it because such shows are quite cheap to produce and deliver better ratings than reruns, news or other syndicated programming. Audiences love it because such programming provides relief from reruns of situation comedies and the sameness of game shows. When produced by syndicators, the shows are prepackaged with ads embedded in them, making them attractive to station owners. In fact, local station owners who have found their station consistently at the bottom of the local news ratings can turn to a game show such as "Wheel of Fortune" and reclaim ratings that their news side never could.

But there are problems. A man who agreed to appear on the "Jenny Jones Show" on the premise of meeting someone who had a crush on him later murdered the would-be lover who was male—a fact that was not revealed until the moment the showed taped. After a highly publicized trial, the television show was exonerated of any blame in the murder, but public opinion was clearly divided on the show's culpability. CNN's Nancy Grace faced an avalanche of criticism when a guest on her show committed suicide the day after an extremely confrontational interview.

The blending of facts and entertainment is not restricted to the small screen. Films such as *Ray, Walk the Line, The Alamo, Nixon, Hoffa* and *Thirteen Days* reflect a particular artistic vision based on fact. *Hoffa* director Danny DeVito sought to make an entertaining film of the major facts of the controversial missing labor leader's life, but took symbolic liberties with many events and people. DeVito justified his changes on the "Today" show by saying what he sought was entertainment— "not sitting down and reading a book."

Based-on-reality films and reality-based television shows differ in format and content but they are alike in invoking the license allowed entertainment programming while retaining the authority of fact—a risky combination. By blending information and entertainment, the possibility for abuse of an unsuspecting audience exists. To understand how this happens, we look to the theory of "uses and gratifications." Phrased simply, the theory says audience members will use the media to gratify certain wants and needs. People bring something to the message, and what they bring affects what they take away.

For example, seeking news and information is a common use of the media, with an expected gratification of getting information necessary for living one's life from traffic to weather to news about government. Entertainment is another common media use, with its own gratification of laughter, crying or any other emotion evoked by entertainment media—something Tolstoy said was the basic aim of the audience.

Infotainment keeps the look of news, yet airs the content of lowbrow entertainment juxtaposing traditional uses and gratifications. With a look of authority (an anchor's desk, a courtroom, a police precinct) and the hype of their importance (e.g., "200 lives saved so far!"), these shows appear to be useful for acquiring information. However, by invoking their license as entertainment, such shows are free to bypass accuracy, fairness, balance and other standards normally associated with news and to focus on more sensational elements to gather larger ratings.

Consequently, infotainment, while fundamentally flawed, gets widely accepted as fact. *New York Times* columnist A. M. Rosenthal (1989) compared airing these tabloid television shows to buying news programming "off the shelf." Stations should add the disclaimer, "We did not put this stuff in the bottle, whatever it is," Rosenthal added.

REALITY TELEVISION: OXYMORON, PROFIT CENTER AND USING THE AUDIENCE

They eat cow's lips, let their families pick their mates and routinely lie about their financial and physical assets. They are Americans with talent. They are "Jon and Kate Plus 8." They race, they dance and they escape. It's all part of the reality television craze that has made strong inroads into prime-time entertainment programming. The craze began with the wildly successful "Survivor" series, which ran first as a summer replacement show and garnered ratings that impressed network executives. "Survivor" quickly spawned other reality shows, among them "Amazing Race," "Danger Island," "Wife Swap," "The Osbornes," "Fear Factor" and "American Idol," to name a few.

Why the rush to reality programming? Ratings and money. For three decades, traditional network television programming lost audience share to cable television, TiVo and the Internet. At their height, the original three American networks, ABC, CBS and NBC, could count on attracting approximately 90 percent of American homes with televisions on any given evening; the rest tuned in a few fledgling independents playing reruns. Today, the audience for five broadcast networks (including Fox and CW) has plunged to less than half of all households, with the number slipping every season.

Then traditional cable outlets such as HBO, TNT and USA got into original scripted programming, cutting further into the audience for scripted entertainment, often sweeping the industry's awards along the way. The reason for the immediate artistic success was a matter of sheer economics: it was easier to program a few hours of quality television a week than to try to program three hours every night as the traditional networks have done for years.

Compounding the problem, those who continued to watch the traditional networks were an older demographic not popular with advertisers. For the networks, reality television was a chance to pull viewers away from cable and computers and back to their programming at a cost lower than scripted television series. Not only did reality shows draw viewers, but the audience they drew centered on 18- to 49-year-olds, a ratings bonanza in the preferred demographic and a potent inducement to produce more reality programming.

Reality programming was not only popular, but cheap to produce. There was little need to pay writers, and the actors who populated them worked for scale or prizes.

But using cheaply produced reality programming to garner ratings has had consequences. Shows such as "NCIS" and "White Collar" were expensive and it often took time to find an audience sufficient to sustain these shows. What the producers hoped for was a chance to air enough episodes—typically 60 or more—to make it to the lucrative syndication market and DVD, where they live on for years and produce a sizable return on the initial investment. What networks ordered were 12 episodes with options for more at a later date—a clause that kept writers, etc. tied to the show and kept lives in limbo until the network exercised or failed to exercise the option.

By eating up entire chunks of the network schedule, reality television pushed many quality shows into an early retirement and kept many more out of production. The result now is fewer quality programs in syndication and fewer producers of quality shows able to get their product into the schedules of the major networks now infatuated with reality. Quality writers fled to the movies or the cable channels willing to try scripted television. The light-viewing months of the summer were once a time when networks took some chances on genre-defining shows to see if they could find an audience. Now that season is given over to "star-making" shows that turn immediate profits with no regard for the future.

If they didn't add to the nation's intellect, reality shows have added to American slang. Getting "voted off the island" became a catch phrase for everyone from politicians to news journalists. "You're fired" entered the American vernacular from "The Apprentice" starring Donald Trump.

The "new" reality television was really a second pass at the genre. The first attempt took place in the 1950s with quiz shows such as "21" and "The $64,000 Question." These shows were enormously popular and, as it turned out, could be rigged. Popular contestants were given the answers to general-knowledge questions beforehand. What the audience saw was a scripted contest with the winner predetermined. Winners came back from week to week and some gained a national following. Not surprisingly, the predetermined winner was the one the producers believed would sustain the ratings or increase them. The quiz show scandals, as they are referred to in media history, were followed by congressional hearings, ruined careers and even legislation.

The new reality shows suffered from some of the same problems. When it was discovered that those who advanced on one or more popular reality shows had actually been determined in advance, it became national news. Soon after, audiences learned that participants in the various reality shows were not always novices to the medium but were often recruited from ranks of fledgling actors. Furthermore, the notion of spontaneity, crucial to getting the audience to believe the premise of the reality show, was false. The producers of shows such as "Survivor," "Joe Millionaire" and the like most often shot hundreds of hours of video with a predetermined "story line" to edit into an allegedly spontaneous program.

Some reality shows were based on legally questionable premises, such as the series that proposed to capture men hiring prostitutes—the reality of "johns"—or cop shows that allowed media to capture arrests inside homes only to be successfully sued for invasion of privacy later. Some shows seemed notable for their complete lack of a moral compass or made us more like voyeurs than traditional viewers. "Temptation Island" put couples and relationships in physical and emotional jeopardy for the entertainment of the audience. But, still, America watched even as lives were altered irreparably.

In June of 2009, a record 10.6 million people tuned into the TLC show "Jon and Kate Plus 8" to learn that Jon and Kate Gosselin were calling it quits after 10 years of marriage, including several years that were documented on television. The concept was a reality series of two parents and their eight children on a $1.1 million Berks County, Penn., home built in part with television funds. At the time of their divorce, papers filed by the couple indicated that they had long lived separate lives, including the possibility that they had been misleading the public about their marriage for up to two years before the filing—a claim disputed by the lawyers as mere "legalese." In an interview with *People* magazine, Kate didn't blame the ubiquitous cameras for the failure of the marriage, saying that the divorce would have happened with or without the television show, which was consistently one of the top shows for the TLC network.

Reality television raises an important ethical question: what constitutes reality? As you'll remember from Chapter 1, definitions of truth and the relationship between truth and reality have changed throughout the millennia. Reality television is a lot like the computer-generated matrix in the film *The Matrix.* Reality shows used participants for its purposes, and along the way, a lot of people in the matrix world of reality TV were entertained.

Kris Bunton and Wendy Wyatt (2012) raise other important questions in their philosophical approach to the ethics of reality television. For example, do reality programs stereotype participants or activities? Even though participants sign legal waivers that are 20 and 30 pages long, do reality programs invade privacy? Can contestants ethically give away the sort of access the shows require? Does reality television inspire us—particularly if we have talent or can create a team that functions well under original circumstances and stress? Suzanne Collins, whose successful book trilogy begins with *The Hunger Games,* takes on many of these same questions in fictional form, often with disturbing answers. Collins has said that she wrote the series, in part, as a response to reality television and that her early literary influences included George Orwell's *1984.*

The early part of this century has been a scary time, and watching Joe Millionaire bungle his relationships is a lot easier than taking the chance of going out on a first date. However, that scary first date has the chance of turning into something wonderful or awful—neither outcome one that Joe Millionaire had to face. Truth in relationships matters because it's how people form connections. Reality television was people, inside a box, having a planned and edited experience. That planning wasn't about truth. It wasn't even particularly personal. Just like in the matrix world, it was a code.

THE DOCUMENTARIAN: ARTIST OR JOURNALIST

Perhaps no media genre blends art and journalism together as does documentary film. In fact, if you ask a documentarian—particularly a fledging one—to define a professional role, directors, producers and editors are quite likely to say that they are producing art that sometimes looks like journalism. Yet, as recent scholarship and professional conferences suggest (Aufderheide 2005), documentarians share many of the same ethical questions as their journalistic first cousins. But, since many of them are either self-taught or the product of film programs, they stumble into the same ethical questions with relatively little guidance.

Documentarians generally agree that they are truth-tellers, but that the truth they seek is not necessarily objective in the way that journalists traditionally have defined it. Rather, documentarians seek to tell truth from a point of view influenced by context. It is not unreasonable to suggest that multiple documentaries can be made about what is essentially the same subject—for example, Oregon's controversial assisted suicide law—each one taking a point of view. However, documentarians assert that the best documentary film is one that acknowledges, and sometimes deeply examines, views in opposition to the director's point of view. The *New York Times,* in 2011, began a new feature on its opinion pages—Op-Docs—where citizens and professionals were invited to provide editorial commentary in the form of short documentaries on subjects of public importance.

Documentary links facts to beliefs and opinions in important ways. Documentarians also wrestle with how deeply involved they should become with the subjects of their films. For example, the director and producer of *Born into Brothels,* Zana Briski, as part of her film recounts her personal efforts to get the children of Indian sex workers into school so they could escape the poverty and work choices the Calcutta slums seem to provide. Documentarians often invest their own funds and months of their unpaid time to capture images, scenes and dialogue that make a narrative work. This commitment to a single source and point of view is rare for journalists and can blur the line between essential source and friend. On the one hand, documentarians are concerned about exploiting those whom they become close to; on the other hand they worry about becoming the prisoner of a single point of view or a source who likes to be on camera to the point where the director loses control over the content of the film itself.

Editing also raises a host of issues for documentarians, everything from the often in-your-face shots of people in joy or pain to the construction of a narrative that requires significant omissions and emphases for aesthetic purposes, edging the resulting film away from the initial truth or even-handed examination that both the filmmaker and the sources sought. Adding music and archival footage and building a narrative structure all require hours in the editing room. As documentaries have become more profitable, they have demanded significant investment in production values and postproduction efforts. Raising the money to make these sorts of films is not easy, and documentarians also worry about becoming the intellectual and artistic prisoners of those who fund their work.

And, there is the role of emotion in documentary film. These are films that are designed to provoke audience response. Strategic communication professionals would recognize the call to action embedded in many documentaries. Documentarians seek to overtly link emotion, fact, logic and action in a way that journalism, perhaps with the exception of investigative reporting, seldom does. Along the way, there are real ethical questions that are not readily answered by the too common response, "but, I am an artist." In the documentary *Inside Job,* which won an Academy Award in 2011, the filmmakers accepted the Oscar by noting that no one had yet been jailed in the financial scandal that precipitated the recession of 2008. The film was an artistic success; however, its political impact was less so. If Plato were alive today, there is little doubt that documentary film, through its artistry as well as investigations, would be on the list of highly suspect professions in the modern-day democratic republic.

AESTHETICS IS AN ATTITUDE

Artists see the world differently. While most people perceive only what is needful, the artist works with what some have called an "enriched perceptual experience." This aesthetic attitude is one that values close and complete concentration of all the senses. An aesthetic attitude is a frankly sensual one, and one that summons both emotion and logic to its particular ends.

For example, the theater audience knows that Eugene O'Neill's plays are "merely" drama. But they also provide us with an intense examination of the role of family in human society—an experience that is both real and personal to every audience member. Such intense examination is what gives the plays their power to move.

The makers of mediated messages, whether they are the executive producers of a television sitcom or the designers of a newspaper page, share this aesthetic impetus. These mass communicators are much like architects. An architect can design a perfectly serviceable cube-like building, one that withstands the elements and may be used for good ends. But great buildings—St. Paul's Cathedral in London or Jefferson's home at Monticello—do more. They are tributes to the human intellect's capacity to harmoniously harness form and function.

In fact, philosophers have argued that what separates the commonplace from the excellent is the addition of an aesthetic quality to what would otherwise be a routine, serviceable work. These qualities of excellence have been described as:

- An appreciation of the function realized in the product.
- An appreciation of the resulting quality or form.
- An appreciation of the technique or skill in the performance.

These three characteristics of aesthetic excellence characterize excellence in mass communication as well.

Take the newspaper weather page. *USA Today* literally recalibrated the standard from tiny black and white agate type to a colorful full page. They understood what the late political columnist Molly Ivins knew: when people aren't talking about football, they talk about the weather. They devoted more space to it and printed it in color. They added more information in a more legible style and form. In short, they gave newspaper weather information an aesthetic quality. While much about *USA Today* has been criticized, its excellent weather page has been copied.

Although mass-communication professionals are infrequently accused of being artists, we believe they intuitively accept an aesthetic standard as a component of professional excellence. As philosopher G. E. Moore (1903, 83) noted in *Principia Ethica:*

> Let us imagine one world exceedingly beautiful. Image it as beautiful as you can; put into it whatever on this earth you most admire: mountains, rivers, the sea, suns and sunsets, stars and moon. Imagine these all combined in the most exquisite proportion so that no one thing jars against another, but each contributes to increase the beauty of the whole. And then imagine the ugliest world you can possibly conceive. Imagine it just one heap of filth, containing everything that is most disgusting to you for whatever reason, and the whole, as far as may be, without one redeeming factor. . . . Supposing (all) that quite apart from the contemplation of human beings; still it is irrational to hold that it is better that the ugly world exist than the one which is beautiful.

Substitute "film," "compact disc," "poem," "news story," "photograph" or "advertising copy" for Moore's word "world" and we believe that you will continue to intuitively agree with the statement. While we may disagree on what specifically constitutes beauty in form and content, the aesthetic standard of excellence still applies.

Philosopher John Dewey (2005) noted, "Aesthetic experience is a manifestation, a record and celebration of the life of a civilization, a means of promoting its development, and is also the ultimate judgment upon the quality of a civilization." In an interview on the PBS series "The Promise of Television," commentator Bill Moyers (1988) said:

> The root word of television is vision from afar, and that's its chief value. It has brought me in my stationary moments visions of ideas and dreams and imaginations and geography that I would never personally experience. So, it has put me in touch with the larger world. Television can be a force for dignifying life, not debasing it.

Though Moyers's comments were made specifically about television, the same argument can be made for a good book, a favorite magazine, music or a film. And whether the media are a force for dignifying humanity or debasing it is largely in the hands of those who own and work in them.

Suggested Readings

BUNTON, KRIS, and WENDY WYATT. 2012. *Reality television: A philosophical examination.* New York: Continuum International Publishing Group.

CALVERT, CLAY. 2000. *Voyeur nation: Media, privacy and peering in modern culture.* Boulder, CO: Westview Press.

JENSEN, JOLI. 2002. *Is art good for us?* Lanham, MD: Rowman & Littlefield, Publishers.

MEDVED, MICHAEL. 1992. *Hollywood vs. America.* New York: HarperCollins Publishers.

MONTGOMERY, KATHRYN C. 1989. *Target: Prime time. Advocacy groups and the struggle over entertainment television.* New York: Oxford University Press.

POSTMAN, NEIL. 1986. *Amusing ourselves to death: Public discourse in the age of television.* New York: Penguin Books.

Cases on the Web

www.mhhe.com/mediaethics8e

"How to remember Malcolm X" by Dennis Lancaster
"Beavis and Butthead: The case for standards in entertainment" by Philip Patterson
"Joe Klein and the authorship of 'Primary Colors'" by Lee Wilkins
"'Bamboozled': Truth (or prophesy) in satire" by Lee Wilkins
"Truth in filmmaking: Removing the ugliness from 'A Beautiful Mind'" by Philip Patterson
"Playing hardball: The Pete Rose–Jim Gray controversy" by Ben Scott
"How much coverage is appropriate? The case of the highly paid athlete" by Matt Keeney
"Up for debate: NBC news logo decorates 'The West Wing'" by Reuben Stern

CHAPTER 10 CASES

CASE 10-A

Searching for Sugar Man: Rediscovered Art

LEE WILKINS
University of Missouri

What makes a hit record has never been reduced to a formula. During the decades of the 1960s and early 1970s, hundreds of talented artists were never heard beyond a small group of fans because their records didn't sell. That was the case with a young Detroit musician, Sixto Rodriguez, who produced one album—"Cold Fact" in 1970— and a second in 1971. With a voice reminiscent of James Taylor and lyrics with the edge and poetry of Bob Dylan, Rodriguez's career never made it out of Detroit. Years later, his Motown-based producer, then living in California, told Danish documentary filmmaker Malik Bendjelloul, that Rodriguez had sold exactly six records in the states.

Which was true—sort of. What his producer may have known—but Rodriguez unquestionably did not—was that the "Cold Fact" album and its title song had become the anthem of young people half a world away. In South Africa, in the early 1970s, Rodriguez was better known than Elvis, sold more records than the Rolling Stones, and had become the voice of a generation that wanted to challenge the apartheid political system in that country. His two records were considered so inflammatory that government censors deliberately scratched vinyl copies housed at radio stations so they could not be broadcast over the air. In the days before the Internet, Rodriguez was an underground pied piper—everyone knew his songs just as everyone in a certain generation in the United States knew that "the answer was blowin' in the wind."

His South African fans also knew something else: Rodriguez was dead. No one was quite sure how he died, but there were conflicting newspaper reports that he had committed suicide—everything from setting himself alight on stage to protest apartheid to shooting himself. In an era of untimely rock musician deaths—Janis Joplin, Jimi Hendrix, Jim Morrison—it seemed only too reasonable. The mystery and the assumption of Rodriguez's demise persisted in South Africa for more than two decades. But, as the country changed, his largely Africanse fans did not forget, including two now-middle-aged fans turned music journalists who set out on an unlikely quest to find out how Rodriguez actually had died.

Solving that mystery became the focus of the documentary film *Searching for Sugar Man* that Bendjelloul reported, shot and produced in the early 21st century. The film chronicles the efforts of the South Africans, one of whom is nicknamed Sugarman, to track down Rodriguez, with the most profoundly startling result.

In response to an Internet posting about the circumstances of the musician's death, Rodriguez's adult daughter e-mailed back that her father is alive, he's living as he has for decades in Detroit supporting himself through heavy construction work, and he has literally no idea about his impact on the nation and the people of South Africa. When the South Africans find and then telephone Rodriguez, he hangs up the phone, thinking that the call is a prank. But, thanks to this initial connection, in the late 1990s, Rodriguez ultimately travels to South Africa where his concert performances are sold out and he plays to audiences in the thousands who can sing every word of every song. Bendjelloul reports it all, including lengthy interviews with Rodriguez, his daughter, his South African fans, and a soundtrack shot through with music that still seems timely even in the next century.

But, to report this different sort of magical mystery (Rodriguez had stopped playing professionally many years before) Bendjelloul makes what he admits are some uneasy compromises (personal communication 2012). In order to track down information about Rodriguez himself, Bendjelloul needs to interview his former producer—who had received some royalty checks for South African sales. The film can't go forward without his cooperation, so Bendjelloul makes the decision not to confront the producer about potential financial chicanery in order to learn more about Rodriguez's early recording and artistic career. Bendjelloul himself is working on a shoestring—while he's shooting the film, he spends some nights on Rodriguez's couch to defray expenses. And, Rodriguez himself is vague about some things. The finished documentary, for example, never mentions a marriage or a lover—although he has three children who appear in the film—nor does it delve deeply into why a person with such enormous talent—having learned he is a phenomenon—fails literally and artistically to capitalize on it during the late 1900s and early 2000s.

The documentary debuted formally in the United States in July 2012. Rodriguez and Bendjelloul were both interviewed in the *New York Times* and on NPR, where audiences learn that Rodriguez had been politically active in Detroit, running unsuccessfully for mayor more than once. Rodriguez's U.S. artistic career also begins to take off; he plays gigs such as South by Southwest and his music is covered at the Newport Jazz Festival. As of this writing, the film has failed to find a national distributor, although clips of it—as well as Rodriguez's music—are available on the Internet and through music distributors such as iTunes.

Micro Issues

1. In crafting the narrative, Bendjelloul behaves more like a feature writer than he does an investigative journalist, even though it is clear that there are things worthy of investigation about Rodriguez's royalty payments. Analyze this choice, from the point of role? Is this a case of leaving out important facts to tell a better story?
2. Should the filmmaker have literally lived with his subject to produce this film? Justify your answer using ethical theory. How would you respond if a journalist had done the same thing with an important source?
3. Is the filmmaker using Rodriguez as a means to his ends?

Midrange Issues

1. How hard should the filmmaker have "pushed" to get information about the potentially less seemly parts of Rodriguez's life?
2. Rodriguez says on camera that he is a shy person. Indeed, in his early Detroit career, he often played at a bar called the Sewer with his back to the audience. Does a film like *Searching for Sugar Man* invade his obviously valued privacy?

Macro Issues

1. Based on the above facts and what you can find on the Internet, analyze how Rodriguez's lack of success in the United States might be explained by the concept of popular culture.
2. In today's environment, where musicians often make it on the Web before making it on the road, do you think Rodriguez and his music would find a U.S. audience? Does it matter?
3. Is the documentary film responsible for changing Rodriguez's life? Should the director have been concerned about this potential as he made the film?

CASE 10-B

Bob Costas and Jerry Sandusky: Is Sports Entertainment or Journalism

LEE WILKINS
University of Missouri

Sports journalism functions, in some ways, by its own set of rules. First, it is enormously important to audience members and profitable for all involved. Some studies suggest that about 30 percent of newspaper readers read the sports pages and literally nothing else. Cable television offers packages allowing sports fan to follow their favorite sports (NFL, NBA, and MLB all have multiple channels) and teams—all for a monthly fee. ESPN is among the most watched broadcast offerings and recently both NBC and CBS have launched all-sports networks.

Sports journalists are boosters—of their local high school teams to professional franchises. Objectivity, or even fairness, sometimes takes a back seat to rooting for the locals. And, the money is enormous. The creation of a college football championship series in 2012 was predicted to be so lucrative—projected in excess of half a billion dollars—that it would certainly provide the broadcast networks with a continuing source of revenue in difficult times.

And, that revenue wouldn't hurt the universities with big-time sports programs, either.

Among the schools that were expected to profit was Pennsylvania State University, a 44,000-student university located in College Station, Penn. There, legendary coach Joe Paterno had led the program for more than four decades. He was the winningest coach in college football history. His student-athletes graduated and many went on to play professional football, and his loyalty to Penn State had raised untold dollars not just for the athletic department but for school's academic mission. As he coached well into his seventies and eighties, Paterno's success also was attributable to his staff, including longtime defensive coordinator Jerry Sandusky. Paterno and the Penn State program had been considered models of how college athletics should be run and managed. There had been little to no critical coverage of the program or Paterno and his staff. Local and national sports journalists were onboard with the narrative of Penn State as an example of "best practices" in college athletics.

It all fell apart in the fall of 2011 when Sandusky was accused of and arrested on charges of child molestation. He subsequently was tried and convicted and is now in prison, was accused of child molestation. Sandusky recruited several of his juvenile victims through a charity he established. One of his inducements was access to the Penn State football program and facilities, where, according to both grand jury and court testimony, Sandusky was seen molesting boys.

According to that same testimony and an independent investigation by former FBI director Louis Freeh, Paterno had known of the problem and, instead of confronting it, had urged the university and its officials not to act. The scandal itself was so profound that the university president of 16 years was fired. Congress and many state legislatures considered legislation that would make it a crime to fail to report suspicions of child sexual abuse. The nation began a conversation about the ethical responsibilities of adults who discover that a crime of this sort is being committed yet do nothing to prevent a recurrence.

If there was a single media event that captured the nature of the problem and the depth of the scandal, it was Bob Costas's interview with Sandusky, conducted before his trial. Costas, widely regarded as among the best sports journalists and legendary for his knowledge and preparation, interviewed Sandusky for a total of 36 minutes, about 8 of which were broadcast on the NBC evening magazine news program, "Rock Center with Brian Williams." (You can access part of the interview at deadspin.com/bobcostas by selecting the Nov. 14, 2011 clip. You can also find links to the full interview and transcript there.) During the interview, Sandusky admitted that he "horsed around" with young boys and made other statements that many viewers and critics characterized as creepy. Costas's questions were characterized as tough. He asked Sandusky directly whether he was innocent of the charges. Costas's work was nominated for an Emmy in 2012.

However, the interview—and the network's editing of it—was not without some controversy. NBC and Costas were criticized for omitting the following exchange from the broadcast, an omission that came to light only after prosecutors subpoenaed the outtakes from the interview. Media critics questioned whether Sandusky, in this passage, admits his guilt, even though he had denied it minutes before.

> 19:00:28:00 But isn't what you're just describing the classic MO of many pedophiles? And that is that they gain the trust of young people, they don't necessarily abuse every young person. There were hundreds, if not thousands of young boys you came into contact with, but there are allegations that at least eight of them were victimized. Many people believe there are more to come. So it's entirely possible that you could've helped young boy A in some way that was not objectionable while horribly taking advantage of young boys B, C, D, and E. Isn't that possible?
>
> JERRY SANDUSKY:
>
> 19:01:01:00 Well—you might think that. I don't know. (LAUGHS) In terms of—my relationship with so many, many young people, I would—I would guess that there are many young people who would come forward. Many more young people who would come forward and say that my methods and—and what I had done for them made a very positive impact on their life. And I didn't go around seeking out

every young person for sexual needs that I've helped. There are many that I didn't have—I hardly had any contact with who I have helped in many, many ways.

Micro Issues

1. Should a sports reporter have done this interview or would this have been better left to an investigative journalist?
2. Should local sports reporters be looking for this sort of story in their local markets?
3. Based on what you can access on the Web, did Costas invade Sandusky's privacy? Was such an invasion appropriate?
4. Who else should Costas and other journalists have interviewed?
5. Would you characterize this interview as fair? Link your response to ethical theory.

Midrange Issues

1. Should NBC have aired this interview in prime time when children might well have been watching?
2. Does this interview harm Sandusky's constitutional right to a fair trial? Depending on your answer, does this mean the network should not have attempted it?
3. Evaluate the portion of the interview the network omitted in light of your answer to the previous question.

Macro Issues

1. Is this the sort of reporting that deserves an award? Would a local journalist having done the same interview have received the same nomination?
2. How would you define the role of the sports journalists in your community? Provide an ethical justification for their approach.
3. The foregoing questions have assumed that sports journalism shares much in common with news. If sports journalism is considered entertainment, do the ethical standards change? Should they?

CASE 10-C

Hardly Art

MITO HABE-EVANS
University of Missouri—Columbia

Hardly Art is an independent record label, a sister label started in 2007 by Sub Pop Records in Seattle. Sub Pop started in 1987 and was among the pioneers of the grunge rock scene, including releasing the first album by Nirvana before the group moved to the major label Geffen/DGC.

Despite its fan popularity, Sub Pop floundered economically. The growing commercial success of alternative music in the 1990s meant that major labels competed with Sub Pop to sign talent. According to a biography of the label on its Web site, the financial woes of Sub Pop were due in part to "unwise spending on meals and travel" among other line items as they sought to grow the business in an increasingly crowded market. Eventually, financial troubles led Sup Pop to sell 49 percent of its ownership to Warner Bros. Records in exchange for a cash infusion (Sub Pop 2008).

The typical business model used by record labels, both independent and major, is one where the label signs a contract with the artist for a set number of albums, fronts the money and resources for recording, producing, manufacturing, distribution, touring and promotion, and the artist earns royalties from recording sales—all of which pay back the music company for its initial investment (Albini 1993). In Sub Pop's case, sales weren't enough to recoup the initial investment—particularly after the smaller label began competing against larger, better funded labels.

Major labels, on the other hand, are able to recover their investment by keeping artists' royalties small. Often, artists remain indebted, even after modest success. David Hesmondhalgh (1999) describes the logic of the music industry as "towards internationalization, because of the economies which accrue to very big, as opposed to moderate, sales: the costs of development, marketing and recording are high; marginal costs for reproducing each copy are very small." Support from major labels—when it comes at all—has turned into survival of the fittest where the commercialization of music mandates that only those artists who make music that attracts the widest possible audience will be supported by the music industry once signed. This is especially true when artists who have signed into multi-album deals and remain in debt to the label must find a way to fulfill their contractual obligations and make enough money to get out of debt.

The emergence of independent record labels has been a response to a lack of support for smaller, less commercially digestible music. These labels value artistic autonomy for musicians, yet must try to balance this with the need to be financially viable. Whereas profit is not the independent record label's sole motivation, it must still be conscious of not losing money in order to survive as a business.

Sub Pop launched Hardly Art as a sister label with a new business model based on a net profit split of 40–60 between the label and the band as opposed to the system of royalties typically used in the industry. All the costs must first be recouped, but once they are, the band sees a much higher percentage of the profit. Because both parties involved have a vested interest in keeping the costs down, they work together to decide what extra activities such as touring and promotions are worth the extra spending. Instead of multi-album deals that bind the band and the label, they work using a one-off project model, which allows for spontaneous releases by small bands. Sarah Moody, the general manager of Hardly Art, says, "as for why we went with this particular model, a large part of it had to do with being artist-friendly, especially to bands just starting out, and a smaller part had to do with seeing whether or not it would be a financially viable venture,"

As of now, with six releases under its belt, Hardly Art is not yet a fully profitable operation, but Moody believes that once the last few months are accounted for, two of their projects will be fully recouped or nearly so. She notes that the first couple of projects carried the additional burden to not being able to share advertising expenses with others, increasing their total budget. She sees this expense as declining on a per project basis after more projects are launched employing the same marketing infrastructure. "There are plenty of other opportunities offered to our bands along the way to help out," Moody says, "whether it's touring, licensing opportunities, and the like . . . so while getting our artists into the black is at the forefront, everyone understands that there has to be a modicum of patience involved."

Micro Issues

1. What are the values that the Sub Pop approach brings to artistic expression? Are any of these values ethical in nature?
2. How important, in an ethical sense, should the freedom to create be to artists? To those who make their work available to others? To music lovers?

Midrange Issues

1. Using the concepts of stakeholder and stockholder theory from the media economics chapter, analyze the ethical implications of the Sub Pop approach.
2. Evaluate whether and to what extent independent music, films, etc., have to consider the dictates of popular culture in their efforts.
3. What is independent music? Is it simply entertainment? Long-lasting art? Business? A blend of the three? How are your answers—in an ethical sense—changed by the way you define "indy" efforts?

Macro Issues

1. Might ownership and profit-sharing structures like this be workable in other areas of the mass media, for example in the creation of advertising or public relations agencies or news organizations? Would you be willing to work for an organization with this sort of business model?
2. Evaluate the ethical claims in the following statement by Moody: "I'd like to think that another goal of the label is to create an environment in which the artists feel comfortable and informed, and feel as though they could make a career of it—as opposed to slinging out random records left and right in an attempt to turn a profit. We view it as much more of a partnership with our bands."

CASE 10-D

Schindler's List: **The Role of Memory**

LEE WILKINS
University of Missouri—Columbia

In 1982 director Steven Spielberg purchased the rights to Australian novelist Thomas Keneally's retelling of the story of the "Schindler Jews," a group of about 1,100 Krakow, Poland, residents who survived the Holocaust because Czech businessman Oskar Schindler was willing to cajole, bribe and bully the Nazis for their lives. Today, Schindler, a Roman Catholic by birth, is known in Israel as a "righteous person"; he is the only Nazi buried in Jerusalem's Mount Zion cemetery.

By 1992 when Spielberg began work on the film, both he and the world had changed. Bosnia was in the midst of "ethnic cleansing," as were nations in Africa and in the Far East, such as Nepal. Some polls indicated that more than half of the U.S. teenagers living in that decade had never heard of the Holocaust; about 23 percent of the U.S. public at the time maintained the gasing of 6 million Jews plus 5 million other "undesirables" in Germany and its occupied territories never happened.

"I think the main reason I wanted to make this film was as an act of remembrance," Spielberg told the film editor of the *Atlanta Journal-Constitution.* "An act of remembrance for the public record. Maybe it won't be seen by millions of people who see my other movies, but it might be the kind of movie shown one day in high schools. I also wanted to leave this story for my children. I wanted to leave them a legacy of their Jewish culture."

What Americans, as well as Spielberg's children, will see is a 3-hour-and-15-minute examination of the conscience of Oskar Schindler, who entered World War II on the side of the Nazis, intending to make a profit. He hires Jews to work in his enamelware factory because they work for less than slave wages. Initially, he befriends the Nazis and the SS to help expedite his purchase and takeover of the plant. Later, after the Nazis have first ghettoized and then attempted to exterminate the Jewish population of Krakow, Schindler uses his personal charm, his connections and most of his war-amassed wealth to have "his" Jewish workers first labeled as essential to the German war machine and later moved from Germany and into Czechoslovakia for safekeeping. None of the bombs manufactured at Schindler's plant ever exploded.

Spielberg shot the film in black and white on location in Poland. Much of the movie has a documentary feel; cinematography is at eye level. It was often Spielberg himself who focused the handheld camera. Hitler appears only once—in a photograph on someone's desk. And, by centering on Schindler, Spielberg captured the conscience of an uneasy hero.

As Keneally's book indicates, Oskar Schindler was a complex man. He managed to maintain outward friendships with many Nazis whom he despised. He was a sensualist who enjoyed good food, expensive possessions and carnal knowledge of women who were not his wife. Spielberg's film, which was rated "R," depicted all of this, including scenes of lovemaking that involved full, frontal nudity and more distant shots of concentration camp existence in which Jewish inmates were required to run naked in front of their guards to determine who remained well enough to work and who was sick enough to be murdered.

Perhaps the most disturbing element of the film was Spielberg's portrait of the violence embedded in Hitler's "final solution" and of the banality of evil (Hannah Arendt's phrase used to describe convicted war criminal Adolph Eichmann) that individual human beings can come to represent. That sundered humanity is symbolized by Amon Goeth (played by Ralph Fiennes), the amoral and, some have suggested, sociopathic commandant of the labor camp from which many of the people who worked for Schindler survived. Whether it is the Nazis hunting the Jews who remain in hiding in the Krakow ghetto or Goeth's random murder of the men and women who lived in his camp as before-breakfast sport, the violence in the film is devastating not just for its brutality but also for its casualness.

When Spielberg's mother told him making "*Schindler's List* would be good for the Jews," Spielberg responded that "it would be good for all of us."

Critics, who had a difficult time accepting that the same man who directed *Jurassic Park* could also produce *Schindler's List* in the same year, praised the film for its aesthetic qualities and for its retelling of the story of the Holocaust in such a powerful fashion. The film also brought Spielberg multiple Oscars, an award that had eluded him despite his enormous popular success. After the film's release, President Bill Clinton said that every American should see it.

Writing in the *Washington Post,* Rita Kempley saw more than a superficial resemblance between Schindler and Spielberg. "And Schindler, played with élan by [Liam] Neeson, is really a lot like Spielberg himself," she wrote, "a man who manages to use his commercial clout to achieve a moral end."

Micro Issues

1. Should a film like *Schindler's List* receive the same "R" rating as films such as *Road Trip?*
2. What is the appropriate role of a film critic for films such as *Schindler's List?* Should different standards be used to evaluate this film than some other Spielberg successes, such as *E.T.* or *Jaws?*
3. Would you allow a child under 17 to see this film?

Midrange Issues

1. Should news accounts focus on events such as the ethnic cleansing in Bosnia with the goal of changing public opinion?
2. Are docudramas that focus on social issues such as spouse abuse or child molestation the appropriate mechanism to engage the public in debate or discussion about such serious questions?
3. Some people have argued that certain historical events, such as the Holocaust or the recent genocide in Rwanda, should never be the subject of entertainment programming because entertainment can never capture the true horror of what has happened. How would you evaluate such an assertion?

Macro Issues

1. Compare the moral development of Oskar Schindler with that of the main characters in a film such as *Gandhi.*
2. John Dewey wrote about "funded memory," by which he meant how a culture remembers and reconstructs its own history. What is the role of entertainment programming in funded memory? What should be the role of news programming in such cultural constructions?
3. Tolstoy argues that good art communicates the feelings of the artist to the masses in such a way that others may experience the same feeling as the artist. How does this film accomplish that purpose?

CASE 10-E

Tom Cruise, Katie Holmes and Suri Cruise: Do Celebrities Have Privacy?

LEE WILKINS
University of Missouri—Columbia

One definition of celebrity reads as follows: People who are famous for being famous. Tom Cruise, one of the most popular actors of the late 20th and early 21st century, may well fit this definition. Although his body of work in film has won some critical acclaim as well as enormous box office success, his real life is followed just as keenly, if not more so, including his multiple marriages.

When Cruise was first dating his now ex-wife Katie Holmes, also an actress, he announced his affection by jumping up and down on the interview couch live on Oprah Winfrey's television show. Holmes and Cruise were often photographed in public; they were relentlessly pursued by photographers known as paparazzi. When their child, Suri, was born, there were no photographs, a consistent stand for Cruise who, with ex-wife Nicole Kidman, did not allow either of their adopted children to be photographed until the younger one was about 2 years old.

In early 2012, Cruise and Holmes divorced, a split that was reported publically in multiple media outlets. Both Cruise and Holmes were interviewed and photographed, particularly in the summer of 2012 when both parents individually took their daughter on outings to tourist destinations in New York and to Disney World in Florida. You can find many photographs of Cruise, Holmes and Suri Cruise through a casual Internet search.

Micro Issues

1. Some theorists suggest that celebrity, because its oxygen is publicity, should not be subject to the same ethical standards regarding privacy and other sorts of individuals. Analyze this argument, using ethical theory to support various approaches.
2. Was it appropriate for media outlets to publish photos of Cruise and Holmes during this time? Of Suri?
3. Are the details of the Cruise–Holmes divorce ethically distinct from the fact that the marriage has ended? Justify your answers in terms of ethical theory.

Midrange Issues

1. How should Cruise's or Holmes's character influence media coverage of them as individuals, particularly their private lives?
2. Is there something more invasive about photographing Suri than photographing her parents? Is a photograph necessary for a journalistic purpose?
3. Should there be different standards for the tabloid press such as "TMZ" or Gawker than for more mainstream media? If there are different standards, what are they?
4. How do you account for the difference in the tabloid press in Tom Cruise and the equally or more accomplished Tom Hanks? Does the individual play a role in his or her privacy?

Macro Issues

1. How does your reasoning apply to the coverage of Michael Jackson's death, particularly his drug use and the charges—none of which were proved in court—of child molestation? Does the same reasoning apply to public officials, for example, diplomats, athletes or elected officials?
2. Photographs of celebrities increase magazine sales and Web hits. Do you think these financial incentives outweigh ethical concerns in the coverage of celebrities? Should they?
3. How does the concept of celebrity relate to the concept of popular and elite art? Critique your analysis from the point of role—of journalists, strategic communication professionals, of artists themselves.
4. How do you think Kant would analyze the concept of celebrity? Our response to celebrities?

CASE 10-F

Hate Radio: The Outer Limits of Tasteful Broadcasting

BRIAN SIMMONS
Portland State University

Trevor Van Lansing has what some would call the greatest job in the world. He is employed by KRFP-AM, an all-talk-format radio station in a large city in the West. His program airs weekdays from 3:00 p.m. to 7:00 p.m., and he is currently rated number one in his afternoon drive-time slot. Van Lansing is, quite simply, the most popular radio personality in the market. He is also the most controversial.

Each afternoon Van Lansing introduces a general topic for discussion and then fields calls from listeners about the topic. However, Lansing's topics (and the calls from his listeners) revolve around a recurring theme: the world as viewed by a Caucasian, Anglo-Saxon Protestant who also happens to be vocal, uncompromising and close-minded.

A sampling of his recent programs typifies his show. On Monday, Van Lansing discusses a woman in a small Indiana town who quits her job in a convenience store to go on welfare because there is more money to be made on the federal dole than in the private sector. Says Van Lansing, "All these irresponsible whores are the same. They get knocked up by some construction worker, then expect the taxpayers to pay for them to sit around the house all day and watch Oprah Winfrey."

Callers flood the airwaves with equally combative remarks in support of and opposition to Van Lansing's comments. On Tuesday, the topic of racial discrimination (always a Van Lansing favorite) comes up. According to Van Lansing, "Those Africans expect us Americans to make up for two hundred years of past mistakes. Forget it. It can't be done. If they are so keen on America, let them compete against Caucasians on an equal basis without the 'civil rights crutch.'"

When one African-American caller challenges Van Lansing's thinking, the host responds, "Why don't you tell your buddies to work for what they get like us

Caucasians? All you do anyway is steal from the guys you don't like and then take their women."

Wednesday finds Van Lansing lashing out against education: "The problem with today's schools is that our kinds are exposed to weird thinking. I mean, we tell our kids that homosexuality is okay, that we evolved from a chimp, and that the Ruskies are our friends. It all started when we elected women to school boards and started letting fags into the classroom. It's disgusting."

Thursday features an exchange between Van Lansing and an abortion-rights activist. At one point they are both shouting at the same time, and the airwaves are peppered with obscenities and personal attacks. By comparison, Friday is calm, as only a few irate Jews, women, and Mormons bother to call in.

Critics have called Van Lansing's program offensive, tasteless, rude, racist, obscene and insensitive. Supporters refer to the program as enlightening, refreshing, educational and provocative. The only thing everyone can agree on is that the show is a bona fide moneymaker. Van Lansing's general manager notes that the station's ratings jumped radically when he was hired, and that advertising revenues have tripled.

In fact, Van Lansing's popularity has spawned promotional appearances, T-shirts, bumper stickers and other paraphernalia, all designed to hawk the station. "Sure, Trevor is controversial, but in this business that's good," says KRFP's general manager.

"Van Lansing is so good that he will make more money this year than the president of the United States. Besides, it's just a gimmick."

Does Van Lansing see a problem with the content and style of his program? "Look," he says, "radio is a business. You have to give the audience what they want. All I do is give them what they want. If they wanted a kinder, gentler attitude, I would give it to them." He continues, "Don't get mad at me. Thank God we live in a country where guys like me can express an opinion. The people who listen to me like to hear it straight sometimes, and that's what the First Amendment is about, right?"

Finally, Van Lansing points out that if people are really offended by him, they can always turn the dial. "I don't force these people to listen," he pleads. "If they don't like it, let them go somewhere else."

Others disagree. The National Coalition for the Understanding of Alternative Lifestyles, a gay- and lesbian-rights group, calls Van Lansing's show "reprehensible." "Trevor Van Lansing is hiding behind the First Amendment. What he says on the air isn't speech; it's hate, pure and simple," says the group's director. "His program goes well beyond what our founders intended."

Adds a representative of the National Organization for Women: "Van Lansing is perpetuating several dangerous stereotypes that are destructive, sick and offensive. Entertainment must have some boundaries."

Micro Issues

1. Would you be offended by Van Lansing's program? If so, why?
2. Would Van Lansing's program be less offensive if the station aired another talk show immediately after his that featured a host holding opposite views?
3. How are the lyrics of rapper Eminem like or unlike Van Lansing's rants? Is an artist subject to different restrictions?

Midrange Issues

1. Who should accept responsibility for monitoring this type of program? Van Lansing? The radio station, KRFP? The FCC? The courts? The audience?
2. What, if any, are the differences between Van Lansing's *legal* right to do what he does and the *ethical* implications of what he does?
3. Legal scholar Mari Matsuda (1989) has called for a narrow legal restriction of racist speech. She notes, "The places where the law does not go to redress harm have tended to be the places where women, children, people of color, and poor people live" (11). She argues that a content-based restriction of racist speech is more protective of civil liberties than other tests that have been traditionally applied. Could such an argument be applied to entertainment programming?
4. In the current American media landscape, talk radio is supposedly the stronghold of the right while the majority of major daily newspapers are supposedly controlled by the left. Does the evidence validate this widely held assumption? Is democracy well served by this arrangement of entire media systems leaning to one side of the political spectrum?

Macro Issues

1. Are entertainers relieved of ethical responsibilities if they are "just giving the audience what they want"? Do Van Lansing's high ratings validate his behavior, since many people are obviously in agreement with him?
2. How does Van Lansing's narrow view of the world differ from a television situation comedy that stereotypes blondes as dumb, blue-collar workers as bigoted, etc.?
3. Van Lansing says that it's great that a guy like him can have a radio show. Is tolerance one of the measures of a democracy? If so, are there limits to tolerance, and who draws those lines?
4. Supreme Court Justice William O. Douglas has said, "If we are to have freedom of mind in America, we must produce a generation of men and women who will make tolerance for all ideas a symbol of virtue." How should democratic societies cope with unpopular points of view, particularly as expressed through the mass media?

CASE 10-G

Crowdsourcing a Book: John Lehrer, Bob Dylan and Nonfiction Truth

PHILIP PATTERSON
Oklahoma Christian University

When Jonah Lehrer resigned from *The New Yorker* in July of 2012, he was the latest young journalist on a professional fast track who had admitted to or was accused of some of journalism's greatest sins: plagiarism, fabrication of quotes and recycling of old material as new. Lehrer's resignation came on the same day that an article in *The Tablet,* a magazine and online site that promises "a new read on Jewish life" written by Michael Moynihan, accused him of fabrication of quotes in his third book, *Imagine: How Creativity Works.*

The Tablet piece was the most consequential of a series of events began a month earlier in June of 2012, Lehrer's first day on the staff of *The New Yorker.* Previously, Lehrer worked as a blogger at *Wired* magazine (a position he still holds) and as a contributor to NPR, primarily focusing on science journalism. His journalistic reputation was enhanced by the strong reviews of his two previous nonfiction books, *How We Decide* and *Proust Was a Neuroscientist.*

In a June 12, 2012, post, media blogger Jim Romenesko noted that Lehrer's blog for *The New Yorker,* titled "Why Smart People Are Stupid," actually included material recycled from a Lehrer post for the October 2012 *Wall Street Journal.* Within a few hours, *New York Magazine*'s Daily Intel blog had found other instances of self-duplication from Lehrer's writing for *Wired,* the *New York Times Magazine,* and other publications. *The New Yorker* allowed Lehrer to remain on staff. The question of repurposing one's own material was a troubling one, but apparently not professionally fatal.

However, questions by Moynihan cut more deeply. Moynihan, a self-described Bob Dylan fanatic who was also reading Lehrer's *Imagine,* became more than curious about the Dylan quotes that introduced the book. Lehrer quoted Dylan as saying of the creative process: "It's a hard thing to describe. It's just this sense that you've got something to say."

But, Moynihan knew of no such Dylan quote; further investigation could find no corroboration. This was troubling, because everything Dylan has said for publication is available online, and the artist himself is notoriously reluctant to grant additional interviews or to provide explanations for his personal creative process. Moynihan then e-mailed Lehrer, asking him where to find the quotations. About three weeks of increasingly vague explanations followed, all of which Moynihan detailed in his story, which concluded that Lehrer had fabricated the quotes. When Moynihan posted his story, Lehrer knew he would have to provide an explanation not to just to his readers but also to his employers.

> The lies are over now. I understand the gravity of my position. I want to apologize to everyone I have let down, especially my editors and readers. I also owe a sincere apology to Mr. Moynihan. I will do my best to correct the record and ensure that my misquotations and mistakes are fixed. I have resigned my position as staff writer at *The New Yorker.*

New Yorker editor David Remnick said: "This is a terrifically sad situation, but, in the end, what is most important is the integrity of what we publish and what we stand for."

Barnes & Noble, Inc. took *Imagine* out of its inventory and Lehrer's publisher, Houghton Mifflin Harcourt, halted shipments of the book and pulled the e-book off the market.

Micro Issues

1. The deceptions of Jonah Lehrer were unearthed by a minor publication and Web site. Why do you think that larger, more mainstream outlets did not discover and advance the story in June and July of 2012?
2. Is Lehrer's religious orientation a factor in www.tabletmag.com pursuing the story? Is his religion relevant to the story?
3. Lehrer was 31 at the time of the scandal. One of his defenders suggested that these were the mistakes of youth and inexperience. Evaluate this comment.

Midrange Issues

1. Five of the blogs that were self-plagiarized are still on *The New Yorker* Web site along with an editorial note that the work had been published elsewhere and providing readers with information on how to find the passages. Should *The New Yorker* have simply deleted the posts?
2. One of the things the Internet has promoted is the development of a "personal brand." How does Lehrer's career reflect this "individual branding" strategy? What are the foreseeable ethical problems for journalists who attempt to create their own brands? For the media outlets that employ them?

Macro Issues

1. Is there a difference in Lehrer passing off his old work as new and passing off someone else's writing as his own?
2. By taking *Imagine* (called a "runaway best seller" by the *New York Times*) off the market, Barnes & Noble is denying the public a chance to read a book on creativity that got some solid reviews in major publications. Should B&N allow its patrons to make their own judgment?
3. Can all journalists now expect to be "crowdsourced" in the way that Lehrer was? What are the potential implications of crowdsourcing for these purposes? How much impact should crowdsourcing have on specific journalistic projects? Are there limits to crowdsourcing?

11

Becoming a Moral Adult

By the end of this chapter, you should:

- **know the stages of moral development as described by Piaget and Kohlberg.**
- **understand the ethics of care.**
- **understand the stages of adult moral development.**

INTRODUCTION

Graduation is not the end of the educational process; it is merely a milestone marking the beginning of a new era of learning. College studies should equip you not only for entry into or promotion within the workforce but also to be a lifelong learner.

The same is true about moral development. There is no "moral graduation," marking you as an upright person capable of making right choices in life's personal and professional dilemmas. It's a lifelong process of steps—some of which you've taken; others lie ahead. Where you are now is a function of both age and experience, but the person you are now is not the person you will be 10 years from now. In a decade, you'll have added insight. Growth may, and probably will, change your decisions. This process is not only inevitable but also desirable. Contemporary scholarship suggests moral development begins within the mind-enhanced brain (Gazzaniga 2011).

This chapter is designed to provide you with an overview of some psychological theories of moral development. It attempts to allow you to plot your own development not only in terms of where you are, but also in terms of where you would like to be.

BASIC ASSUMPTIONS ABOUT MORAL DEVELOPMENT: THE RIGHTS-BASED TRADITION

People can develop morally just as they can learn to think critically (Clouse 1985). Scholars base this assertion on the following premises.

First, *moral development occurs within the individual.* Real moral development cannot be produced by outside factors or merely engaging in moral acts. People develop morally when they become aware of their reasons for acting a certain way.

Second, *moral development parallels intellectual development.* Although the two may proceed at a slightly different pace, there can be little moral development until a person has attained a certain intellectual capacity. For this reason, we exempt children and people of limited mental ability from some laws and societal expectations. While you can be intelligent without being moral, the opposite is not likely.

Third, *moral development occurs in a series of universal, unvarying and hierarchical stages.* Each level builds on the lower levels, and there is no skipping of intermediate stages. Just as a baby crawls before walking and babbles before speaking, a person must pass through the earlier stages of moral development before advancing to the later stages.

Fourth, *moral development comes through conflict.* As moral development theorist Lawrence Kohlberg notes (1973, 13), "A fundamental reason why an individual moves from one stage to the next is because the latter stages solve problems and inconsistencies unsolvable at the present developmental stage." Just as a baby learns strategies other than crying to get its needs met, the developing moral being learns more complex behaviors when older, more elementary strategies no longer work.

The two most cited experts in the field of moral development did their work decades and continents apart yet came to remarkably similar conclusions. Jean Piaget conducted his research in Switzerland in the 1930s by watching little boys

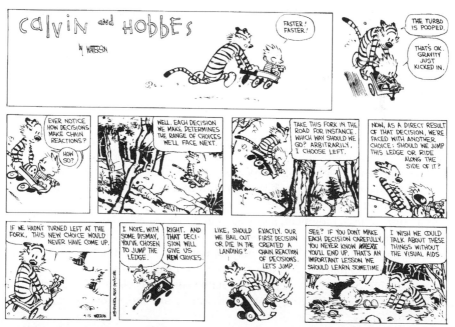

CALVIN AND HOBBES © 1990 Watterson. Dist. By UNIVERSAL UCLICK. *Reprinted with permission. All rights reserved.*

play marbles, and Lawrence Kohlberg studied Harvard students in the 1960s. They are often called "stage theorists" for their work in identifying and describing the stages of moral development.

THE WORK OF PIAGET

Piaget watched as boys between the ages of 3 and 12 played marbles, and he later tested his assumptions about their playground behavior in interviews. The box on the next page presents the basics of Piaget's theory.

The children under ages 5 to 7 didn't really play a game at all. They made up their own rules, varied them by playmate and game and delighted in exploring the marbles as tactile objects. Their view of the game was centered exclusively on what each child wanted.

The younger boys (ages 7 and 8) did follow the rules and played as if violations of the rules would result in punishment. The boys believed the rules were timeless, handed down from some "other," and that "goodness" came from respecting the rules. Boys in this stage of moral development believed "Right is to obey the will of the adult. Wrong is to have a will of one's own" (Piaget 1965, 193).

Children progressed to the next stage of moral development about age 11 when the boys began to develop notions of autonomy. They began to understand the reasoning behind the rules (i.e., fair play and reciprocity) that were the foundation of the rules themselves. Children in this stage of moral development understood that the rules received their power from their internal logic, not some outside authority.

These children had internalized the rules and the reasons behind them. Understanding the rules allowed the boys to rationally justify violating them. For example, children in this stage of moral development allowed much younger children to place their thumbs inside the marble circles, a clear violation of the rules. But the younger boys' hands were smaller and weaker, and by allowing them a positional advantage, the older ones had—in contemporary language—leveled the playing field. They had ensured fairness when following the rules literally would have made it impossible.

Although Piaget worked with children, it is possible to see that adults often demonstrate these stages of moral development.

Take the videographer whose primary motivation is to obtain a great shot, regardless of the views of those he works with or his story subjects. This journalist operates within an egocentric moral framework that places the primary emphasis on what "I" think, "my" judgment, and what's good for "me."

Beginning journalists, the ones who find themselves concerned with the literal following of codes of ethics, may be equated with the heteronomy stage of development. This journalist knows the rules and follows them. She would never accept a freebie or consider running the name of a rape victim. It's against organizational policy, and heteronymous individuals are motivated largely by such outside influences.

Just as the boys at the third stage of moral development were more willing to alter the rules to ensure a fair game for all, journalists at the final stage of moral

Piaget's Stages of Moral Development

EARLY DEVELOPMENT (before age 2)

- Interest in marbles is purely motor (e.g., put the marbles in your mouth).

FIRST STAGE—egocentrism (years 3–7)

- Children engage in "parallel play"; there is no coherent set of rules accepted by all.
- The moral reasoning is "I do it because it feels right."

SECOND STAGE—heteronomy (years 7–8)

- Children recognize only individual responsibility; obedience is enforced through punishment.
- Each player tries to win.
- Rules are regarded as inviolate, unbreakable and handed down from outside authority figures, usually older children.

- The children do not understand the reason behind the rules.

THIRD STAGE—autonomy (begins about age 11)

- Children internalize the rules; they understand the reasons behind them.
- They develop an ideal of justice and are able to distinguish between individual and collective responsibility.
- They ensure fair play among children.
- Children can change the rules in responses to a larger set of obligations.
- Authority is internal.
- Children understand universal ethical principles that transcend specific times and situations.

development are more willing to violate professional norms if it results in better journalism. The journalist at this stage of moral development has so internalized and universalized the rules of ethical professional behavior that he or she can violate some of them for sound ethical reasons.

However, people seldom remain exclusively in a single stage of moral development. New situations often cause people to regress temporarily to a previous stage of moral development until enough learning can take place so that the new situation is well understood. Perhaps the immediacy of the Internet or the power of social networking sites caused such a regression for some at first. But in any case, such regression would not include behaviors that would be considered morally culpable under most circumstances, for example, lying or killing, even despite the new context.

THE WORK OF KOHLBERG

Harvard psychologist Lawrence Kohlberg mapped six stages of moral development in his college-student subjects. The box on the next page outlines Kohlberg's stages of moral development, divided into three levels.

Kohlberg developed a lengthy set of interview questions to allow him to establish which stage of moral development individual students had achieved.

He asserted that only a handful of people—for example, Socrates, Gandhi, Martin Luther King or Mother Teresa—ever achieved the sixth stage of moral development. Most adults, he believed, spend the greater portion of their lives in the two conventional stages where they are motivated by society's expectations.

Doing right, fulfilling one's duties and abiding by the social contract are the pillars upon which the stages of Kohlberg's work rest. Under Kohlberg's arrangement, justice—and therefore morality—is a function of perception; as you develop, more activities fall under the realm of duty than before. For instance, reciprocity is not even a concept for individuals in the earliest stage, yet it is an essential characteristic of people in upper stages of moral development. Conversely, acting to avoid punishment is laudable for a novice, yet might not be praiseworthy for a news director functioning at a more advanced stage. The further up Kohlberg's stages students progressed, the more they asserted that moral principles are subject to interpretation by individuals and subject to contextual factors yet able to be universalized.

Kohlberg's stages are descriptive and not predictive. They do not anticipate how any one individual will develop but suggest how most will develop. Kohlberg's formulation has much to recommend it to journalists, concerned as they are with concepts such as free speech, the professional duty to tell the truth and their obligations

---

The Six Moral Stages of Kohlberg

LEVEL 1: PRECONVENTIONAL

Stage 1: Heteronymous morality is the display of simple obedience.

Stage 2: Individualism is the emergence of self-interest. Rules are followed only when they are deemed to be in one's self-interest and others are allowed the same freedom. Reciprocity and fairness begin to emerge, but only in a pragmatic way.

LEVEL 2: CONVENTIONAL

Stage 3: Interpersonal conformity is living up to what others expect, given one's role (e.g., "brother," "daughter," "neighbor"). "Being good" is important and treating others as you would have them treat you becomes the norm.

Stage 4: Social systems is the recognition that one must fulfill the duties to which one has agreed. Doing one's duty, respect for authority and maintaining the social order are all goals in this level. Laws are to be upheld unilaterally except in extreme cases where they conflict with other fixed social duties.

LEVEL 3: POSTCONVENTIONAL

Stage 5: Social contract and individual rights is becoming aware that one is obligated by whatever laws are agreed to by due process. The social contract demands that we uphold the laws even if they are contrary to our best interests because they exist to provide the greatest good for the greatest number. However, some values such as life and liberty stand above any majority opinion.

Stage 6: Universal ethical principles self-selected by each individual guide this person. These principles are to be followed even if laws violate those principles. The principles that guide this individual include the equality of human rights and respect for the dignity of humans as individual beings regardless of race, age, socioeconomic status or even contribution to society.

to the public and the public trust. However, Kohlberg's work was not without its problems. At least two aspects of his research troubled other moral development theorists.

Many scholars have argued that any general theory of moral development should allow people who are not saints or religious leaders to attain the highest stages of moral development. While perhaps only saints can be expected to act saintly most of the time, history is replete with examples of ordinary people taking extraordinary personal or professional risk for some larger ethical principles. Some felt that Kohlberg's conception—unlike Piaget's—was too restrictive.

Still more troubling was that in repeated studies, men consistently scored higher than women on stages of moral development. This gender bias in Kohlberg's work prompted discussion about a different concept of moral development founded on notions of community rather than in the rights-based tradition. It is called the ethics of care.

PARALLEL ASSUMPTIONS ABOUT MORAL DEVELOPMENT: THE ETHICS OF CARE

The psychologists who developed the ethics of care disagree with at least two of the fundamental assumptions underlying Piaget and Kohlberg. First, they say, moral development does not always occur in a series of universal, unvarying and hierarchical stages. Second, moral growth emerges through understanding the concept of community, not merely through conflict. The rights-based scholars believe that moral development emerges from a proper understanding of the concept "I." Proponents of the ethics of care say that moral development arises from understanding the concept of "we."

Carol Gilligan (1982) provides the clearest explanation of the ethics of care. Gilligan studied women deciding whether to abort. As she listened, she learned that they based their ethical choices on relationships. The first thing these women considered was how to maintain a connection. Gilligan argued that the moral adult is the person who sees a connection between the "I" and the "other." The women spoke in a "different voice" about their ethical decision making. Like many feminist ethicists, Gilligan reasoned that the ethical thinking emerged from a lived experience, not through the imposition of the top-down moral structure or set of rules.

For example, Gilligan presented the women with Kohlberg's classic ethical dilemma: the case of the desperate man and the greedy pharmacist. In this scenario, a man with a terminally ill spouse doesn't have enough money to purchase an expensive and lifesaving drug. When he explains the situation to the pharmacist, the pharmacist refuses to give him the medication.

Under Kohlberg's system, it would be ethically allowable for a man at the highest stages of moral development to develop a rationale for stealing the drug, an act of civil disobedience for a greater good. However, women made this particular choice less often. Instead, they reasoned that the most ethical thing to do was to build a relationship with the pharmacist, to form a community in which the pharmacist viewed himself or herself as an active part. In that situation, the women reasoned, the pharmacist ultimately would give the man the drug in order to maintain the connection.

Gilligan proposed that the women's rationale was no more or less ethically sophisticated than that expected under Kohlberg's outline. However, it was different, for it weighed different ethical values. Whether those values emerged as the result of how women are socialized in Western culture (an assertion that has often been made about Gilligan's work) or whether they merely reflected a different kind of thinking still remains open to debate. For our purposes, the origin of the distinction—and whether it is truly gender-linked—is not as important as the content.

Gilligan's notion of moral development is not neatly tied into stages. Her closest theoretical counterpart is probably the theory of communitarianism (see Chapter 1 for a description) with its emphasis on connection to community and its mandate for social justice.

If you were to carve stages from Gilligan's work, they would resemble:

- **First**—an ethic of care where the moral responsibility is for care of others before self.
- **Second**—an acknowledgment of the ethic of rights, including the rights of self to be considered in ethical decision making.
- **Third**—a movement from concerns about goodness (women are taught to believe that care for others is "good" while men are taught that "taking care of oneself" is good) to concerns about truth.

A complete sense of moral development, Gilligan observed, requires the ability "to [use] two different moral languages, the language of rights that protects separations and the language of responsibilities that sustains connection" (Gilligan 1982, 210).

Contemporary journalists have struggled with the issues of connection. Since much of our profession is based on an understanding of rights as outlined in various legal documents, ethical reasoning for journalists almost always assumes a rights-based approach. (You probably took this ethics course along with or immediately after a media law course, for example.) This historical rights-based bias, however, has led journalists into some of their more profound errors, including arrogance toward sources and readers and an unwillingness to be genuinely accountable to anyone.

If journalism as a profession is to mature ethically (or even survive economically), it must see itself as the vehicle to help people become the citizens they can be and to help reconnect and sustain communities that have become increasingly fragmented.

In 1992, deadly riots rocked the streets of Los Angeles in the wake of a police brutality trial (look up "Rodney King" for information on this historic event). In a *Newsweek* essay entitled "Whose Values?" the week after the trial, Joe Klein wrote:

> Television brought the nation together in the '50s; there were evenings when all of America seemed glued to the same show—Milton Berle, "I Love Lucy" and yes, "Ozzie and Harriet." But cable television has quite the opposite effect, dividing the audience into demographic slivers. . . . Indeed, if you are a member of any identifiable subgroup—black, Korean, fundamentalist, sports fan, political junkie—it's now possible to be messaged by your very own television and radio stations and to read your own magazines without having to venture out into the American mainstream. The choices are exhilarating, but also alienating. The basic principle

is centrifugal: market segmentation targets those qualities that distinguish people from each other rather than emphasizing the things we have in common. It is the developed world's equivalent of the retribalization taking place in Eastern Europe, Africa and Asia (Klein 1992, 21–22).

In the late 1990s, a movement called "civic journalism" mushroomed as an attempt to return journalism to what touched the everyday lives of people. Today the buzzword is "engagement," a broad professional heuristic that aims to foster a community of readers/viewers and listeners concerned with their networked civic life and employing the media as a way to share common thoughts and propose change.

DEVELOPING AS AN ETHICAL PROFESSIONAL

In the 1970s, James Rest, a psychology professor at the University of Minnesota, took Kohlberg's schema of moral development and used it to create a paper-and-pencil test to measure moral development among various professions. In the ensuing years, the test, called the Defining Issues Test (DIT), has been administered to more than 40,000 professionals, among them doctors, nurses, dentists, accountants, philosophers and theologians, members of the U.S. Coast Guard, surgeons, veterinarians, graduate students, junior high students, prison inmates and others. Those taking the test read four to six scenarios and are then asked to make a decision about what the protagonist should do, and then to rate the factors that influenced that decision. Because the test is based on Kohlberg's work, test takers who rely on universal principles and who consider issues of justice score well. Most people who take the DIT score in the range of what Kohlberg would have called conventional moral reasoning—stages 3 and 4 of his scale.

Wilkins and Coleman (2005) asked journalists to take the DIT and compared journalists' scores to those of other professionals. Journalists do well on the DIT, scoring below only three other professions: philosophers/theologians, medical students and practicing physicians. Because the single biggest predictor of a good score on the DIT is education, and journalists as a group have less formal education than the three professions with scores "above" them, the findings are significant. Other professions, for example orthopedic surgeons, scored lower than journalists on the test. In a follow-up study (Coleman and Wilkins 2009), public relations professionals also did well on the DIT.

The scenarios on the DIT are not directed at any particular profession but rather determine how people think about "average" moral questions. When journalists are presented with scenarios that deal directly with journalism, for example, problems involving the use of hidden cameras or whether to run troubling photographs of children, they score even better. In these tests, journalists often score in the fourth and fifth stage of Kohlberg's moral development schema. In an interesting side note, scholars found that having a visual image, such as a photograph, of some of the stakeholders in an ethical dilemma elevates ethical reasoning.

Other scholars have studied journalists' ethical decision making. Investigative reporters make moral judgments about the subjects of their stories, even though when they talk about their work they are reluctant to drop their professional objectivity (Ettema and Glasser 1998). Another study found that journalists who have been sued for invasion of privacy don't often think about the ethical issues their reporting creates (Voakes 1998). This leads to an indirect but plausible conclusion that solid ethical thinking may keep journalists out of court.

Finally, research shows that journalists do agree on what constitutes "good work" in their profession—an emphasis on truthtelling, taking a role as government watchdog, investigative reporting and treating the subjects with dignity. However, journalists believe that the single biggest threat to continuing professional excellence is the increasing pressure to make a profit. Journalists are out of joint with a mission that includes the competing interests of public service and profit making (Gardner, Csikszenthmihalyi and Damon 2001). How that tension is resolved is the essential question facing news operations today.

WHERE DO YOU GO FROM HERE?

Perry (1970) postulates that one of the major accomplishments of college students is to progress from a simple, dualistic (right versus wrong) view of life to a more complex, mature and relativistic view. Perry states that students must not only acknowledge that diversity and uncertainty exist in a world of relativism but also make a commitment to their choices (i.e., career, values, beliefs, etc.) out of the multiplicity of "right" choices available.

Unlike physical development, moral development is not subject to the quirks of heredity. Each individual is free to develop as keen a sense of equity as any other individual, yet not all reach their full potential. Kohlberg (1973) claims we understand messages one stage higher than our own. Through "aspirational listening"— picking a role model on a higher level—you can progress to a higher stage of moral development. This observation is not new. In fact, Aristotle suggested that virtues could be learned by observing those who possess them.

This book uses the case study method. Often in case studies, it is the reasoning behind the answer rather than the answer itself that is the best determiner of moral growth (Clouse 1985). *An important part of moral development is the recognition that motive, not consequence, is a critical factor in deciding whether an act is ethical.*

Elliott (1991) illustrates the difference in the following scenario. Imagine a situation where you are able to interview and choose your next-door neighbor. When you ask Jones how she feels about murder, she replies she doesn't kill because if she got caught she would go to jail. When you interview Smith, he says he doesn't kill people because he believes in the sanctity of life. It takes little reflection to decide which neighbor you would prefer. Elliott concludes: "Ethics involves the judging of actions as right or wrong, but motivations count as well. Some reasons for actions seem better or worse than others" (1991, 19).

To the above quote we might add: "and some justifications are more deeply rooted in centuries of ethical thought than others." The goal of this book—and probably one of the goals your professor had for this class—is to ensure that your choices are not merely "right," as that's a debate for the ages, but to ensure that your choices are grounded in the ethical theories that have stood the test of time and are not subject to the vagaries of current popular thought. The work of Kohlberg and Piaget suggests that your journey is not finished, but that you *have* started. And with the set of tools you have now acquired, you have an excellent chance of reaching your destination.

Suggested Readings

BELENKY, MARY F. et al. 1988. *Women's ways of knowing: The development of self, voice and mind.* New York: Basic Books.

COLES, ROBERT. 1986. *The moral life of children.* New York: Atlantic Monthly Press.

ETTEMA, JAMES, and THEODORE GLASSER. 1998. *Custodians of conscience: Investigative journalists and public virtue.* New York: Columbia University Press.

GARDNER, H., MIHALY CSIKSZENTHMIHALYI, and WILLIAM DAMON. 2001. *Good work: When excellence and ethics meet.* New York: Basic Books.

GAZZANIGA, MICHAEL, S. 2011. *Who's in charge? Free will and the science of the brain.* New York: HarperCollins.

GILLIGAN, CAROL. 1982. *In a different voice: Psychological theory and women's development.* Cambridge, MA: Harvard University Press.

LEVINSON, DANIEL J. 1978. *Seasons of a man's life.* New York: Alfred A. Knopf.

WILKINS, LEE, and RENITA COLEMAN. 2005. *The moral media.* Mahwah, NJ: Lawrence Erlbaum Associates.

Bibliography

Albini, S. (1993). "The problem with music." Retrieved November 14, 2008, from Negativland Web site: **http://www.negativland.com/albini.html.**

Alderman, E., and Kennedy, C. (1995). *The right to privacy.* New York: Alfred A. Knopf, Inc.

Anderson, C. (2006). *The long tail: How the future of business is selling less of more.* New York: Hyperion.

Ansen, D. (2006, October 23). "Inside the hero factory." *Newsweek,* pp. 70–71.

APME. (2009). *The Associated Press Statement of News Values and Principles.* Retrieved September 10, 2009, from **http://www.apme.com/news/news_values_statement .shtml.**

Arendt, H. (1970). *The human condition.* Chicago: University of Chicago Press.

Aristotle. *The Nicomachean ethics.* Book II 4–5 (1973). Trans. by H. Rackham. Ed. by H. Jeffrey. Cambridge, MA: Harvard University Press.

Associated Press Ethics Statement. (2012). Retrieved August 22, 2012, from **http://wwwapme .com/?page=EthicsStatement.**

Associated Press. (2009). *Associated Press to build news registry to protect content.* Retrieved September 10, 2009, from **http://www.ap.org/pages/about/pressreleases/ pr_072309a.html.**

Aufderheide, P. (2005). *Reclaiming fair use.* Oxford, England: Oxford University Press.

Auletta, K. (1991). *Three blind mice: How the TV networks lost their way.* New York: Random House.

Axelrod, R. (1984). *The evolution of cooperation.* New York: Basic Books.

Bagdikian, B. H. (1990). *The media monopoly* (3rd ed.). Boston: Beacon Press.

Baker, S., and Martinson, D. (2001). "The TARES test: Five principles of ethical persuasion." *Journal of Mass Media Ethics, 16*(2 & 3), pp. 148–175.

Baldasty, G. J. (1992). *The commercialization of news in the nineteenth century.* Madison: University of Wisconsin Press.

Belenky, M., et al. (1988). *Women's ways of knowing: The development of self, voice and mind.* New York: Basic Books.

Benoit, W. (1999). *Seeing spots: A functional analysis of presidential television advertisements.* Westport, CT: Praeger.

Berger, A. (1989). *Seeing is believing.* Mountain View, CA: Mayfield Publishing Co.

Berger, J. (1980). *About looking.* New York: Pantheon Books.

Bok, S. (1978). *Lying: Moral choice in public and private life.* New York: Random House.

———. (1983). *Secrets: On the ethics of concealment and revelation.* New York: Vintage.

Booth, C. (1999, November 15). "Worst of times." *Time,* pp. 79–80.

Borden, S. (2009). *Journalism as practice: MacIntyre, virtue ethics and the press.* Burlington, VT: Ashgate Publishing.

Bovée, W. (1991). "The end can justify the means—but rarely." *Journal of Mass Media Ethics, 6,* pp. 135–145.

Brady, J. (2006, February 12). "Blog rage." *Washington Post,* p. B1.

Braxton, G. (2007, August 24). "Right words to inspire reading?" *The Los Angeles Times.* Retrieved from **http://www.latimes.com.**

Brooks, D. E. (1992). "In their own words: Advertisers and the origins of the African-American consumer market." (A paper submitted to the Association for Education in Journalism and Mass Communications), Montreal, Canada, August 5–8.

Bryant, G. (1987, Spring–Summer). "Ten-fifty P.I.: Emotion and the photographer's role." *Journal of Mass Media Ethics,* pp. 32–39.

Bugeja, M. (2005). *Interpersonal divide: The search for community in a technological age.* Oxford, England: Oxford University Press.

Bunton, K., and Wyatt, W. (2012). *Reality television: A philosophical examination.* New York: Continuum International Publishing Group.

Calvert, C. (2000). *Voyeur nation: Media, privacy and peering in modern culture.* Boulder, CO: Westview Press.

Carey, J. W. (1989, Autumn). "Review of Charles J. Sykes' Profscam." *Journalism Educator,* p. 48.

Cassier, E. (1944). *An essay on man.* New Haven, CT: Yale University Press.

Chandrasekaran, R. (2006). "Comments resuming in *Post* blog." *Washington Post.* Retrieved February 17, 2012, from **http://www.Poynter.org.**

Chester, G. (1949). "The press–radio war: 1933–1935," *Public Opinion Quarterly,* pp. 252–264.

Christians, C. G. (1986). "Reporting and the oppressed." In D. Elliott (ed.), *Responsible journalism* (pp. 109–130). Newbury Park, CA: Sage Publications, Inc.

Christians, C. G. (2010). "The ethics of privacy." In Christopher Meyers (ed.), *Journalism ethics: A philosophical approach* (pp. 203–214). Oxford, England: Oxford University Press.

Christians, C. G., Ferré, J. P., and Fackler, M. (1993). *Good news: Social ethics and the press.* New York: Longman.

Christians, C.G., Glasser, T., McQuail, D., and Nordenstreng, K. (2009). *Normative theories of the media: Journalism in democratic societies.* Champagne: University of Illinois Press.

Christians, C. G., Glasser, T. L., McQuail, D., Nordenstreng, K., and White, R. A. (2009). "Part Three: Roles." In *Normative theories of the media: Journalism in democratic societies* (pp. 139–218). Urbana: University of Illinois Press.

Clegg, A. (2005). "Dove gets real." Retrieved from **http://www.brandchannel.com.**

Clouse, B. (1985). *Moral development.* Grand Rapids, MI: Baker Book House.

Coleman, A. D. (1987, Spring–Summer). "Private lives, public places: Street photography ethics." *Journal of Mass Media Ethics,* pp. 60–66.

Coleman, R., and Wilkins, L. (2009, July 3). "The moral development of public relations practitioners: A comparison with other professions." *Journal of Public Relations Research, 21,* pp. 318–340.

Coles, R. (1986). *The moral life of children.* New York: Atlantic Monthly Press.

The Commission on Freedom of the Press. (1947). *A free and responsible press.* Chicago: University of Chicago Press.

Cranberg, G., Bezanson, R., and Soloski, J. (2001). *Taking stock.* Ames: Iowa State University Press.

Crouse, T. (1974). *The boys on the bus: Riding with the campaign press corps.* New York: Ballantine.

Cunningham, B. (2003, July–August). "Re-thinking objectivity." *Columbia Journalism Review,* pp. 24–32.

Davies, J. C. (1963). *Human nature in politics.* New York: John Wiley & Sons.

Deuze, M. (2008). "The changing nature of news work: Liquid journalism and monitorial citizenship." *International Journal of Communication, 2,* pp. 848–865.

Dewey, J. (2005/1932). *Art as experience.* New York: Penguin Putnam Inc.

de Toqueville, A (1985). *Democracy in America.* New York: George Dearborn and Co.

Dionne, E. J. (1991). *Why Americans hate politics.* New York: Simon & Schuster.

———. (1996). *They only look dead.* New York: Simon & Schuster.

Dyck, A. (1977). *On human care.* Nashville, TN: Abingdon.

Elliott, D. (1986). "Foundations for news media responsibility." In D. Elliott (ed.), *Responsible journalism* (pp. 32–34). Newbury Park, CA: Sage Publications, Inc.

———. (1991, Autumn). "Moral development and the teaching of ethics." *Journalism Educator,* pp. 19–24.

Ellul, J. (1965). *Propaganda* (K. Kellen and J. Lerner, Trans.). New York: Alfred A. Knopf.

Etcoff, N., Orbach, S., Scott, J., and D'Agostino, H. (2004, September). "The real truth about beauty." A paper commissioned by Dove, A Unilever Beauty Brand. New York: Strategy One.

Ettema, J., and Glasser, T. (1998). *Custodians of conscience: Investigative journalists and public virtue.* New York: Columbia University Press.

Fallows, J. (1996). *Breaking the news: How the media undermine American democracy.* New York: Pantheon.

Fancher, M. (2004, April 18). "Powerful photograph offered chance to tell an important story." *Seattle Times,* p. A1.

Farhi, P. (2006, January 28). "Deluge shuts down *Post* blog." *Washington Post,* p. A8.

Festinger, L. (1957). *A theory of cognitive dissonance.* Stanford, CA: Stanford University Press.

Fischer, C. T. (1980). "Privacy and human development." In W. C. Bier (ed.), *Privacy: A vanishing value?* (pp. 37–46). New York: Fordham University Press.

Fitzpatrick, K., and Bronstein, C. (2006). *Ethics in public relations: Responsible advocacy.* Thousand Oaks, CA: Sage Publications, Inc.

Fletcher, G. P. (1993). *Loyalty: An essay on the morality of relationships.* New York: Oxford University Press.

Fry, D. (ed.). (1983). *The adversary press.* St. Petersburg, FL: The Modern Media Institute.

Fuss, P. (1965). *The moral philosophy of Josiah Royce.* Cambridge, MA: Harvard University Press.

Gazzinga, M. S. (2011). *Who's in charge? Free will and the science of the brain.* New York: HarperCollins.

Gans, H. (1979). *Deciding what's news: A study of CBS Evening News, NBC Nightly News, Newsweek and Time.* New York: Vintage.

Gardner, H., Csikszenthmihalyi, M., and Damon, W. (2001). *Good work: When excellence and ethics meet.* New York: Basic Books.

Genocide Watch. (2004, February 24). "Today is the day of killing Anuaks." Retrieved from **http://www.genocidewatch.org.**

Gert, B. (1988). *Morality, a new justification of the moral rules.* New York: Oxford University Press.

Gilligan, C. (1982). *In a different voice: Psychological theory and women's development.* Cambridge, MA: Harvard University Press.

Godwin, M. (1998). *Defending free speech in the digital age.* New York: Times Books.

Goffman, E. (1959). *The presentation of self in everyday life.* New York: Anchor.

Gogoi, P. (2005, August 17). "From reality TV to reality ads." Retrieved from **http://www .businessweek.com.**

Gogoi, P. (2006, October 17). "Wal-Mart vs. the blogosphere." Retrieved from **http://www .businessweek.com.**

Gormley, D. W. (1984). "Compassion is a tough word." *Drawing the Line,* pp. 58–59. Washington, DC: American Society of Newspaper Editors.

Gramm, B., and J. Weisman (2003, March 4). "Display of 5 POWs draws firm rebuke." *Washington Post,* p. A1.

Grcic, J. M. (1986). "The right to privacy: Behavior as property." *Journal of Values Inquiry, 20,* pp. 137–144.

Grunig, L., Toth, E., and Hon, L. (2000). "Feminist values in public relations." *Journal of Public Relations Research, 12*(1), pp. 49–68.

Gulati, G. J., Just, M. R., and Crigler, A. N. (2004). "News coverage of political campaigns." In L. L Kaid (ed.), *Handbook of political communication research* (pp. 237–256). Mahwah, NJ: Lawrence Erlbaum Associates.

Gunther, M. (2006, October 18). "Corporate blogging: Wal-Mart fumbles." Retrieved from **http://www.cnnmoney.com.**

Gurevitch, M., Levy, M., and Roeh, I. (1991). "The global newsroom: Convergences and diversities in the globalization of television news." In P. Dalhgren and C. Sparks (eds.), *Communication and citizenship.* London. Routledge.

Gutwirth, S. (2002). *Privacy and the information age.* Lanham, MD: Rowman & Littlefield Publishers, Inc.

Hadley, C. (2006). Personal interview with case study author.

Haiman, F. (1958). "Democratic ethics and the hidden persuaders." *Quarterly Journal of Speech, 44,* pp. 385–392.

Halberstam, D. (2001). *War in a time of peace.* New York: Scribner.

Halbert, D. J. (1999). *Intellectual property in the information age.* Westport, CT: Quorum Books.

Hammargren, R. (1936). "The origin of the press–radio conflict," *Journalism Quarterly, 13,* pp. 91–93.

Hanson, K. (1986). "The demands of loyalty." *Idealistic Studies, 16,* pp. 195–204.

Harris, T. (Producer). (2007, September 1). *CNN Newsroom.* Atlanta: Cable News Network.

Hart, A. (2003, July–August). "Delusions of accuracy." *Columbia Journalism Review,* p. 20.

Hemmel, P. (2006, June 11). Personal interview with author.

Hendrickson, E., and Wilkins, L. (2009). "The wages of synergy." *Journalism Practice, 3*(2), pp. 3–21.

Herman, E. S., and Chomsky, N. (2002). "The propaganda models." In *Manufacturing consent: The political economy of the mass media* (pp. 1–36). New York: Pantheon.

Hesmondhalgh, D. (1999). "Indie: The institutional politics and aesthetics of a popular music genre." *Cultural Studies, 13*(1), pp. 34–61.

Hess, S. (1981). *The Washington reporters.* Washington, DC: The Brookings Institution.

Hickey, N. (2001, November–December). "The cost of not publishing." *Columbia Journalism Review.*

Hickey, N. (2003, July–August). "FCC: Ready, set, consolidate." *Columbia Journalism Review,* p. 5.

Hobbes, T. (1958). *The Leviathan* (Reprints from 1651). New York: Bobbs-Merrill.

Hodges, L. W. (1983). "The journalist and privacy." *Social Responsibility: Journalism, Law, Medicine, 9,* pp. 5–19.

———. (1986). "Defining press responsibility: A functional approach." In D. Elliott (ed.), *Responsible journalism,* (pp. 13–31). Newbury Park, CA: Sage Publications, Inc.

———. (1997). "Taste in photojournalism: A question of ethics or aesthetics? In *Media Ethics: Issues and Cases,* 3rd ed. New York: McGraw-Hill, pp. 37–40.

Hollifield, C. A., and Becker, L. B. (2009). "News media performance in hyper-competitive markets: An extended model of effects." *International Journal on Media Management, 8,* pp. 60–69.

Jamieson, K. H. (1992). *Dirty politics.* New York: Oxford University Press.

———. (2000). *Everything you think you know about politics . . . and why you're wrong.* New York: Basic Books.

Jensen, J. (2002). *Is art good for us?* Lanham, MD: Rowman & Littlefield, Publishers.

Journal of Mass Media Ethics. (1987, Spring–Summer). Special issue on photojournalism.

Kaid, L. L. (1992). "Ethical dimensions of political advertising." In R. E. Denton (ed.), *Ethical dimensions of political communication* (pp. 145–169). New York: Praeger.

Kim, G., and Paddon, A. (1999, September). "Digital manipulation as new form of evidence of actual malice in libel and false light cases." *Communications and the Law, 21,* p. 3.

Klein, J. (1992, June 8). "Whose values?" *Newsweek,* pp. 19–22.

Koehn, D. (1998). *Rethinking feminist ethics.* New York: Routledge.

Kohlberg, L. (1973). "The contribution of developmental psychology to education." *Educational Psychologist, 10,* pp. 2–14.

Kovach, B., and Rosenstiel, T. (2007). *The elements of journalism: What news people should know and the public should expect.* New York: Three Rivers Press.

Lacy, S. (1989, Spring). "A model of demand for news: Impact of competition on newspaper content." *Journalism Quarterly,* pp. 40–48, 128.

Lebacqz, K. (1985). *Professional ethics: Power and paradox.* Nashville, TN: Abingdon Press.

Lee, S. T. (2005). "Predicting tolerance of journalistic deception." *Journal of Mass Media Ethics, 20*(1), pp. 22–42.

Leigh, D., and L. Harding (2011). *WikiLeaks: Inside Julian Assange's war on secrecy.* London: Guardian Books.

Leiss, W., Kline, S., and Jhally, S. (1986). *Social communication in advertising: Person, products and images of well-being.* New York: Methuen Publications.

Lester, P. (1991). *Photojournalism: An ethical approach.* Hillsdale, NJ: Lawrence Erlbaum Associates.

———. (1992). *Photojournalism: An ethical approach.* Hillsdale, NJ: Lawrence Erlbaum Associates.

———. (1996). *Images that injure.* Westport, CT: Greenwood Press.

———. (2003). *Images that injure.* Westport, CT: Greenwood Press.

Levinson, D. J. (1978). *Seasons of a man's life.* New York: Alfred A. Knopf, Inc.

Linsky, M. (1986). *Impact: How the press affects federal policymaking.* New York: W. W. Norton.

Lippmann, W. (1922). *Public opinion.* New York: Free Press.

———. (1982). *The essential Lippmann.* Cambridge, MA: Harvard University Press.

Lowery, S., and DeFleur, M. (1988). *Milestones in mass communication research* (2nd ed.). New York: Longman.

Manly, L. (2005, October 3). "U.S. network TV shows turn props into dollars." *International Herald Tribune,* pp. A14, 16.

Martin, E. (1991). "On photographic manipulation." *Journal of Mass Media Ethics, 6,* pp. 156–163.

Martin, M. (2007, September 17). "Man behind BET's 'Read a Book' responds to critics." *Tell Me More @ NPR News.* Interview streamed from **http://www.npr.org.**

Marx, G. T. (1999). "What's in a name." *The Information Society, 15*(2), pp. 99–112.

Matsuda, M. (1989). "Public response to racist speech: Considering the victim's story." *Michigan Law Review, 87,* pp. 2321–2381.

May, William F. (2001). *Beleaguered rulers: The public obligation of the professional.* Louisville, KY: Westminster John Knox Press.

McChesney, R. (1991). *Rich media, poor democracy: Communication politics in dubious times.* Champaign–Urbana: University of Illinois Press.

———. (1997). *Corporate media and the threat to democracy.* New York: Seven Stories Press.

McCluskey, C. (2009, August 29–30). "At best plagiarism, at worst outright theft: *Courant* covers towns with other papers' reporting." *Journal Inquirer.*

Medved, Michael. (1992). *Hollywood vs. America.* New York: HarperCollins Publishers.

Merrill, J. C. (1974). *The imperative of freedom: A philosophy of journalistic autonomy.* New York: Hastings House.

Meyers, C. (2003). "Appreciating W.D. Ross: On duties and consequences." *Journal of Mass Media Ethics, 18*(2), pp. 81–97.

Mill, J. S. (1859). *On liberty.*

Mills, C. W. (1956). *The power elite.* New York: Oxford University Press.

Mills, K. (1989, Winter). "When women talk to women." *Media and Values,* p. 12.

Molotch, H., and Lester, M. (1974). "News as purposive behavior: On the strategic use of routine events, accidents and scandals." *American Sociological Review, 39,* pp. 101–112.

Montgomery, K. C. (1989). *Target: Prime time. Advocacy groups and the struggle over entertainment television.* New York: Oxford University Press.

Moore, G. F. (1903). *Principia ethica.*

Moyers, B. (1988). Quoted in "The promise of television," episode 10. Produced by PBS.

National Association of Broadcasters. (1985). *Radio: In search of excellence.* Washington, DC: NAB.

Negroponte, N. (1995). *Being digital.* New York: Alfred A. Knopf.

Nelkin, D. (1987). *Selling science: How the press covers science and technology.* New York: W. H. Freeman.

Nerone, J. C. (1995). "Social responsibility theory." In *Last rights: Revisiting four theories of the press.* Urbana: University of Illinois Press.

Neville, R. C. (1980). "Various meanings of privacy: A philosophical analysis." In W. C. Bier (ed.), *Privacy: A vanishing value?* (pp. 26–36). New York: Fordham University Press.

Newsom, D., Turk, J. V., and Kruckeberg, D. (1996). *This is PR: The realities of public relations.* Belmont, CA: Wadsworth.

Newton, J. (2000). *The burden of visual truth: The role of photojournalism in mediating reality.* Hillsdale, NJ: Lawrence Erlbaum Associates.

Niles, R. (2009). "What are the ethics of online journalism?" *Online Journalism Review.* Retrieved September 10, 2009, from **http://www.ojr.org.**

Nissenbaum, H. (2010). *Privacy on context: Technology, policy and the integrity of social life.* Stanford, CA: Stanford Law Books.

O'Toole, J. (1985). *The trouble with advertising.* New York: Times Books.

Oldenquist, A. (1982). "Loyalties." *Journal of Philosophy, 79,* pp. 73–93.

Orwell, G. (1949). *1984.* San Diego: Harcourt Brace Jovanovich.

Patterson, P. (1989). "Reporting Chernobyl: Cutting the government fog to cover the nuclear cloud." In L. M. Walters, L. Wilkins, and T. Walters (eds.), *Bad tidings: Communication and catastrophe.* Mahwah, NJ: Lawrence Erlbaum Associates.

Patterson, T. (1980). *The mass media election.* New York: Prager.

Perry, W. (1970). *Forms of ethical and intellectual development in the college years.* New York: Holt, Reinhart & Winston.

Pfanner, E. (2005, October 3). "Product placements cause a stir in Europe." *International Herald Tribune,* pp. A14–A15.

Piaget, J. (1965). *The moral judgment of the child.* Translated by Marjorie Gabain. New York: Free Press.

Picard, R. (1988). *The ravens of Odin: The press in the nordic nations.* Ames: Iowa State University Press.

Picard, R. G. (2010). *The economics of financing media companies.* New York: Fordham University Press.

Plaisance, P. L. (2002). "The journalist as moral witness: Michael Ignatieff's pluralistic philosophy for a global media culture." *Journalism: Theory, Practice & Criticism, 3*(2), pp. 205–222.

Plato. *The republic.*

Pojman, L. (1998). *Ethical theory: Classical and contemporary readings.* Belmont, CA: Wadsworth Publishing Co.

Postman, N. (1986). *Amusing ourselves to death: Public discourse in the age of television.* New York: Penguin Books.

Powell, T. F. (1967). *Josiah Royce.* New York: Washington Square Press, Inc.

Privacy Implications of Online Advertising Full Committee. (2008, July 9). Retrieved from **http://commerce.senate.gov/public/index.cfm?FuseAction=Hearings.Hearing& Hearing_ID=e46b0d9f-562e-41a6-b460-a714bf370171.**

Radin, M. J. (1982). "Property and personhood." *Stanford Law Review, 34*(5), pp. 957–1015.

Rainey, J. (2006, September 14). "Local leaders urge owner of the *Times* to avoid cuts." Retrieved from **http://www.latimes.com.**

Rainville, R., and McCormick, E. (1977). "Extent of racial prejudice in pro football announcers' speech." *Journalism Quarterly, 54,* pp. 20–26.

Rawls, J. (1971). *A theory of justice.* Cambridge, MA: Harvard University Press.

Rawls, J. (1999). *A theory of justice.* Cambridge, MA: Harvard University Press.

Reaves, S. (1987, Spring–Summer). "Digital retouching: Is there a place for it in newspaper photography?" *Journal of Mass Media Ethics,* pp. 40–48.

———. (1991). Personal correspondence to the author quoted in digital alteration of photographs in consumer magazines. *Journal of Mass Media Ethics, 6,* pp. 175–181.

Reid, T., and Doran, J. (2003, March 24). "Mistreating prisoners is a war crime, says Bush." *The Times* (London), p. 2.

Ricchiardi, S. (2009). "Share and share alike; once considered unthinkable, content-sharing arrangements are proliferating rapidly, often uniting newspapers long seen as bitter rivals." *American Journalism Review, 31.1* (February–March), 28(8).

Rieder, R. (1999, November–December). "A costly rookie mistake." *American Journalism Review,* p. 6.

Robinson, M., and Sheehan, G. (1984). *Over the wire and on TV.* New York: Basic Books.

ROBOFISH. (n.d.). *Read a Book (Dirty Version).* Comment posted.

Rosen, J. (2000). *The unwanted gaze: The destruction of privacy in America.* New York: Random House.

Rosenthal, A. M. (1989, October 10). "Trash TV's latest news show continues credibility erosion." Syndicated column by *New York Times* News Service.

Ross, W. D. (1930). *The right and the good.* Oxford, England: Clarendon Press.

———. (1988). *The right and the good.* Indianapolis, IN: Hackett Publishing.

Royce, J. (1908). *The philosophy of loyalty.* New York: Macmillan.

Rush, G., and Molloy, J. (2003, May 16). "Cut and cover." *New York Daily News,* p. D1.

Russell, B. (ed.). (1967). *History of Western philosophy.* New York: Touchstone Books.

Sabato, L. J. (1992). *Feeding frenzy: How attack journalism has transformed American politics.* New York: Free Press.

Sabato, L. J. (2000). "Open season: How the news media cover presidential campaigns in the age of attack journalism." In D. A. Graber (ed.), *Media power in politics* (4th ed., pp. 161–171). Washington, DC: CQ Press.

Salmon, F. (2006, March 27). "Blood money." Retrieved from **http://www.democracynow .org.**

Sandel, M. J. (1982). *Liberalism and the limits of justice.* Cambridge, MA: Harvard University Press.

Sandel, M. J. (2012). *What money can't buy: The moral limits of markets.* New York: Farrar, Straus and Giroux.

Schoeman, F. D. (ed.). (1984). *Philosophical dimensions of privacy: An anthology.* Cambridge, MA: Harvard University Press.

Schudson, M. (1978). *Discovering the news.* New York: Basic Books.

———. (1984). *Advertising: The uneasy persuasion.* New York: Basic Books.

———. (1995). *The power of news.* Cambridge, MA: Harvard University Press.

Schwartz, T. (1973). *The responsive chord.* Garden City, NY: Anchor Press.

Seabrook, J. (2003, July 7). "The money note." *New Yorker,* p. 46.

Seelye, K. (2006, October 5). "Publisher is fired at *Los Angeles Times.*" Retrieved from **http://www.nytimes.com.**

Shaw, D. (1999, December 20). "Journalism is a very different business—Here's why." *Los Angeles Times,* p. V3.

Shirky, C. (2009). *Here comes everybody: The power of organizing without organizations.* New York: Penguin.

Shoemaker, P. J., and Reese, S. D. (1996). *Mediating the message: Theories of influences on mass media content.* White Plains, NY: Longman.

Smith, C. (1992). *Media and apocalypse.* Westport, CT: Greenwood Press.

Smolkin, R. (2005, April–May). "Reversing the slide." *American Journalism Review.*

Society of Professional Journalists. (2009). *SPJ Code of Ethics.* Retrieved September 10, from **http://www.spj.org/ethicscode.asp.**

Society of Professional Journalists Code of Ethics. (2012). Retrieved August 22, 2012, from **http://www.spj.org/ethicscode.asp.**

Spence, E. A., Alexandra, A., Quinn, A., and Dunn, A. (2011). *Media, markets and morals.* London, England: Wiley-Blackwell.

Spencer, J. (2001, October 1). "Decoding bin Laden." *Newsweek.*

Stanard, A. (2006, October 12). "Facebook privacy charges raise student ire." Retrieved from **http://www.detnews.com.**

Stone, I. F. (1988). *The trial of Socrates.* Boston: Little, Brown and Co.

Sub Pop Records. (2008). "The Sub Pop story." Retrieved November 14, 2008, from Sub Pop Records Web site: **http://www.subpop.com/artists/sub_pop.**

Sunstein, C. (2001). *Republic.com.* New Haven, CT: Princeton University Press.

Swanberg, W. A. (1972). *Luce and his empire.* New York: Scribner.

Szarkowski, J. (1978). *Mirrors and windows.* New York: Museum of Modern Art.

Thorson, E., Duffy, M., and Schumann, D. (2007). "The Internet waits for no one." In D. W. Schumann and E. Thorson (eds.), *Internet advertising: Theory and research* (pp. 3–14). New York: Routledge.

Tolstoy, L. N. (1960). *What is art?* (Almyer Maude, Trans.). New York: MacMillan Publishing Company, p. 96.

Tomlinson, D. (1987). "One technological step forward and two legal steps back: Digitalization and television news pictures as evidence in libel." *Loyola Entertainment Law Journal, 9,* pp. 237–257.

Toulmin, S. (1988, Summer). "The recovery of practical philosophy." *The American Scholar,* p. 338.

van den Hoven and J. Weckert, eds. (2008). *Information technology and moral philosophy.* Cambridge, England: Cambridge University Press.

Voakes, P. S. (1998). "What were you thinking? A survey of journalists who were sued for invasion of privacy." *Journalism and Mass Communications Quarterly, 75*(2), pp. 378–393.

Vonnegut, K. (1952). *Player piano.* New York: Dell Publishing Co.

Wallace, T. (2012, August 8). "Komen breast cancer foundation president resigns; founder shifts roles." Retrieved August 9, 2012, from **http://nola.com/business.**

Ward, S. J. (2004). *The invention of journalism ethics.* Montreal, Canada: McGill-Queens University Press.

Ward, S. J., and H. Wasserman (2010). *Media ethics beyond borders: A global perspective.* New York: Routledge.

Weaver, D. H., Beam, R. A., Brownlee, B. J., Voakes, P. S., and Wilhoit, G. C. (2007). *The American journalist in the 21st century: U.S. news people at the dawn of a new millennium* (LEA's Communication Series). Mahwah, NJ: Lawrence Erlbaum Associates.

Werhane, P. (2006). "Stockholder ethics in health care." Presented to the Association of Applied and Professional Ethics, February 2006, San Antonio, TX.

Wilkins, L. (1987). *Shared vulnerability: The mass media and American perception of the Bhopal disaster.* Westport, CT: Greenwood Press.

Wilkins, L., and Christians, C. G. (2001). "Philosophy meets the social sciences: The nature of humanity in the public arena." *Journal of Mass Media Ethics, 16*(2 & 3), pp. 99–120.

Wilkins, L., and Coleman, R. (2005). *The moral media.* Mahwah, NJ: Lawrence Erlbaum Associates.

Williams, B. (2009). "The ethics of political communication." In L. Wilkins and C. G. Christians (eds.), *Handbook of mass media ethics.* New York and London: Taylor & Francis.

Winslow, D. (2004). "Peter Turnley's photo-essays to debut in *Harper's Magazine.*" Retrieved from **http://www.digitaljournalist.org.**

Woodward, K. (1994, June 13). "What is virtue?" *Newsweek,* pp. 38–39.

Index